IMAGE FORMATION AND COGNITION

IMAGE FORMATION
AND COGNITION

MARDI JON HOROWITZ, M.D.

Research Psychiatrist
Mount Zion Hospital and Medical Center;
Assistant Clinical Professor of Psychiatry
University of California School of Medicine
San Francisco, California

APPLETON-CENTURY-CROFTS
Educational Division/MEREDITH CORPORATION
New York

Second Printing

To Nancy
with love

Acknowledgments

I am deeply grateful for the opportunity to learn and to conduct research provided by the Research Career Award Program of the National Institute of Mental Health. The encouragement and support of everyone associated with that program was of lasting value to me. The grants involved were Research Career Development and Research Scientist Development Awards, Levels I and II from the United States Public Health Service (NIMH-K3-22,573). I am also very thankful for specific research project grants from the National Institute of Mental Health, the Vocational Rehabilitation Agency (now the Social and Rehabilitation Service), the Office of Naval Research, and Mount Zion Hospital and Medical Center. (Specific grant numbers are cited at appropriate places in the text.) I thank the Department of Psychiatry at Mount Zion Medical Center for support, sponsorship, and facilities; I also have depended at various times on the support of Langley Porter Neuropsychiatric Institute, the University of California Medical Center, and Oakland Naval Hospital.

My debts to individuals are numerous and include many more than the few I mention. First, I must cite Jurgen Ruesch and Enoch Calloway, III, who directed my earliest research efforts. At Mount Zion Medical Center, Edward Weinshel, Harold Sampson, and Robert Wallerstein have been especially helpful to my theoretical formulations. I particularly thank them for close scrutiny of various phases of the entire manuscript and for valuable comments. In many ways, they have provided intellectual and moral support for all of my work. At other institutions, Jerome Singer, Sydney Segal, Morton Reiser, George Mahl, Jack Block, Leo Goldberger, Ernest Haggard, and George Klein have helped with provocative discussion and advice.

In addition I want to thank those who carefully read all or part of the manuscript: Leo Goldberger for a complete and critical reading; Adrienne Applegarth and Daniel Greenson for suggestions on the chapters concerning clinical theory; Robert Byrne for editorial advice as well as the personal encouragement of a friend; and Stephanie Scharf Becker, whose professional concern for clarity of thought and expression forced me to face assumptions and rethink relevant problems. I sincerely thank her but also realize that by now only she is fully aware of her many contributions. For excellent secretarial work I thank Marilyn Jones, who with good humor organized and typed often illegible drafts right up to the final copy; and Peter Armetta who helped to compile the bibliography. David Stires and Daniel Shapiro of Appleton-Century-Crofts also were very helpful from inspiration to completion.

I also wish to thank my patients and friends who over the years shared with me their innermost thoughts and feelings. To sufficiently thank my wife, Nancy, for her constant encouragement, comments, and faith is indeed difficult, and by dedicating this work to her, I hope to express at least a part of my deep gratitude. Finally, I thank my children Ariana, Jordan, and Joshua for cheering me on.

Preface

The nature of image formation is relevant to any study of thinking, emotion, and perception. A short example can illustrate the important cognitive issues. A man chased by a lion will retain an image of the lion rather than looking over his shoulder to remind himself why he is running. The image has information derived from perception which in turn motivates continued action for escape. Much later, after this frightening event, the man might relive his experience as an intrusive image. If he misinterpreted the intrusive image as a perception, he might once again run in terror. This time the image would ·be maladaptive: others seeing his strange action would regard his behavior as deviant. This simple instance contains the three classic issues of image formation: when are images useful in cognition, how do we differentiate internal images from perceptions, and how do we control image formation?

For centuries, the main interest in image formation revolved around the topic of hallucinations since these are the most extreme instance of lapses in differentiation and control. Some societies regarded hallucinators as sick, others saw them as inspired by devils or divine spirits. The medical models, first formulated by Galen and Hippocrates, described hallucinations as the result of derangements in mental functioning due to intoxication. The contrasting religious model hypothesized that some unusually powerful spirit inspired the hallucination. The Spanish Inquisition, for example, classified the motivation as "divine" if the hallucinator reported desirable contents, and "demonic" if evil image contents were reported. This classification could mean the difference between sainthood and torture or death. Teresa of Avila saved many persons from torture by reintroducing the medical model: hallucinators were infirm and therefore not liable for their image contents.

Later theorists continued to question the cause of hallucinations, but, in addition, they tried to relate hallucinations to overall image formation and cognitive processes. While image formation was a major topic of research in both academic psychology and psychoanalysis at the turn of the century, the field was virtually deserted after World War I. During the next decades, experimental cognitive research was carried out by sparse numbers of investigators who generally worked in isolation, and whose papers met with little interest. In psychoanalysis there was a growing interest in the functions of the ego with special emphasis on the defensive aspects of thought processes, perception, and the regulation of emotion. Even in psychoanalytic theory, however, there was less interest in dream thinking and comparatively greater emphasis on thought in words as it emerged in the course of free-associations during the analytic hour.

In the last decade there has been a tremendous upsurge of interest in cognitive studies. Paradoxically, we discovered how little we know about thought and how incomplete our theories are. We are especially in need of theoretical formulations about the nature of nonlexical thought and the relationship of nonlexical thought to other aspects of cognition.

My own studies of image formation began in 1959 at the Langley Porter Neuropsychiatric Institute when I was confronted with the problem every clinician faces: how to communicate verbally with withdrawn and mute psychotic patients. Realizing that communication need not necessarily be verbal, and bringing into play a previous interest in painting and graphics, I began using "art therapy." But instead of more conventionally analyzing what the patient drew, I decided to be a participant-observer, to enter into the very processes of graphic communication, in effect, to send messages as well as receive them. Often I saw how a patient would struggle, both with and against his image experiences, and I was confronted by a problem central to image formation: self-control over one's own thoughts.

Later, as a psychoanalytically oriented therapist, I was again impressed by this formidable phenomenon: deep motives, early and repressed memories, and new ideas or feelings emerged not only in dreams and fantasies but in spontaneous or even intrusive images emerging "on the spot" during my patient's free associations. Once again, these images sometimes seemed strange, alien, even meaningless to the very person who generated their formation; they were like "messages from the unconscious" which were often in symbolic code, and not always easy to decipher. Such experiences are not restricted to patients: similar events occur in everyday life. These observations led to study, theoretical speculation, and research into a variety of image experiences in normal and abnormal persons, in natural and experimental situations. This book is my effort to synthesize these experiences and contribute to the growing body of psychologic knowledge that will eventually produce a comprehensive theory of cognition.

The book is organized into four sections. The first part consists of three chapters designed to introduce a working vocabulary (Chapter 1), and to describe the wide range of image experiences (Chapter 2) and the circumstances that are likely to increase such experiences (Chapter 3). Since the focus of this book is the subjective experience of images, this beginning with phenomenology is appropriate.

The second part deals with psychodynamic influences on image formation, and begins with a review of early concepts of the role of the image in thought (Chapter 4). In Chapter 5, I present a model of how images relate to other aspects of thought representation, in Chapter 6 a brief review of the psychoanalytic view of image formation and in Chapter 7, the problem of control over image formation, a paramount issue throughout the remaining chapters. Chapter 8 presents three case histories intended to explain unbidden images and to illustrate in some detail the psychodynamic meaning of image experiences presented elsewhere through short vignettes. Chapter 9 describes how clinical observation and theory, as described in foregoing chapters, can lead to hypotheses and predictions testable in the experimental laboratory.

The third section of the book concerns neurobiologic influences over image formation and directs attention to the physical factors that change conscious experience. Chapter 10 describes the contribution of perceptual factors arising outside of the higher brain centers in the formation of illusions and hallucinations. Chapter 11 focuses on image experiences arising during brain stimulation and Chapter 12 on flashbacks that occur after prolonged drug use.

The final section of the book is on the therapeutic uses of images. Though, of course, more knowledge about image formation will be the basis for a precise method of therapy, Chapter 13 offers what I know about art therapy, and Chapter 14 reviews psychotherapy methods that influence a patient's image formation.

BIBLIOGRAPHIC NOTE

The bibliography is assembled alphabetically by author at the end of each chapter. The entire list of references is again reassembled at the end of the book. Works from the *Standard Edition of the Complete Psychological Works of Sigmund Freud*, edited by James Strachey, and published by the Hogarth Press are indicated by the abbreviation *Stand. Ed.*, followed by the volume and page numbers.

San Francisco   MARDI J. HOROWITZ
September 1970

Contents

IMAGE FORMATION AND COGNITION

Phenomenology of Image Formation

CHAPTER
1
Images and Image Formation

Any thought representation that has a sensory quality we call an image. Images can involve the senses of seeing, hearing, smell, taste, touch, and movement; but since my focus is on visual images, I use the word "image" for mental contents that have a *visual* sensory quality (unless otherwise indicated). While "image" refers to a specific experience, "imagery" refers to different types of image experience collectively.

A person can describe an image in many ways, including information about contents, vividness, clarity, color, shading, shapes, movement, foreground and background characteristics, and other spatial relationships. Furthermore a person can often tell how the image entered his awareness, its duration, associated emotions, the relationship of the image to objects in the external world, efforts to change or dispel it, and the sequential or simultaneous arrangement of a series of images.

While people can describe image *contents*, they are usually unaware of all the underlying processes or motives which go into image *formation*. Neurobiologic and psychologic explanations can elaborate how and why a given image appears, in a particular person, at a particular time. While neurobiologists focus on the anatomic and physiologic substrates as causes, psychologists focus on the cognitive use, psychodynamic meaning, and motivational aspects of image formation. These two approaches interrelate but in a complicated and ambiguous manner since the two bodies of theory developed from extremely different types of observations and methods. At present, neither approach alone or in combination will fully explain an image experience. But it is useful to retain the conceptual dis-

3

tinctions between "image" and "image formation" and the need for both psychologic and biologic explanations.

DOES ONE "SEE" AN IMAGE?

Philosophers, faced with the logical problem of seeing something that is not there and not seeing something that is there, have labored over conceptual models of what constitutes "seeing" and how seeing relates to belief and knowledge.* By definition, to see is to perceive with the eye. Unfortunately the verb "to see" is commonly used to describe both external perceptions and internal visual representations; what often results is confusion about both events and their relationship to each other (Sarbin, 1967). People can agree that they see a tree in the yard or a car on the road, but they agree much less on whether they all see a mirage, an illusion, or a hallucination. To avoid ambiguity, and the questionable application of "to see," I shall use a less misleading vocabulary. When I mean an image is produced within the psychic system, I shall use the verb "to form" as in, "he formed an image of a vase." When I mean an image is derived directly from external visual stimuli, I shall use the verb "to perceive" as in "he perceived a vase." When I use "to see," as in quoting a patient's report, I shall try and do so in a clear context by describing the degree of vividness, the sense of localization, the sense of reality, and the presence or absence of corresponding external objects.

The word "image" is also problematic because, in its root meaning, it means "replica" (Sarbin and Juhasz, 1970). It is important to remember that images are not merely imitations, but memory fragments, reconstructions, reinterpretations, and symbols that stand for objects, feelings, or ideas. In order for this book to have continuity with other works on images and image formation, I shall retain these terms and use them carefully within defined limits. To avoid confusion, the word "image" in this text will never refer to external replicas but only to mental representations.

AN IMPORTANT PROBLEM IN THE STUDY OF IMAGERY

An image is such a private experience that there is only one primary source of information about it: the introspective report. Such reports of subjective experience have been found, in scientific investigations, to be quite fragile. People fabricate events that have not occurred in order

---

* Soltis (1966) has a review of the proposed philosophic solutions.

to please, do not report events that have occurred to escape censure, change their thinking to suit a variety of motives, use terms that do not have shared meanings, forget, contradict themselves, distort experiences, and vary experience with changes in the interpersonal and nonhuman environment. While more will be said of this later, the reader is warned at this point neither to be overly dismayed, nor to accept any image report uncritically.

REFERENCES

Sarbin, T. R. 1967. The concept of hallucination. *J. Personality*, 35 (3):359–380.
———— and Juhasz, J. B. 1970. Toward a theory of imagination. *J. Personality*, 38 (1):52–76.
Soltis, J. F. 1966. *Seeing, Knowing & Believing: A Study of the Language of Visual Perception*. Reading, Mass., Addison-Wesley.

CHAPTER

2

Types of Images

Because an image experience can be described from so many different perspectives, it is often confusing to try and give it one general label. For example, a vivid image of one's own body while falling asleep can be called hypnagogic because it occurs in the context of falling asleep, pseudohallucinatory because it is very vivid, or autoscopic because the contents are of the physical self. A full description might be: autoscopic hypnagogic pseudohallucination. A simpler description might use only one label (hypnagogic, or autoscopic, or pseudohallucination) depending on what the observer wishes to emphasize.

If a complete theory of image formation were available, the best method of categorization would be to designate the causes of a given experience. Since no such theory is yet formulated or agreed upon, we must categorize images phenomenologically, by their most striking descriptive characteristic. This practice leads to a formidable array of terms that are only loosely organized and are not mutually exclusive. In order to approach the psychology of image formation with a meaningful grasp on a variety of experiences, I have grouped the different types of images into four categories (Table 1).

The categories stem from four different approaches to an image experience. That is, one can emphasize an image's vividness, its context, the influence of perception on the internal image, or image contents, depending on what he thinks is the most relevant aspect of the image experience. Relevance depends on the interpretation one makes of the

Table 1   Categories and Types of Images

A. IMAGES CATEGORIZED BY VIVIDNESS

1. Hallucination
2. Pseudohallucination
3. Thought image
4. Unconscious image

B. IMAGES CATEGORIZED BY CONTEXT

1. Hypnagogic or hypnopompic image
2. Dream image; nightmare
3. Psychedelic image
4. Flashbacks
5. Dream scintillations

C. IMAGES CATEGORIZED BY INTERACTION WITH PERCEPTIONS

1. Illusion
2. Perceptual distortion
3. Synesthesia
4. Déjà vu
5. Negative hallucination
6. After-image

D. IMAGES CATEGORIZED BY CONTENT

1. Memory image; eidetic image
2. Imaginary image
3. Entoptic image
4. Body image; body schema experience
5. Phantom limb
6. Paranormal hallucination
7. Imaginary companion
8. Number and diagram forms

image for that person at that time. While later chapters will discuss the theory and reasons for how we choose to label an image (i.e., how an observer determines what part of the image he wishes to emphasize), this chapter will define and explain clinical terminology, as well as provide a brief overview of the issues related to the general categories.

A. IMAGES CATEGORIZED BY VIVIDNESS

Man dwells in fantasy as well as in reality, and the problem is knowing the difference between the two realms. Sometimes images are mistaken for perceptions, sometimes perceptions seem imaginary. The correct separation of the two sources of information depends to a large extent on the degree of vividness of the experience. As internal images become more vivid, they are more likely to be localized as external and appraised as real. Because such errors are frequent among persons in states of psychopathology, the vividness of an image is a central clinical issue. The descriptions below range from most to least vivid.

1. HALLUCINATIONS

A hallucination is an internal image that seems as real, vivid, and external as the perception of an object.* Hallucinations occur in any sensory modality. Schizophrenics, for example, report auditory hallucinations more frequently than visual hallucinations. Not all hallucinations are unpleasant, and some persons derive great comfort from, even respond ecstatically to their visions. Hallucinations occur in any state of consciousness, including full wakefulness.

"Hallucination" is a slippery term and, as Sarbin points out (1967), subject to misapplication. One problem is that there are few words or phrases which distinguish perceptions of external objects from images that exist only in the mind. A person who states, "I saw my mother," does not clearly indicate whether he 1) perceived his mother, 2) mistook a woman on the street for his mother, 3) conjured up an internal image of his mother or, 4) hallucinated his mother. In ordinary communication we escape difficulty by adding descriptive statements or asking questions. Unfortunately, persons with psychiatric disturbances frequently have such disordered communication that it may be impossible for a patient to elaborate on a statement like, "I saw my mother" (Ruesch, 1957).

Descriptive difficulties also occur in psychiatric diagnoses. The common association of hallucinatory symptoms with psychotic episodes, especially schizophrenia and toxic psychosis, leads to some erroneous conclusions. Persons who hallucinate tend to be diagnosed as having a psychosis, although normal persons can also have hallucinations. On the other hand, persons who appear psychotic and report images may be misdescribed as having hallucinations. Proper assessment of hallucinations can be made only after extended and clear descriptions in the context of reliable communication. In making diagnoses, these standards are often not met, and clinicians should be careful to apply only tentative labels. Sometimes the correct description of a patient's presenting syndrome is possible only after he has been in treatment for a period of time. A person who has had a hallucination might describe it this way:

> I was staring off into space, then I saw my brother in the corner of the room. His mouth moved but I heard no words. I spoke to him and he didn't answer. He just stood there, about eight feet away from me. Then he kind of fogged up and disappeared.

Note in the above example that for labeling purposes the crucial state-

---

* By the strict definition proposed by Esquirol in 1838 (Zilboorg, 1941) an experience is hallucinatory only when it appears to be real without any immediate contribution from external perception. If there is a real perceptual contribution, even if it is very distorted in the image formation process, then the experience is labeled illusion rather than hallucination. In actual practice, however, a person who has extreme illusions, especially if the distortions persist, is often said to be hallucinating.

ments concern the apparent reality to the subject of his mental representation.

2. PSEUDOHALLUCINATION

The distinction between pseudohallucinations and hallucinations, on the one hand, and between pseudohallucinations and thought images, on the other hand, is attributed to Kandinski (1880) and has recently been reexamined by Sedman (1966). Frequently, there is a clinical "in-between" type of phenomenon in which images are very vivid yet lack the sense of reality found in hallucinations. Some patients may oscillate between hallucinations and pseudohallucinations or between pseudohallucinations and thought images. While not subjectively localized in the external environment or, if projected externally, not possessing a sense of reality, pseudohallucinations have a more intense and compelling quality than thought images. Perhaps a useful criterion is the reaction of the subject: even though the person does not believe what he images is real, and even though the images differ in quality from an actual perception, he nonetheless reacts to them emotionally as if they were real. Perhaps this emotional reaction is closely related to the common quality of pseudohallucinations: they seem to occur contrary to the actions of the will and do not dissipate at once in spite of efforts to dispel them (Jaspers, 1962). A pseudohallucination might be described like this:

> I get this fantastic image of my mother with a green snake coiled around her neck. It's choking her. So lifelike and in color; I know it is just in my mind, but I get terrified. I get it every night now; I wish I could make it go away. I can get myself to think of it now, but it's not the same as at night. Now it's scary but not so bright or frightening.

3. THOUGHT IMAGE

A thought image is an ordinary ingredient of mental life. Vividness may range from relatively weak to very clear, but by definition thought images are always localized internally. Content ranges from fantasy to visualizations of logical problems in geometry. Poetry, for example, frequently calls forth a succession of vivid thought images. An example of a thought image: "I recall now the room where I lived in college, I can see the disorder of books and the drab color of the walls."

4. UNCONSCIOUS IMAGE

For the sake of completeness, I include a term that the reader may come across in psychoanalytic literature, the unconscious image. This

Table 2 Distinguishing Hallucination, Pseudohallucination,
Thought Image, and Unconscious Image by Several Criteria

Event	Usual Vividness	Usual Subjective Localization	Objective Localization	Sense of Reality
Hallucination	great	extrapsychic	intrapsychic	seems real
Pseudohallucination	great to moderate	extra- or intrapsychic		seems unreal (but may behave "as if" real)
Thought image	moderate to dim	intrapsychic		seems like memory or imagination
Unconscious image	none	none	repressed memory storage	presence is denied

seems to be a contradiction in terms: if an image is unconscious, how is it experienced as an image? Psychoanalytic theory assumes that an unconscious image was once conscious but, because of its involvement in psychologic conflict, is deliberately "forgotten" through the process known as repression (Freud, 1908). Though the unconscious image (perhaps expressive of a fantasy) may be inhibited from awareness, we assume that it may nonetheless influence thought and behavior. Often the image is revealed when defensive censorship decreases, as in the course of psychoanalytic treatment.*

These four types of imagery, contrasted above by degree of vividness, are also distinguished by other factors as illustrated in Table 2. The table presents only generalizations, and a specific experience may oscillate from moment to moment on any factor.

B. IMAGES CATEGORIZED BY CONTEXT

The context in which one forms an image is another important issue in explanations of psychodynamics and psychopathology. Suppose a

* Joseph (1959) suggests that the word "fantasy" be reserved for unconscious images and "daydreams" be used for conscious images. The English psychoanalytic authors distinguish "phantasy" for unconscious images, and "fantasy" for conscious ones. As is often the case, terms are not consistently used. The entry of images into awareness, their repression, and their reentry will be described in detail in Chapter 8. The reader interested in unconscious fantasy may also wish to consult Beres (1965).

person reports what we determine to be a hallucination. We would be alarmed if that person were a surgeon who experienced the event during an operation, or a jet pilot during a landing approach, or a carpenter at his lathe. If, on the other hand, the person hallucinated while falling asleep, or while on LSD, we might more readily accept the report as within the realm of normal experience. The various labels defined below attempt to make an image experience understandable by describing the context of occurrence.

1. HYPNAGOGIC OR HYPNOPOMPIC IMAGES

A hypnagogic image is one that occurs in the twilight state between wakefulness and sleep; hypnopompic images are exactly the same but occur while waking up. Because these experiences can be extremely vivid and seem real, they are sometimes called hypnagogic hallucinations. On the other hand, the experiences may also be pseudohallucinations or thought images. Hypnagogic images are characterized by a sense of non-volitional control over contents and tend to progress from logical thought to fantasy. Figures 1–3 are drawings by an artist of his flow of nonhallucinatory hypnagogic images.

Here is an example of a verbal report:

> Customarily as I drift off to sleep I find a succession of visual experiences. When I close my eyes I see darkness but then it lightens to gray. Next I see colored lights and sometimes very complex geometric forms that dance, rotate, or sparkle about. Soon a succession of images of people and scenes parades before me. I find these quite interesting and often go to sleep while watching them. At times, however, I get vivid hallucinations which may frighten me awake. For instance, once all of a sudden I saw a spider on my pillow; another time a crab. They were ugly and scary and caused me to start up in bed thinking they were real. Within seconds I knew them to be hallucinations—still, I had to wait several long seconds after waking up for them to fade.

The Isakower (1938) phenomenon is a particular type of hypnagogic image which is a visual sensation of large approaching masses. Isakower suggests that the image contents may be memory images of the mother's breasts or face.*

2. DREAM IMAGES; NIGHTMARES

Nightly dreams are largely visual experiences. Recent sleep research has demonstrated that most persons dream about five times a night during

---

* Lewin (1946, 1948a and b) suggests that memory images of the white (brown, or yellow) expanse of the mother's face or breast might be revived as sleep approaches because of the similarity of the state to falling asleep while suckling. The images then serve as a "dream screen" unto which other images are projected.

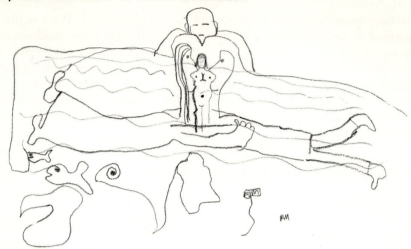

Figs. 1 (above), 2 (below), and 3 (opposite). An artist's drawings of his flow of hypnagogic images.

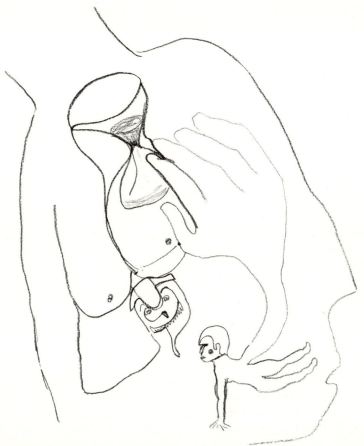

cycles of rapid eye movement sleep (REMS). REMS means a state of activated brain activity as manifested by the electroencephalogram and rapid eye movements during the sleeping period. If persons are awakened during REMS, they are very likely to report a dream-like experience, an experience of visual quality. If they are awakened out of non-REM sleep, they may report thoughts but these are less frequently in visual form (Dement and Kleitman, 1957).

Example of a dream report from a REM awakening:

> I was riding with a guy on the back of a motorcycle. I was in my new blue dress, he was dressed all in black. Then suddenly we were sitting in my back yard eating a lot of stuff spread out on a blanket. In the next scene there were a bunch of letters on a sign or something but I couldn't see them well enough to know what it said.

Example of a report from a non-REM awakening:

> Thinking of going on a picnic tomorrow. What food to buy. That's all.

Nightmares are a special form of dream. Ordinarily we define nightmares as a dream which is very unpleasant. There is, however, a relatively common cluster of experiences that constitute the classic nightmare. The three elements, as described by Jones (1950) are: 1) frightening visual images, 2) associated feelings of paralysis and, 3) smothering sensations. A typical nightmare:

> A terrible devil sat on my chest and glowered at me with burning red eyes. I couldn't get the strength to stir, my hands couldn't clench, and I felt like I couldn't breathe. Next I was being pursued by the devil, I was running as if through molasses—so slow but I just couldn't move any faster although I was desperate. I awoke just before he got me, sobbing with fright, still with the feeling of being unable to get my breath, and with my heart throbbing.

The resemblance of dreaming to the waking experience of hallucinations has led to various versions of a release hypothesis. According to such hypotheses, hallucinations are dreams released in the daytime due to some pathologic process.*

3. PSYCHEDELIC IMAGES

Hallucinogenic drugs (such as LSD) frequently produce a kind of image, often of hallucinatory quality, that is rare in the ordinary experience of most persons. A psychedelic image experience often begins with unusual perceptions such as fluorescent colors or scintillating effects, and progresses on to development of intense visual thought images, illusions, pseudohallucinations, or true hallucinations. The content often seems novel, weird, and compelling—accompanied not infrequently by a sense of uncanny and even mystical meaningfulness. Sometimes a visionary sense of "knowing" or symbolic synthesis remains after the drug has worn off, although the actual images experienced may be forgotten (Freedman, 1968). The contents and form are not unique to drug hallucinations since similar phenomena are reported during delirium caused by fever, starvation, or trances.

Example of a psychedelic image:

> First I was disappointed, the cube (LSD) wasn't going to give me any effect. Then I noticed a particular halo of light surrounding the dark head of my trip guide. I shut my eyes and saw a kaleidoscope of scintillating colors streaming endlessly in fantastically complex and reduplicated shapes. I was startled, opened my eyes and saw the pattern, ever changing on the wall. Then there was a parade of images and images within images, a whole world of pictures which I can scarcely recall. I do remember one where everyone was garbed in color with black dots like a butterfly. We were perched on the edge of a hill, by a tree, over-

---

* See Chapter 3 for more detailed information on dreams.

looking a deep blue valley. We had butterfly wings and were proud beings from the unknown future. I knew I could fly upwards and upwards with the greatest of confidence.

4. FLASHBACK, FLASHING, OR THROWBACK

Images formed during a drug-induced state may be reexperienced repeatedly after the drug has worn off. The terms flashback, flashing, and throwback are "hippie" slang and refer to the subjective sensation of unbidden returns of visual images first formed during the drug intoxication but later repeated long after the drugs have worn off. A secondary meaning is that the image is a repetition of a perception long past.

> A man with bat wings, swooping down onto me. I just get it anytime now—over and over again. Maybe a little more when I'm high on pot. It happened as part of my acid trip—that bat man really scared me too. And it was with a whole bunch of other things. Now it just comes into my mind anytime, the flashback. It scared me at first; now I'm used to it, but I can't make it happen and I can't make it stop.*

5. DREAM SCINTILLATIONS

Dream scintillations are a rapid succession of images which intrude upon awareness and are difficult to remember. Physical stress usually precedes the experience, which may occur in a state of fatigue but not necessarily drowsiness. Consciousness takes on a dreamlike state but without disruption of on-going emotion or behavior. Forbes (1949) coined the term, "dream scintillations" and postulated the cause to be transient, local circulatory disturbances. Saul (1965) noted that both his own experiences and those reported by Forbes immediately followed strenuous physical activity. I have suggested revising the term to "flickering images" since the person is not asleep and hence not dreaming, and also because the event could be a transient change in consciousness due to a minor variant of temporal lobe epilepsy (Horowitz et al., 1967). While rarely documented, this type of experience may be more common than the literature suggests.

Saul summarized his personal occurrences, each lasting 20 to 30 minutes as follows:

> There was slight visual disturbance, irregular areas not seen, a kind of scotoma. The experience itself is strange and fascinating. One feels as though he has just had a dream which he is trying hard to recall. He keeps trying to recall it, but while thus striving in vain, that which he

---

* Flashbacks are discussed in detail in Chapter 12. The slang use of the term is now being extended to include sudden ideas whether they are experienced as images or not.

is trying to recall seems to change. Then the realization dawns that this effort to grasp the dream is itself part of a dream state, a dream state which goes on like a real dream, shiftingly and distractingly, but while one is fully awake and in full command of his behavior and feelings so that no one else could observe or suspect anything unusual unless it is a slight distraction.

Here is a more detailed example of a single episode of dream scintillations or flickering images.

I was walking quietly, thinking nothing in particular, about half an hour after a strenuous swim in unusually cold water. I noticed the gradual development of a bilateral, right-sided blurring of vision. Form could not be distinguished clearly although there was only a mild diminution in illumination. Next I began to have the sensation of a rapid succession of visual images in my mind's eye, but I could not retain or recapture them. I was anxious about the visual impairment but had undiminished volitional control over my actions. I was unable either to block out these images or to decipher their meaning. It seemed that these flickering images caused me to feel queasy and vaguely nauseated. They lasted about one half hour. I was able to "think around them" in verbal thought but only with effort and with a very short concentration span.

The images were sometimes colored. They did not resemble delayed after-images, as might have occurred from light reflections off wave forms in the water. At times they were images of recognizable objects such as faces, fragments of landscape, et cetera. Even when I recognized what the brief images were, however, they seemed to have no relationship to those that immediately preceded or followed them. These images were located in my mind. I never had the feeling that they were real. Although I was anxious, the images did not have affective charge other than the queasy feeling.

C. IMAGES CATEGORIZED BY INTERACTION WITH PERCEPTION

The third important feature for clinicians assessing image reports, in addition to degree of vividness and context, is concern for an interaction of the image contents with perception, and the possible motives for such contamination. For example, if a person reports an illusionary image, we are concerned with how closely his subjective experience resembled the objects perceived. We infer that psychologic motives are different when a person mistakes a nearby policeman in uniform for his father and when he mistakes a distant bird for an airplane.

1. ILLUSION

An illusion occurs when a perceiver transforms stimuli until they resemble something other than the external object. The experience is subjective, often vivid, localization is external, and usually there is at least a brief sense of reality.

> I was uneasy walking home alone late at night. The wind led to strange sounds and I was easily startled by the moving shapes of the shadows of trees as they blew back and forth. I screamed and dropped my purse when I saw a grotesque man crouched and ready to spring at me. I then realized with great relief that the man was a shape created by sheets of newspaper blown up against a bush. My sensation of seeing the man had been quite distinct, however unreal it was: in my mind I had the definite impression of the line of his head and shoulders, even his menacing glare. Now as I pass that bush on my walk home, the first glance may still evoke the image of the attacker.

Illusions are common in everyday life and more common in certain mental states such as fear or anticipation. Inattentiveness, boredom, and fatigue increase the incidence, but in such cases the illusion is quickly dispelled by heightened or focused attentiveness. Many illusions apply a learned schemata; for example when proofreading a manuscript the reader may see words spelled correctly when there is an error. Illusions are not always experienced as a surprise. Many children (and adults) spend hours deliberately making images out of clouds, cracks in the ceiling, or the wandering patterns of wood grain.

Does the above definition of "illusion" include mirages? Since several persons may consensually validate seeing a mirage, this might disqualify it as an illusion. But a mirage may or may not be an illusion, depending upon how distant the subjective experience is from the shared optical sensations. On a desert or ocean, for example, certain atmospheric conditions may lead to strange shapes of light and form that can actually be photographed—seeing these "mirages" is an actual perception. If, however, the person believes that he sees "the minarets of the lost city of Atlantis," then this experience may be labeled an illusion.*

2. PERCEPTUAL DISTORTIONS

Perceptual distortions include changes in shape, size, shimmerings, apparent bendings of actual straight lines, and altered color experiences. Sometimes vertical objects appear tilted or even inverted; stationary objects may have apparent movement. These may appear during auras of persons with epilepsy or migraine headache, during drug intoxications, and as flashbacks after prolonged or repeated use of hallucinogens.† In

---

* A more detailed analysis of illusions will be found in Chapter 10.
† Visual perceptual distortions, such as changes in contour, size, tilt, color, or movement, are called *metamorphosias* by neurologists. For a detailed description of the variety of this phenomenon, see Willanger and Klee (1966).

states of fatigue, people commonly experience perceptual distortion. Here are several examples:

> When I'm tired things get blurry, I even lose focus so I see double.

> I didn't drop any acid (take LSD) for a week after the twelfth trip (LSD experience). But things went on—like I'd see blue as a fantastic electrical radiance. And sometimes I'd be looking at a seam or a line between walls and the line would kinda vibrate or collapse, bend in on itself.

> During the preliminary phase before my migraines I know they are inevitable because everything appears very tiny and far away (*micropsia*). The shapes are quite distinct, not any dimmer; everything just shrinks up.

Distortions in perception are often present as part of a syndrome of image events in psychiatric or neurologic patients. That is, a patient may, during an acute phase of illness, describe various events that are categorized separately as hallucinations, illusions, pseudohallucinations, and perceptual distortions. Sometimes a disintegrative episode begins with perceptual distortions and, as the condition deteriorates, advances to hallucinations.

3. SYNESTHESIAS

Synesthesias are blends of images from more than one mode of representation. For example, images from one sense are translated into images from another sense giving an unusual quality to immediate experience. Synesthesia is most commonly reported as "color hearing." That is, auditory stimuli are imaged in both auditory and in visual form, usually as a sensation of changing colors. The movie *Fantasia* and light shows with rock music give an external version of this internal phenomenon. Some persons always experience their thoughts synesthetically or invariably translate perceptions in one sense into images of another sense. Usually, however, the synesthetic experience is episodic rather than constant and persons who are not used to it may become startled when they experience a synesthesia.

An example of a constant type of synesthesia:

> Everything I hear has a color—nouns, music, and numbers especially. For example, whenever I hear the name 'Marsha' I see a green blob on the left of my mind and a yellow blob on the right, the edges are ragged. Marsha is always green and yellow. Also, when I hear music I think I get about the same color patterns every time I hear the record. Every number has its own color, always the same, and when you tell me

the numbers, I hear you but see the colors too, the colors help me remember.

4. DÉJÀ VU EXPERIENCES

Mention of this type of experience seems desirable although the experience is perhaps more one of mood or interpretation than images. A déjà vu experience consists of seeing a new situation as one that repeats a past experience when actually this is not true. The déjà vu experience is not restricted to visual perception but, when it does involve perception, it is a particular kind of illusion: an illusion of familiarity rather than misinterpretation of form.

> As I entered the hospital room I had the uncanny sensation that I had seen all these things before, that I had this entire same experience at some previous time. Yet I had never before set foot in this particular hospital. Seeing the bed and the hanging curtains seemed especially meaningful in terms of this sensation of memory. For a moment I felt as if I were unreal and transformed into some other time dimension.

Déjà vu phenomena, like many of the visual image experiences described in this chapter, may occur in full wakefulness in healthy persons. It occurs more frequently during stress, altered states of consciousness, psychedelic experiences, and the auras of epileptic seizures.

Other special feeling tones that may accompany visual perceptions include *depersonalization* or *derealization*. Depersonalization occurs when perception of the physical self is dislocated from the concept of personal identity. An example occurs when a person believes a part of his body belongs to someone else. Children at times delight in playful mimicry of this experience as when the hands are crossed and fingers move in apparently strange ways. Derealization occurs when current experience seems in some way no longer real. In terms of perceptual experience, there may be illusions of distance, graying, diminishing of visual intensity, or loss of three-dimensional quality. There may be confusion of image and perception, self and other, reality and fantasy. An extreme and very special form of derealization is the negative hallucination.

5. NEGATIVE HALLUCINATIONS

Negative hallucinations might have been considered under vividness along with hallucinations proper. Instead they are considered under this, the perceptual dimension, because negative hallucinations consist of not seeing something which is within the field of vision. This is a rarely reported phenomenon, because clinical interviewers are unfamiliar with the experience, seldom ask about it, and because patients would find this type of experience most difficult to notice or describe.

Sometimes very mild versions of negative hallucinations occur in everyday life. For example, one may be looking for some object, look right at it, but yet not consciously see it. Some positive hallucinations and illusions involve an aspect of negative hallucination: the real stimuli of perception are omitted from conscious representation and replaced by internal images. Relatively discrete negative hallucinations can apparently be produced in hypnotic trances and through the use of posthypnotic suggestion as illustrated by the following example:

> During a hypnotic trance the subject was told firmly that he would be unable to see Dr. Jones, an observer, even after being awakened from the hypnotic trance. If he looked directly at Dr. Jones, the suggestion continued, he would see right through him. In order to end the post-hypnotic effect, the subject was told that this "not seeing" would end after he counted to ten.
>
> The subject was then awakened and chatted normally with the hypnotist. When asked if he could see Dr. Jones, he said he could not. When asked what he saw on the chair Dr. Jones occupied, the subject insisted the chair was empty. The hypnotist then asked the subject, since the chair was empty, would he please go sit on it. The subject got up to comply but then walked around the room. He was asked why he refused to sit on the chair. The subject replied, "It looks too uncomfortable." Next, the suggestion was terminated by asking the subject to count to 10. He then reacted in a startled manner saying Dr. Jones was now in the chair and must have entered unobserved. When asked about his discomfort about the instruction to sit in the chair, the subject claimed he could not see Dr. Jones during the previous period but had a very anxious feeling that he must avoid the apparently empty chair.

One problem with hypnosis is how to interpret the subjective and introspective reports of the person in the trance. There is no situation where compliance is more of a problem. Is the hypnotic subject merely complying with the expectations of the hypnotist, or can hypnosis change perception? Whatever the answer, many skeptical subjects have reported the experience of negative hallucinations, and such reports are also found in persons unfamiliar with the term and the theory. Therefore, the phenomenon does appear to exist in subjective experience.

Such extremes of perceptual inhibition are not restricted to hypnosis. Certain forms of neurotic psychopathology, particularly hysterical neurosis, also may lead to strategic nonperception. For example, one woman patient reported that she saw men from the waist up but was blind to them below the waist. Her selective negative hallucination did not apply to women. Other hysteric patients may report the symptom of *tunnel vision* in which only the center of the visual field is seen, as if one were looking through a long tunnel. The wider field of vision is blotted out.

These inhibitions of perception occur without any evidence of neurologic pathology and are reversible with psychotherapy.

6. AFTER-IMAGES

An after-image is a residue that persists after removal of an external signal. The reader may have experienced both "negative" and "positive" after-images, terms borrowed from photography. For example, if for several seconds you look at a red object and then glance at a white wall you may "see" projected onto the wall the color green, opposite to red on the color wheel—this is a *negative after-image. A positive after-image*—a residue of the reddish impression—may also occur. Richardson (1969) gives a review of the relevant research literature.

Usually after-images last only a few seconds after the stimulus leaves the visual field. Sometimes the images persist for a long time or recur after a latency period (Hanawalt, 1954), and are of special interest because of their uncontrolled and unexplained entry into awareness.

Paliopsia is a rare and weird after-image that is noted in certain types of organic lesions of the brain (Feldman and Bender, 1969) and under the influence of some hallucinogenic drugs. In paliopsia an image continues after the gaze is deflected. For instance, if you were to look at a person's profile and then move your gaze away towards a nearby lampshade you might see the profile or a single eye on the lampshade. You might even see a chain of profiles as illustrated in Figure 4.

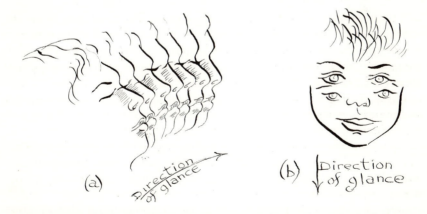

Fig. 4. An example of paliopsia. The subject had taken hashish and noted this type of after-image. When he shifted his gaze across the features of his companion, he noted a chain of images (a). When he moved his gaze up and down, a single feature, the eyes, was reduplicated.

D. IMAGES CATEGORIZED BY CONTENT

The remaining types of images described in this chapter receive their names from their characteristic content. Their vividness may range from hallucination or pseudohallucination, down to the status of "unconscious" images. As for context, they may occur in any of the various states described earlier. And, to a greater or lesser extent, their presence may result from perceptual interactions.

1. MEMORY IMAGE

A memory image is a reconstruction or resurrection of a past perception. Often people use memory images to recollect forgotten details.

> I could not recall whether the earrings had been packed away or not and was worried about them. I brought to mind my last look at the box and, in my mental picture tried to look into each compartment; then I saw them, over in the corner, and was relieved to know that they had been packed.

Memory images may be quite dim, almost nonsensory in nature, or they may be extremely distinct, even projected onto blank spaces such as walls or paper in an effort to localize them externally. When memory images are especially vivid they are called *eidetic images* and persons with eidetic capacity are sometimes said to have a photographic memory. *Eidetic images* are more common in children, as the capacity is often lost at the onset of adolescence. Some adults, however, retain this capacity. For example, the famous psychologist Titchener, reportedly had the ability to remember books he had read with distinct and accurate revisualization of the pages (McKellar, 1957).

Jaensch (1930) performed a classic study of young persons with eidetic images. He typologized his subjects as basedowoid or tetanoid by the vividness and sense of localization of their reported experiences. The "basedowoid type" experienced eidetic images with moderate vividness. The "tetanoid types" experienced eidetic images as vivid and externally localized, like perceptual images. Jaensch's terms are seldom used, however.

Persons with vivid memory images may find good use for their trait. More than one medical student has found an answer during a practicum by "reprojecting" an illustration from his anatomy text and finding from his image the information he needs. Architects, mathematicians, dancers, artists, and spies would probably also benefit to the degree that they could retain vivid memory images.

2. IMAGINARY IMAGE

An imaginary image contains contents that have never been perceived with that particular organization. The component parts of an imaginary image are derived from images of past perceptions and recombined to form new concepts and fantasies. Sometimes people use imaginary images to invent creative solutions, such as the architect who forms an image of a new idea for a drainage system. People also use imaginary images to daydream. Usually, a stream of thought or a daydream will be partly composed of memory images and partly composed of imaginary images that are new constructions of memory components. Often a person will confuse the imaginary and the memory images, that is, he may think his image is historically correct when aspects of it are fictive, or he may believe he only imagines something that he really once saw.

The phrase "imaginary image" can be confusing because it is used in two ways. One way, as above, differentiates content, which is either perceptual memories or a recombination of percepts. The other use of this term distinguishes the sources of image content, which are intrapsychic ("imaginary") and extrapsychic.*

3. ENTOPTIC IMAGES

Entoptic images, experienced as intrapsychic, relate to perception, since they arise from stimulation of optic structures within the eye or in some portion of the optic neural circuits as they travel to higher brain centers. "Seeing stars" on blows to the eye or head is an entoptic experience. (See Figure 5.) Ophthalmologic researchers were at one time disconcerted by this phenomenon. They would go to great lengths to seal off all visual perceptions using complex blindfolds only to hear subjects report little dancing lights, geometric figures, sparklers, or vague luminescent shapes. Such reports were sometimes blamed on the "ideoretinal light"—excitations of optic neurones arising from within the retina without benefit of light from the external world.

Entoptic events may also occur secondary to the physical properties of the eye itself. For example, the shadows cast upon the light sensitive receptors of the retina by blood vessels or "floaters" may lead to entoptic images. (Floaters are debris or residues of embryonic development

---

* Some investigators use the term "non-object bound" to refer to images whose derivation is entirely intrapsychic and "object-bound" for images based on external sources (Scheibel and Scheibel, 1962; Caston, 1969).

The arrows seem to move towards each other, the round things blink off and on with small purple lights moving downwards

Fig. 5. An entoptic image.

that may still float uselessly in the aqueous or vitreous fluids that balloon out the eye. They are technically termed *muscae volitantes*.)

Example of entoptic images:

> A physician was in the hospital suffering from leukemia. He knew his diagnosis and wanted to keep track of the count of his white blood cells as he was treated with anti-leukemic drugs. Although this information was withheld from him, he made relatively close approximations by an unusual method. By staring off at blank spaces of the ceiling and moving his face from side to side, he could see the shadows of cells moving in the capillaries of the retina. He could tell if the blood cells were densely or loosely packed in the vessels. (This is made possible by the orbital anatomic arrangement: the capillaries of the retina stand between the source of light, the pupil, and the nerve cells.)*

4. BODY IMAGE; BODY IMAGE EXPERIENCE

The body image † is a hypothetic construct of usually unconscious images that operates as a specialized, internal, analog data-center for information about the body and its environment (Schilder, 1950; Fisher and Cleveland, 1958). It is in constant transactional relationship with current perception, memory, emotions, drives, thoughts, and actions. The body image includes information about the shape, appearance, position, and organization of the body and its immediate surroundings. Theoretically, there may be a series of body images: the most current one being stacked upon and developed out of a series of body images and concepts of personal space extending backwards in time to the earliest body images of childhood (Horowitz, 1966). Some of these body images

---

* Chapter 10 discusses entopic images in greater detail.
† Sometimes referred to as the body schema or schemata.

may be preconscious, in a psychoanalytic sense: they can be raised into consciousness with volitional effort. Other body images are unconscious, cannot be deliberately raised to conscious representation, and emerge only under unusual circumstances.

When body image experiences gain consciousness, the degree of vividness will determine whether the image is a thought image, a pseudo-hallucination, or a hallucination. Thought images of the body commonly occur when a person anticipates performing an unusual, nonautomatic physical act. Pseudohallucinatory body image experiences may occur in states of unusual body sensations or when injuries change the physical structure of the body. For example, after a disfiguring facial burn or plastic surgery, some patients experience vivid images of the body as it was and as it is. In altered states of consciousness, whether induced by drugs or other processes, strange body experiences are common. These may include a feeling of leaving the body, of seeing it from a distance, of shrinkage or expansion, or specific changes in a given body part.

One of the most intriguing body image experiences is the *autoscopic phenomenon*—a visualization of the self, perhaps with hallucinatory vividness depicted as if seen from some external point. The autoscopic phenomenon, also known as "the double," may occur during fatigue, anxiety, toxic states, or in organic pathology of the brain (Todd and Denhurst, 1955). An example:

> I had taken several deep breaths of nitrous oxide and had for several minutes been in an euphoric and light-headed state. I felt I couldn't speak. Then I was able to go on with my work. I felt the experience was over when suddenly I saw myself in a most unusual way: I saw myself from the ceiling, from outside my body. I could see my hands working and even the expression on my face. I felt very objective and detached. The perception seemed entirely clear, as if I were seeing a double of myself.

5. PHANTOM LIMB

This is a version of body image disturbance which is so discrete that it has received a separate clinical label. The phantom limb experience occurs following amputation or loss of a body part. For example, about one quarter of the women who have had a breast removed surgically report phantom breast sensations (Jarvis, 1967). In the postamputation period the person continues to have "sensations" in the missing part just as if it were still present. Clinical study suggests that these sensations can be considered in both neurophysiologic and psychologic terms. Subjectively the experience can be realistic and even painful. Here is a typical example:

> Of course I knew my left leg had been amputated, yet even while I could see where it ended just above the knee and where the sheets

descended around it, I could still feel all the rounded and solid sensations of the missing lower part of my leg. The itch in my toes seemed real and the strangest thing of all was that an image of my toes formed in my mind's eye, and I could see exactly where they needed scratching.

6. PARANORMAL HALLUCINATION OR VISION

The mystic, religious, extraterrestial, or supernatural nature of the content gives this special variety of hallucination or pseudohallucination its title. Religious visions, ghosts, goblins, demons, fairies, guardian angels, and other apparitions fall into this category. Here is one person's description:

> I knew I couldn't go on as I had been. So I stayed in my room and fasted. I seemed to suffer greatly, to reach the brink of absolute despair. Then I had a sensation of great luminosity and began to see white flickering flames. With a feeling of great joy, of bliss, I saw a white robed figure pointing to a cross. I knew then my course, that I was not to marry, but was to devote myself entirely to the pursuit of religious truth. Often I have tried to recreate this splendid vision but have only the weakest of images. At the time it was the most brilliant thing I had ever seen and the memory of it still gives me the greatest comfort during moments of fatigue and uncertainty.

7. IMAGINARY COMPANIONS

Children sometimes insist that an imaginary playmate, human or animal, is always with them. Situation comedies on television have made use of this fact: "Oh, oh, don't sit on Herman, he's sitting there." Barnaby and Mr. O'Malley, and Harvey and his rabbit are good examples. Sometimes imaginary companions can achieve great vividness, and children will "actually see," that is hallucinate, the imagined person or pet. But most will say they are only imagining the companion in their minds. In both instances complete descriptions of color, form, shape, size, texture, and movement are given with such clarity that some form of visual image of the imagined object must be present.

8. NUMBER FORMS AND DIAGRAM FORMS

A number form is a characteristic schemata that a person uses to form visual images of numbers. People who use number forms for all arithmetic calculations are often surprised to learn not everyone shares this type of mental representation. And people without number forms are sometimes surprised and incredulous to hear of them. Some persons with number forms have very idiosyncratic visuo-spatial patterns as in the following example:

> Whenever I have to do any calculation with numbers, I visualize the numbers as a kind of ladder. It starts at the bottom of the left leg with one and goes up—two, three, four, each equidistant and written out in my handwriting until it gets to 13, then it jogs over to 14 and goes up on that leg of the ladder to 21, then it curves back to the left on 22. Then it goes to 30, rungs over for 31 to 40, then back for 41 and on to 100. After one hundred I don't seem to get the number form except for the last two digits. When I multiply two numbers like 12 x 23, then I see all of the numbers in the ladder but 12 and 23 are kind of lit up brighter than the others. I also see the days of the week but probably this is pretty conventional. Each day goes from left to right starting with Sunday in a kind of revolving drum so that a new level of the drum or spiral is started each Sunday. Whenever I make an appointment I mark it visually at the proper place on the drum. Today always stands out brighter on my visual image; "yesterday" and "tomorrow" are a little brighter than the other days but less bright than "today."

From this discussion of basic types of images, we will move on to a discussion of when visual images are most likely to occur.

REFERENCES

Beres, D. 1965. Symbol and object. *Bull. Menninger Clin.*, 29:3–23.

Caston, J. 1969. Completion effects and attention in hallucinatory and non-hallucinatory patients and normal subjects. *J. Nerv. Ment. Dis.*, 148:147–157.

Dement, W., and Kleitman, N. 1957. The relation of eye movements during sleep to dream activity. *J. Exp. Psychol.*, 53:339–346.

Feldman, M., and Bender, M. 1969. Hallucinations and illusions of parieto-occipital lobe origin. Paper presented at Eastern Psychiatric Research Association meeting, New York, November, 1969.

Fisher, S., and Cleveland, S. E. 1958. *Body Image and Personality*. Princeton, N.J., D. Van Nostrand Co.

Forbes, A. 1949. Dream scintillations. *Psychosom. Med.*, 11:160–162.

Freedman, D. X. 1968. On the use and abuse of LSD. *Arch. Gen. Psychiat.*, 18:330–347.

Freud, S. 1908. Hysterical phantasies and their relation to bi-sexuality. *Stand. Ed.*, 9, 1959.

Hanawalt, N. G. 1954. Recurrent images: New instances and a summary of the older ones. *Amer. J. Psychol.*, 67:170–174.

Horowitz, M. J. 1966. Body image. *Arch Gen. Psychiat.*, 14:456–460.

——— Adams, J., and Rutkin, B. 1967. Dream scintillations. *Psychosom. Med.*, 29:284–292.

Isakower, O. A. 1938. A contribution to the patho-psychology of phenomena associated with falling asleep. *Int. J. Psychoanal.*, 19:331–345.

Jaensch, E. R. 1930. *Eidetic Imagery & Typological Methods of Investigation.* London, Kegan, Paul, Trench and Truber & Co.

Jarvis, J. H. 1967. Post mastectomy breast phantoms. *J. Nerv. Ment. Dis.*, 144(4):266–272.

Jaspers, K. 1962. *General Psychopathology.* Manchester, England, Manchester University Press.

Jones, E. 1948. *Papers on Psychoanalysis*, 5th ed. Baltimore, Williams & Wilkins.

Joseph, E. D. 1959. An unusual fantasy in a twin with an inquiry into the nature of fantasy. *Psychoanal. Quart.*, 28:189–206.

Kandinski, V. 1880. Zur lehre von jen halluzinationen. *Arch. Psychiat.*, 11:453.

Lewin, B. D. 1948a. Inferences from the dream screen. *Int. J. Psychoanal.* 29:224–231.

——— 1948b. Reconsideration of the dream screen. *Psychoanal. Quart.*, 22:174–199.

——— 1946. Sleep, the mouth and the dream screen. *Psychoanal. Quart.*, 15:419–434.

McKellar, P. 1957. *Imagination & Thinking.* New York, Basic Books.

Richardson, A. 1969. *Mental Imagery.* New York, Springer Publishing Co.

Ruesch, J. 1957. *Disturbed Communication, the Clinical Assessment of Normal & Pathological Communicative Behavior.* New York, Norton.

Sarbin, T. R. 1967. The concept of hallucination. *J. Personality*, 35(3):359–380.

Saul, L. 1965. Dream scintillations. *Psychosom. Med.*, 27:286–289.

Scheibel, M., and Scheibel, A. 1962. Hallucinations and brain stem reticular core. In West, L., ed. *Hallucinations*, New York, Grune & Stratton.

Schilder, P. 1950. *The Image and Appearance of the Human Body: Studies in the Constructive Energies of the Psyche.* New York, International Universities Press.

Sedman, G. 1966. A comparative study of pseudohallucinations, imagery and true hallucinations. *Brit. J. Psychiat.*, 112:9–17.

Todd, J., and Denhurst, K. 1955. The double: its psychopathology and psychophysiology. *J. Nerv. Ment. Dis..* 122:47–55.

Willinger, R., and Klee, A. 1966. Metamorphopsia and other visual disturbances with latency occurring in patients with diffuse cerebral lesions. *Acta. Neurol. Scand.*, 42:1–18.

Zilboorg, G. 1941. *A History of Medical Psychology.* New York, W. W. Norton & Co.

3

The Circumstances that Increase Image Formation

Certain mental states encourage image formation. As with any psychologic phenomenon, paradoxic effects occasionally occur, and a few persons may experience decreased image formation under circumstances that increase image formation in most persons. These paradoxical effects occur because image formation is influenced not only by internal and external stimuli and motives but also is regulated by defensive or controlling motives. For example, most persons in conditions of perceptual deprivation report an increase in the frequency and vividness of imagery; a few persons, however, report a decrease in image formation, presumably because their controlling or defensive processes increase at a sharper rate than their impulsive processes.

Although individuals vary, generalizations can be made about the likelihood of image experiences under various circumstances. These generalizations help the clinician to evaluate a given image report in terms of the "expectability" of that occurrence. As emphasized in Chapter 2, the average person may hallucinate in some circumstances, but the same hallucination in another context may suggest the presence of some abnormality. This chapter describes generalizations about image formation in several states ranging from normal wakefulness to dreaming sleep. These generalizations are derived from clinical observations and experimental studies. In the last twenty years, many investigators studied the effects of sensory, sleep, or dream deprivation and accumulated evidence about what circumstances change image formation.

NORMAL WAKEFULNESS

Most persons form images at some time during their normal waking mental life, though they differ in frequency of images. Some persons think largely in a flow of visual images, others rarely experience a visual image and think mostly in words.*

Whatever the habitual style in problem-oriented or reality-oriented thinking, most people (about 95 percent) can form a visual image in full wakefulness when given a specific instruction (Betts, 1909; McKeller, 1957; Sheehan, 1967a and b). For example, when asked to form an image of a Christmas tree, most people will have at least a dim quasi-visual representation, some will have a technicolor tree with glowing lights, and only a very few will be unable to form any image. To form *visual* images is easier for more persons than to form images in any other sensory mode. For example, Brower (1947) found that on specific instruction, 97 percent of 15 subjects formed a visual image, 59 percent could form an auditory image, and 39 percent could form an image of smell. Sheehan (1967a) also found that subjects could form more vivid visual images than images in other sense modes. A conflicting finding is reported by Lindauer (1969); he found that tactile and gustatory type words aroused more vivid images than visual type words.

Daydreaming or fantasy while awake tends to further increase the visual quality of thought. Singer (1966) has studied daydreaming extensively and finds that about 96 percent of his adult subjects report at least some daydreaming activity every day although they differ widely in their frequency of fantasy. Most of these daydreams take the form of visual images of people, objects, or events. Singer reports variations based on sex, age, intelligence, social class, and other variables. For example, persons between 18 and 29 years of age reported more frequent daydreams than persons 30 to 39. Persons 40 to 49 reported the least daydreaming activity of his three age subgroups.

Images may also increase when planfulness decreases and persons enter a state of directionless thought. Some persons enter a state of directionless thought purposively (as with efforts at meditation). They stop efforts to attend to external stimuli, or efforts to remember or solve a particular problem, or efforts to rehearse future events. At other times, a reduction in planfulness may be involuntary—sometimes a train of

---

* This topic will be discussed in Chapters 4 and 5, which are about the role of the image in thought.

problem-solving thought reaches an impasse, and persons report an increase of images when baffled. Here is an example.

> A psychoanalytic patient embarked on a long chronology of her activities over the weekend. When she reached the end of her series of events she ran out of her planful organization of what she was going to say. At this point she said her mind became empty, blank, and she didn't know how to proceed. Then, to her surprise, a visual image sprang into mind of an open door leading into an empty room.

Images may also occur when a person expects certain external stimuli, when there is an unrewarded straining towards perception. In situations of boring perceptual search, unusually vivid internal images may occur, especially when the search leads to fatigue or a kind of trance-like state. This can be an occupational hazard of lookouts, aircraft spotters, radar operators, and jet pilots. For example, pilots flying at high altitudes, especially if the ground is concealed by clouds and they have little to do, may experience the "breakoff phenomenon," a state of detachment and confusion into which unbidden but vivid images may intrude (Clark and Graybiel, 1957).

REVERIES AND HYPNAGOGIC STATES

Image formation changes in quality and quantity as alertness wanes. At first the speed of thinking slows and the inclination to daydream increases. Images become more frequent and more vivid. Persons experience the contents and arrangement of the images as less controlled. In the deepest hypnagogic states, hallucinations may occur and suddenly activate the person to full wakefulness.

One of the earliest studies of reverie and hypnagogic states is a paper by Silberer (1909) in which he reported the use of hypnagogic reverie for the investigation of symbolism and hallucination formation (see Rapaport's translation and annotated version, Rapaport, 1951).* Silberer found that two conditions, drowsiness and the "antagonistic" active or forced effort to think, led to an "autosymbolic" phenomenon. This autosymbolic experience is quasi-hallucinatory: a visual symbol or metaphor comes forth automatically and represents a previously verbal thought. For example, Silberer was drowsy and yet forcing himself to think through how to correct an awkward phrase in an essay he was writing. He then experienced a visual image of smoothing a piece of wood with a plane: a metaphor for the goal of his thoughts.

---

* Rapaport's book, *The Organization and Pathology of Thought,* contains many of the classic papers on this topic, together with Dr. Rapaport's theoretic commentary. It is highly recommended to the reader.

Rapaport (1957) attempted to train himself to write automatically during periods of altered consciousness so that he could review the records later when fully awake. He collected records of his thoughts at various levels of alertness from waking to sleeping. The reports include daydreams, reveries, hypnagogic hallucinations, and dreams. During this progression, Rapaport noted that his reflective self-awareness decreased,* the ability to exert effort decreased, logical thinking decreased, and visual images increased in frequency and vividness.

Rapaport observed the same cognitive motif treated quite differently at different levels of awareness as had also been observed by Varendonck (1921) and Freud (1900). The motif concerned his wish to remain conscious and record his thoughts in spite of his urge to sleep. In full wakefulness he could conceptualize this as an antithesis: I must—I cannot. The next phase was a hypnagogic visual image of two waves that he was trying to bring together. He also saw somebody trying frantically to approach a door that slowly shut. He then fell asleep and dreamt he was on the way to an examination and was afraid he would be late. Then he "fell off," as if into deeper sleep. He then dreamt "a father in a monastery, panting, saying to his son, 'I am so glad you got in before they shut the door.'" Each of the four treatments of the motif becomes more concrete, more symbolic or metaphoric, and more visual. The final treatment seems like a wish-fulfillment. Note also the increased penetration of the current conceptual theme, "I must—I cannot" into other personal life issues and childhood memories as he entered dreaming sleep.

DREAMS

Like hallucinations, dreams are an extremely vivid form of imagery. Unlike hallucinations, all people experience dreams on a regular basis: each time a person sleeps, he dreams.

Dreams are a series of images, chiefly visual, although auditory, tactile, kinesthetic, and other forms of images and words may also occur. During a dream, ideas and feelings that are unfamiliar to waking life may emerge: raw hostility, strange erotic fantasies, new ideas, prophetic statements, and forgotten memories are commonplace in dreams.

Until recently we were dependent for dream reports on daytime recollection. Based on this source of introspective data, many clinicians believed, as did laymen, that people differ in how much they dream each night. Apparently this is not true. Recent studies of rapid eye movement sleep have given researchers the opportunity to wake people at various times throughout the night. Even people who do not remember dreams in

---

* Reflective self-awareness is the sense of being the thinker of one's thoughts.

the daytime and do not report having any dreams will report visual image events of fantasy-like quality during such procedures. Dreams reported in the daytime, as in analytic therapy, have a more cohesive story line than those reported on awakenings immediately after conclusion of a rapid eye movement period. Some dream researchers also find that laboratory dream narratives tend to be long and incoherent, less intense than the tightly organized and more drive-laden reports from dreams experienced at home. (Hall and Vandercastle, 1964; Domhoff and Kamiya, 1964.)

There are between three and five discrete dreams each night in almost every sleeper (Dement, 1955), and the several dreams of the night often have some kind of continuity and theme (Offenkrantz and Rechtshaffen, 1963). Early in the evening the dreams tend to revolve around residues of the day's events (Freud, 1900). As the night progresses, the dreams tend to center more on childhood and past events (Verdone, 1965). Dreams can incorporate internal or external stimuli or they may be impervious to such stimuli. Dream investigators have stimulated volunteers during dreaming sleep with lights, sounds, or temperature changes. The stimulus was clearly incorporated in 20 to 60 percent of dreams in one study of Dement and Wolpert (1958). When an external stimulus is incorporated into a dream, it is often changed symbolically and incorporated into the ongoing dream fantasy.

While dreaming, people enter various types of emotional states. Psychoanalytic studies of dream formation indicate that latent thoughts are more readily disguised than emotions. Thus, the ideas represented in the image contents may be accompanied by feelings that appear incongruent. Pleasant image contents may be associated with anxiety or anger. On the other hand, the person may have very pleasant or erotic feelings while having image contents that are of destructive or frightening themes. Such incongruities lead many people to regard dreams as "crazy" or meaningless. Plato accepted dreams as a normal form of madness and suggested that psychotics were persons who continued the bizarre mental life of the dream into wakefulness. (The reasons for the bizarre nature of some dreams will be considered with the psychodynamics of image formation in Chapter 6.)

Studies of the manifest content of dreams across groups of persons reduce some of the mystery of the individual dream experience. They show dreaming to be a variety of thought carried out in hallucinatory images and guided by primitive (as well as sophisticated) rules and regulations. Thus starving men report an increase in dreams of food and less dreams of sex; young children between 5 and 6 dream of magical happenings and ghosts; children 11 to 12 dream of play and travel; and aged persons have, as frequent dream contents, images reflecting feelings of helplessness and weakness as well as lost resources (for a review of manifest dream content in normal and pathologic states see Kramer, 1970).

RAPID EYE MOVEMENT SLEEP AND ITS ASSOCIATION WITH DREAM THINKING

The ability to sample dream states increased markedly when the psychologic experience of dreaming was related to neurophysiologic indices. Aserinski and Kleitman (1953) noted that during the night there were periodic cycles of a brain wave recording characteristics of "alertness" and rapid eye movements (REM). Dement and Kleitman (1957) found that subjects awakened from this "Stage 1 REM" sleep reported dreams relatively frequently (about 80 percent of the time). When subjects were awakened from non-REM sleep, they reported mental contents suggestive of dreams only infrequently (20 percent or less of reports in most subjects).

Many studies have been conducted in multiple sleep laboratories since these initial discoveries. Some kind of thinking seems to go on during every stage of sleep. The four to five REM periods that most subjects have in an average night seem to be accompanied by visual images of hallucinatory vividness. These images are often arranged in some kind of story line organized by primary process principles.* Reports of subjects on awakenings from non-REM sleep contain conspicuously fewer visual images. The thoughts are experienced more as words or simple ideas with less admixture of primary process thinking (Rechtschaffen et al. 1963). Of interest, Fiss et al. (1968) have found that persons awakened from REM sleep show more primary process responses on projective psychologic tests (such as inkblot interpretation) than persons wakened from non-REM sleep.

The presence of hallucinatory visual images during REM sleep led to efforts to find linkages between neurophysiologic events and these subjective experiences. During REM sleep various areas of the brain associated with vision enter an excitation state as shown by depth electrode studies in animals. So far nothing can be said with certainty, but some evidence suggests that the optical receptive areas of the brain are excited before the associative, cortical, or "thinking" areas (Cordeau, 1964). Were this so, cyclic, optical-type excitations (either peripheral or central) might provide raw sensory material out of which the psychologically meaningful dream is constructed.

That some sensory stimuli, of endogenous origin, provide a nidus for dream formation is an interesting but still speculative notion. Only milli-

---

* To be described later in more detail. Primary process may for the moment be regarded as primitive, magical, and wishful thinking without regard for logical or realistic critera.

seconds are required for transmission of impulses along nerve tracts, and the sequence of excitation of structures is difficult to measure. Once measured, the significance of recordings is hard to determine, or, and even if an area appears to be activated "first," we are unsure what this means. The highly interactional relationship of images, perception, eye movements, and schemata for tracking and matching visual stimuli with head movement and position may make any "which comes first" question hard to answer, or even inappropriate.

There are some other data that relate the subjectively experienced images of the dream with neurophysiologic or behavioral events that can be objectively recorded. While there have been conflicting reports, some investigators have found the direction of eye movements, as recorded with the electro-oculogram or electromyogram of eye muscles, may correspond at times with the reported dream contents on subsequent awakening (Dement and Wolpert, 1958). For example, Roffwarg et al. (1962) found that vertical eye movements might be associated with a dream report such as climbing stairs while horizontal eye movements might be associated with reports such as watching a tennis match.

An added perspective to the relationship between REMS and visual images involved studies of persons with brain lesions and the congenitally blind. Greenberg (1966) found that persons with brain damage in visual association areas had diminished or absent eye movements towards the impaired visual field. In congenitally blind subjects investigators did not, at first, find rapid eye movements during sleep, although the characteristic brain wave pattern was present (Berger et al., 1962; Offenkrantz and Wolpert, 1963). New methods of measuring eye movements, however, demonstrated that the congenitally blind do have rapid eye movements, even though they do not dream in visual images (Amadeo and Gomez, 1966; Gross et al., 1965). Thus, rapid eye movements may be a part of the neurophysiology of Stage 1-REM sleep regardless of the presence of visual images in the subjective dream. Perhaps this is one example of physiologic functions which precede and are then coordinated with psychic processes. In the case of REMS, optic excitations which are controlled by the lower brain on a physiologic and automatic level may provide the material which is later given subjective meaning on a psychic level.

DREAM DEPRIVATION

Dream deprivation is a selective form of sleep deprivation. Whenever a person enters Stage 1 of rapid eye movement sleep, he is awakened. The first night may require five such awakenings and the person may lose about 80 percent of his normal amount of dream time. On subsequent nights the sleeper enters stage 1 REM more frequently so that eventually 12 or more awakenings may be necessary. If allowed to sleep, the person shows a rebound effect; instead of "dreaming" for 20 to 25 percent of his sleep time, he may "dream" 50 to 60 percent of the time. Early dream research findings were thought to indicate a possible need for dreaming (Fisher and Dement, 1963). It was reasoned, that a dream-deprived person might "dream," that is hallucinate, while he was awake during the day. Studies by Fisher and Dement yielded supportive results: subjects were thought to have a latent hallucinatory propensity during the dream-deprived state. Pivik and Foulkes (1966) found that dream deprivation led to intensified dream content on subsequent REM awakenings. Other studies yield less supportive data and the question of the waking effects of dream deprivation, at present, is undecided. Greenberg et al. (1968) reported an increase in primary process thinking as shown only on responses to Rorschach tests given during the day. Sampson (1966) reported that objective psychologic tests showed no significant changes after dream deprivation but that the behavior of subjects shifted: some subjects developed oral cravings, childish behavior, and an increase in aggressive themes in their reported dream fragments. My own unpublished studies suggest an increase in fantasy images, but awakening control subjects in non-REMS led to similar increases in fantasy. The apparent increase in primary process or imagery seemed due to the emotional effects of the experiment: multiple awakenings, close contact with the investigators for many nights, and so forth, rather than dream deprivation per se.*

Past studies have found that total sleep deprivation increases visual imagery experiences, even to the point of hallucinations. The presence of other disturbances in reality-relatedness has led some investigators to consider sleep deprivation as a means of producing a transient "model psychosis" in normal persons (Luby et al., 1962; West et al., 1961; Brauchi and West, 1959; Kollar et al., 1969). Again, there is often a progression from entoptic-type images and perceptual distortions to hallucinations suggesting a release phenomenon. There is, however, a tremendous amount of individual variation. Disc jockeys on marathons and high school students engaged in feats of sleeplessness may go many days and not report hallucinations.

NEUROSIS AND THE FUNCTIONAL PSYCHOSIS

Increased image formation may occur as a person loses the subjective sense of volitional control over mental processes. This loss of the

---

* Two examples from this research are presented in Chapter 6.

sense of volitional control may occur with either neurosis or psychosis. In neurotic states enhanced image formation seldom reaches hallucinatory intensity during waking life; in the psychoses hallucinations and pseudo-hallucinations occur more frequently.

There are few rules about what kinds of neurotic disorders may lead to increased image formation. Individuals vary too widely and the diagnostic categories now in use do not correlate with the presence or absence of any specific type of image experience. Obsessional patients may report recurrent intrusive images of sadistic scenes, often without emotional accompaniment. Also obsessional patients tend to use isolation and to compartmentalize certain concepts in images by denying these images' translation into words (Beres, 1965). Hysterical patients may have images of sexual danger and phobic patients may have unbidden images of disaster accompanied by a feeling of guilty fearfulness. But none of these comments can be extended to generalizations since neurotic patients differ very widely.

Some generalizations can be applied to increased image formation· as seen in psychosis. Hallucinations are notoriously, perhaps too notoriously, common in schizophrenic episodes and are more frequent in acute than chronic episodes (Bleuler, 1950). But no hard and fast rule is applicable: persons with involutional psychosis, hysterical psychosis, or transient psychotic regressions (psychotic character, or borderline personality) also may hallucinate. The diagnosis of schizophrenia should never be based on the presence of hallucinations alone.

Visual hallucinations are less frequent than auditory hallucinations in the group of schizophrenic syndromes. Jansson (1968) reviewed the admission records of 293 young schizophrenic patients and found that 84 had evidence of hallucinations. Of these 84, 87 percent had auditory hallucinations and 44 percent had visual hallucinations. Some patients had both auditory and visual, a few had hallucinations of smell, touch, or taste. Small et al. (1966) found a similar, but smaller visual percentage: 30 percent of schizophrenic subjects reported visual hallucinations. Jansson found a slight but not statistically significant trend towards a more favorable course in patients with visual hallucinations only. He found no association between the mode of hallucination, auditory or visual, and premorbid personality. Schizophrenic patients may continue to hallucinate as they pass from the acute to chronic phase of their syndromes. Malitz et al. (1962) found that 50 percent of 100 chronic schizophrenics had auditory hallucinations; only 9 percent reported visual hallucinations. Havens (1962) also notes the comparative reduction of visual hallucinations in chronic schizophrenics while auditory hallucinations appear to be common. Clinically, the more disoriented, excited, and confused the patient is, the more likely he is to have visual hallucinations.

The contents of hallucinatory or pseudohallucinatory images vary widely with the current internal motives of the patient. Persons who feel that they are losing mental control may project this feeling into bodily sensation and into images of bodily disintegration—volcanoes erupting, or persons or things coming apart, or scenes of world destruction. Those who feel totally neglected and alienated may form images that show hollowness, emptiness, or objects being eaten away. Such image contents depict feelings and impulses in a concrete but sometimes displaced or symbolic form. Other common hallucinations may provide an explanation for the sense of disintegration: the images may be of machines or persons who are emitting controlling rays or influences. Still other image contents, that commonly are reported, provide something that is needed or restorative. Just as the starving man may hallucinate food, a schizophrenic patient may hallucinate people who are praising him, telling him how to behave, or condemning him for his impulses. These figures may range from relatives to cosmic religous figures. The person who fears he has destroyed the world may envision complicated metaphysical structures to restore it.

There will be differences in hallucinations according to social, sexual, and age factors since these influence internal motives. Forgus and Dewolfe (1969) attempted a content analysis of themes in schizophrenic hallucinations. In their small sample of 18 men and 12 women, they found that 67 percent of the women reported hallucinations containing themes of conscience disturbance ("repent") while this theme was found in only 7 percent of men. Men were more likely to hallucinate themes such as compensatory grandiosity ("You are God") or coping with problems ("Do your job").

Researchers have also studied the manifest content of dreams of schizophrenic patients. While never diagnostic, some dream contents apparently occur or are reported more frequently in groups of schizophrenic persons. For example, hostility may be blatant and self-directed; scary dreams may occur with frequent change of scenes, or banality of content; or an isolated actionless person may be pictured surrounded by open spaces or strangers (Kramer, 1970). By and large, however, many dream reports of schizophrenic persons are just like those of normal persons, and nonschizophrenic persons experience, at times, dreams such as those described above.

Persons with depressive psychosis also may have an increased incidence of certain dream contents when the reports of groups are compared. Hostility is present about one-half the time and divided equally between the dreamer and some other dream character; the dreams often include family members and themes of escape (Kramer, 1970).

NEUROBIOLOGIC CHANGES IN THE EYE OR BRAIN

Any type of electrophysiologic, biochemical, or physical change involving the eye, the optic tracts, or the brain may lead to increased imagery experiences. In fact, visual hallucinations may be a major presenting symptom in toxic delirium. The imagery experiences range from perceptual distortions, through elementary sensations, to full hallucinations. Any of the phenomena reported in Chapter 2 may occur. These observations are detailed in Chapters 10 (the eye) and 11 (the brain).

INCREASES IN IMAGE FORMATION INDUCED EXPERIMENTALLY

Much recent research has involved image formation in one way or another: that is why the topic of imagery is once again important in contemporary psychology and psychiatry (Holt, 1964a). The research aims to create experimental extensions of unusual but natural occurrences that tend to evoke hallucinations in some people. One reason for excitement was the hope of learning more about hallucinations and what kinds of circumstances foster this type of break with reality. Many investigators hoped to discover a kind of artificial psychosis or laboratory equivalent of psychosis so that the pressing problem of mental illness could be solved. Unfortunately, the syllogism is not necessarily accurate: schizophrenics may hallucinate, but making people hallucinate may not reveal the cause of schizophrenia. However, the research has revealed the lack of clarity about how to define different types of imagery and has indicated the need to differentiate clearly two types of loss of control over image formation: loss of control over contents, and loss of control over vividness and other formal properties.

SENSORY DEPRIVATION

A person may be deprived of one sensation, say vision, of more than one, or of all sensations. Natural occurrences include variations ranging from social isolation to specific deprivations of sensation. Persons trapped in mine disasters, on liferafts or lifeboats, or confined to isolation and nonmotility after heart surgery, or to darkness after cataract removal operations may share one sensation in common: they may experience vivid and unbidden images of hallucinatory intensity (Solomon, et al., 1961; Miller, 1962).

The first experimental studies on perceptual deprivation were done early in the 1950's at McGill University (Bexton et al., 1954). The investigators put subjects alone in a blank room and had them listen to a meaningless hum of "white" noise (a sound like a radio between stations). In this state of strangely reduced perception and isolation, subjects reported increased visual imagery, loss of control over thought contents, and hallucinations.

In sensory deprivation, image experiences often emerge progressively. At first the normal level of visual images in thought intensifies. Then sensations of geometric figures, lights, or colors may emerge (entoptic images). Volitional control—the ability to direct a sequence of thought or images—diminishes and hallucinations occur in some subjects (Freedman and Greenblatt, 1960; Vernon et al., 1958). Experimenters noted that in certain individuals the "hallucinations" might occur as soon as the first hour and subsequently diminish. This led to the hypothesis that the early hallucinations were the result of an attempt to obtain stimulation from the external world and that this wish to cling to the external world might be subsequently relinquished (Zuckerman et al., 1962).

Such observations led to more studies, and repeated experimentation demonstrated that hallucinations could occur without prolonged exposure to sensory deprivation. Within a ten minute period after the placement of the eye patches, binocularly eye-patched subjects reported imagery similar to that of persons subjected to prolonged sensory deprivation (Ziskind and Augsburg, 1962). Also the kinds of images reported and the extent to which subjects reported imagery after deprivation varied with suggestion (Rossi et al., 1963; Mendelson et al., 1963) but could not be accounted for merely by suggestion (Zuckerman and Cohen, 1964a).

Goldberger and Holt (1961) correlated the occurrence of imagery during sensory deprivation-isolation conditions with measures from an extensive assessment including a battery of objective tests, qualitative data from projective techniques, interviews, and autobiography. It was difficult to find any special correlation of other measures such as personality traits to the process of forming images. The authors interpreted the correlations that did occur in a general way: subjects who were emotionally free, intellectually flexible, and wished to cooperate had some tendency to report more images than those who were relatively more emotionally constricted, intellectually rigid, and less motivated to be a "good subject."

From these studies came two theories which are not necessarily antagonistic. One maintains that wakeful consciousness requires continued incoming stimuli to maintain alertness. To preserve this level of stimulus nutriment, internal images may be facilitated when external signals are not available. The second theory posits that image formation increases because a person enters an altered state of consciousness. The relative reduction in reality-oriented (secondary process) thought leads to an increase of primitive thought forms (primary process) (Goldberger and Holt, 1961). Both theories suggest that there is an ever-available internal source of images and that these images are released or facilitated under appropriate circumstances.

A tremendous effort went into sensory deprivation research, but many energetic investigators feel that the field still lacks defining principles and organized theory (Kubzansky, 1964). Two serious problems confounded the work. One is that the various investigators never agreed upon a set of definitions to differentiate image experiences. Some called almost all image reports "hallucinations"; others used far more stringent definitions (Suedfeld and Vernon, 1964; Ziskind and Augsburg, 1962; Zuckerman and Cohen, 1964b). The second problem was the tremendous variability between subjects in terms of what was experienced during isolation, sensory depatterning, sensory restriction, or sensory deprivation (Miller, 1962; Goldberger and Holt, 1961). Partly this variation in subjects was due to variances in thought styles, which will be discussed in the next two chapters, and partly it was due to the unreliability and variability of introspective reports.

The problem of introspective reports haunts every research study on image formation and is worth considering briefly at this point. Visual thought images are essentially private: no one but the subject can know of them except through some form of description. These descriptions of intrapsychic events have long been suspect as an instrument of science (see Bakan, 1967, for a review). Why? The answer can be summarized under the headings of false positive and false negative reports.

FALSE POSITIVES, MISCOMMUNICATIONS, AND SEMANTIC CONFUSIONS

Language is loaded with words that refer to vision (Sarbin, 1967) and these words seem to be "primed" in any communication about thought. When a person says, "I see," he may be referring to a wide range of psychic phenomena from hallucinations to perception to a vague word representation. Moreover, subjects vary greatly in their reports. One person may describe a moderately vivid thought image as if it were a hallucination; another person may give a bland description of a hallucination. The observer must modify descriptions by other observations of the style of the patient in order to get to the phenomenologic "facts" (Shapiro, 1965). The descriptions of very disturbed patients are often labeled as hallucination when the patient may have vivid visual thought images that are *not* actually experienced as occurring in the external environment. The investigator and his subjects rarely are found to share spontaneous definitions and labels of cognitive events. Training of the subjects by certain criteria is very difficult: they often say they "get it" when they do not. Even if they do "get it," for a while they frequently lapse into their previous and indiosyncratic method of labeling cognitive events.

This variable is compounded by a further source of error: the tremendous susceptibility of image formation to suggestion based on the demand characteristic of the experiment (Orne, 1962). Also, changes in mental state of any sort will affect subjective experience and communication (e.g., change in consciousness, attention, affect, attitude toward others, appraisal of situation, expectation, plans, or wishes to comply or resist).

FALSE NEGATIVES

1. When reporting images, subjects often neglect sensations with minor or mild intensity since they expect an image to be vivid and durable.

2. Attentiveness and memory for visual images are variable. Some subjects do not include their peripheral awareness of visual thought images as part of "what is (has been) on the mind." Even after repeated instruction and reinstruction, some subjects give additional responses at a later time, e.g. "Oh, did you want me to tell that, too?" Fleeting images are easily forgotten.

3. Some subjects find it hard to translate visual images into words and either do not do so or else give distorted verbal reports of their subjective experience.

4. Certain subjects have a cognitive style of representation in which personal, intimate, affect, and impulse loaded ideas are presented predominantly in imagery. Some such subjects are reticent about telling their imagery content on the grounds that it would betray too much or be like "reading their minds," although they are willing to describe their "real thoughts" (by which they mean thoughts in word representation).

These control problems make vulnerable any experimental design that contrasts one group of subjects, (e.g., by diagnostic labels) with another group of subjects. The differences noted might be due only to variation in some aspect of communication style. Even cross correlations between one type of image and another come under this hazard. For example, suppose an individual reports vivid images during sensory deprivation experiences and during hypnagogic experiences, and scores high on voluntary image formation tasks and on questionnaires. This does not mean that his images are necessarily more vivid than those of a person who tends to use low-key or "moderate" descriptors.

While there is always the possibility of false negatives and false positives, introspective reports remain our richest (only?) source of information about the internal subjective experiences of another person. As theoretic psychologists like Bakan (1967) and Maher (1966) have pointed out, the *knowing* by an experimenter of the *meaning* of a subject's report is acceptable in the framework of clinical dynamic psychology and psychiatry and must eventually find its place in our scientific method. The problem with this use of "knowing," through rapport or empathy, through construction within oneself of another's experience, is that bias and distortion readily occur, and are difficult to detect. So far, the best way out of the dilemma seems to be constant efforts to describe clearly the criteria of clinical judgments. These statements can then be assembled and used as a kind of manual for content analysis. So far, no agreed upon or demonstrably reliable manual for scoring reports for the presence of visual image experiences is available. A provisional manual for content analysis is presently in use (Appendix, pp. 192–196), as will be described in Chapter 9.

DRUGS AS ENHANCERS OF IMAGE FORMATION

After taking psychedelic drugs such as LSD, psilocybin, mescaline, and peyote, some people report remarkable increases of image formation and a variety of other altered experiences (Hoffer and Osmond, 1967). One theory to explain this increase is that the drugs alter the regulation of optic pathways by inhibition and facilitation (Freedman, 1968). This is the release theory of hallucinations and is often credited to Hughlings Jackson (1932). Jackson assumes that thought images, hallucinations, and perceptions may to some extent share the same neural substrates, a view shared by Freud (1900) and recently restated by Evarts (1962). Ordinarily, excitation by internal images is inhibited before it activates perceptual neural structures.* In altered states of conscious-

---

* Cohen (1938) has reviewed the contrasting view of de Clerambault, Kandinsky and Baillarger that hallucinations and thought images arise from separate mechanisms.

ness, such as those induced by drugs, inhibition decreases and internal imagination or memory images may gain access to the perceptual neural substrates. What results is hallucination.

Support for this view is gained in such experiments as those of Marrazzi (1962) who showed that LSD may lower the threshold for the occurrence of experimentally induced illusions. Another support for the release theory is the progression of image experiences observed as the drugs take effect. The first sign of drug effect is usually some kind of perceptual distortion; then entoptic-type images and illusions commonly appear (Hoffer and Osmond, 1967). Thought images become more vivid and less controlled. Finally they advance towards hallucinations in terms of vividness and external projection (Maclay and Guttman, 1941). This progression is similar to that experienced on falling asleep, entering a delirium from a high fever or alcoholism, or sensory deprivation.

While some drugs seem to have a primary effect on the visual representation system, drugs also create other effects that contribute to enhanced image formation. Loss of concentration, loss of short-term memory, and loss of ability to sequence thoughts in a meaningful train of associations are such factors (Paul, 1964). Other drug effects that probably increase image formation include loss of capacity to exert volitional control, passivity, feelings of elation, body image changes, and turning towards primitive types of thought organization (Linton and Langs, 1962). Thus, psychologic factors are important in addition to whatever specific neurobiologic changes in the visual system are induced by drugs. For example, Slater et al. (1957) found that subjects who were alone taking LSD averaged 1.8 severe hallucinatory or illusion experiences, while subjects taking LSD in a group averaged only 0.8 experiences.

Many drugs other than the psychedelic agents increase image experiences. Indeed, visual hallucinations are sometimes a clinical clue that a toxic drug-induced delirium is the cause of a patient's psychotic episode. Bromide psychosis is one example. Also, excessive use of amphetamine type drugs (dexedrine, benzedrine, "speed," and so forth) may induce hallucinatory psychosis, although visual images are not remarkably enhanced on a single ingestion.* Ellinwood (1967) found auditory and visual hallucinations in one-half of patients treated in a psychiatric hospital for amphetamine psychosis. Most patients with auditory hallucinations also had visual hallucinations. Fear and suspiciousness were prominently associated with the hallucinations, and the patients reported a heightened awareness of faces and eyes. Chapter 12 will dwell at greater length on delayed drug effects.

---

* For a review of hallucinogens see Hoffer and Osmond (1967) and Schultes (1969).

HYPNOSIS

The word hypnosis customarily refers to an induction procedure performed by a hypnotist, to a state of consciousness called a "trance," and to several effects which can be achieved in this state. In the trance state, persons can be instructed to form visual images, to dream, or even to hallucinate. Their descriptions of the experience which ensues may resemble the descriptions of persons who spontaneously dream or hallucinate. Apparently the factors of suggestion, the role of being hypnotized, and the regressed state of consciousness of the trance all contribute to enhanced image formation.

How many of the reported image effects are specific to hypnotic procedures and the hypnotic state? Barber (1969) has done extensive systematic research work with hypnosis. He contends that the hypnotic state is a superfluous construct which does not add to our understanding because it involves circular reasoning: because the hypnotic state is used to account for high levels of response (e.g., increased image formation), subjects who manifest high responses to suggestions are said to be in a hypnotic state. On the other hand, Orne (1959) suggests that under hypnosis there is a relatively specific change in the subjective experience of hypnotized individuals. Both contentions have merit: the hypnotic experience is a distinct one, for those who have experienced it; the experiences under hypnosis, however, can be effected without trance induction. For example, Spanos and Barber (1968) set out to contrast the image experiences, on specific instructions, of subjects hypnotized and subjects not hypnotized. They found that one-third of a group of 102 student nurses reported that they clearly experienced a strongly suggested visual hallucination (seeing a cat in their laps) even though they were not induced into a hypnotic state. Subjects who were hypnotized had an increase of such visual reports beyond this baseline level, but the degree of increase was not remarkable in comparison with this high level of response in nonhypnotized subjects. The operational definition of hallucination in this study seems to have a low threshold for positive categorization. I would prefer the term pseudohallucination since I doubt that one third of the student nurses lost their reality testing capacity. But the study does show how powerful suggestion alone can be without the addition of specific efforts to alter the state of consciousness.

Sometimes, in a hypnotic trance, subjects are instructed to form positive or negative hallucinations; to "see" something that is not there, or not to see something that is there. Many subjects report complete compliance with the suggestions. The question is, are the positive hallucinations really as vivid to the subject as a perception? If evidence were found that the hallucinations replicated perceptual experience, then this would show that psychologic motivation can lead internal images into entry of the perceptual substrates. Some ingenious experimental psychologists have attempted to answer this question.

Brady and Levitt (1966) showed subjects a rotating drum marked with vertical stripes. As the drum turns, the stripes move across the subject's visual field; these moving stripes cause a reflex movement of the eyes that is called nystagmus. Nystagmus is involuntary, and subjects asked merely to imagine the drum, after it had been removed, did not develop nystagmus types of eye movements. Brady and Levitt then hypnotized subjects and asked them to hallucinate the rotating drum: in the trance state many subjects did develop the same kind of nystagmus eye movements that they showed while watching the drum in reality. Underwood (1960) tried a similar method using optical geometric illusions and telling subjects to see or not to see various aspects of the geometric figure. He found evidence for positive but not negative hallucinations. In spite of these findings, however, some investigators remain uncertain as to the apparent perceptual reality of hypnotic hallucinations, and the reader may wish to withhold judgment until further research is published.

CONCLUSION

Any situation that induces an altered state of consciousness will change image experiences. While this statement sums up a great many clinical and experimental observations, it also is a tautology: altered states of consciousness are defined by the contents of consciousness, the organization of these conscious contents, and the precursors and residues of the awareness of these contents. Thus, altered states of consciousness are partially defined by the presence or absence, vividness, content, and volitional control of images. While there is great variance between persons, certain generalizations can be made as to changes in the quality of image experience as a person becomes less wakeful, reality-oriented, and committed to reason and problem-solving thought. Images begin to occur more frequently, to attain greater vividness, and to escape directions of the will and limitations of censorship. The contents of images tend to be derived more and more from inner sources, less and less from external stimuli. In their organization they follow progressively more primitive or simple styles, and tend to be controlled more by wish or fear than the requirements of reality. In addition, there is a tendency towards fantasy elaboration of elementary sensations such as entoptic phenomena which may end in hallucination. As these changes take place, there is a gradual loss of the sense of self-direction of the course of image formation.

REFERENCES

Allers, R., and Teller, J. (1924). On the utilization of unnoticed impressions in associations. *Psychol. Issues*, Monogr. 7, 2:121–155, 1960.

Amadeo, M., and Gomez, E. 1966. Eye movements, attention and dreaming in subjects with lifelong blindness. *Canad. Psychiat. Ass.* J., 11:500–507.

Aserinski, E., and Kleitman, N. 1953. Regularly occurring periods of eye motility and concommitant phenomena during sleep. *Science*, 118:273–274.

Bakan, D. 1967. *On Method*. San Francisco, Jossey-Bass, Inc.

Barber, T. X. 1969. *A Scientific Approach to Hypnosis*. Princeton, Van Nostrand.

———— and Calberley, D. S. 1965. Hypnotizeability, suggestibility, and personality. II. An assessment of previous imaginative-fantasy experiences by the As, Barber-Glass, and Shor questionnaires. *J. Clin. Psych.*, 21:57–58.

Beres, D. 1965. Symbol and object. *Bull. Menninger Clin.*, 29:3–23.

Berger, R. J., Olley, P., and Oswald, I. 1962. The EEG, eye-movements and dreams of the blind. *Quart. J. Exp. Psychol.*, 14:183–186.

Betts, G. H. 1909. *The Distribution and Functions of Mental Imagery*. New York: Columbia University Teacher's College Press.

Bexton, W. H., Heron, W., and Scott, T. H. 1954. Effects of decreased variation in sensory environment. *Canad. J. Psychol.*, 8:70–76.

Bleuler, E. 1950. *Dementia Praecox or The Group of Schizophrenias*. New York: International Universities Press.

Brady, J. P., and Leavitt, E. E. 1966. Hypnotically induced visual hallucinations. *Psychosom. Med.*, 28:351–363.

Brauchi, J. T., and West, L. J. 1959. Sleep deprivation. *J.A.M.A.*, 171:11–14.

Brain, R. 1955. *Diseases of the Nervous System*. London, Oxford University Press.

Bromberg, W., and Schilder, P. 1933. Psychologic considerations in alcoholic hallucinosis. *Int. J. Psychoanal.*, 14:206–224.

Brower, D. 1947. The relative predominance of various imagery modalities. *J. Gen. Psych.*, 37:199–200.

Clark, B., and Graybiel, A. 1957. The breakoff phenomenon. *J. Aviat. Med.*, 28:121–126.

Cohen, L. H. 1938. Imagery and its relations to schizophrenic symptoms. *J. Ment. Sci.*, 84:284–346.

Cordeau, J. P. 1964. Abstracted in *Electroenceph. Clin. Neurophysiol.*, 17:442–443.

Dement, W. 1955. Dream recall and eye movements during sleep in schizophrenic subjects and normals. *J. Nerv. Ment. Dis.*, 122:263–269.

────── and Wolpert, E. 1958. The relation of eye movements, body motility, and external stimuli to dream content. *J. Exp. Psychol.*, 55:543–553.

────── and Kleitman, N. 1957. The relation of eye movements during sleep to dream activity: An objective method for the study of dreaming. *J. Exp. Psychol.*, 53:339–346.

Domhoff, B., and Kamiya, J. 1964. Problems in dream content study with objective indicators. *Arch. Gen. Psychiat.*, 11:519–532.

Evarts, E. V. 1962. A neurophysiologic theory of hallucinations. In West, L. J., ed. *Hallucinations*, New York, Grune & Stratton.

Eagle, M. 1962. Personality correlates of sensitivity to subliminal stimulation. *J. Nerv. Ment. Dis.*, 134:1–17.

────── Wolitsky, D. L., and Klein, G. S. 1966. Imagery: Effects of a concealed figure in a stimulus. *Science*, 151(2):837–839.

Ellinwood, E. H. 1967. Amphetamine psychosis: 1. Description of the individuals and process. *J. Nerv. Ment. Dis.*, 144:273–283.

Fisher, C. 1960. Subliminal and supra-liminal influences on dreams. *Amer. J. Psychiat.*, 116:1009–1017.

────── 1954. Dreams and perception: The role of preconscious and primary modes of perception in dream formation. *J. Amer. Psychoanal. Assoc.*, 2:389–445.

────── and Dement, W. 1963. Studies on the psychopathology of sleep and dreams. *Amer. J. Psychiat.*, 119:1160–1168.

────── and Paul, I. H. 1959. The effect of subliminal visual stimulation on images in dreams: A validation study. *J. Amer. Psychoanal. Assoc.*, 7:35–83.

Fiss, H., Ellman, S. J., and Klein, G. S. 1968. Effects of interruption of rapid eye movement sleep on fantasy in the waking state. *Psychophysiology*, 4:364 (Abstract).

────── Goldberg, F. H., and Klein, G. S. 1963. Effects of subliminal stimulation on imagery and discrimination. *Percept. Motor Skills*, 17:31–44.

Forgus, R. H., and Dewolfe, A. S. 1969. Perceptual selectivity in hallucinatory schizophrenics. *J. Abnorm. Psychol.*, 74:288–292.

Freedman, D. X., 1968. On the use and abuse of LSD. *Arch. Gen. Psychiat.*, 18:330–347.

Freedman, S. J., and Greenblatt, M. 1960. Studies in human isolation, II. Hallucinations and other cognitive findings. *U.S. Armed Forces Med. J.*, 2:1479–1497.

Freud, S. (1900) The interpretation of dreams. *Stand. Ed.*, 4, 1953.

Goldberger, L. 1961. Homogeneous visual stimulation (Ganzfeld) and imagery. *Percept. Motor Skills*, 12:91–93.

────── and Holt, R. 1961. *A comparison of isolation effects and their personality correlates in two divergent samples.* New York: N.Y. Univ. ASD Technical Report, 61–417.

Greenberg, R. 1966. Cerebral cortex lesions: The dream process and sleep spindles. *Cortex*, 2:357–366.

────── et al. 1968. The effects of dream deprivation. Presented to American Psychoanalytic Association 1968 Annual Meeting, Boston, Mass.

Gross, J., et al. 1965. Eye movements during emergent stage I EEG in subjects with lifelong blindness. *J. Nerv. Ment. Dis.*, 141:365–370.

Hall, C. S., and Vander Castle, R. L. 1964. A comparison of home and monitored dreams. Paper presented at the Association for the Psychophysiological Study of Sleep, Palo Alto, Calif., March, 1964.

Havens, L. L. 1962. Placement and movement of hallucinations in space: Phenomenology & theory. *Int. J. Psychiat.*, 43:426–435.

Hoffer, A., and Osmond, H. 1967. *The Hallucinogens*. New York, Academic Press.

Holt, R. R. 1964a. Imagery: The return of the ostracized. *Amer. Psychologist*, 19(4):254–264.

———— 1964b. The emergence of cognitive psychology. *J. Amer. Psychoanal. Ass.*, 12:650–665.

Horowitz, M. J. 1967. Visual imagery and cognitive organization. *Amer. J. Psychiat.*, 123:938–946.

Jackson, J. H. (1932) *Selected writings*, Taylor, J., ed., Vol. 2, New York, Basic Books, 1958.

Jansson, B. 1968. The prognostic significance of various types of hallucinations in young people. *Acta. Psychiat. Scand.*, 44:401–409.

Kollar, E. J., et al. 1969. Psychosis in dream deprivation. "Psychological, psychophysiological, and biochemical correlates of prolonged sleep deprivation." *Amer. J. Psychiat.*, 126:488–497.

Kramer, M. 1970. Manifest dream content in normal and psychopathologic states. *Arch. Gen. Psychiat.*, 22:149–159.

Kubzansky, P. E. 1964. Discussion of papers presented at symposium, Sensory deprivation research: Where do we go from here? American Psychological Association Convention.

Lindauer, M. 1969. Imagery and sensory modality. *Percept. Motor Skills*, 29:203–215.

Linton, H., and Langs, R. 1962. Subjective reactions to lysergic acid diethylamide (LSD-25). *Arch. Gen. Psychiat.*, 6:352–368.

Luby, E. D., et al. 1962. Model psychoses and schizophrenia. *Amer. J. Psychiat.*, 119:61–67.

Maher, B. A. 1966. *Principles of Psychopathology*. New York, McGraw-Hill.

Malitz, S., Wilkens, B., and Esecover, H. 1962. A comparison of drug induced hallucinations with those seen in spontaneously occurring psychoses. In Wesت, J., ed. *Hallucinations*. New York, Grune & Stratton.

Marrazzi, A. S. 1962. Pharmacodynamics of hallucination. In West, L. J., ed. *Hallucinations*. New York, Grune and Stratton.

Maclay, W. S., and Guttman, E. 1941. Mescaline hallucinations in artists. *Arch. Neurol. Psychiat.*, 45:130–137.

McKeller, P. 1957. *Imagination and Thinking*. New York, Basic Books.

Mendelson, J. H., et al. 1963. Effects of visual deprivation on imagery experienced by deaf subjects. In Wortis, J., ed. *Recent Advances in Biological Psychiatry*, Vol. 6. New York, Plenum Press, 1964.

Miller, S. C. 1962. Ego autonomy in sensory deprivation, isolation and stress. *Int. J. Psychoanal.*, 43:1–20.

Offenkrantz, W., and Rechtschaffen, A. 1963. Clinical studies of sequential dreams. I: A patient in psychotherapy. *Arch. Gen. Psychiat.*, 8:497–508.

——— and Wolpert, E. 1963. The detection of dreaming in a congenitally blind subject. *J. Nerv. Ment. Dis.*, 136:88–90.

Orne, M. T. 1962. On the social psychology of the psychological experiment: with particular reference to demand characteristics and their implications. *Amer. Psychologist*, 17:776–783.

——— 1959. The nature of hypnosis: Artifact or essence? *J. Abnorm. Soc. Psychol.*, 58:277–299.

Paul, I. H. 1964. The effects of a drug-induced alteration in state of consciousness on retention of drive-related verbal material. *J. Nerv. Ment. Dis.*, 138:367–374.

——— and Fisher, C. 1959. Subliminal visual stimulation: A study of its influence on subsequent images and dreams. *J. Nerv. Ment. Dis.*, 129:315–340.

Pivik, T., and Foulkes, D. 1966. "Dream deprivation": Effects on dream content. *Science*, 153:1282–1284.

Pötzl, O. (1917) The relationship between experimentally induced dream images and indirect vision. *Psychol. Iss.* Monograph 7, 2:41–120, 1960.

Rapaport, D. (1957) Cognitive structures. In Gill, M., ed. *The Collected Papers of David Rapaport.* New York, Basic Books, 1967.

——— 1951. *The Organization and Pathology of Thought.* New York, Columbia University Press.

Rechtschaffen, A., Vogel, G., and Shaikun, G. 1963. Interrelatedness of mental activity during sleep. *Arch. Gen. Psychiat.*, 9:536–547.

Roffwarg, H. P., et al. 1962. Dream imagery: Relationship to rapid eye movements of sleep. *Arch. Gen. Psychiat.*, 7:235–258.

Rossi, A. M., Sturrock, J. B., and Solomon, P. 1963. Suggestion effects on reported imagery in sensory deprivation. *Percep. Motor Skills*, 16:39–45.

Sampson, H., 1966. Psychological effects of dreaming sleep. *J. Nerv. Ment. Dis.*, 143:305–317.

Sarbin, T. R. 1967. The concept of hallucination. *J. Personality*, 35:359–380.

——— and Juhasz, J. B. 1970. Toward a theory of imagination. *J. Personality*, 35(1):52–76.

Schultes, R. E. 1969. Hallucinogens of plant origin. *Science*, 163:245–254.

Shapiro, D. 1965. *Neurotic Styles.* New York, Basic Books.

Sheehan, P. 1967a. A shortened form of Betts' questionnaire upon mental imagery. *J. Clin. Psychol.*, 23:386–389.

——— 1967b. Reliability of a short test of imagery. *Percept. Motor Skills*, 25:744.

Shevrin, H., and Luborsky, L. 1961. The rebus technique: A method for studying primary-process transformations of briefly exposed pictures. *J. Nerv. Ment. Dis.*, 133:479–488.

——— and Luborsky, L. 1958. The measurement of preconscious perception in dreams and images, and investigation of the Pötzl phenomenon. *J. Abnorm. Soc. Psych.*, 56:285–294.

——— and Stross, L. 1964. The fate of fleeting impressions in dreams, waking images and hypnosis: A study of thought organization in different states of consciousness. Unpublished progress report.

Silberer, H. (1909) Report of a method of eliciting and observing certain symbolic hallucination phenomena. In Rapaport, D., ed. *The Organization and Pathology of Thought*. New York, Columbia University Press. 1951.

Singer, J. 1966. *Daydreaming*. New York, Random House.

Slater, P. E., Morimoto, K., and Hyde, R. W. 1957. The effect of group administration upon symptom formation under LSD. *J. Nerv. Ment. Dis.*, 125:312–315.

Small, I. F., et al. 1966. Clinical characteristics of hallucinations of schizophrenia. *Dis. Nerv. Syst.*, 27:349–353.

Solomon, P., et al., eds. *Sensory Deprivation*. Cambridge, Mass., Harvard University Press, 1961.

Spanos, N., and Barber, T. 1968. Hypnotic experiences as inferred from subjective reports: Auditory and visual hallucinations. *J. Exp. Res. Personality*, 3:136–150.

Suedfield, P., and Vernon, J. 1964. Visual hallucinations during sensory deprivation: A problem of criteria. *Science.*, 145:112–113.

Underwood, H. W. 1960. The validity of hypnotically induced visual hallucinations. *J. Abnorm. Soc. Psychol.*, 61:39–46.

Varendonck, J. 1921. The psychology of daydreams. In Rapaport, D., ed. *Organization and Pathology of Thought*. New York: Columbia University Press, 1951.

Verdone, P. 1965. Temporal Reference of manifest dream content. *Percept. Motor Skills*, 20:1253–1268.

Vernon, J. A., Hoffman, J., and Shiffman, H. 1958. Visual hallucinations during perceptual isolation. *Canad. J. Psychol.*, 12:31–34.

West, L. J., et al. 1961. The psychosis of sleep deprivation. *Ann. N.Y. Acad. Sci.*, 96:66–71.

Ziskind, E. 1965. An explanation of mental symptoms found in acute sensory deprivation: Researches 1958–1963. *Amer. J. Psychiat.*, 121:939–947.

———— and Augsburg, T. 1962. Hallucinations in sensory deprivation—method or madness? *Science*, 137:992–993.

Zubek, J. P., ed. 1969. *Sensory Deprivation: Fifteen Years of Research*. New York, Appleton-Century-Crofts.

Zuckerman, M., and Cohen, N. 1964a. Is suggestion the source of reported visual sensations in perceptual isolation? *J. Abnorm. Soc. Psychol.*, 68:655–660.

———— and Cohen, N. 1964b. Sources of reports of visual and auditory sensations in perceptual-isolation experiments. *Psychol. Bull.*, 62:1–20.

———— et al. 1962. Stress and hallucinatory effects of perceptual isolation and confinement. *Psychol. Monogr.*, 76:30, 1–15.

PART
II
Psychodynamics of Image Formation

CHAPTER

4

Early Concepts of the
Role of Images in Thought

Many early psychologists believed that thought was composed of images arranged by linear associational connections, and that persons could be typed according to the specific kind of image they habitually used. By implication, they also believed that thought was conscious, directed by free will, and could be understood by introspection. This chapter relates these early theories and the observations that shattered them. But first, a brief account of the philosophic antecedents to the various theories.

PHILOSOPHIC BEGINNINGS

Aristotle considered images to be the basic elements of thought, connected by associational relevance. The mind determines the objects it will pursue or avoid by contemplation of these images, which exist in the mind in the absence of external objects. In this formulation, Aristotle advanced an enduringly important concept about images: they have the power to motivate a person to emotion and effort.

Later philosophers such as Locke and Hume formulated theories of cognition in which images were again basic elements. Locke (1690) believed that thought developed as perception was recorded in residual images. These images were then recalled, as part of thought, and simple images could be recombined to form complex ideas. Hume (1739) attempted to separate images from perceptions (he used the terms idea and impression) on the basis that perceptions had greater vividness, force, and liveliness. The image, however, was regarded as an exact copy of a perception. During sleep, fever, madness, or violent emotions the difference between images and perceptions was lost, and images seemed to be real.

Hume observed that memory must not only preserve perception as recorded images but must also retain some schema of their order in time and position in space. However, the images need not be recalled invariably in the order perceived; by reprocessing images into different combinations it was possible to imagine, as well as to recall accurately, the past.

Hartley (1834) speculated that there was thought in imageless form through the use of word signification without sensory quality. He believed that word meaning was acquired through the process of labeling objects. Some word objects had "no proper ideas"; by this he meant that words such as pronouns and participles were not affixed to specific objects but were learned simply as words through speech or reading. Hartley thus presumed two overlapping systems for the representation of thought: words in nonsensory quality, and images of the various sensory types.

Mill (1829), like Hume, was interested in the difference between perceptions and images (he called them sensations and ideas). Sometimes he noted images were as vivid as perceptions, as in hallucinations or dreams. He regarded these as episodes in which thought escaped the laws of association and the government of the will. Ordinarily, thought was regulated by associational relevance. To define associational direction of thought further, Mill classified images as interesting (pleasurable or painful) and uninteresting (not particulary pleasurable or painful). Uninteresting ideas did not attract much attention, and trains of images were organized, in their flow, towards even more interesting images. In a sense, Mill regarded consciousness as a sensory organ that was attracted to interesting images just as it was attracted to interesting perceptions.

EARLY PSYCHOLOGY: IMAGES AS THE ELEMENTS OF THOUGHT

In the late nineteenth century, many psychologists attacked the problem of thought with a strategem based on Aristotelian science. They would describe the basic elements or "atoms" of thought and then find how these basic elements combined. They designated images as the primary elements of thought and trained introspectors to report as accurately as possible their stream of consciousness. For a while the theory became a self-fulfilling prophecy because thought is easily biased by the instructions of an authoritative person and the expectations of the subject. Since subjects were asked to describe the sensory quality of various kinds of images, they tended to report all of their thoughts as images. Thought in words was categorized by the image quality of the word: as a visual image if the word had the quality of being "seen," as an auditory image if the word had the quality of being "heard," and as a kinesthetic image if the word had the quality of being articulated.

In the above model of thought, images were assembled according to various laws of association. These laws suggested that once an image was in mind it would tend to call forth, as the next unit of thought, an image that was categorically similar, concretely similar, that occurred frequently, that occurred recently, or that had some perceptual continuity with the previous image. This second image would call forth a third, and so forth. Naturally, one image might evoke multiple associations, and multiple images might be "primed" by the conscious awareness of the preceding image. But, in general, thought proceeded by selecting the image highest in a hierarchy of activation.

DISCOVERY OF IMAGELESS THOUGHT

Marbe (1901) and Külpe (1922) at the University of Würzberg were among the first investigators to realize that their data contradicted the theory that images were the elements of thought. They used introspective reports to examine the processes occurring between a stimulus word presentation and a subject's reaction to it. Their subjects reported that they were sometimes aware of experiences hard to label as images. This conscious experience was not an image, not a word, and not even a clear awareness of will or choice—it was a kind of formless sense of predisposition. At other times, of course, they blurted out associations without any awareness of any intervening conscious thought process.

Messer (1906) tried to study the "dispositions of consciousness" that had no representational form. He groped towards the idea that much of thinking went on below the conscious level, and developed a model of conscious thinking as a sampling of these out-of-awareness processes with various degrees of clarity. His model, like Freud's (1900), considers consciousness as a kind of superordinate sense organ: Consciousness samples thought.

The ideas of the Würzberg School about imageless and unconscious thinking outraged authorities in other academic centers of psychology. Wundt, the father of experimental psychology, responded with critical argument. He disputed the possibility of "imageless thought" and impugned the scientific methods of the Würzberg School. He, of course, was well aware of how easily introspective reports might be biased (Mandler and Mandler, 1964).

Titchener (1909), another influential theoretician, seconded Wundt; he gave the verdict that there were no such things as imageless thoughts. The contents of thought called imageless by the Würzberg psychologists were actually "highly complex integrations of sensory components which faulty introspective techniques had failed to recognize." When introspection failed to yield any clear images, Titchener felt that images were nonetheless present but might be images of kinesthetic or spatial quality that were hard to recognize or describe.

Ach (1905) tried to unite the opposing schools of thought by this type of formulation:

> When a content is only an imageless knowledge (immediately preceding or simultaneous with the meaning awareness) there exists in consciousness a visual, acoustic, or kinesthetic sensation (tension-sensation), or a memory image of the content. These sensations are image-representations in consciousness of the imageless knowledge. They are indicators of the meaning-content. The sensations may come without such meaning-content as pure sensory qualities.

Ach also tried to indicate the tremendous speed and multiplicity of thought:

> Furthermore, it happens at times that complex contents, the verbal expression of which would take several sentences, appear momentarily, like a flash of lightning.

The intensive experimentation by both sides of this image-imageless thought controversy resulted in two relatively new ideas which were highly important: 1) that there were determinants of conscious thought that operated outside of conscious awareness, and 2) that there were schemata, plans, expectations, attitudes, goals, and values that existed on a different level of abstraction than "elementary particles" of thought.

Bühler (1907) formulated statements about cognitive schemata when he classified imageless knowledge as 1) consciousness of a rule, of knowing that one can solve a problem and how it is done, without actually having the steps in mind; 2) consciousness of knowing the meaning of something, intending it without having the meaning content clearly in mind; and 3) consciousness of relation.

Watt (1905) was able to trace a mental set as it "left awareness." Upon beginning an experiment a subject might be completely conscious of the task set for him, but this awareness gradually tended to drop out of consciousness. At the same time, the mental set lost none of its effectiveness in determining the course of the subject's reactions. Thus, a vital controlling factor was found to exist that was not directly available to reflective self-awareness (consciousness).

Watt presented his subjects with a series of stimulus words and grouped their responses into three categories: 1) simple reproductions of the stimulus or the response (associated with rapid reaction time); 2) visual images after which came a spoken word (associated with longer reaction time); and 3) psychic word representations appearing between the presentation of the written word (optical) and the spoken reaction (reaction time between type one and two). The vividness and frequency of visual images seemed to be dependent on the nature of the task in question. A subject who showed an absolute absence of visual images while performing one kind of task might show lively and detailed visual images with another.

Selz (1927) summed up the accumulated experience and asserted both the possibility of understanding thought and the need to extend investigation of thought beyond the introspective reports of conscious awareness:

> Together with the theory of diffuse reproduction, a conception of intellectual processes as a mere running off of images must also be abandoned. It is not images, not even the awareness of thoughts that have sometimes been designated as imageless "elements", that make up the constituent units of our system of specific responses; rather, these units are acts, intellectual operations that are just as needful of and amenable to analysis as the simple reflexes from which complex body movements are built up.

GESTALT PSYCHOLOGY: ANOTHER CHALLENGE TO THE ASSOCIATIONIST THEORY

The Gestalt school of psychology maintained and demonstrated that perceptions consist of entire patterns and forms rather than of particulate information that is pieced together into a whole (Köhler, 1969). Instead of sequential and associational assembly of bits from simple to complex, the Gestalt school suggests that thought, as well as perception, might be assembled wholistically, from less clear to more distinct versions of the same form. This important focus on large scale organization in perception and thinking was, perhaps, a final telling blow to the early theory that "atoms" of images were assembled by associational connection.*

Academic psychology was staggered by the idea of thought outside of conscious awareness, the conceptualization of endless levels of men-

---

* An excellent reference to all the material covered so far in this chapter is Mandler and Mandler (1964).

tal sets and determining tendencies, the multiple motives causing progression of thought along associational networks, and the unreliability of the introspective method that was required for collection of data. If such a bewildering array of variables had to be considered, how could thought processes ever be unraveled by scientific methods? Many psychologists despaired of the task and turned instead to the study of sensation (e.g., visual psychophysics), human intellectual performance (e.g., memory of visual images), and animal learning as measured by behavior (e.g., conditioning to visual stimuli). Bakan (1967) suggests that this flight was due, in part, to anxiety about investigating unconscious motives. The study of imagery itself was ostracized from academic psychology (Holt, 1964) only to return more recently along with a renewed interest in cognitive processes.

THE CONCEPT OF IMAGE TYPES

One corollary of the theory that thought took place by forming sequences of images was that persons differed in their habitual choice of sense modes for representation of thought. Common sense observation led to this formulation. Some persons obviously formed concepts pictorially while others generated thought as a series of words that seemed to be "heard" and scarcely ever had a picture in their "mind's eye."

Sir Francis Galton (1893) was interested in how persons varied in their capacity to form mental images in different sense modes and conducted an interesting investigation by sending a questionnaire to prominent scientists and thinkers. Among other things, he asked his subjects to describe the vividness of their mental imagery as they attempted to recall, as clearly as possible, their morning's breakfast table with all its contents. He found a wide range of styles. Most people had not thought much about the sensory quality of their thoughts and were very surprised to find that everyone did not use exactly the same types of images as they did.

Galton, by careful questioning, was also able to demonstrate the presence of number forms, calendar forms, and synesthetic systems. Galton's diligent work on imagery led to the theory that each person used characteristic modes, so that persons could be typologized as visualizers, kinesthetes, audiles, and so on. The theory that persons have different styles of thought relates to the problem of differentiating personality; for if persons think in a different mode they will react to situations differently, remember differently, and behave differently.

When people describe their thought, they usually mention contents or ideas, but not the mode of representation. When asked what form his thought takes, a person is often puzzled by the question at first, but is usually able to go on to say whether a thought is a visual image, a word, whether there is a taste, movement, or tactile quality to the representation, and so forth. Persons unsophisticated in this type of discourse are surprised when told that all persons do not have similar experiences when thinking. A person who is used to a parade of visual images that are then translated into words may react with disbelief or even pity when told that some people think mainly in words. Persons who think mainly in words may wonder how it is possible to form visual images and, once formed, how any kind of rational thinking is likely to take place.

Anne Roe (1951) used interviews to find out the representation of thought in various scientists. As an example of this type of approach, her results indicated that about one third were visualizers, one third were verbalizers, and about one quarter were "imageless" in that they just knew something was going on without being able to qualify the nature of their representations. (The rest were mixed.) She found more visualizers among physical scientists, more verbalizers among social scientists.

Most persons, however, do not seem to have a discrete style; they use images of various sense modes, and they use words in a mixed fashion as appropriate to circumstances. In unusual cases, however, the reliance on a single style is easy to observe.

One of the best recent works on an extreme degree of single-style thinking is Luria's (1968) *The Mind of a Mnemonist*, which describes in detail an extraordinary man whose thought was dominated by visual images. He could perform prodigious feats of memory using both eidetic visual perceptions and supplemental imagery. After seeing a table of numbers, he could retain the visual impressions for years and read off numbers from the recalled image in any direction requested. When presented words, he remembered the visual images evoked by the sounds and then retranslated these images to reproduce the words he was asked to memorize and retain. Even mathematical or logical problems were solved through association of numbers with concrete objects. Simpler versions of the same mnemonic tricks are common. But what is of the greatest interest to us here is that this person was dominated by his cognitive style; he was *compelled* to form visual images and, at times, this actually interfered with volitional and goal-directed thinking. Only with great effort, and at times not even then, could he keep from elaborating visual images in response to any sensory stimulus. When reminded of that stimulus thereafter, he inevitably recapitulated the responsive images whether he wished to or not. These visual images were so vivid and so stable that sometimes he could not follow the meaning of what he was reading because images dominated his attention. Also, during his childhood, he periodically could not distinguish his images from perceptions.

DISSENSION ABOUT THE RELIABILITY OF
IMAGE TYPOLOGIES

In the research on images in thought carried out at the turn of the century, it was important to categorize subjects as to whether they were visualizers, audiles, kinesthetes, and so on. Experimenters devised many ingenious methods, but finally there was such a plethora of procedures for measuring images and image types that the psychologic literature became confused with little replication of promising experiments. In the midst of this confusion the American Psychological Association asked a special committee to standardize some of the procedures used in experimental work. J. Angell, chairman of this committee, took upon himself the long task of reviewing all the methods then in use for the determination of mental imagery (1910).

As described, many of the methods assumed that individuals could be typologized according to the type of images they used in thought. For example, one assumption was that measurement of whatever sense mode of stimulus presentation was easiest to memorize would indicate that person's habitual mode of representation. Thus, a person who did comparatively well memorizing a visually-presented list was considered to be a visualizer, while a person who did relatively well on a list presented auditorily was assumed to be prone to use auditory images in thought. The same held true for the ability to maintain memorization during distractions in different modalities. A person who relied mainly on auditory imagery, for example, was thought to be more distracted by sound during a visual memorization task than he would be by visual stimuli during an auditory memorization task.

Creativity was thought to provide another means of typing subjects. Literary works could be studied for the sense mode of images most prevalently used as metaphors. Similarly, the ability of a person to create imaginary products in different contexts could lead to imagery typing. For example, a comparison could be made between relative ability to imagine things growing out of an inkblot, out of amorphous sounds, or out of movement sensations.

Angell's criticism of each of the above "objective methods" * is pertinent. He pointed out that many subjects could translate from one mode of imagery to another and, as a result of this effort, might remember a list they had translated better than one which was presented and recalled in the same type of imagery, without translation efforts. He also

---

* The methods were called objective because they resulted in scores of task performance rather than analysis of introspective reports.

pointed out that intensification of the learning process might occur with efforts to concentrate during a distraction, actually improving learning rather than detracting from it. Angell concluded that, at that time, there were no objective methods of imagery analysis that were reliable.

Angell then went on to list more subjective methods, which usually required some degree of introspective report. He noted that subjects varied in their performances according to the ideas they had of what was expected of them by the investigators. Also, the images employed for describing one set of experiences sometimes differed from that used for another set. Subjects seemed able to shift their styles of cognition from one modality of imagery to another.

Concluding his summary of the methods then available, Angell made certain recommendations that are still worth following. Investigators should seek to ascertain all the forms of images that any individual could command at will, to determine the forms that person uses in daily life, and to determine the function of the subject's images in his thought processes. It was felt that no one of these aims could be realized by any simple, single, or quickly-executed test. Even an extended group of tests would not yield such data if the subject were deficient in introspective powers. Angell suspected that the clear imagery types listed by Galton (1893) were probably not to be found in experimental subjects. He indicated that the different image modes could be expected to shift and substitute for each other under slight changes of conditions: "This is not to deny the reality of types, but simply to urge that they do not follow with any great regularity the lines heretofore laid down. They represent problems we still have to solve, rather than solid foundations on which we can build."

At about the same time, Betts (1909) was studying the ability to form vivid images in various sensory modes. He found a few people who formed thought in only one mode, but most of his subjects who reported vivid visual images also tended to form vivid images in other senses. Those with dim visual images tended to have dim images in general. Sheehan (1967) confirmed these findings: persons with vivid images in one mode usually formed vivid images in general. Persons differed more in terms of general vividness of reported imagery than in specificity of mode of imagery.

THE RELATIONSHIP BETWEEN HALLUCINATIONS AND IMAGE STYLE

Despite the conclusions of such investigators as Angell and Betts, the concept of image types remained popular and led to some interesting research. Several researchers focused on the relationship of the mode of hallucinatory experiences to the person's ordinary style of thought images. Anthony (1959) suggests, for example, that children with a visual tendency are more likely to develop syndromes such as hallucinatory night terrors while those with a motor tendency are more likely to become sleep walkers.

Psychotic hallucinations were studied by Cohen (1938) using the Griffitts word-image association test for prevailing mode of concrete images. In the Griffitts (1924) test a subject is given a phrase and asked to report the content and sensory mode of his intrapsychic response. For example, the stimulus could be "whistle of a train" and the subject would report whether she had an auditory image response, such as hearing the whistle, or a visual image, say of a train. The results are scored in terms of the percentage of response in each sensory mode of thought image. Cohen contrasted schizophrenic patients who had reported hallucinations in different sense modes, with normal subjects who did not report hallucinations. He found that the subgroup of visual hallucinators had less than the group average for visual thought images and that auditory hallucinators had fewer than average auditory thought images. In contrast to these negative correlations, kinesthetic hallucinations correlated positively with increased kinesthetic imagery, and "somatic hallucinations" correlated with increased "body imagery." Cohen concluded that "the relationships of imagery and hallucinations are different for the visual and auditory modalities than for the kinesthetic, tactual-temperature, and olfactory-gustatory modalities."

In 1945, Roman and Landis reported another study correlating style of mental images with the modality of reported hallucinations. They used a standardized psychiatric interview that focused on the subjective intensity of various modes of images. They studied only auditory and visual hallucinations since these are most prevalent. Roman and Landis concluded, as did Cohen, that the results tended to contradict the hypothesis that hallucinations are exaggerations or projections of the person's usual thought images.

Based on these previous studies, Seitz and Molholm (1947) conducted an extensive study of 1) persons with schizophrenia, 2) persons with alcoholic hallucinations, and 3) normal controls. They used the same test of concrete images developed by Griffitts and used by Cohen. In patients with auditory hallucinations, the mean percentage of auditory image responses to stimuli was less than the percentage in patients with no hallucinations. Similar results occurred in patients with visual hallucinations, who gave less visual responses than patients without visual hallucinations. Of interest, the numbers in the percentage data were quite similar to those reported earlier by Cohen. Seitz and Molholm concluded:

These findings indicate quite definitely that one of the factors on which auditory hallucinations may depend is a relatively low percentage of auditory imagery. According to this concept, most of those persons who attempt to resolve their personal mental conflicts by projecting them as auditory hallucinations would be found, if they were tested by means of an impersonal projective technique, to have had the hallucinations in a modality of imagery in which they were relatively deficient . . . Not only do these findings disprove the old theory that auditory hallucinations are exaggerations of predominating auditory imagery, but they suggest the new concept that one of the factors responsible for auditory hallucinations is relatively deficient auditory imagery.

The data of these several studies were consistent, but the investigators may have misinterpreted these results since they did not consider defense and control. People who have symptoms such as hallucinations are likely to attempt to prevent lapses in control by suppression of image formation in the modality of the feared hallucination.* Also, the authors neglect to consider the attitudes of such patients. Many hallucinators will fear to disclose thought images in a modality that they have come to associate with a pathologic symptom. Certainly they will have already been questioned about their hallucinations. Thus, some patients who have had hallucinations will tend to report fewer responses in the image mode of the hallucinations. This is a good example of how difficult it is to interpret even replicated empirical data in the field of image formation in particular and thinking in general.

CONCLUSION

We can now summarize some of the hard-won findings of these early researchers:

1. Thought does not consist only of discrete image particles. Expression of ideas and feelings may take various forms of representation, some of which are imageless.

2. Thought is not limited, in construction, to sequential associations between basic elements; thoughts do not occur only one at a time, but rather multiple thoughts may be experienced simultaneously.

3. Thought enters awareness (or consciousness samples thought) to various degrees. Many aspects of thinking take place out of awareness and are not available to introspective efforts.

---

* It is possible, however, that the investigators are correct in their interpretation of the results. While I consider this less likely, persons may have relatively more control over habitual image formation than over less habitual image formation. A "breakthrough" might occur in the less controlled modality. This topic, of control and defense, is discussed in more detail in Chapter 7.

4. Introspection alters the very thinking it seeks to study, and instruction on how to introspect alters thought even further.
5. There are hierarchical levels of thought organization ranging from definite images or words, to organizational schemata that assemble these presentations, to the regulatory influences that govern both.
6. Persons cannot be reliably separated into discrete image types according to a given sense mode. Few persons may habitually or even exclusively think in one mode. It does seem possible, however, to distribute people along a continuum from high to low capacity for forming voluntary images in general: some people form vivid images in several modes, others seldom have a clear image in any sensory mode.

We do not yet know why some persons use image formation more than others. We may speculate that some persons have constitutional factors that predispose them to heightened vividness or retention of images, or that reduce their capacity for regulation of image formation. Environment also must play a major role although we can not yet chart the route of its influence. Probably important factors would include the kind of perceptual stimulation provided, the extent to which the infant used internal images as a substitute for perceptions (e.g., of an absent mother), and the child's later capacity to acquire symbolism and language to substitute for images.

Infantile experiences at the separation-individuation phase of psychologic development may thus be very important influences on subsequent cognitive style (Mahler, 1960). Experience that involves perceptual shock or trauma would also influence subsequent emphasis on one or another form of imagery.

Finally, cultural factors will play a heavy influence and, at this time, our society seems to be undergoing a transformation from word orientation to image orientation, under the influence of the mass communication media.

REFERENCES

Ach, N. (1905) Awareness. In Mandler, J., and Mandler, G., eds. *Thinking: From Association to Gestalt*. New York, John Wiley & Sons, 1964.

Angell, J. C. 1910. Methods for the determination of mental imagery. *Psychol. Monogr.*, 13:61–107.

Anthony, J. 1959. An experimental approach to the psychopathology of childhood: Sleep disturbances. *Brit. J. Med. Psychol.*, 32:19–36.

Aristotle. Thinking; Recollection. In Mandler, J., and Mandler, G., eds. *Thinking: From Association to Gestalt*. New York, John Wiley & Sons, 1964.

Bakan, D. 1967. *On Method*. San Francisco, Jossey-Bass, Inc.

Betts, G. H. 1909. *The Distribution and Functions of Mental Imagery*. New York, Columbia University Teacher's College Press.

Bühler, K. (1907) Tatsachen und probleme zu einer psychologie der denkvorgänge. I. uber gedanken. In Mandler, J., and Mandler, G., eds. *Thinking: From Association to Gestalt*. New York, John Wiley & Sons. 1964.

Cohen, L. H. 1938. Imagery and its relations to schizophrenic symptoms. *J. Ment. Sci.*, 84:284–346.

Freud, S. (1900) Interpretation of dreams. *Stand. Ed.*, 4, 1953.

Galton, F. 1919. *Inquiries into Human Faculty*. New York, E. P. Dutton & Co. (Everyman).

Griffitts, C. H. 1924. *Fundamentals of Vocational Psychology*. New York, MäcMillan.

Hartley, D. (1834) Excerpts from "Observations on Man." In Mandler, J., and Mandler, G., eds. *Thinking: From Association to Gestalt*, pp. 72–92. New York, John Wiley & Sons, 1964.

Holt, R. R. 1964. Imagery: The return of the ostracized. *Amer. Psychol.*, 19:254–264.

Hume, D. (1739) Excerpt from "A treatise of human nature." In Mandler, J., and Mandler, G., eds. *Thinking: From Association to Gestalt*, pp. 51–69. New York, John Wiley & Sons, 1964.

Köhler, W. 1969. *The Task of Gestalt Psychology*. Princeton, N.J., Princeton University Press.

Külpe, O. (1922) The modern psychology of thinking. In Mandler, J., and Mandler, G., eds. *Thinking: From Association to Gestalt*. New York, John Wiley & Sons, 1964.

Locke, J. (1690) Excerpts from "An essay concerning human understanding." In Mandler, J., & Mandler, G., eds. *Thinking: From Association to Gestalt*. New York, John Wiley & Sons, 1964.

Luria, A. R. 1968. *The Mind of a Mnemonist*. New York, Basic Books.

Mahler, M. S. 1960. Symposium on psychotic object relationships. III. Perceptual de-differentiation and psychotic "object relationships." *Int. J. Psychoanal.*, 41:548–553.

Mandler, J. M., & Mandler, G., eds. 1964. *Thinking: From Association to Gestalt*. New York, John Wiley & Sons.

Marbe, K. (1901) The psychology of judgements. In Mandler, J., and Mandler, G., eds. *Thinking: From Association to Gestalt*. New York, John Wiley & Sons, 1964.

Messer, A. (1906) Experimental psychological investigations on thinking. In Mandler, J., and Mandler, G., eds. *Thinking: From Association to Gestalt*. New York, John Wiley & Sons, 1964.

Mill, J. (1829) Excerpts from "Analysis of the phenomena of the human mind." In Mandler, J., and Mandler, G., eds. *Thinking: From Association to Gestalt*, pp. 94–124. New York, John Wiley & Sons, 1964.

Roe, Anne. 1951. A study of imagery in research scientists. *J. Personality*, 19:459–470.

Roman, R., and Landis, C. 1945. Hallucinations and mental imagery. *J. Nerv. Ment. Dis.*, 102:327–331.

Seitz, P. F., and Molholm, H. B. 1947. Relation of mental imagery to hallucinations. *Arch. Neurol. Psychiat.*, 57:469–480.

Selz, O. (1927) The revision of the fundamental conceptions of intellectual processes. In Mandler, J., and Mandler, G., eds. *Thinking: From Association to Gestalt*. New York, John Wiley & Sons, 1964.

Sheehan, P. 1967. A shortened form of Betts' questionnaire upon mental imagery. *J. Clin. Psychol.*, 23:386–389.

Titchener, E. B. (1909) Imagery and sensationalism. In Mandler, J., and Mandler, G., eds. *Thinking: From Association to Gestalt*. New York, John Wiley & Sons, 1964.

Watt, H. J. (1905) Experimental contribution to a theory of thinking. In Mandler, J., & Mandler, G., eds. *Thinking: From Association to Gestalt*. New York, John Wiley & Sons, 1964.

5

Modes of Representation
of Thought

One reason for the slow rate of progress in imagery research has been the isolation of this topic from a general theory of perception, memory, and thought. Visual images are only one form for representation of percepts, memories, ideas, and feelings. A given train of thought, for example, might include images of various sensory qualities, words without sensory quality, and implicit ideas, feelings, or predispositions. Examination of visual images alone would be misleading and would not result in an understanding of the motives for the train of thought or the utility of visual images in the thought process. Since an ongoing stream of consciousness may contain many modes of representation, it is desirable to formulate a model that shows the relationship of visual images to other forms of representation. This chapter offers such a provisional model.

BACKGROUND

Freud (1900) postulated that the earliest thinking in infancy was in hallucinatory images for purposes of temporary, if imaginary, gratification. In a parallel line of reasoning, Piaget (1930) suggested that whenever the preverbal child experienced desire he might form in his mind an image, a kind of pseudohallucination that transformed or gratified the desire. Werner (1957) and Lukianowicz (1960) find resemblances among the thought patterns of children, primitive men, and psychotic persons in that all three groups use magical constructions and are prone to fuse inner images with perceptions of external reality. Werner also noted that when the child is around three or four years old, he begins to decrease physical manipulation of material, as a way of acting out thought, and instead begins to play make-believe games that probably involve thinking through images. Schilder (1942), like the other authors, also postulated that, in the development of thinking, images are gradually replaced by symbols and concepts with less sensory quality.*

Most experimentalists and theorists in the last few decades have assumed a childhood progression from images to words, have paid little attention to the phases of image thinking, and have assumed that adult thinking depends largely on lexical signification. The image-imageless thought controversy described in the last chapter was dropped in favor of the assumption of the primacy of words.†

In one of the first works marking a resurgence of interest in thought processes, Humphrey (1951) pondered over the assumption that thought proceeds in lexical form and reconsidered the place of image formation in cognition. He concluded that while thinking is permeated with language, it is not identical with word usage. He did not believe that images preceded words in adult thinking, but that images might either impede thinking by being "distractions" or might enhance thinking by connotative enrichment. Humphrey reasoned that perception involved images but, in the course of problem solving, the images were intellectualized. As this occurred, the images dropped away, became symbols or schemata, and eventually were transformed into imageless knowledge.

Not all contemporary investigators agree, however, about the primacy of words. For example, Vernon (1967) studied the problem of the relationship of verbal language to thought processes by reinterpretation of 33 independent research studies involving 8,000 subjects. Among these subjects, some were deaf from birth, some acquired deafness after they had learned words, and some could hear normally. Thinking ability was, in these studies, measured by conceptual tasks such as nonverbal intelligence tests. Vernon takes a relatively extreme position when he concludes that "there is no functional relationship between verbal languages and cognition or thought process; verbal language is not the mediating sym-

---

* The development of secondary process thinking out of primary process thinking is a related concept to be discussed in Chapter 6.
† Lacan (1966), for example, suggests that *the unconscious* has a structure based on word representations.

bol system of thought; and there is no relationship between concept formation and level of verbal language development."

Recent research efforts have reaffirmed the utility of images for learning and memory processes. (Jenkins et al., 1967; Deno, 1968; Paivio, 1969; Frandsen and Holder, 1969). Paivio suggests that memory may operate according to two processes, one based on images, the other on words; and that images are specialized for spatial representations while words are specialized for sequential processing.

Tversky (1969) has demonstrated that the same stimuli may be recorded, in short term memory, as either pictorial images or as words depending on the anticipation the subject has, when he receives the stimuli, of what he is going to do with the information. Beritashvili (1969) points out that when learning is accomplished by use and retention of mental images, then only a single trial is necessary for relatively permanent retention of what has been learned. He contrasts this with conditioned-reflex learning which requires multiple trials and is impermanent. Thus, current research reaffirms the utility of thought images for processing information, and suggests that visual images are useful for parallel (simultaneous) processing of information, and lexical representations for serial (sequential) processing.

Bruner (1964), in considering the course of cognitive growth during childhood, posits three systems for processing information and constructing inner models of the external world. He defines a thought representation as the end product of information processing, and the three forms of representation are labeled as *enactive representation, iconic representation,* and *symbolic representation.*

The model presented in this chapter is an elaboration of Bruner's tripartiate system. Bruner focuses on the dimension from concreteness to abstraction of signification. Since I wish to focus on the subjective quality of thought representation, I have shifted the labels of the three systems to *enactive, image,* and *lexical* modes of representation, and consider the organization of these modes of thought.

This model is similar to the SI (structure of the intellect) model put forward by Guilford (1959). Guilford's model is composed of three kinds of categories: content categories, operation categories, and product categories. What he calls the content category is closest to our present topic, the mode of representation. Guilford lists under content four headings: figural, symbolic, semantic, and behavioral. Behavioral content is similar to what will here be labeled, after Bruner, enactive; semantic to what is here labeled lexical; and figural to what is here labeled images. Guilford's use of "symbolic" refers to numbers and letters which, in the present conceptualization, would fall into lexical representation. Once again the present model differs in purpose to Guilford's model: the intent is description of *modes* of representation of thought rather than the *contents* that are represented.

REPRESENTATIONAL SYSTEMS

ENACTIVE THOUGHT

Infants act reflexively. Innate response mechanisms such as sucking, crying, clinging, following, and smiling are released by maturational sequence plus internal or external perceptions. Almost immediately, however, such responses lose their reflexive quality and are modified by interaction with the environment. We may regard modification of motor response systems by experience as the rudiments or precursors of thinking, since the modification requires perception, response, and intervening change. Take, for example, a relatively reflexive motor response to a stimulus, such as withdrawal from pain. Through self-perception a memory of this response to this stimulus is retained. The recorded motor knowledge may be reactivated in subsequent situations that seem similar. Perhaps several possible motor responses are activated. Trial action may take place through relatively minor movements until the appropriate response is selected. These trial actions, through anticipatory tensing of various muscle groups, may be regarded as thinking through enactions. The memory pool for use as enactive representation would grow from two sources: memory of motor action by the self, and retention of mimicry responses to the motor activity of someone else (Schilder, 1942).

Several examples may clarify enactive representation as a mode of thinking that can be used by adults as well as small children.

> 1. A child wanted some candy that he had been emphatically told not to touch. As he tentatively reached for it with one hand, he made a stern reproving face and stopped his reaching with the other hand. The gestures and facial expression represent a train of thought: I want it, mother would say no, better not. The mimicry of mother's facial expression adds emotive power to the restraining ideas.
>
> 2. A person while conversing sought to use the expression "he likes to pin people down." The phrase, however, was apparently repressed for the moment. While attempting to recall the term, he made a hand gesture of pinning something down which represented enactively the desired thought. Then the words he sought entered his awareness and he was able to speak them.
>
> 3. While thinking of a coming tennis match, a person noted that he anticipated making various strokes by very slight muscle tensions and micromovements.

4. A woman patient, while discussing in psychotherapy her feelings for her therapist, began to twist her wedding ring and move it on and off her finger. She noticed herself performing this gesture and said, "You know, this must mean I wish I were not already married, and that indeed is how I feel sometimes." In this instance the thought "not married" is represented first in body movement and then is translated and elevated to word representation.

IMAGE REPRESENTATION

Because images retain a sensory quality, they are useful in solving problems requiring inner depiction of external reality. We have previously referred to this as trial perception and trial action.* The sensory quality of images may also be useful for evocation of emotional responses resembling the response to actual perceptions. A person avoiding danger may, for example, maintain a useful level of fear by forming an image of the dangerous situation. This fear is useful because it provides motivation for avoiding or mobilizing resources to meet potential harm. Images are also found in close relationship to emotional processes in terms of memory and recollection. In the course of psychoanalytic psychotherapy, for example, painful and repressed memories and impulses may enter awareness first as images—either in fantasy, free association, or dream—and only later be labeled with words.

The close relationship of images to wishes, fears, and emotional processes may be regarded three ways. Images (as thoughts in general) may be formed in response to emotions; images may express emotions; and images may evoke emotions.

EXAMPLE 1.

Following a car accident in which he saw several people injured, a patient was troubled by recurrent and vivid revisualizations of the traumatic scenes. Whenever he tried to talk of fear and guilt feelings associated with the event, he noted that very vivid mental images of the frightening experience entered his awareness and made verbal communication more difficult. During the months after the accident, whenever he became frightened in other unrelated life situations, he found that images of the accident came into his awareness.

In this example, the image occurred in response to intense and unresolved feeling states and also expressed and correlated with associated emotions. In the next example, thought expressed as an image arises in response to and as correlation with an emotional state but also evokes further emotional response.

---

* Thinking may also take the form of selective perception; this will be discussed in connection with illusion formation in Chapter 10.

Example 2.

> A mountain climber successfully maneuvered himself to safety after a rope broke. When he was back in base camp, he formed an image of what could have happened: the image depicted himself falling and being crushed on the rocks. On developing this image he felt intense panic, an emotion not present during the actual danger period when rapid and "cool" action was required.

Because of its emotion evoking ability, image formation can also be used purposefully (although not necessarily consciously) to transform emotions.

Example 3.

> A woman patient kept herself from feeling sexually aroused in the presence of attractive men by visualizing her mother's disapproving face. Vivid visualization made her feel disgust, but merely thinking words such as "mother" or "mother says sex is bad" did not generate sufficient emotion to provide her with a defense against her sexual excitation.

The use of images as a mode of thought representation increases in dreams, reveries, and hallucinogenic experiences, as noted in Chapter 3. Increased admixtures of primary process types of thinking are also noted in such altered states of consciousness. This double movement towards both greater use of images and greater admixture of primary process has led to a conceptual tendency to ally the two concepts. Thus, in psychoanalytic theory, visual images are often tacitly considered to be the characteristic mode representing primary process type thoughts. It should be emphasized, however, that visual images also may serve secondary process thinking (Beres, 1960).

For example, some persons use images to represent conceptual problems, especially those involving spatial relationships as in architecture or geometry. Many persons also habitually rely on visual images for memory recall. The reader may wish to try to remember how many windows he has in his house. A usual maneuver for solving this problem is to visualize each room and count the windows in the image.

LEXICAL THOUGHT

In the course of development, the relationship between words and what they signify is finally established. The child moves beyond the use of interpretation of sounds, inflections, and tonalities to include words as a means of thinking. The acquisition of lexical representation allows progression to new levels of conceptualization and reasoning.

Cognitive theorists regard thought in words as the most rational, secure, and conceptually clear form of thinking. Indeed, one of Freud's formulations indicated that attachment of a word-representation to a thing-representation was how an idea was raised to the level of consciousness (Freud, 1923). He pointed out that the clearest thinking and clearest trains of thought were achieved when ideas and affects became labeled with words.

ORGANIZATION OF THE REPRESENTATIONAL SYSTEMS

Each system of representation—enactive, image, and lexical—has different schemata for organizing the units within the system. The smaller units of representation within each of the systems are assembled into sets of units according to such schemata. These patterns of organization would not *necessarily* differ from one system to another, but each system might have different tendencies or special uses as a means of ordering thought. For example, the unit in lexical thinking is a morpheme (a unit of meaning). A sentence is a "set of morphemes" or a "set of lexemes" that are organized by grammatical schemata. Similarly, a visual daydream picture might be a "set of images."

Table 1 presents the types of representation vertically and levels of complexity horizontally.* The schemata are categorized only to illustrate

Table 1   Modes of Thought Representation

Mode	Sample of Units	Sample of Sets of Units	Sample of Schemata	Sample of Relationships of Units
Enactive	Anticipatory movements, tensions, kinesthesia	Acts Gestures Postures Facial expressions	Direction and force	This does that.
Images	Images: Tactile Gustatory Olfactory Visual Auditory	Signs Body image Fantasies Introjects	Space Volume Simultaneity Signs & signals	This is there. This is like that. This and that happen together.
Lexical	Morphemes	Grammar (phrases, sentences, paragraphs)	Linearity Sequential schemata Syllogisms	First x then y, then z. x leads to y if w but not if not w.

* The figure starts at a high level of functioning. It could start with smaller units such as particulate sensations for imagery (e.g., geometric forms, colors, and so forth) or with phonemes (units of sound) for lexical constructions.

major trends of organization for each mode. Thus, direction and force are dominant themes in enactive thinking, simultaneous relationships are well depicted in images, and sequential arrangements are most clearly indicated by lexical representation (Luria, 1966).

Preverbal systems of thought persist, and enactions and images are used at times in adult thinking. Organizational plans for words will be based, in part, on preverbal schemata. Also, schemata developed with lexical thinking may then be applied to images or enactions, even though they were not previously available. Thus, the developing child may be able to organize a series of images better after the acquisition of language because learning the patterns of speech requires development of sequential organizational schemata.

REGRESSION

At times thought changes from its most progressive and complex format to a style of some earlier time or to a more primitive form of organization. This return to the primitive is called a regression. The present model allows specification of the type of regression noted in the expression of thought. The classification includes:

a. A return from later acquisitions of representational capacity to earlier, more primitive systems of representation. For example, a retreat from words to images or enactions.
b. A return within one system to earlier contents, for example, a regression from a contemporary body image to a developmentally primitive body image.
c. A return within one system to earlier modes of organization such as a shift from complex systems of associational rules to simple rules of associational connection. For example, in some pathologic states, words may no longer be linked according to conceptual meaning but by phonic (rhyming) similarity (Luria and Vinegradova, 1959).
d. A shift to primitive levels of control and regulation. For example, instinctual drives may be expressed in primitive rather than advanced (differentiated) forms, or there may be a loss of distinction between internal images and external perceptions. (See Chapter 7 for a full discussion of this type of regression).

BOUNDARIES AND LINKAGES OF THE SYSTEMS

The model illustrated in Table 1 is an abstract set of compartments. Each compartment is a facet useful to describe subjective thought events.

Normal streams of thought will flow simultaneously in many compartments without clear-cut division between modes of representation. Enactions blur into imagery in the form of kinesthetic, somesthetic, and vestibular or visceral images. Image representation blends with words in the form of faint auditory or visual images of words. Words and enactive modes merge through motor images of speaking.

Organic pathology sometimes reveals the boundary between representational systems. Some brain tumors or head injuries result in loss of the ability to form visual images without loss of word thinking or enactive capacities (Brain, 1954; Humphrey and Zangwell, 1951). Persons with such injuries can process verbal information, but have great difficulty solving problems that require simultaneous and spatial organization. Sperry (1964) has studied persons whose cerebral hemispheres were disconnected surgically as a radical treatment for severe epilepsy. They find that patients after this procedure function as if they have two separate brains which no longer intermix their thought representations. Stimuli can be presented selectively to either the dominant or nondominant hemisphere by masking certain areas of the visual field. Stimuli presented to the dominant hemisphere are processed better if they are in lexical form; stimuli presented to the nondominant hemisphere are processed better if they are in visual-spatial form (such as "how would you untie this knot shown here"). In a very dramatic demonstration, patients also "know" things with the hand ennervated by the dominant hemisphere (usually the left brain in right-handed persons) that they do not "know" with the hand ennervated by the other hemisphere. For example, suppose the patient is blindfolded and a scissors is placed in his hand. The hand associated with the dominant hemisphere does not know how to make cutting movements but the person can say those are scissors. When the scissors are placed in the other hand, the person cannot verbally say what they are, but knows how to make cutting motions. Apparently in normal persons the hemispheres communicate with each other so that the "two separate brains" effect in these special patients does not occur.

An example of impaired translation between the systems for representation may also be found in organic pathology which leads to difficulties in the use of verbal information. These difficulties are called dysphasia. Clinicians identify three kinds of dysphasia: nominal, receptive, and productive. Nominal dysphasia is the inability to find the right word. If, in a dysphasic person the intended idea is presented in consciousness as a visual image, the failure in nominal dysphasia can be conceptualized as a failure in translation from images to words. Receptive dysphasia is defective ability to comprehend the meaning of words expressed by others, although self-expression in words may be unimpaired. According to my model, receptive dysphasia is an impairment involving the system for representing auditory images or an impairment in the processes of transition from auditory images to lexical meaning. In a similar manner, productive dysphasia, an inability to speak words already present in conscious thought, is a defect of translation between thought and the enactive representation of speech.

The assembly of a sentence depends on the lexical system. Deciphering what is heard or read, however, will require use of the image systems, either auditory or visual, because perceptual registrations must be held as images until appropriate labels are established. Also, enactive representations are necessary to movements for vocalization or writing. Ordinarily such enactive representations proceed automatically outside of awareness. When no automatic plan is available, however, some conscious enactive representation is required before execution of the motor behavior. In verbal communication then, there must be transitions among each system of representation. The different types of dysphasia that have been noted in organic brain impairments may reflect defective translation between systems of representation.

TRANSFORMATION FROM THE IMAGE MODE TO OTHER MODES OF THOUGHT

Perceptions are retained for a short time, in the form of images, which allows continued emotional response and conceptual appraisal. In time, retained images undergo two kinds of transformation: reduction of sensory vividness and translation of the images into other forms of representation (such as words). Ordinarily the transformation of images is automatic. In extreme situations, however, transformation is not easily completed.

Clinically, we see that following a traumatic experience that is witnessed visually, certain distortions of ordinary cognitive experience may occur. Instead of becoming reduced in intensity, the images of the traumatic event may return to awareness with unusual visual vividness. Also, and this is significant, these vivid images apparently escape volitional control. At times they emerge in a peremptory manner in spite of efforts to avoid or dispel them. At other times there is an amnesia for the event; descriptive statements and recollection images cannot be formed at will. Sometimes amnesia and peremptory revisualization occur in the same person in separable phases after the traumatic episode. With recovery from the post-traumatic state the images become dim, the events can be discussed verbally, and the person regains the capacity to recall the events when he wishes to and, importantly, to repress the memory if he has to.

Failure of transformation could be discussed in terms of emotional stress alone were it not for the observation of very similar experiences in emotionally *neutral* settings. Peremptory and vivid formations of images occur not only after arousing perceptions but also after repeated perceptions. People who pick berries all day may experience involuntary but vivid images of berries when they are putting their minds at ease before falling asleep (Hanawalt, 1954). Students, after long hours at a microscope, may be troubled by returning images during moments of relaxation. Night drivers also report images of oncoming headlights while attempting to sleep later on. Skiers experience a similar effect in kinesthetic sensations: after a day on the slopes, while relaxing before sleep, they refeel muscle movements and changes in bodily position repeated so often during the day. Although the initial perceptions may be neutral or pleasurable, the later images are often unpleasant and hard to dispel.

These observations of vivid and peremptory visual images suggest that image transformation processes are overloaded either when the perceptions that form the images are extremely arousing or when certain (relatively novel) perceptual schemata are too frequently repeated. Observation of failures in transformation permits speculation about the processes involved.

In order to evaluate and to store perceptions by multiple markers for future memory use, perceptual images are transformed by labeling processes: they are assigned to various categories and translated into other representational modes, such as words, by association with relevant memories. When perceptions are simple and do not involve stress or conflict, the labeling processes are completed virtually instantaneously; otherwise the images might be put out of mind for the moment and stored in a special memory system for later review. Those images that overload transformation processes would then remain in the hypothetical image storage. Speculatively, this special storage would tend to press towards revisualization of those images so that they can be "worked through" and the storage system cleared for further records of experience. Some of the stored images might be reviewed and transformed in dream or preconscious thinking (Eissler, 1966; Breger, 1967).

In the case of traumatic or intensely arousing images, the association of strong emotions with the images would increase the difficulty of categorization and association operations. Whichever images were incompletely transformed in a given cognitive "effort" would remain in the special storage condition with its continued "push" for revisualization. Under repressive circumstances, release of images from the storage system would be inhibited. When inhibition failed, the images would emerge in a manner experienced as involuntary.*

RELEVANCE OF THIS MODEL TO CURRENT RESEARCH AREAS

The change in mode of representation is the topic of many studies of infant and child development. Its relevance may be somewhat less clear to studies of nonverbal behavior, altered states of consciousness, and verbal transactions (e.g., psycholinguistics and content analysis). These, therefore, deserve brief mention.

Enactive representation is related to studies of nonverbal behavior. While enactions do not require visible movement, visible changes in facial expression or gesture do often accompany enactive thinking. Such visible changes are part of the data sought by investigators of nonverbal behavior. The existence of enactive representation as a mode of thinking should be a part of their working theory since it would seem essential to differentiate those gestures and expressions that reflect ongoing enactive coding of thoughts (and are not intended as communication) from those movements or changes that are intended as communication. Furthermore, the nonverbal behavior of people who habitually use large amounts of enactive representation might differ from those people who use less.

In some states of consciousness there is a shift towards image formation. Thus, many researchers in the fields of sensory deprivation, dreams, drugs, and correlates of attention find themselves measuring or counting images. In using image experiences as one index of alteration in the state of consciousness, however, it is necessary to consider the habitual modes of thinking of the research subjects.

As stressed earlier, most persons will use all three types of representation in an overlapping manner, and their thought will shift from one mode to another to suit the needs of the moment. Some persons, however, tend to favor a given mode to the near exclusion of others. Subjects who habitually use lexical thinking may present data that differ in meaning from the data presented by subjects who habitually think in images. For example, a subject who finds himself always thinking in words, without any awareness of visual images, may be experiencing a major shift in

---

* Janis (1958) points out that impending stress, such as that which a patient experiences before anticipated surgery, may lead to a process which he calls "unrepression," in which the individual regains memories that had previously remained unconscious. A stress or a trauma may thus evoke internal images, including fantasied anticipations, which also must be worked through by translation and assimilation with other conscious memory systems. Similarly, internal images such as those occurring during LSD intoxication may have a "traumatic effect" in that they press for return and mastery. This will be discussed further in Chapter 12.

the organization of his thoughts when he begins for the first time to report relatively dim visual images. Reports of an identical intensity of image formation or number of images might not indicate any shift in a person who habitually used images in his thinking. Thus, the shift in the "lexical thinker" might actually be equivalent in importance to a shift from ordinary images to lurid images in the "image thinker."

Similar considerations are applicable to studies of psycholinguistic structure or to research methods that use content analysis of verbal productions. For example, in item analysis of a stream of communication from psychoanalytic therapy it might be important to differentiate persons who readily transform their lexical thoughts into speech from those people who must first translate an ongoing stream of images into words and then into speech. Thus, measurement of linguistic structure (such as noun and verb counts) may be different in persons simply because of different representational styles.

SUMMARY

Thought is neither represented exclusively in images, as was once postulated, nor is it represented only in words. This chapter presents a model with enactive, image, and lexical modes of representation. Each has certain organizational tendencies and cognitive uses. The image systems, and their underlying organization, place them relatively close to emotion.

In ordinary thought, the modes interrelate flexibly. In extreme situations, illustrated by organic pathology and psychic trauma, the different modes are subjectively experienced in a less integrated form, and failures in transformation from one mode to another may occur. Pathologic states may indicate what processes are involved in transformation from one mode of representation to another and transformation from intense to less vivid image formation. Failure to consider these transformations may lead to misinterpretation of data in several important research areas.

REFERENCES

Beres, D. 1960. Perception, imagination, and reality. *Int. J. Psychoanal.*, 41:327–334.

Beritashvili, I. S. 1969. Concerning psychoneural activity of animals. In Cole, M., and Maltzman, I., eds. *A Handbook of Contemporary Soviet Psychology*. New York, Basic Books.

Brain, R. 1954. Loss of visualization. *Proc. Roy. Soc. Med.*, 47:228–290.

Breger, L. 1967. Function of dreams. *J. Abnorm. Psychol., Monogr.,* 72 (5, Whole #641).

Bruner, J. S. 1964. The course of cognitive growth. *Am. Psychol.,* 19:1–15.

Deno, S. L. 1968. Effects of words and pictures as stimuli in learning language equivalents. *J. Educ. Psychol.,* 59:202–206.

Eissler, K. R. 1966. A note on trauma, dream, anxiety, and schizophrenia. *Psychoanal. Stud. Child,* 21:17–50.

Frandsen, A., and Holder, J. 1969. Spatial visualization in solving complex verbal problems. *J. Psychol.,* 73:229–233.

Freud, S. (1923) The ego and the id. *Stand. Ed.,* 19, 1961.

———— (1900) The interpretation of dreams. *Stand. Ed.,* 3, 5, 1962.

Guilford, J. P. 1959. Three faces of intellect. *Amer. Psychol.,* 14:469–479.

Hanawalt, N. G. 1954. Recurrent images: new instances and a summary of the older ones. *Amer. J. Psychol.,* 67:170–174.

Horowitz, M. J. 1968. Visual thought images in psychotherapy. *Amer. J. Psychother.,* 22:55–59.

Humphrey, G. 1951. *Thinking: An Introduction to Experimental Psychology.* New York, Wiley and Sons.

Humphrey, M. E., and Zangwill, O. L. 1951. Cessation of dreaming after brain injury. *J. Neurol. Neurosurg. Psychiat.,* 14:322–325.

Janis, I. L. 1958. *Psychological Stress.* New York, John Wiley and Sons.

Jenkins, J. R., et al. 1967. Differential memory for picture and word stimuli. *J. Educ. Psychol.,* 58:303–307.

Lacan, J. 1966. The insistence of the letter in the unconscious. *Yale French Studies: Structuralism,* Issues 36 and 37, pp. 112–147.

Lukianowicz, N. 1960. Visual thinking and similar phenomena. *J. Ment. Sci.,* 106:979–1001.

Luria, A. R. 1966. *Higher Cortical Functions in Man.* New York, Basic Books, Inc.

———— and Vinogradova, O. S. 1959. An objective investigation of the dynamics of semantic systems. *Brit. J. Psychol.,* 50:89–105.

Paivio, A. 1969. Mental imagery in associative learning and memory. *Psychol. Rev.,* 76:241–260.

Piaget, J. 1930. *The Child's Conception of Physical Causality.* New York, Harcourt.

Schilder, P. 1942. *Mind: Perception and Thought in Their Constructive Aspects.* New York, Columbia University Press.

Sperry, R. W. (1964) Brain bisection and mechanisms of consciousness. In Eccles, J. C., ed. *Brain and Conscious Experience.* New York, Springer-Verlag, 1966.

Tversky, B. 1969. Pictorial and verbal encoding in a short term memory task. *Percept. Psychophysics,* 6:225–233.

Vernon, M. 1967. Relationship of language to the thinking process. *Arch. Gen. Psychiat.,* 16:325–333.

Werner, H. 1957. *Comparative Psychology of Mental Development.* New York, International Universities Press.

CHAPTER

6

Psychodynamics of Image Formation

When a person forms images as a part of reality-oriented, rational thought, then he and others find his image contents understandable. Experimental psychologists, such as those cited in the past two chapters, generally prefer to work with rational, relatively neutral aspects of image formation because there is a basis for consensual agreement. The investigator may assume that the subject is oriented toward reality and wishes to appraise it correctly, react logically towards it, and respond with optimal performance.

However, some image experiences are not oriented towards reality, are not readily understandable by the self or others, and are emotional and idiosyncratic. These images are derived from a style of thinking that reflects internal motives more than external demands. Such image formation has been the province of psychoanalytic investigation and occurs prominently in the construction of dreams, hallucinations, myths, magic, and fantasy. When images are used in these fantastic forms of thinking they tend to be arranged by primary process types of association, with evidence of condensation, displacement, and symbolization. Image formation, in these circumstances, may gratify wishes; it may also express conflicted and previously hidden ideas or memories. This chapter provides an elementary introduction to these topics, since they are essential to understanding an important aspect of image formation.

THE RANGE OF THOUGHT

The organization and regulation of thought has a spectrum from analytic, reality-oriented, logical thought to fantastic, wish-oriented, magical thinking. The forms of thought regulation that influence the latter end of the spectrum are called "the primary process," and the thought products are occasionally (and loosely) called "primary process thought." The forms of thought regulation that influence the reality-oriented end of the spectrum are called "the secondary process," and the products are sometimes called "secondary process thought." * In the broad central range, there is thought influenced by both the primary and secondary process.

Primary and secondary process are differentiated according to two key issues: the degree to which they impose delay of discharge on impulsive motives, and the organization they impose on the thought that intervenes between stimulus and response. In what follows, the stimulus will be regarded as an internal, impulsive motive †; the response (also internal) will be in general a thought, in particular an image or series of images. What occurs between stimulus and response is the process of image formation.

PRIMARY PROCESS

Primary process forms of thought regulation are more primitive than secondary process forms, as they develop earlier in childhood. The

---

* Freud devised these labels in a manuscript that remained unpublished until after his death, *The Project for a Scientific Psychology* (1895) and used them in *The Interpretation of Dreams* (1900). For more recent reviews see Gill (1967), Holt (1967), and Noy (1969).

† In the absence of agreed upon terminology and a firm theory of thought, word selection is difficult. Three words are commonly used in psychoanalytic theory for what I mean here: instinct, drive, and motivation. These are sometimes compounded: instinctual drive, drive derivatives, instinctual motives, instinctual impulses. Following Rapaport (1960), I have selected to use the word "motive" to designate the various internal pressures towards thought. This word includes both instinctual-drives-pressures and instinctual-drive-restraining factors and structures (such as defenses, controls, habits, and internalized rules of culture) which sometimes, but not always, act as motivational causes for thought. When necessary for clarity, I will specify the kind of motive as an impulsive motive or a defensive motive, depending on whether the motive favors thought expression or seeks to reduce or modify expression. Sometimes a drive derivative may serve as a defensive motive in this definition of terms. I shall limit use of the word "motive" to internal motives. In this definition, external objects or perception, or even internal irritations of the perceptual substrates, may be causal influences but not motives, except insofar as they serve to trigger internal motives.

principal feature of primary process thought is its directness: the motives cannot be tolerated or restrained for long, they cannot be modulated, some kind of response is imperative, and the response need not be realistic. For example, the prototype of the first thought has been modeled, by Freud (1900), on the basis of hallucination. The infant is hungry and cries reflexively. In a short period of development, the infant associates the sight of the breast, or a bottle, or the mother's face with the relief of hunger pangs. In primary process thinking, the baby may temporarily relieve his motivational tension, in the absence of the gratifying object, by a hallucinatory recollection of the breast. Here is the principal influence of primary process: immediate gratification, by any means, with minimal delay, without detour or extended planning. These qualities of primary process thought lend it a magical quality and an orientation towards more pleasure, less pain, and neither too much nor too little tension. The adherence of drives, ideas, and feelings to word labels, images, and enactions is loose in primary process, more adherent or "bound" * in secondary process. This loose (unbound) cathexis permits the shifts in representation known as condensation, displacement, and symbolization (to be discussed below).

SECONDARY PROCESS

Secondary process forms of thought regulation are imposed gradually upon the primary process as the child develops. The child learns that immediate magical gratification is less optimal than delayed but real fulfillment. The child learns how to think realistically, and it also learns how to modulate motivation so that action can be delayed until the right time and the right place. These central characteristics (reality testing,† ability to delay, and organizational ability) differentiate the secondary process from the primary process (Zern, 1968). That is, instead of immediate wish-fulfillment, the child learns to use memory, reason, logic, assessment of meaning, appraisal of environment, comparison, hierarchy formation, rehearsal, planning, and other mechanisms aimed at optimum interaction with the physical environment. The child also develops thresholds of greater tolerance for drives and learns to modulate drives. (Hartmann, 1964, calls this tolerance for and differentiation of impulses the neutralization of drive energies.)

Like the primary process, the secondary process form of regulation serves the goals of maximum pleasure, minimum pain, and the right level

---

* For a review of this important topic in psychoanalytic theory see Holt (1962).
† See Chapter 7 for a discussion of reality testing.

of tension. But it subordinates these goals to the reality principle (Schur, 1966). That is, the secondary process orients thought towards real possibilities and serves the goal of the greatest good over time. When regulated by the primary process, a person eats green apples when he is hungry, because he cannot wait for them to ripen and because he cannot restrain his impulse to eat enough to avoid the long-range risk of a stomach-ache. The secondary process form of regulation permits the person to restrain the urge to eat green apples, because he envisions that the later stomach-ache is more painful than the immediate taste is pleasurable; the secondary process allows him to wait for ripe apples.

COMPARISON OF PRIMARY AND SECONDARY PROCESS

Primary process is not necessarily disadvantageous. Suppose an explorer is lost and starving to death. In his extreme hunger he hallucinates a turkey dinner with all the trimmings. If he hallucinates when he should be lighting a signal fire, then this form of gratification is maladaptive in the long run. If, however, his signal fire is already lit and the hallucination helps him keep his will to live, then it is advantageous in the long run.

Primary process is also enormously advantageous to the creative process. Thought formation under the primary process is rapid and there is a relative absence of logical restraints. These two conditions make for many juxtapositions between one thought element and another in a given period of time. The rapidity of thought and the low requirements for conventional or reasonable association mean that a really novel combination of seemingly divergent ideas might be achieved while thought is under primary process mediation. Of course, secondary process mediation and revision might be necessary to complete the creative thought.

As mentioned, primary process precedes secondary process developmentally. Primary process influence over thought probably rests on simpler structures and is never entirely lost. During situations of intense impulsive motivation, primary process influence may again become apparent in the final thought products. Also, when there is reduction in capacity for the high-level organization required for secondary process thought, primary process thinking may emerge. One example of the emergence of primary process influence occurs during dreaming sleep. Freud made one of his major contributions to science in his investigation of dream-thinking. He found that primary process thought is not disorganized, rather the primary process influence imposes its own style of organization.

In *The Interpretation of Dreams*, Freud (1900) noted the central use of visual images in primary process thinking and certain characteristic mechanisms of primary process thinking in the formation of dream pictures. He described how dreams were wish fulfillments, how latent thoughts * were formed into the manifest dream by the dream work, and how the dream work used condensation, symbolization, and displacement to achieve disguised expression of usually censored ideas and feelings. These characteristic mechanisms of the primary process are easily achieved when thought is expressed as visual images and are also used to various extents in image thinking, in states other than dreaming (Breuer and Freud, 1893–1895; Freud, 1908).

Though certain features often accompany thought influenced by the primary process, they should not be regarded as synonymous with primary process. For example, images are a frequent mode of representation in primary process thought but are not categorically limited to primary process thinking. Images are also used for representation that is influenced by secondary process. In an analogous relationship, condensation and displacement are mechanisms basic to the primary process, but they can also serve the purposes of the secondary process. This is even more true of symbolization which is used widely in both primary process and secondary process (Gill, 1967).

CONDENSATION

Condensation is the compression of several latent meanings into a single manifest image. The simplest form of condensation is omission of some ideational elements and allowing a part to stand for the whole. Usually, however, condensation includes an active process in which meanings fuse and form a composite. For example, the image of a face may be a composite, in which the eyes are derived from one person, the hair from another, and the overall facial expression from still a third person. Or, in another common type of condensation, ideas related to several persons can be relegated to a single person. A figure, in an image, may stand for the self now, the self as a child, and also for other persons.

Many mechanisms enter into the structure of any image. The example to follow is not a pure illustration of condensation, but will convey the idea.

The person in this example is a woman art student who volunteered to participate in an experiment on the effects of dream deprivation on

* By latent thoughts, Freud means the essential thoughts that would completely replace the dream if there were no censorship. Any reader who has not done so is strongly advised to read *The Interpretation of Dreams*.

image formation. She agreed to report her dreams, her reveries before sleep and on waking up, and her daydreams; to perform various image-forming tasks; and to provide associations to emergent images. Her first dream in the laboratory provides an example of condensation of several themes into one image. Her dream image was a leg disappearing out of a window. (Figure 1 is her drawing of the image.) Based on considerably more material revealed through the process of association and the overall body of psychodynamic data, the image of the leg going out the window condensed several themes. These themes included escape, depression, sex, wish for understanding, and representation of the experimental setting.

The best approximation of the latent dream thoughts are:

DEPRESSION—I feel sad that I do not now have a good relationship with a man, and that past relationships have not ended well. Sometimes I feel so sad that I would contemplate jumping out a window (suicide).

ESCAPE—Why did I volunteer for this anyway, I'd like to get out of here, jump out the window if necessary.

SEX—I would like to have someone love me. (The window symbolizes her open feminine receptivity and organ anatomy, the foot symbolizes the penetrating male penis).

WISH FOR UNDERSTANDING—I would like to open myself up to these doctors and have them understand me, but they might get too penetrating. (Open window, penetrating foot).

EXPERIMENTAL SETTING—Her dreams are going to be interrupted, a penetration into her sleep by the experimenters, like the foot through the window.

In the latter two themes there is a reversal, a common mechanism of displacement, the leg going out the window in the manifest dream, is going "in" in the latent thoughts. The several themes can be condensed into this idea: I would like to understand myself better, maybe this psychologic experiment will help, maybe I could even relate affectionately to these men, but that is not their purpose, they only want a subject, they might reject me and I would be depressed, or they might get dangerously penetrating, I'd like to get out of here right now, this is dangerous. This entire train of thought is expressed at once in the single dream image.

Some of the later image-drawings help support these interpretations of the latent dream thoughts. The next night the subject reported a dream in which she was alone in a house, explored it, and found a bed in the hallway with two figures in it. (This dream image is drawn in Figure 2.) The bed in the hallway repeats the theme of the leg in the window. The hall is an open area, a corridor, the bed an elongated object. A leg should not be in the window, a bed should not be in the hall (a prohibi-

Fig. 1 (above). The dream of a leg disappearing. Fig. 2 (below). The dream of the bed in a hallway.

Figs. 3 (left) and 4 (below). Drawings of two figures done during reverie.

tion against the sexual aspect of the latent thoughts). Again, this is a condensation. The bed in the hallway also expressed her loneliness at seeing two people who were close, while she was separate from them. In her associations this referred to childhood memories of her standing alone in the hall outside of, and excluded from, her parent's bedroom. The scene also reflects, in a condensed form, the experimental situation. For the sake of propriety, she slept in a laboratory room with twin beds; in the other bed was her roommate, whom she referred to as her "baby-

Fig. 5. Drawing of woman and child done during reverie.

sitter." A male experimenter was alone, part of the time, in an adjoining room where he monitored the systems that record EEG, eye movements, and audio tape. During the day the subject produced drawings in a reverie-like state. Some of these contained pictorial references to being mothered (she was the "baby") and also to being held sexually. Figure 3 shows a masculine figure cradling a smaller feminine figure, and Figure 4 shows a more explicit image. Note, however, the size difference: the bottom figure is child-like. There is condensation of sexual wishes with wishes to be cradled or to have a baby. This latter composite appears more clearly in Figure 5, another reverie image. These later pictures reveal the sexual and nurturance themes condensed into the first dream image.

DISPLACEMENT

Displacement is a mechanism that results in a change of relative emphasis. An unimportant idea or feeling may be accentuated, while an important idea or feeling may be diminished in intensity. This mechanism is so important to the image construction of dreams that, in interpretation, Freud warned against assuming that the most vivid or central element in a dream is the most meaningful. The core of the latent thoughts might be expressed, instead, in a fleeting, trivial or peripheral detail. The purpose of displacement is to escape censorship by disguising ideas that are prohibited from clear expression.

Sometimes ideas about the self are displaced onto other persons or objects. In the previous example, a strong motive towards being taken care of was, possibly, displaced onto a weaker wish for sexual gratification. Phobias are commonly the result of displacement: the latent fear is disguised as the overt phobic anxiety towards an associated object.

One of the most common forms of displacement is achieved through reversal. Homosexuality can thus be represented in a dream or an image by apparently heterosexual themes, anger by kindness, or active wishes by depictions of the self as passive and receptive.

SYMBOLIZATION

Symbolization is a process by which one object, feeling, or situation may be chosen to signify another. It differs from displacement in that the meaning is relatively fixed, and in that the meaning may be collective as well as idiosyncratic. For example, suppose a boy is angry at his mother because she disciplined him. If he slams the door or kicks a dog, the mechanism is displacement: instead of hostility towards his mother he is hostile to the door or the dog. If he fantasizes about a queen who comes to grief, he has formed a symbol for his mother. Like his parent, the queen rules her subjects, but queens are also common in stories so he can displace his hostility onto a convenient symbol and avoid recognition of the object of his hostility. Another kind of symbol would be to make a voodoo doll and stick pins in it.

Symbols may be selected for reasons of relevance, disguise, or simply because they are easy to visualize. For example, a king may represent the idea of fatherly authority and grandeur, small animals may represent children, a gun may symbolize a penis. Symbols that can stand for several meanings are often used in images because they also serve the mechanisms of condensation and displacement. Freud warned against universal symbolism and, referring to his own mannerisms, allegedly said "sometimes a cigar is just a cigar." Personal meanings may be different from cultural meanings. Thus, a gun in a dream may mean a penis, a source of harm or pain, a source of power, a threat, a memory about guns, or even

Fig. 6. (above). Girl on a porpoise. Fig. 7 (below). Abstract version of porpoise.

(Porpoise in H₂O)

a person named "Gunther." Only the context and the personal associations in each case reveals the significance of a symbol.

The following example shows data from a dream deprivation experiment where the subject did a series of six drawings, after first staring at a central dot (to reduce outward attention and encourage spontaneous images).

Fig. 8. Fish swimming upstream.

The subject was a nurse, who at the end of the experimental period was talking openly about her wish to meet a nice young man, get married, and have children. While she did not relate these thoughts during the early days of the experiment, they probably were not far from her awareness. Of course latent fantasies about sexual relationships are common to men and women in studies where subjects sleep in the laboratory.

On the evening of the third night in the laboratory and the first night of dream awakenings, the subject did a series of six drawings, one of which depicted a girl riding a porpoise through waves (Figure 6). The theme returned the next morning in more abstract form (Figure 7). Interestingly enough, she had forgotten the contents of Figure 6, done the previous evening. One day later, on the morning after the second night of a dream deprivation procedure involving multiple awakenings, she produced a drawing of fish swimming up a waterfall (Figure 8). Two days later, after the sixth laboratory night and the fourth night of dream deprivation, she drew a balloon with a figure in the basket, in the third of six drawings (Figure 9). The fifth picture of that set is Figure 10, a direct reference to pregnancy, and the sixth is Figure 11, a vase covered with vines.

These drawings are all symbolic of some phase of sexual relations, fertilization, and pregnancy. Without the associations the reader cannot be absolutely sure, but perhaps will accept the *possibility*, that in her fantasy thinking the fish swimming upstream could symbolize sperm, that the girl on a porpoise and the figure in a balloon might depict the exhileration of intercourse, and that the vase could symbolize the female sexual anatomy (the fruitful uterus).

So far we have considered the range from primary to secondary process and certain thought mechanisms that occur frequently in the

Fig. 9 (left). Ascending balloon.
Fig. 10 (below). Direct depiction
of pregnancy wish.

Fig. 11. A vase.

primary process end of the spectrum: condensation, displacement, and symbolization. The next example, the dream of a patient in psychotherapy, shows these mechanisms and how they apply to both primary and secondary process thought. The dream was brief and reported as follows:

> "I was sitting in a red Volkswagen bus with a friend (a man), and I have considerable difficulty adjusting our seats to the same level."

> Through associations to the dream images, it became clear that the red Volkswagen bus is a symbol that condenses several themes. She associated red to her friend's expensive red sportscar, a phallic contrast with the box-like quality of the bus. The Volkswagen bus was associated to "an intelligent way to carry a large family" but also a "low-status form of transportation." The bus symbolizes her self-concept: intelligent but low status.

> The difficulty in adjusting seats to the same level is an action that also symbolizes current feelings. She fears that her friend might not be interested in her because she is beneath his social level. She, on the other hand, wonders if she is not above him because of her greater intellectual quickness and sensitivity. The manipulation of the seat, the seat handle, and moving up and down referred to sexual intercourse. This portion of the dream could be a wish-fulfillment of erotic feelings as well as a statement about their sexual compatibility.

> The dream shows secondary process as well as primary process organization of thought. It was the first conscious expression of a train of thought that emerged more clearly in subsequent therapy sessions. She and her boyfriend have fun sexually, but she wonders if they should consider marriage and family since they have trouble reaching the same level intellectually and socially. She regards him as superior because he is rich, upper class, and has a penis. She knows she is superior intellectually and is aware of her temptation to "cut him down." This train of thought is presented with marvelous simplicity and concreteness in the image of "difficulty adjusting our seats to the same level."

> There was also displacement in the dream. Associations revealed that some of the sexual impulses were directed towards the therapist. "Not on the same level" referred to the difference between couch and chair, and "VW" referred to the therapist's car. There was displacement of emphasis from the patient-therapist relationship to the relevant relationship with the boyfriend.*

UNRAVELING THE MEANING OF IMAGES

Very often, the motives behind image formation are well-disguised. The tracks are hidden and only the ingenious end-product, the image, enters awareness. To undo the work of symbolism, condensation, and

---

* The dream also had deeper meanings. The red color and being inside a car referred to particularly important childhood memories, and there were additional impulsive motives not cited here.

displacement, the information inherent in every part of the image must be released. The key to this process is the free associative method.

Freud found a way of setting aside resistance and unraveling the concealments in the construction of dream images, which applies to all images. The essence of this technique is as follows. A person is asked to place his mind in a relaxed and uncritical state. He is instructed to report every thought regardless of its implications, apparent relevance, logic, or propriety. The therapist may break down the image report into phrases or components and give them back to the subject who reports his associations. When the associational chain seems to run dry, the next component might be presented.

With this method, information relevant to the image experience increases markedly. The information concerns both possible meanings behind image details and the attitude of the subject towards understanding various aspects of his perience. The observer and the subject listen to these associations with "the third ear," seeking meaningful patterns.

The additional information may provide clues that unmask the disguise achieved by condensation and symbolization. The observer and the observing part of the subject's psychic system notice which feelings and ideas emerge repeatedly as associations to various aspects of the image experience.* The following example illustrates how increased information from associations allows the interpretation of an image.

> A psychotherapy patient was on the way to her session when she passed a sign on a window that read "Evangelist's Services." She had a visual image of a woman kneeling while a man prayed over her head. She burst into tears without knowing why. Even when she talked of her experience in the therapy hour, she could not understand her tears or her image. The therapist asked her to free associate even though the image experience was relatively simple. First, she was presented with the idea of a woman kneeling. When she seemed to run out of spontaneous associations to that part of the image, the therapist suggested the idea of a man praying. After the next pause she was asked what "over her head" brought to mind. Then she was asked to associate to the words "evangelist" and "services." Here are several of her associations to each component.
>
> *A Woman Kneeling.* Kneeling is a subservient position. I remember kneeling in church. A scrub woman kneels. The woman isn't looking up, maybe she is afraid to.
>
> *A Man Is Praying.* That seems silly, I don't believe in God anymore. I think of choir music and feeling inspired. Hands touch each other in prayer. The man is not touching her. It gives me a hypocritical feeling —about him, that is.

---

* The technique of image interpretation is described further in *The interpretation of Dreams* (Freud, 1900), by Erikson (1954), Sharpe (1961), and by Saul, Snyder, and Sheppard (1956). Chapter 8 of this book will give illustrations of how the meaning behind formation of recurrent images may be unraveled.

Over Her Head. Over someone means to be better than someone. She wants him to do something for her. But she can't see if he is. I can't see you either, because you're always looking at me and I have to look down (the patient faces the therapist but usually bows her head to avoid looking at him).

Evangelist. That's someone really inspirational, a little bit of a quack. I saw Burt Lancaster in a movie, he seduced Katherine Hepburn. People get all excited in evangelistic meetings. It's really dumb.

Services. Praying. Religious services. Stud services. I don't like that idea. A woman would go to an evangelist because she really was in need. I mean to deceive herself. The idea of a woman doing that is degrading. Like if she were really sexed up and had to fool herself by calling it religion.

From these associations one can make a tentative formulation of at least one meaning of the image. The patient alludes several times to the feeling of humiliation: kneeling is "subservient," someone better than another, "really dumb," "degrading." There is also the hint of sexual excitement: inspiration, touching, stud services, and the patient's insightful remark about a woman being "sexed up."

The combination of the affects associated with the image contents suggests this interpretation. She is beginning to feel sexually excited toward the therapist (as part of a reliving in the transference of a prior set of experiences). She feels inferior intellectually because she is emotionally "sick." She also feels, guiltily, that she is coming for love rather than for treatment, and feels hypocritical because she has always believed that psychiatry was a hoax and a waste of time. At the moment she is afraid that she will reveal her sexual excitement, to herself and to the therapist. She fears that she will express her yearning for love and receive either a humiliating rejection or become a sucker swallowing the hoax of psychiatry in return for artificial affection. When she saw the sign "Evangelist's Services," the perceptual stimuli acted as a trigger for these latent thoughts, which influenced the formation of an image that condensed, displaced, and symbolized her feelings. While the thought content was sufficiently disguised, the image nonetheless released enough accompanying emotions so that she wept in response.

GRATIFICATION THROUGH IMAGE FORMATION

As stated earlier, both primary process and secondary process regulate image formation. When primary process influence is preponderant, the impulsive motives act as imperative stimuli, moving towards resolution not so much as soon as is feasible, but "right now," whether feasible or not. Sometimes a person cannot achieve gratification from the external environment, and he turns to internal sources. One internal, immediately workable source is image formation. These images are derived from memories of situations or fantasies that gratified similar desires or needs in the past.

Freud (1895) illustrated this process, in a hypothetical, primitive form, by conceiving of the infant's "first" thought process as a hallucination of the maternal breast. In this model, as mentioned earlier, the baby associates seeing the breast with the ensuing relief from his pangs of hunger. When this association and the relevant perceptual images are adequately recorded in memory, when hunger pangs are strong, and when the breast does not immediately appear, the baby "hallucinates" the absent breast by reviving the memory trace. This image, with its associations of relief from tension, momentarily reduces hunger-anxiety and helps the baby tolerate the delay until the next feeding. Rapaport (1954, 1951) considers such hallucinatory image formation of a previous perception associated with gratification as the prototype for all later thought. Holt (1967) points out that such hallucinations, if they occur, would be really gratifying because the infant would suck, and thereby comfort himself, on its own lips and tongue.

Less primitive kinds of gratification occur in daydreams about sex and success in everyday life. Here is a typical example:

> A scientist had devised an ingenious but laborious experiment. It would be a major contribution to his science if the conclusion he anticipated were reached. It was necessary, however, for him to spend a great deal of time in the laboratory. He frequently became bored, fatigued, and irritated and found himself thinking of reasons to leave the laboratory, such as for coffee. He resisted these impulses by returning to a visual daydream of himself, modestly accepting the honorarium that was offered for the solution to the problem he hoped to solve. The man who offered the award, as demonstrated by the patient's associations and description of the visual images during psychotherapy, resembled his father.

The images involved in the fantasy took but a few seconds, but left him feeling refreshed. He repeatedly used the fantasy to stimulate himself. The visual and implicit sensation of being given something of value by the older man changed his mood and increased his motivation by reminding him of an eventual reward for the arduous work and by gratifying in fantasy his frustrated wish for closeness and identification during lonely moments. The daydream also granted him his father's permission to do well. As suggested by Joseph (1959), the fantasy was a trial action modified to provide gratification.

Visual fantasies can provide a safe outlet for impulses that might be dangerous if they were discharged in real action. The employee who is submissive in reality, but imagines telling off his boss, is one example. Similarly, images can be used to gratify prohibited desires or to attain in fantasy what is unobtainable in reality.

Image formation for gratification may occur with or without accompanying actions. Many wishful visual fantasies occur during masturbation, which provides real physical gratification. In fact, the frequent association of fantasy with the physical act of masturbation leads some persons to suppress fantasy activity because they unconsciously endow the act of fantasy with guilt. Other persons indulge frequently in fantasy, even to the disruption of daily tasks, and such activity has earned the nickname "mental masturbation."

This type of gratification through image formation also occurs in the context of sexual intercourse. For example, some persons are unable to achieve orgasm unless they have certain perverse or pregenital visual fantasies during love making. Thus, some males may be having the "gratification" in fantasy of holding a film "sex-kitten" while having intercourse with their wives. This type of fantasy allows indulgences of impulses that the person would not put into real action because they conflict with other motives such as those of ideals and conscience.

> A young married woman was sometimes sexually frigid. At other times she was able to achieve an orgasm during intercourse with her husband. Her only route to sufficient erotic excitation for orgasm was to have a specific visual fantasy during love making. In this fantasy she pictured herself as a prostitute permitting humiliating acts to be performed upon her for money. She felt guilty and tried to avoid recall of these fantasies or acknowledgement of their implications. She also feared revealing the images to the therapist because she was ashamed of them and feared that they might be regarded as abnormal. Also, translation of the images into words would destroy the compartmentalization of her mental life: she would have to recognize the images and their implications, and that meant that she might have to give up her only current route to sexual pleasure.

Image formation, even in daydreams, is not exclusively dominated by sexual or aggressive urges. The gratification may be compliance with the rules of conscience or concepts of the ideal self. Also, the gratification may be that of mastery, such as the completion of a difficult problem or task (Kris, 1950). The internal activity itself, separate from contents, may be a pleasurable compensation for reduced external stimulation (Singer, 1966).

Psychoanalytic theory has focused largely on the issue of gratification through image formation because of Freud's insistence that, whatever evidence of problem solving might be present in the *manifest* dream, the *latent* dream thoughts and the dream work involved a striving for wish-fulfillment. In a broader view we might regard image formation as motivational as well as gratifying. Pleasant images may increase rather than decrease longing; unpleasant images may motivate avoidance (Tomkins, 1962; Arieti, 1967). Several examples of the motivational properties of images will be presented in Chapters 7 and 8.

EXPRESSION OF EMERGENT CONCEPTS AS IMAGES

A new thought may gain representation in any mode: enactive, image, or lexical. Clinicians observe, however, that thoughts involved in an impulse-defense conflict often enter awareness first in the form of visual images.

Freud used this observation during an interval when he wished to give up hypnosis but had not yet developed the free associative method. Freud and Breuer (1893–1895) believed that repressed memories of traumatic experiences provided the basis for hysterical symptoms. To relieve the symptom, they wanted patients to recall the memory and undergo a working-through of the emotions involved. Freud gave up trance-induction and simply used suggestion. He pressed his hand on the patient's forehead and told him a picture would come to mind when he released the pressure:

> Once a picture has emerged from the patient's memory, we may hear him say that it becomes fragmentary and obscure in proportion as he proceeds with his description of it. The patient is, as it were, getting rid of it by turning it into words . . . (If) a picture of this kind will remain obstinately before the patient . . . this is an indication to me that he still has something important to tell me about the topic of the picture. As soon as this has been done, the pictures vanish like a ghost that has been laid. (Freud and Breuer, 1893, pp. 280–1.)

Freud later developed the method of free association and abandoned suggestion. He continued to pay attention to visual images and, in *The Ego and the Id* (1923), stated:

> We must not be led away . . . into forgetting the importance of optical memory residues . . . or to deny that it is possible for thought processes to become conscious through a reversion to visual residues and that in many people this seems to be the favored method.

Freud (1898, 1901) observes that when a memory is repressed, there often emerges into consciousness an unusually vivid visual image of a relevant object (überdeutlich). In an instance from his own experience, he was blocked in the recall of the name of the artist Signorelli, but saw instead an ultraclear thought image of the artist's self-portrait. This kind of vivid image partially expresses, but also screens from awareness, conflicted memories or ideas. That is why they are sometimes called "screen memories" (Freud, 1899, 1916).

Later psychoanalysts also noted that images sometimes are the first vehicle for expression of repressed mental contents. They also emerge in resistance to expression of ideas in words (Deutsch, 1953; Lewin, 1955). Kanzer (1958) suggests that there may be an oscillation between image formation and lexical representation and that image formation tends to occur during transitions in the state of consciousness. One common experience in the conduct of insight therapy is that patients may report a vivid visual image during the seconds after they have heard an interpretation.

Warren (1961) and Kepecs (1954) have noted how visual images present new material, yet also seem to be a form of resistance to having this material emerge. Both analysts asked patients to describe what they noted in their mind during moments when they lapsed from verbal reports. Patients often responded with reports of visual images. One of Kepecs' patients reported that her mind had gone blank, so he asked her to describe the blankness. It appeared that it had a particular substance, like looking at a closed door. The patient then recalled that she had followed her father into the bathroom, hoping to see what a penis looked like. The door was shut in her face. A similar motive, the wish to look, was currently active and directed towards the analyst. The image of the blank, closed door was a partial expression of this motive, in the form of a memory that also reminded her that looking was prohibited.

Here is an illustration of how images may serve as the first expression of conflicted thoughts.

> A young woman in her twenties had been in psychoanalytically oriented therapy for a character disturbance for over a hundred hours. One day when entering the office, she imagined herself as being without her head and, after a silence, said she had nothing to talk about and that no thought would come to her. She then had an image of herself with a button on the side of her head. The button was pressed and little white letters sorted into bundles came out of her mouth. She felt like an automaton. Her next associations concerned people being laid off work because of "motivation." She laughed and said motivation was a slip of the tongue for "automation." Next she reported an image of a word game like scrabble. Then she said, "That was like trying to sort words meaninglessly." The therapist asked if the slip, "motivation" for "automation," could have to do with her feelings about therapy. She replied that she felt treatment might be discontinued because of her apparent lack of motivation. She said her feelings of being like an automaton doing the therapist's bidding must have been behind the image of entering without her head emitting meaningless words. She felt forced to talk but wanted to say nothing. Why should she tell the therapist how bad off she was when he cared so little for her? Then she spoke more freely about a recent accident in which she was nearly killed. She had resisted mentioning this episode during several previous therapy hours.

This same patient could also alter her perception to achieve certain gratifying sensory effects. During a different period of therapy, she found her attention focused on a brass bookend on a shelf behind the therapist's head. Next she had a thought image of the bookend striking the therapist's head. She realized, as a consequence of verbalizing this image, that she was angry at the therapist for his failure to congratulate or reward her for recent therapeutic progress. The therapist's "brass-headedness" seemed to be a connecting associative link. She then revealed her capacity to purposively change the direction of gaze of a single eye. This allowed her to move, in her internal double image, the bookend toward and away from the therapist's head. She was thus capable of partially gratifying her hostile urges by forming images of bashing in the therapist's head.

There are many other instances in free association when a patient reports a visual image that represents a repressed urge or idea. Of course, this effect is not limited to images. Recall the slip of the tongue in the above example. The patient may describe the image and report associations to it before he realizes the full impact of the idea and associated feelings. Sometimes, however, the image is understandable at once:

A young surgeon was launching himself into private practice and was forcing himself to work extremely long hours. Although the success and financial gain were highly gratifying, and although he was propelled by an intense ambition, he periodically thought about his long hours without knowing why he was bothered. While falling asleep after a hard day of work, he experienced a hypnagogic hallucination. The image was a yellowish, lifeless hand like those he saw during autopsies. He instantly awoke and felt that the image was a message to the ambitious and driving part of himself from some other aspect of his personality. The message was clear to him: he would kill himself if he maintained his current hectic pace.

Why should some conflicted ideas gain representation first as visual images and not as lexical thoughts?* To summarize, image formation is a more primitive system, and it tends to be under the influence of a primitive system of regulation, the primary process. Images may be harder to inhibit, and they may also be easily disguised through the mechanisms of condensation, displacement, and symbolization. Lexical representation develops later, when prohibitions have been internalized and inhibitory systems and the secondary process have developed. Also, words tend to be clear, once they enter awareness: images may be fleeting and poorly recorded in memory. Finally, images are more likely, than lexical representation, to provide partial gratification because they are more analagous to perception.

---

* The expression of emergent ideas is not exclusive to image formation, of course, and certainly it is not exclusive to visual images. Any of the concepts expressed in this chapter may be equally applicable to other forms of imagery such as auditory images, olfactory imagery, and so forth.

CONCLUSION

This chapter focused on the expression of impulsive motives as images. As inner motives develop into images, the thought process may follow primary process or secondary process types of organization. Some aspects of the impulsive motives may be disguised by condensation, symbolization, and displacement. This disguise can often be unraveled using the free associative method. The images may serve as partial gratification of wishes, they may also be the first expression in awareness of emergent and previously hidden ideas or feelings. The image formation process is not, however, guided solely by the surge of impulsive motives. Other motives may seek to attenuate or divert expression through regulation and control of image formation. The interplay between impulsive and defensive motives may lead to total repression of image formation, to compromises in terms of what is expressed, and even to the sudden emergence of unbidden and unwelcome images. This latter phenomenon is one of the most mysterious aspects of image formation. We consider regulation and control of image formation more closely, and the unbidden image phenomenon in particular, in the next 3 chapters.

REFERENCES

Arieti, S. 1967. *The Intrapsychic Self*. New York, Basic Books.

Deutsch, F. 1953. Instinctual drives and intersensory perceptions during the analytic procedure. In Lowenstein, R. M., ed. *Drives, Affects, Behavior*, Vol. 1. New York, International Universities Press.

Erikson, E. H. 1954. The dream specimen of psychoanalysis. In Knight, R. P., and Friedman, C. R., eds. *Psychoanalysis, Psychiatry, and Psychology*, Vol. 1. New York, International Universities Press. 1954.

Freud, S. (1923) The ego and the id. *Stand. Ed.*, 19, 1961.

———— (1916) A mythological parallel to a visual obsession. *Stand. Ed.*, 14, 1957.

———— (1908) Hysterical phantasies and their relation to bi-sexuality. *Stand. Ed.*, 9, 1959.

———— (1901) The psychopathology of everyday life. *Stand. Ed.*, 6, 1960.

———— (1900) Interpretation of dreams. *Stand. Ed.*, 4, 5, 1952.

———— (1899) Screen memories. *Stand. Ed.*, 3, 1962.

———— (1898) The psychical mechanism of forgetfulness. *Stand. Ed.*, 3, 1962.

———— (1895) Project for a scientific psychology. In Bonaparte, M., Freud,

A., and Kris, E., eds. *The Origins of Psychoanalysis*. New York, Basic Books, 1954.

———— and Breuer, J. (1893–1895) Studies on hysteria. *Stand. Ed.*, 2, 1955.

Gill, M. M. 1967. The primary process. *Psychol. Issues*, Monogr. 18/19, 5:60–298.

Hartmann, H. 1964. Comments on the psychoanalytic theory of the ego. In *Essays on Ego Psychology; Selected Problems in Psychoanalytic Theory*. New York, International Universities Press.

Holt, R. R. 1967. The development of the primary process: A structural view. *Psychol. Issues*, Monogr. 18/19, 5 (2–3):344–383.

———— 1962. A critical examination of Freud's concept of bound versus free cathexis. *J. Amer. Psychoanal. Ass.*, 10:475–525.

Joseph, E. D. 1959. An unusual fantasy in a twin with an inquiry into the nature of fantasy. *Psychoanal. Quart.*, 28:189–206.

Kafka, E., and Reiser, M. 1967. Defensive and adaptive ego processes: Their relationship to GSR activity in free imagery experiments. *Arch. Gen. Psychiat.*, 16:34–40.

Kanzer, M. 1958. Image formation during free association. *Psychoanal. Quart.*, 27:465–484.

Kepecs, J. G. 1954. Observations on screens and barriers in the mind. *Psychoanal. Quart.*, 23:62–77.

Kris, E. 1950. On preconscious mental processes. In Rapaport, D., ed. *Organization and Pathology of Thought*, pp. 474–493. New York, Columbia University Press, 1951.

Kubie, L. S. 1967. The relation of psychotic disorganization to the neurotic process. *J. Amer. Psychoanal. Ass.*, 15:626–640.

Lewin, B. D. 1955. Dream psychology & the analytic situation. *Psychoanal. Quart.*, 24:169–199.

Noy, P. 1969. A revision of the psychoanalytic theory of the primary process. *Int. J. Psychoanal.*, 50:155–178.

Rapaport, D. (1960) On the psychoanalytic theory of motivation. In Gill, M., ed. *The Collected Papers of David Rapaport*, pp. 853–915. New York, Basic Books. 1967.

———— 1954. The conceptual model of psychoanalysis. In Knight, R. P., and Friedman, C. R., eds. *Psychoanalytic Psychiatry and Psychology*. New York, International Universities Press.

———— 1951. Consciousness: A psychopathological & psychodynamic view. In Abramson, H. A., ed. *Problems of Consciousness*, pp. 18–57. New York, Josiah M cy Jr. Foundation.

Saul, L., Snyder, T., and Shepard, E. 1956. On reading manifest dreams and other unconscious material. *J. Amer. Psychoanal. Ass.*, 4:122–137.

Schur, M. 1966. *The Id and the Regulatory Principles of Mental Functioning*. New York, International Universities Press.

Sharpe, E. F. (1937) *Dream Analysis*. London, The Hogarth Press, 1949.

Singer, J. 1966. *Daydreaming*. New York, Random House.

Stekel, W. 1951. The polyphony of thought. In Rapaport, D., ed. *Organization and Pathology of Thought*. New York, Columbia University Press.

Tomkins, S. 1962. *Affect, Imagery, Consciousness.* New York, Springer Publishing Company.

Warren, M. 1961. The significance of visual images during the analytic session. *J. Amer. Psychoanal. Ass.,* 9:504–518.

Zern, D. 1968. Freud's considerations of the mental process. *J. Amer. Psychoanal. Ass.,* 16:749–782.

CHAPTER

7
Regulation of Image Formation

Ordinarily people are not aware of the ways in which they regulate the vividness and contents of their images, but they do become aware of images that are unusually vivid, or images that depict contents they wish to avoid. When such images occur, a person may feel as if he has lost control of his thinking. Such episodes occur in everyday life, as when a person cannot dispel a recurrent melody, or when a person cannot bring to mind an image of a familiar object. In states of psychopathology, recurrent hallucinations may torment a person, or there may be total amnesia for important memories. By studying lapses in control, we may deepen our understanding of the processes that regulate image formation.

A CONCEPTUAL MODEL OF IMAGE FORMATION

Because regulation of image formation is a topic central to the rest of this book, I will present briefly a model of image formation and control to use as a conceptual tool for the descriptions that follow. There is no proof of the model, but it does not contradict known neurophysiologic, psychophysical, or psychodynamic facts.

Conscious images derive content from two sources: perception and memory. Perception includes the reception of external visual signals, and stimuli that arise within the body such as excitations of the optic pathways (entoptic images). Memory includes recollection of

107

events, recall of fantasy, and reconstructions using various fragments of memory. Some conscious image experiences are composites, mingling elements from both sources. The prevalence of illusions, for example, suggests that perception, memory activation, and fantasy share, at least in part, the same channels of image formation.*

Consider a central matrix or series of matrices on which images may be formed. Unless these matrices are activated, no image appears in conscious experience. The degree of image vividness depends on the degree of activation, reduplication of images, or rhythmic repetition.

The matrices may be activated from external or internal sources. Perhaps there might be a gradient. Certain matrices might be turned towards perception but accessible, in states of high intensity, to memory images; others might be turned towards internal image formation but accessible to perception images under situations of very high stimulus input (or low barrier against stimulus input).

The two basic resources, the various perception and image-formation processes, and the apparatus for image formation would be interrelated by feedback processes. This feedback would include provisions for matching perception images with memory images and searching for a "best-fit" composite image. This feedback would also interrelate with sensorimotor control systems, especially those involving schemata for eye movements, head position, proprioception, and other modes of sensation.

To prevent excessive entry or flooding with stimuli from external or internal sources, regulatory influences would affect transmission of information at all levels of this model. Such regulatory influences would also amplify or "seek out" stimuli when required by states of need. Regulation would effect the entire system at several sites: the input from perceptual sources, from internal sources, and the apparatus for image formation itself. And this regulation could take place by either active inhibition or active facilitation to modify content, organization, or vividness of image formation.

These basic regulatory mechanisms, inhibition and facilitation, would each have a range of settings. The setting, ranging from very high to very low, would depend on current neurobiologic capacity and psychologic motives. For example, fatigue might reduce the ability to facilitate in spite of strong psychologic motives for amplification of the process. Inhibition and facilitation can be exerted in concert or in conflict.

_____

* Arlow (1969) calls this the two projector model: the image formation apparatus is like a window shade, and projectors from within (e.g., fantasy) and from without (e.g., perception) may influence the forms that appear on the shade. West (1962) presents the same model using the analogy of a pane of glass which transmits signals from outside during daylight, and signals from inside at night: at any time the images on the glass may be composites from both sources. Recent experimental work by Antrobus and Singer (1969) and Segal (1969) also suggests that image formation and perception occupy, at least to some extent, overlapping channels for cognitive processing (see Chapter 10).

Perception could be "tuned up" by facilitation while memory activation or fantasy was "tuned down" by inhibition. Or, a given portion of a process could be in a state of excess facilitation with deficient inhibition producing a situation analogous to an uncontrolled car, going too fast without brakes or steering. A combination of excess facilitation with excess inhibition would be like pressing on the gas pedal and the brakes at the same time.

Hernandez-Peon (1964) suggests that from a neurophysiologic point of view a major occurrence in mental development is the progressive differentiation of inhibition and facilitory mechanisms. Gardner (1969) and Holt (1968) arrive at the same conclusion from a psychoanalytic point of view, and suggest that such a model of reciprocal control may clarify theoretic problems involving the energy-structure duality.* Gardner sees mental processes activated in hierarchically organized "columns of structures." In alert wakefulness, activation is greater in upper process levels of a column. At these upper levels processes are regulated by fine controls of inhibition and facilitation yielding secondary process thought, as described in the previous chapter. Lower levels are regulated by the more primitive controls that characterize primary process.

To summarize, this model of a central image-depicting apparatus is somewhat differentiated: part shows preferential receptivity to perception, part to internal image formation. Two basic sources, external and internal, may provide contents to this apparatus. The entire system can be regulated through inhibitory and facilitatory influences at various locations. These active regulatory operations may be operating at high or low levels, synchronously or in conflict, with refined or gross control processes. Their operation depends on both neurobiologic influences and psychologic motives.†

OVERCONTROL: LOSS OF THE VOLITIONAL ABILITY TO FORM IMAGES

Suppose, in what follows, that the neurobiologic structures that subserve the various parts of the model are intact and capable of the normal

---

* The theoretic problem of the energy-structure duality is how to explain the durability over time of what Rapaport calls "cognitive structures" and how to explain how cognition takes place without flooding of consciousness by either external or internal stimuli. When energy levels are low, structures seem to become more primitive and consciousness does become flooded, at times, with uncontrolled stimuli. When energy levels increase, the operation of sophisticated structures and controls is again apparent (Rapaport, 1960).

† The classification of motives as ego, id, or superego, functions; as impulsive or defensive aims; as guided by the pleasure, unpleasure, reality principles; as conscious, preconscious, or unconscious; as sexual or aggressive drives; or as primitive or recent; is beyond the scope of this model but not incompatible with it. See Schur, 1966.

range of function and that variations in function are due to psychologic influences.* A person may fail in his conscious desire to obtain images from either perception or memory. Such a failure could be due to excessive inhibition, or deficient facilitation.

Example 1. Inability to Generate a Memory Image

A young marine stationed on a Pacific Island became panicky because of strong sexual impulses towards the native girls he worked with. He tried to conjure up an image of his fiancée in the United States but was unable to do so. He could, however, form images of his home, his mother, his father, and other close acquaintances. He became panicky and felt that the girl was completely gone from his memory. He could remember their dates and could visualize places they had gone, but he could not remember what her appearance was like.

In this example, the marine consciously attempts to facilitate internal image formation (remember his fiancée), but volitional facilitation is weak in comparison with unconscious inhibition (forgetting his fiancée). Put more simply, one set of his motives (unconscious) wants him to forget his fiancée and have a good time with the local girls. Another set of motive (conscious), the part he identifies as "himself," says that he will be happier in the long run if he remembers his fiance and forgets the island girls.

Example 2. Inability to Generate Perceptual Images

A woman consulted an ophthalmologist because of tunnel vision: she could see objects directly in front of her but not at the periphery of her gaze. As the objects were further from the center of her glance, they became grayer and less distinct. No neurologic deficits were found, and no known neurologic disease could account for her impairment of perception. Psychotherapy uncovered the fact that she was afraid of seeing particular sexual scenes and that this specific fear had generalized to vision, leading to inhibition of images of peripheral perception. The symptom was relieved when her specific fear was brought to light.

The two previous examples indicate how a lapse of control characterized by inability to facilitate, or excessive inhibition, may involve processes that form images from either memory or perception.

---

* Influences on image formation from alterations of biologic substrates will be considered in Chapters 10, 11, and 12. This model presumes that subjective experience alters regulatory levels such as thresholds of excitation. Since these regulatory mechanisms have an electrophysiologic or biochemical basis, the model presumes that conscious experience can causally affect brain processes. While many neural scientists have tended to reject such hypotheses and have preferred to regard consciousness as an "epiphenomenon," investigators such as Sperry (1969) have emphasized the need for models that show an interaction between consciousness and neurobiologic processes and that consider the directive role of consciousness in determining the flow pattern of cerebral excitation.

UNDERCONTROL: LOSS OF VOLITIONAL ABILITY TO PREVENT IMAGE FORMATION

The next two examples indicate either a failure to inhibit or instances of excessive facilitation.

EXAMPLE 3. INABILITY TO PREVENT AN INTERNAL IMAGE FROM FORMING

When a young, adolescent girl tried to pray at night, she was troubled by a vivid, intrusive image of God's penis, hanging down from heaven as an inverted erection, pointing at her like an accusatory finger. The intrusion occurred only during prayer, especially when she tried to recite a prayer beginning, "Our Father who art in Heaven . . ." She was frightened both by the contents of the image and by her inability to dispel it.

A similar inability to prevent images may occur from the side of perception.

EXAMPLE 4. INABILITY TO STOP PERCEPTION

A 10-year-old boy watched, terror stricken but unable to remove his gaze, while his father slaughtered piglets whose mother had died. As his father disemboweled each piglet, he threw the guts into a bucket. During that night, the boy screamed and complained that he was seeing it over again in his dreams. During the next day, he told his mother that he could not forget seeing his father cut up the pigs. Both parents recalled that the child stood and stared wide-eyed at the event even though they urged him to leave. He seemed unable to take his eyes off what was happening and, afterwards, he seemed to be in a state of shock.

PSYCHOPATHOLOGY

A loss of control over image formation is one of the important symptoms of psychopathology. I find it useful, conceptually, to consider loss of control from two points of view even though any given clinical syndrome will contain elements related to both points of view (and others as well). One point of view considers formal properties, especially the vividness of images and the problem of differentiating internal image formation from visual perception. Failures in this differentiation are commonly called a loss of reality testing. The second point of view focuses on contents: the key issue is the intrusive entry into awareness of unwelcome mental images which I will call "unbidden images."

REALITY TESTING

When we vividly experience a perceptual image, localize it as external, and recognize it as plausible, then we have no trouble saying "it is real." When we vaguely form an image and know it is intrapsychic and fictive, then we have no trouble saying "I imagine it." But let one part of the triad—vividness, localization, and plausibility—be incongruent with the other factors, and the question of reality occurs. For example, suppose an image is depicted with a vividness that resembles the intensity of perceptual images. In the model presented earlier, this vividness might include activation of the perception-oriented portion of the image depiction structures. Suppose that in spite of this vividness there is not sufficient information about whether the image contents have entered the depiction structure from the side of perception or the side of memory. And, in addition, suppose the image contents are appraised as unlikely to be real: an angry pink elephant charging down Main Street. The person who experiences the image is faced with a problem: is the elephant real or imagined? He must find a way to test the difference, to find the true origin of his image in order to plan or execute appropriate behavior. Reality testing has great conceptual importance in psychiatry because hallucinations and delusions are regarded as "failures in reality testing." This phrase, coined by Freud in 1911, has been so overworked that one gets the impression that there is some discrete, single reality-testing apparatus that is working well, weakly, or not at all. Instead, there are at least three clinically discrete operations to test the reality of images. I discuss these next under the headings 1) automatic reality testing, 2) checking, and 3) logical appraisal and learned counterweights.*

AUTOMATIC REALITY TESTING

I use this phrase to refer to the effortless and immediate differentiation usually made between perceptual images and memory or fantasy images. This automatic differentiation is suggested in the model by placement and vividness. Perceptual images are placed at different locations

---

* There is another meaning to the term reality testing: the differentiation between internal images that are real memories and those that are imaginary. In this text the term will be restricted to the differentiation between internal images and current perception.

in the area of image depiction and have a greater vividness than thought images. Additional information may be provided by the direction of input: perceptual images are derived from binocular gaze and are altered by eye movements and blinking. Subjectively, perceptions seem to be a passive experience (although we know that physiologically and cognitively the process is active, i.e., requires regulation). Internal images are more often willful, or at least there is incipient or implicit planfulness; they follow internal motives rather than external or physical events, and they come from within.

Thus, in ordinary circumstances, several different sets of information differentiate external and internal sources of input. When the different sets agree, then there is automatic, seemingly effortless labeling of what is real and what is unreal. When the different sets of information disagree, then a person activates the additional process of checking.

CHECKING

Suppose an image is depicted with unusual vividness, yet it is not clearly a perception. Automatic differentiation of the two possibilities is not successful. A variety of processes can check out the image, including altering the level of facilitation or inhibition of the two basic sources of image material.* For example, the person may inhibit the perceptual input by closing his eyes or shifting his glance. If this reduces vividness, then the image probably came through this external channel. Of course, checking is not always successful or correct, as shown in one of the following examples:

EXAMPLE 5. SUCCESSFUL CHECK BY EXTERNAL PERCEPTUAL INHIBITION

A man walking late at night visualized moving lights. Was he seeing flying saucers he wondered? He closed his eyes—the lights remained vivid in his awareness, so he knew they were not really coming from the night sky.

EXAMPLE 6. UNSUCCESSFUL CHECK BY EXTERNAL PERCEPTUAL INHIBITION

A woman awoke with a start. There beside her in bed was a giant crab. She shut her eyes, the crab disappeared. But when she opened her eyes it was still there. She repeated this three times: the crab was there whenever she opened her eyes. Convinced that it was real, she screamed, awakening her husband. While she told him of her experience, the image

---

* Martin (1968) considers this process as alteration of thresholds, thus keeping Freud's metaphor of the stimulus barrier. Unlike Freud (1920), Martin suggests a stimulus barrier not only to perception, but also to internal images.

faded. (Why cessation of hypnagogic hallucinations sometimes occurs with eye closure is unknown.)

Facilitating perception is another method of testing reality; as when a person may "look closer" at the image to see if this makes it increase in vividness, or when he may try to dispel what he thinks are internal images. As with inhibition, none of these methods is invariably successful.

EXAMPLE 7. INTERNAL INHIBITION TO CHECK REALITY

A patient stared at his girlfriend and felt her face was turning into a dog's head. He tried mentally to plastically restore her face to its usual shape. The doglike features disappeared. When he relaxed, he had a repetition of the same impressions. Again he could make it go away with an effort of will. He decided his mind was playing tricks on him.

EXAMPLE 8. INTERNAL FACILITATION TO CHECK REALITY

A student taking LSD saw his girlfriend's hair change into snakes. Somewhat whimsically, although he was a little frightened, he mentally commanded the snakes to smile with pleasure and give their heads a little shake. When they did so, he relaxed and felt this was part of his "trip," and not a menacing reality.

Sometimes internal image formation can achieve great vividness and even apparent external localization. Automatic and checking types of reality testing fail to distinguish the source of image input. A sense of reality and unreality can still be perserved, albeit with less stability, by use of logical appraisal.

LOGICAL APPRAISAL AND LEARNED COUNTERWEIGHTS

When an internal image is both very vivid and subjectively seems to occur "outside," a person can still test reality by appraisal of image contents. The appraisal of content as "not real" may counterbalance the effects of unusual vividness of internal images and may be based on logical calculation ("I never saw a purple cow before."), on previous experience ("I sometimes hallucinate crabs when I am just awakening."), or on consensual validation ("No one else here seems to see a Martian."). Many schizophrenic patients come to know the contents of their hallucinations and, though they continue to hallucinate, develop counterweights that help them to distinguish a perception from a hallucination. They thus reduce the deleterious effect of hallucinations on their behavior patterns by repeating a formula such as "whenever I think I see my brother it is probably a hallucination."

PROGRESSIVE LOSS OF REALITY TESTING

Inquiry into the development of hallucinations sometimes indicates two rather different routes. In one type, gradual deterioration in the differentiation of image sources begins with intensification of internal image experiences. Images become progressively more vivid and automatic processes become insufficient. For a while checking may maintain a sense of what is real and what is unreal, but if loss of control continues the person appraises vivid images as unreal only through logical inference. As logical inference becomes less reliable, a single image may fluctuate so that the experience seems now real and now unreal. Finally, hallucinations always seem like real perceptions.

EXAMPLE 9. DETERIORATION OF REALITY. TESTING BEGINNING AS
    INTENSIFICATION OF INNER IMAGES

A woman entered the hospital with an involutional melancholia, a type of depressive psychosis in which hallucinations and delusions sometimes occur. Her husband had died some years ago, leading her into immense grief and loneliness. For a while after his death, she was saddened but able to care for herself in spite of her former dependency on him. She still regularly set two places for dinner and laid out his clothes. At times she indulged herself in the pleasant daydream of talking to him at dinner. At other times she tried, sometimes in vain, to rid herself of such visions.

Next she began to see her husband out of the corner of her eye, or hear him speak. She would turn with a start, look quite carefully, and determine that no one was there. Next she hallucinated him visually, for hours on end it seemed, but still retained a sense of reality by reminding herself of his death. Finally, however, her sense of reality was entirely lost, and she had both pleasant and unpleasant hallucinations of him.

Another form of progressive deterioration in reality testing begins with distortion of perception. Blurring may occur as well as changes in size, shape, vividness, and color. Persons in this condition often complain of depersonalization and derealization. Illusions may occur which can deteriorate into hallucinations as an end result. Regaining the reality testing capacity may at times retrace the course of the original deterioration.

EXAMPLE 10. DETERIORATION OF REALITY TESTING BEGINNING AS
    PERCEPTUAL DISTORTION

A man was upset when his wife left him, and he became suspicious of men at work. He spent several days in morbid ruminations. One morning, when he went out for the paper, the sunlight seemed brighter and buildings had a fiery edge. When he looked at people they appeared dark and blurred, while the edges of their contours were bright as if surrounded by an aura or halo. He began to feel people were especially interested in him: he had fleeting illusions of faces watching him from windows, began to hear accusing voices, and felt as if he were Jesus. Finally, he formed delusions of persecution and grandiosity and hallucinated leering faces and religious figures.

The regulation of vividness of internal images, as indicated in the above example, is one of the major problems to confront the discrimination processes. I will mention briefly two current hypotheses which account for loss of control of vividness: the release theory of neurobiology, and the purposive theory of psychodynamics. They are not contradictory.

UNDERCONTROL OF VIVIDNESS: THE RELEASE THEORY

Many studies of the evolution and development of the nervous system indicate that primitive patterns of function remain but are held in quiescence by inhibition and patterns of function acquired at a higher developmental level. Jackson (1958) suggested that vivid internal images, such as hallucinations, also derived from primitive functions of the nervous system. When higher cortical functions, such as those subserving lexical thought or thought in images that was parsimonious in vividness, were disrupted as in fatigue, toxicity, or disease, then the lower cortical functions, including those subserving image formation of hallucinatory vividness, were activated as the result of failure of inhibition.

West (1962) summarized contemporary views of this hypothesis in his general theory of hallucinations and dreams. He postulates that vivid internal images tend to occur when a) the nervous system is in a state of relative arousal or excitability, and b) when there is insufficient input from perception to occupy the image-forming apparatus or to inhibit entry of internal images. For example, in sensory deprivation when the subject may be awake but have little perceptual input, internal images tend to gain in vividness. Similarly, in dreams, there may be greater cortical arousal without perceptual input resulting in unusual vividness of internal images.

The release theory is not incompatible with the model suggested at the beginning of this chapter. Vividness of internal images could occur under various circumstances. Internal input could be facilitated with unusual intensity in states or organic irritation or high motivation. Internal input could undergo relatively low inhibition due to organic diminution of inhibitory capacity or because of a low psychologic defense level.

The matrices for image formation could have a shift in gradient so that internal images were favored. Scheibel and Scheibel (1962) suggest that a shift in dendritic biasing could accomplish this effect. Finally, external perceptual inputs could be modified in a way conducive to increased vividness of internal images: there could be global reduction of input, there could be a high signal to noise ratio of input (see Chapter 10), and there could be input that triggers and intensifies psychologic motives.

UNDERCONTROL OF VIVIDNESS: PURPOSIVE THEORY

Purposive theories of increases in vividness of internal images have been advanced from neurobiologic as well as psychoanalytic points of view. Neurobiologically, increased vividness of internal images in states of perceptual reduction may be useful for maintaining arousal by supplying a source of stimulation that acts like external perception. This stands in contrast to the release theory which states that the vivid images are the *result* rather than the *cause* of high arousal.

Psychoanalytic theories of vivid events such as pseudohallucinations or hallucinations tend to focus on the meaning and purpose of the *contents*. The increase in vividness per se has been designated as part of a two-fold process called "topographic regression" (Freud, 1900; Gill, 1963). One aspect of topographic regression is conversion of thoughts in words to thoughts in images. The second step occurs in hallucinations. The "sense organ of perception" is stimulated from within, and thoughts, thereby, become as vivid as perceptions. Perceptual regression, in terms of enhanced vividness or apparent perceptualness of thoughts, may make fantasies appear more real and also make reality more like fantasy (since the two are no longer distinguished) (Arlow and Brenner, 1964; Freeman et al., 1966; Schaffer, 1968). For instance, the woman in Example 9 may have greater gratification by hallucinating her husband because, during the hallucination, her sad loss is magically undone. The increase in vividness of the image of her husband, and her ensuing appraisal of the image as a real perception, avoid feelings of grief.

UNBIDDEN IMAGES

Another type of loss of control of thought, regardless of increased vividness, is intrusive, *unbidden visual images*. This term avoids the connotations of Gordon's earlier term, "autonomous imagery" (1949, 1950), which indicates that the images entered awareness under their own autonomy, in contrast to images formed consciously and volitionally. Unfortunately, the word autonomous conveys the almost opposite meaning in psychoanalytic theory, where autonomous ego functioning, for example, refers to mental processes that are carried out independent of id, reality, or super ego influences. In psychoanalytic theory, a loss in ego autonomy over image formation means what Gordon calls autonomous images. (Hartmann, 1958; Rapaport, 1951, 1958; Miller, 1962).

In terms of content, people form either voluntary, spontaneous, or intrusive images. Voluntary images are deliberate, for example when a person tries to recollect a familiar person or scene. Less deliberate are spontaneous images, which emerge without conscious effort: they seem to pop into the mind, are perhaps related to the stream of thought, and do not seem particularly intrusive or distressing. They often occur when the mind is drifting.

In contrast, unbidden images seem to "intrude" into awareness. Their presence is often distressing and their meaning may be obscure. They range from hallucinatory vividness to a dim quasi-sensory quality. A person may exert various defensive maneuvers against continuation or repetition of the image, but efforts to dispel it may or may not be successful. These images seem unwanted or alien to the very person who forms them.

Emotional responses to unbidden images range from extreme pleasure to great pain and may include feelings of ecstasy, surprise, awe, anxiety, fright, or panic. The experience of the images may lead to anxiety over the lapse in control in addition to the emotions expressed in, and responsive to, the contents of the images. While the majority of reported unbidden images are reported as unpleasant, some unbidden images herald remarkable creative achievements. Such creative responses often arise after a period of struggle with an apparently unsoluble problem. Lewin (1969) points this out in retelling Kekule's experience of a creative unbidden image while in a drowsy state:

> Kekule had been puzzling over the linkage of carbon atoms in forming the benzene ring, as the story goes. Then he dozed and saw snakes form a mouth-to-tail chain. The front snake took the hind snake's tail in its mouth. He realized the carbon atoms must be linked together in such a chain to account for the various properties of benzene and awoke with a start knowing he had solved the problem.

Lewin also retells the story of William Lamberton, who had worked for two weeks unsuccessfully on an algebraic problem. He gave up and decided not to think of it again. For a week he succeeded in his resolve. Then on awakening one morning from sleep, he had an unbidden image that solved the problem in an unusual way: the solution was geometric rather than algebraic and was seen as a picture projected onto a painted-over blackboard some distance from him. As Kubie (1958) has pointed out, such creative solutions are not uncommon during dream thinking and often take a visual form. Kris (1951) would regard such creative products as "regression in the service of the ego"; Weissman (1969) would regard creative products as regression in the service of the ego-ideal rather than the ego. The following section describes less desirable regressions.

PATHOLOGIC FORMS OF UNBIDDEN IMAGES

Freud devoted his earliest studies (1895) to the effect of unconscious wishes on symptom formation. In several places he describes repeated and peremptory images; for example, in "A Mythological Parallel to a Visual Obsession" (1916), he describes a young man in whom the products of unconscious mental activity have become conscious as obsessive images.

Hollender and Böszörmenyi-Nagy (1958) studied acute and chronic schizophrenics with hallucinations and noted that in the acute state of hallucinatory schizophrenia the "ego's own reaction . . . is not always at one with the hallucinated experience. The initial response is that of fear bordering on panic. To some extent this state may persist for a considerable period of time and is responsible for much of the anxiety (and perhaps depression) noted in acute schizophrenic episodes. To an extent, the ego maintains its observing function and reacts to its own experience (the hallucination) as something foreign, strange, or 'crazy.' "

Later the hallucinations "are fitted into the ego's previous orientation by use of a variety of theories . . . When this type of reconciliation has occurred, the hallucinations are no longer regarded as 'crazy' (by the subject)."

In the next chapter I shall describe the unbidden image syndrome in detail, using data from my clinical investigations. It will help to consider in advance three points of view which explain unbidden images as: 1) sequels to psychic trauma; 2) eruptive expressions of usually-repressed ideas and feelings; and 3) a means for transformation of feeling states.*

UNBIDDEN IMAGES AS SEQUELS TO PSYCHIC TRAUMA

Breuer and Freud (1895) first considered repetition of trauma in their theoretic model for hysteria. They followed Binet's therapeutic technique of directing a patient's attention back to the moment when the symptom (of hysteria) first appeared. They insisted that abreaction

---

* These points of view developed historically. In current theory, as summarized at the end of Chapter 8, points 1 and 3 are special versions of 2.

(reliving the experience) was the significant aspect of this therapy. If there were no impediment to abreaction, the mental disturbance caused by the trauma was dissipated through absorption of the memory into the usual complex of memory storage and associations and the well known ways of "working-off emotions" (expressing anger, experiencing grief, and so forth). The dissipation of pathologic or "strangulated" emotion was prevented by two basic types of situations—defensive and hypnoid:

     1. DEFENSIVE—social situations prohibited expression of the emotion or else the trauma was associated with something so personally painful that the patient "repressed" it. The trauma itself was specified as fright, shame, or psychic pain.

     2. HYPNOID—the trauma took place during a hypnoid state. Freud became more dubious about this second type of situation and later repudiated the idea as superfluous and misleading (Jones, 1953). Actually, the hypnoid state idea had been put forward in 1890 by Moebius (in Breuer and Freud, 1895):

> The necessary condition for the (pathologic) operation of ideas is . . . a special frame of mind . . . It must resemble a state of hypnosis; it must correspond to some kind of vacancy of consciousness in which an emerging idea meets with no resistance from any other . . . We know that a state of this kind can be brought about not only by hypnotism but by emotional shock (fright, anger, et cetera) and by exhausting factors (sleeplessness, hunger, and so on). (p. 215).

Recurrent intrusive dreams, a prominent symptom of the traumatic neurosis of World War I, called Freud's attention to what appeared to be a new kind of repressive failure. In traumatic dreams, as in wish-fulfilling dreams, ideas or memories repressed by day, gained expression during sleep. But the breakthrough was clearly unpleasant; the traumatic dream appeared to be an exception to the pleasure principle. Thus, Freud hypothesized the principle of the *repetition compulsion* (Freud, 1920).

The compulsion to repeat trauma worked as follows. A harrowing or frightening experience exceeded a person's state of preparedness and/or capacity to master the resulting stimulations and affects. A temporary protective mechanism shunted the experience out of awareness where it resided as a kind of undigested foreign body; the memory traces were still extremely vivid and the affects were still of potentially overwhelming intensity. At some later date, the "repetition compulsion" asserted itself—the person relived the experience repeatedly until it was mastered—until associated feelings such as helplessness diminished. Until such mastery of affects, recall of the experience tended to evoke very vivid images. With mastery the memory traces were processed for storage in the usual way: they were stripped of sensory intensity and related to various schemata and concepts. Arlow (1969) has suggested that, to some extent, the traumatic images always remain in unconscious fantasy and are "looked at" internally whenever potentially similar situations arise. Bibring (1943) and other psychoanalysts * suggest that the repetition of trauma is for the purpose of working off the trauma by mastery and acceptance.

Greenacre (1949) notes that overwhelming visual experiences in childhood may daze and bewilder the child and undergo compulsive repetition in fantasy. If incompletely mastered, these visual traumas may lead to a symptom complex of visual disturbances, headaches, and halo effects. Niederland (1968), Krystal (1968), and Chodoff (1970) studied the concentration camp victims of the Nazis and, concurrent with other symptoms, found that intrusive visual images of concentration camp scenes persisted for decades. These intrusive images sometimes occurred after a relatively symptom-free interval.

Psychologic responses to great stress differ in various personality types but seem to have a course that can be abstracted (Cobb and Lindemann, 1943; Friedman and Linn, 1957; Popovic and Petrovic, 1964; Parkes, 1964; Davis, 1966). Often there is an initial period of psychologic or physical *overactivity* followed by a period of *inertia*. Next is the period of *preoccupation* where the person talks repetitively about the disaster and may complain of vivid unbidden imagery derived from the experience. In the fourth stage, the person often uses a characteristic *defense* or adaptation mechanism (e.g., suppression or substitution). In the fifth phase, the person recovers memories hitherto repressed. As each memory is reviewed, it fades in intensity. Note that in each stage an individual's control over the contents of awareness varies.

Continued clincial studies of psychoanalytic patients who reported traumatic experiences revealed that traumatic memories sometimes serve as partial screens for ideas and feelings that are currently dangerous or anxiety provoking (Glover, 1929; Reider, 1960; Malev, 1969). By attending to the traumatic memory, the patient may externalize and project into the past what is current and internal; he thus escapes full recognition of the present conflict. Because of such motives, a dormant memory may be revived as a current image (Rapaport, 1967; Sears, 1936).

The intense vividness and traumatic contents of revived images lead to arousal of a feeling state that resembles the emotions produced by the original experience. The feeling state generally includes a sense of impending danger which may be used to motivate preparation of defenses against currently undesirable internal urges or hurts (Schur, 1953; Murphy, 1961).

---

* See Furst (1967) for a complete review.

UNBIDDEN IMAGES AS AN ERUPTIVE EXPRESSION OF USUALLY REPRESSED IDEAS AND FEELINGS

Concepts that are not presently conscious may be dormant, and easily activated or they may be repressed and held from consciousness. In the state of repression two forces, at least, are present. One force presses for expression of the idea or feeling, the other force presses against expression. In the model presented at the beginning of this chapter, the urges for expression would facilitate a particular internal image; the motives for avoidance of contemplation would inhibit it. The high level of facilitation and of inhibitions results in a dynamic equilibrium with the image held out of awareness.

Disruption of the equilibrium could result in a sudden release of repressed images. The intrusion of these images into the conscious stream of thought would be experienced as an unbidden image. The sudden release could arise from a rapid change in motivation or from a change in the capacity to inhibit. For example, perception of a current sexually arousing situation might increase the impetus to express sexual strivings; or ingestion of alcohol might reduce inhibitory capacity.

Psychoanalytic theoreticians such as Kubie (1958), Arlow (1969), and Knapp (1969) suggest that there may be continuous unconscious daydreaming in visual images. The processing of these images might lead to some sudden activation, catapulting the unconscious image into consciousness. The conscious self might regard this intrusion as an attack of unpleasant stimuli. In this regard there is a similarity, in subjective experience, between the reception of external traumatic perceptions and the reception of internal "dangerous" ideas or feelings. Both are regarded as unwelcome intrusions.

IMAGE FORMATION TO TRANSFORM FEELING STATES

Image formation is well suited to the tasks of disguise or transformation of feeling states. For example, while remaining unaware of his own purpose, a person might form an unbidden image in order to raise his level of anxiety. Freud describes such breakthroughs as the result of switch-off processes in his paper, "Some Neurotic Mechanisms in Jealousy, Paranoia, and Homosexuality" (Freud, 1922):

> The pathogenic phantasies, derivatives of repressed instinctual impulses, are for a long time tolerated alongside the normal life of the mind, and have no pathogenic effect until by a revolution in the libidinal economy

they receive a hypercathexis; not till then does the conflict which leads to the formation of symptoms break out . . . I should also like to throw out the question whether this . . . does not suffice to cover the phenomenon which Bleuler and others have lately proposed to name "switching." One need only assume that an increase in resistance in the course taken by the psychical current in one direction results in a hypercathexis of another path and, thus, causes the flow to be switched into that path. (pp. 228–9)

Klein (1967), in his paper on peremptory ideation, develops this switch-off model into an ideomotor cycle with various types of sequences and linkages. He calls the region of start of the cycle a "primary region of imbalance." The series of steps in the cycle are cognitive efforts aimed at terminating the imbalance through some kind of switch-off such as a thought (e.g., an image), an action, or a perception. If the primary region of imbalance has extreme intensity, its effects have a peremptory quality. Such intensity is gained due to inadequate completion of the cycle, especially dense or converging facilitations at the primary region of imbalance, or repeated interruption of the cycle due to inhibitory negative affects (e.g., anxiety, guilt, and so forth). The processes involved in the cycle may be either in or out of awareness, and Klein emphasizes the special properties of repressed trains of thought: they endure without fading and have a special kind of impetus. Klein postulates that repression tends to interrupt the cycle, the lack of switch-off terminations results in increased intensity of the primary region of imbalance, and peremptory ideation such as unbidden images result.

Since this description of three explanatory viewpoints for loss of control over the contents of images was very abstract, I present here a single vignette to illustrate them.

RECURRENT UNBIDDEN IMAGES IN A NEUROTIC PATIENT: THE INTRUSIVE MOTHER

The patient, a young married woman, complained of a recurrent unbidden image of her mother's scowling face. This image occurred at the moment of vaginal penetration during sexual intercourse with her husband. The image of her mother's scowling face appeared before her, as if it were several feet over the bed. The images were quite vivid, but she knew they were generated in her own mind. The first time they occurred, she reacted by crying and feeling frightened. Later, even though she knew the images would occur, she found that she could not prevent or dispel them. The images dissipated "of their own accord" in a minute or less. This symptom persisted for a long time and, even when she "got used to the image," she still experienced disgust, shame, and anxiety when it appeared. As the image faded, she could suppress her disgust, re-establish genital arousal and reach a sexual climax "in spite of her mother!"

By piecing together material from many hours of psychotherapeutic work, it is possible to give some idea of the latent thought processes that led to development of the unbidden image. While these thoughts were not consciously experienced, they can now be given the following expressive form:

I am sexually excited by my husband. But whenever I think of my husband, I am reminded of my father towards whom I also have had sexual feelings. I feel and felt that sexual feelings towards my father are wicked and dangerous. I might be caught doing or thinking something bad, or he might hurt me with his big penis. Mother would disapprove strongly of my images and make me miserable if she found out about them. After all, sex is disgusting. What I want is wrong, and I had better not allow myself to get excited. Maybe if I think of how bad she would make me feel if she were to catch me thinking erotically, that would scare the sexual feelings out of me. Just imagine her seeing me; that makes me feel disgust, shame, and anxiety.

Now consider the case with regard to the trauma, repressive breakthrough, and transformational explanations.

Trauma. As it happened, the patient once had a traumatic perceptual experience when her scowling mother caught her masturbating. Sexual arousal reminded her of the earlier event, reactivated the vivid shock memory, and released the associated images into awareness.

Expression of Repressed Mental Contents. Symbolically, her husband represented her father, and sexual excitation toward her husband was unconsciously and magically regarded as sexual excitation toward her father. Her sexual impulses led to guilt, and both feelings were repressed. The sexual excitation involved in intercourse activated the repressed feelings and also lowered her defensive capacity (due to the altered state of consciousness). Only the more defensive aspect of her feelings erupted: her guilt as expressed by imaging her mother's face.

Transformation and Disguise of Affective State. The image of her mother's scowling face did not directly express her sexual wishes towards her father. In fact, it did not directly express guilt feelings as her own but rather projected them onto her mother. Forming the images evoked feelings of fear, disgust, and shame, which reduced her sexual excitation. Thus, by forming the image, she avoided sexual feelings. At a more conscious level, she tried to suppress the fearsome images and regain arousal.

The intrusive mother became a symbol that condensed not only the train of thought summarized earlier, but also other trains of thought. For example, in the course of her psychotherapy it became clear that the image was used not only to transform sexual arousal to fear, but also to satisfy certain exhibitionistic wishes. She defiantly wished to show her mother that she was having sexual activities in spite of the mother's prohibitions. At the conscious level she wished none of these things but only to have a mutually gratifying experience with her husband. The emergence of less conscious and less adaptational motives was therefore experienced as a loss of control over the contents of her thought.

SUMMARY

Sometimes image formation appears to get out of hand. The internal images gain in vividness so that they are hard to distinguish from perceptions. Or they express ideas and feelings that the person wishes to avoid. In many instances unbidden images combine both features: unusual vividness and an ego-alien quality. Thus, they are a central problem for any theory of image formation. Three explanations—of traumatic repetition, breakthrough of repressed ideas or feelings, and defensive transformation of feelings—have been outlined. The next chapters present more detailed examples of unbidden images and attempt to examine the explanation in greater depth.

REFERENCES

Antrobus, J., and Singer, J. 1969. Mind wandering & cognitive structure. Paper presented to N.Y. Acad. Sci., Oct. 20, 1969.

Arlow, J. 1969. Unconscious fantasy & disturbances of conscious experience. *Psychoanal. Quart.*, 38:1–27.

———— and Brenner, C. 1964. *Psychoanalytic concepts and the structural theory*. New York, International Universities Press.

Bibring, E. 1943. The conception of the repetition compulsion. *Psychoanal. Quart.*, 12:486–519.

Breuer, J., and Freud, S. (1895) Studies on hysteria. *Stand. Ed.*, 2, 1954.

Chodoff, P. 1970. The German concentration camp as a psychological stress. *Arch. Gen. Psychiat.*, 22:78–87.

Cobb, S., and Lindeman, E. 1943. Neuropsychiatric observation after the Coconut Grove fire. *Ann. Surg.*, 117:814–824.

Davis, D. R. 1966. *An Introduction to Psychopathology*, 2nd Ed. London, Oxford University Press.

Freeman, T., Cameron, J. L., and McGhie, A. 1966. *Studies on Psychosis*. New York, International Universities Press.

Friedman, P. and Linn, L. 1957. Some psychiatric notes on the Andrea Doria disaster. *Amer. J. Psychiat.*, 114:426–432.

Freud, S. (1922) Some neurotic mechanisms in jealousy, paranoia, and homosexuality. *Stand. Ed.*, 18, 1962.

———— (1920) Beyond the pleasure principle. *Stand. Ed.*, 18, 1962.

———— (1916) A mythological parallel to a visual obsession. *Stand. Ed.*, 14, 1957.

———— (1911) Formulations on the two principles of mental functioning. *Stand. Ed.*, 12, 1958.

———— (1900) The interpretation of dreams. *Stand. Ed.*, 4, 1953.

———— (1895) Project for a scientific psychology. In Bonaparte, M., Freud, A., and Kris, E., eds. *The Origins of Psychoanalysis.* New York, Basic Books, Inc., 1954.

Furst, S. S. 1967. *Psychic Trauma.* New York/London, Basic Books, Inc.

Gardner, R. W. 1969. Organismic equilibration and the energy structure duality in psychoanalytic theory. *J. Amer. Psychoanal. Ass.*, 17:3–40.

Gill, M. 1963. Topography & systems in psychoanalytic theory. *Psychol. Issues*, 3(2): Monogr. 10.

Glover, E. 1929. The screening function of traumatic memories. *Int. J. Psychoanal.*, 10:90–93.

Gordon, R. A. 1950. An experiment correlating the nature of imagery with performance on a test of reversal perspective. *Brit. J. Psychol.*, 41:63–67.

———— 1949. An investigation into some of the factors that favor the formation of stereotyped images. *Brit. J. Psychol.*, 39:156–167.

Greenacre, P. 1949. A contribution to the study of screen memories. *Psychoanal. Stud. Child*, 3–4:73–84.

Hartmann, H. 1958. *Ego Psychology & the Problem of Adaptation.* New York, International Universities Press.

Hernandez-Peon, R. 1964. Psychiatric implications of neurophysiological research. *Bull. Menninger Clin.*, 28:165–185.

Hollender, M. H., and Boszormenyi-Nagy, I. 1958. Hallucination as an ego experience. *Arch. Neurol. Psychiat.*, 80:93–97.

Holt, R. R. 1968. Comments made during the panel "Psychoanalytic Theory of the Instinctual Drives in Relation to Recent Developments." Reported by Dahl, H. *J. Amer. Psychoanal. Ass.*, 16:613–637.

Jackson, J. H. 1958. *Selected writings of John Hughlings Jackson.* Taylor, J., Holmes, G., and Walshe, F. M. R., eds. New York, Basic Books Inc.

Jones, E. 1953. *The Life and Work of Sigmund Freud*, Vols. I, II, III. New York, Basic Books, Inc. 1953, 1955, 1957.

———— 1929. Fear, guilt, and hate. *Int. J. Psychoanal.*, 10:383–397.

Klein, G. S. 1967. Peremptory ideation: Structure & force in motivated ideas. *Psychol. Issues*, 5:80–128.

Knapp, P. H. 1969. Image, symbol and person. *Arch. Gen. Psychiat.*, 21:392–406.

Kris, E. 1951. On preconscious mental processes. In Rapaport, D., ed. *Organization and Pathology of Thought*, pp. 475–493. New York, Columbia University Press.

Krystal, H. K., ed. 1968. *Massive Psychic Trauma.* New York, International Universities Press.

Kubie, L. S. 1967. The relation of psychotic disorganization to the neurotic process. *J. Amer. Psychoanal. Ass.*, 15:626–640.

———— 1958. *Neurotic Distortion of the Creative Process.* Lawrence, University of Kansas Press.

Lewin, B. D. 1969. Remarks on creativity, imagery and the dream. *J. Nerv. Ment. Dis.*, 149:115–121.

Malev, M. 1969. Use of the repetition compulsion by the ego. *Psychoanal. Quart.*, 38:52–71.

Martin, R. M. 1968. The stimulus barrier and the autonomy of the ego. *Psychol. Rev.*, 75:478–493.

Miller, S. 1962. Ego autonomy in sensory deprivation, isolation and stress. *Int. J. Psychoanal.*, 43:1–20.

Murphy, W. F. 1961. A note on trauma and loss. *J. Amer. Psychoanal. Ass.*, 9:519–532.

Niederland, W. G. 1968. Clinical observations on the "survivor syndrome." *Int. J. Psychoanal.*, 49:313–315.

Parkes, C. M. 1964. Effects of bereavement on physical and mental health: A study of the medical records of widows. *Brit. Med. J.*, 2:274–294.

Popovic, M., and Petrovic, D. 1964. After the earthquake. *Lancet.*, 2:1169–71.

Rapaport, D. 1967. *Emotions and Memory.* New York, International Universities Press.

———— (1960) On the psychoanalytic theory of motivation. In Gill, M., ed. *Collected Papers of David Rapaport.* New York, Basic Books, 1967.

———— 1958. The theory of ego autonomy: A generalization. *Bull. Menninger Clin.*, 22:13–35.

———— 1951. The autonomy of the ego. *Bull. Menninger Clin.*, 15:113–123.

Reider, N. 1960. Percept as a screen; economic & structural aspects. *J. Amer. Psychoanal. Ass.*, 8:82–99.

Sachs, L. J. 1956. A case of obsessive-compulsive neurosis showing forced visual imagery. *J. Hillside Hosp.*, 5:384–391.

Scheibel, M., and Scheibel, A. 1962. Hallucinations and brain stem reticular core. In West, L., ed. *Hallucinations.* New York, Grune & Stratton.

Schafer, R. 1968. *Aspects of Internalization.* New York, International Universities Press.

Schur, M. 1966. *The Id and the Regulatory Principles of Mental Functioning.* New York, International Universities Press.

———— 1953. The ego in anxiety. In Lowenstein, R. M., ed. *Drives, Affects, Behavior*, Vol. 1, pp. 67–103. New York, International Universities Press.

Segal, S. Imagery & reality: Can they be distinguished? Paper presented at conference of the Eastern Psychiatric Research Association on Origin and Mechanisms of Hallucinations, New York, 1969.

Sears, R. R. 1936. Functional abnormalities of memory with special reference to amnesia. *Psychol. Bull.*, 33:229–274.

Sperry, R. W. 1969. A modified concept of consciousness. *Psychol. Bull.*, 76:532–536.

Weissman, P. 1969. Creative fantasies and beyond the reality principle. *Psychoanal. Quart.*, 38:110–123.

West, L. J. 1962. A general theory of hallucinations and dreams. In West, L. J., ed. *Hallucinations.* New York, Grune & Stratton.

CHAPTER
8

Unbidden Images

> Why do I yield to that suggestion
> Whose horrid image doth unfix my hair
> And make my seated heart knock at my ribs
> Against the use of nature? Present fears
> Are less than horrible imaginings.
> SHAKESPEARE: *Macbeth I.iii.*

On the surface, unbidden images have a certain irony in that the person who forms them disowns them and regards them as unwelcome intrusions. An incomplete analysis would suggest that these experiences are simply eruptions of impulsive motives. Analysis of the underlying psychodynamics, however, reveals that a variety of unconscious regulatory maneuvers modulate image formation. By detailed study of cases, such as those reported in this chapter, it is possible to describe and infer the cognitive operations involved, and to understand why images are experienced as intrusions.

SUBJECTS

The investigator asked psychiatric inpatients whose complaints centered on pathology of image formation to participate in a study of their thought processes and symptom formation.* If they consented, certain research methods supplemented their regular treatment program.

---

* I thank Dr. Norman Mages, Director, and the staff and patients of the Mount Zion Medical Center Psychiatric Inpatient Service for their help. Judy Payne, R.N. and Carol Farwell, R.N. made special contributions.

INTERVIEWS

Research study interviews were separate from psychotherapy interviews. (The patients understood that their psychotherapist received information from the research interviews, and vice versa.) This freed the investigator to inquire into various aspects of thought processes that might, at that moment, not be directly relevant to the psychotherapeutic process. Also the investigator was not involved in potential "bargain" decisions about medications, privileges, and passes to go home.

The research interviews used both structured and unstructured methods. The focus was on developing detailed descriptions of current subjective experiences, thought processes in general, image formation in particular, and the responses to external events and psychotherapeutic interventions. The interviewer used both free associative methods and direct questioning, as seemed appropriate. In addition, various ancillary procedures examined control over image formation and perception.

VISUAL EVOCATION TASK

The visual evocation task gathers information about voluntary, spontaneous image formation in a semi-structured situation.* It consists of three sets of instructions. In the first set, the patient is asked to form first an image of a person, then a pleasant image, then an unpleasant image, and lastly an image from earliest childhood.

The second set of instructions in this task uses emotional words as stimuli for image formation. Generally, the patient is asked to repeat a phrase beginning with "I feel" and ending with a different label for emotion like "angry." Five types of emotion are presented, as indicated by the following words: pleased, fearful, angry, ashamed, and gloomy. Thus, the patient would first say, "I feel pleased," allow himself to form a spontaneous image, and then report what image occurred to him. This would be repeated for each word. To avoid repeating the same words with successive tasks, four matched sets are used, each containing different words. For example, the first set consists of satisfied, anxious, resentful, guilty, and depressed. The second set is pleased, fearful, angry, ashamed, and gloomy. There were two additional sets of adjectives.

The third part of the visual evocation task provides a looser structure: the subject is only told *when* to form images, not what *kind* of image to form. The patient is told that when an instruction is given to

---

* Further rationale for this type of task will be discussed in Chapter 14.

form an image, he should just let his mind rest and allow a spontaneous image to develop and grow in vividness. Half a minute is given for silent imagery formation, followed by one minute of description of the image. Then about one minute is spent drawing the image that is produced. This is repeated six times. Later, associations to certain images can be requested.

In each set, the patient is told to allow images to spring into his mind in response to whatever suggestion is given and that he should describe in detail his actual subjective experience. If necessary, he is asked additional questions as to how vivid the image was, whether it was in color, what was in the background, whether he himself was visualized, what the mood was like, how old he was at the time depicted, and whether the image was fleeting, durable, surprising, expected, from imagination, or from memory.

DRAWINGS

After a patient describes an image experience, additional data may come from a drawing of the image. Information is often available in the graphic product which amplifies or corrects the verbal description. One way to obtain drawings is the dot-image sequence (Horowitz, 1966), in which patients stare at a dot in the middle of a page, draw what comes to mind, and produce a series of six pictures. Another technique for obtaining a graphic series over time in withdrawn or nonverbal patients is interaction drawing (Horowitz, 1963). The patient and therapist jointly draw on the same page and usually take turns. Ideally, they continue the process of joint drawings several times a week. (This technique is demonstrated in chapter 13.) Interaction drawing can obtain more imagery production than the patient ordinarily gives in interviews or in his own free drawings. The responses of the therapist stimulate counter-responses, decrease the distrust and distance experienced by the patient, and also can be used to counter or diminish his defensive maneuvers.

PERCEPTUAL DISCRIMINATION TASK

The task is a series of auditory tones or visual stimuli where the patient must match each stimulus with the preceding stimulus. The matching requires careful attention to the external environment and avoidance of internal distractions. Every few minutes the patient is asked to report whatever thoughts enter his awareness during the period in which he is doing the task. Thus, it is possible to obtain descriptions of any intrusive thoughts, images, or ideas that may have occurred.

PROJECTIVE TESTS

Projective tests consist of visual stimuli that are presented to the patient who is then asked to report his internal image responses. The most common form is the inkblot, such as the Rorschach or Holtzman inkblots. The blots are symmetric splotches of form, color, and shading. While they do not actually depict any particular object, they are suggestive and certain usual responses have been catalogued for each stimulus. The patient reports what forms are suggested to him, and from his responses some inferences can be made about his current impulses, defenses, conflicts, thought processes, and cognitive style.

These several methods are ways to add to clinical impressions of a patient's spontaneous communications. Manipulation of image formation through instructions and situations may add information about the degree of control the patient has over this aspect of thinking.

CASE 1
Isabel

The case presented here is a good illustration of how images derived from a traumatic perception may serve defensive functions.

Isabel,* a married woman in her twenties with three children, was hospitalized on a psychiatric ward because of confusion, panic, and recurrent frightening images. Her diagnosis was hysterical psychosis. She complained of "seeing an old man who had died in her home." The images, always of the old man, frightened her and occurred in two forms. In one, the old man looked angrily at her; in the other he was dead. These same images came as hallucinations or pseudohallucinations and also as illusions, hypnagogic visions, and recurrent nightmares.

The old man depicted so intensely and repeatedly was a boarder in her home and had died there a year previously. After his death, the patient was upset but did not receive psychiatric treatment. Within a few weeks she felt better. Then, almost a year later, the unbidden images of the old man returned and were associated with panic, confusion, and disordered thinking and behavior. The onset was a dream of the old man, and afterward he came to "haunt" her during the day.

She originally met the old man while walking her children in the park. He was friendly toward them, and after a brief conversation she found out that he was on social security with no place to live. As she had

---

* Names and some details are changed.

an empty room in her home, she invited him to purchase room and board. For a while all went well, and he even helped with babysitting. Then he became bedridden with a chronic debilitating illness. She had to care for him as his physical health and mental functioning deteriorated. He became incontinent of urine and feces. Also he was easily enraged. During his rages, he accused her of tormenting him, robbing him, and giving him poor care. At times she responded with equal rage and, for instance, tried to persuade her husband to punish the old man physically.

The night before the old man died, she had dreamed that her little girl was killed by a car. In her subculture this was known as a "death-dream" and meant that someone would die. She thought of this when, in the morning, she found the old man dead. Since her mother and sister had insisted at times that the patient's dreams were prophetic, she believed that she had caused the man's death. She felt the recurring visualizations were his ghost returning to haunt her.

HOSPITAL COURSE

Initial Phase. During the initial phase of hospitalization, the intrusive image of the old man was the principle content of her communications. She usually was in a confused and panicky mental state, pacing about while wringing her hands and sobbing anxiously. She gave little history other than repeated fragmentary descriptions of her images. Any questions about other aspects of her life were twisted back to this topic or ignored. Her speech was blocked and punctuated by pleas for reassurance and protection against the images.

She found references to the old man in every aspect of her waking life. For example, during an interview she looked suspiciously at some papers. When asked what was there she said, "a chair" and on further inquiry drew an outline of a chair by connecting some random marks on the papers. In the angry image the old man is seated in such a chair, she added.

In an effort to see if the visual evocation task might obtain more information, she was asked to do the first set. The first instruction was "form an image in your mind's eye of a familiar person." She said several times that she could not do this. Then she said, "Oh, the head of the old man! Bald, a scary face!" She got to her feet, raised her hands to cover her face, and sobbed. While crying and pacing back and forth, she said that she had had angry thoughts about the old man because he swore at her. When he yelled at her she wished he would die; when he did die she knew she had killed him. His ghost haunted her. She needed help. After these remarks she told of her "death dream."

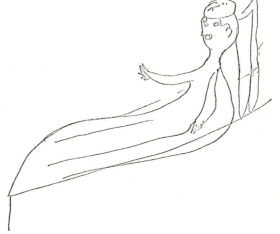

Fig. 1. The old man screaming.

She then frequently related this story to members of the ward staff in order to gain repeated reassurances from nurses that she was not to feel guilty about having the dream, that the death and dream were coincidental, and that there was no such thing as a ghost. This repetition deflected attention away from other considerations about why she was in the hospital.

SECOND PHASE. During the second week of hospitalization the patient was considerably less panicky. She cried less, her pleading behavior diminished, but she still reported illusions: she thought other persons on the ward were the old man, especially if she saw them unclearly or in the corner of her eye. Also, she sometimes walked up and down the halls and peeked into rooms, claiming to see the old man within them. Recurrent unbidden images of him continued as intense thought images or pseudohallucinations. Recurrent dreams of him screaming at her troubled her sleep. Above is one drawing she made of the recurrent images (Figure 1).*

As she became more coherent in interviews, she began to describe her brittle temper, her impulses to hit people, and her fear that part of her body was dying. The image evocation task was repeated during this phase. Her comments revolved around preoccupation with the old man theme. For example, when asked to form a visual image in response to the concept of "I feel angry" she replied:

---

* Some of the patients' drawings in this chapter were faint and the lines therefore darkened for reproduction. Every effort was made to retain the original quality of line.

> I don't know—the old man is looking at me real mad. He said "damn you." I hit him a couple of times. He got mad and then he threatened to get me.

At this point rapport with Isabel was good enough so that she could take a projective test, the Holzman inkblots. This is a series of 42 cards; a single response is obtained for each card. Her response to seeing ten of the inkblots was "I don't know"; she saw unpleasant faces in eleven of the cards. In seven of the cards she saw spiders, bugs, or reptiles. Her responses were instant without careful scrutiny of the contours and shapes. Almost every card seemed to frighten her. Because of this latter observation, she was asked to pick out the card that frightened her the most. When she selected an inkblot and was asked what she saw in it now, she said, "two children hanging." (Previously her response had been "two people dancing.") She then said, "No, I don't mean that, I see people dancing or sitting down." She got up and began to cry and pace about.

After a while she was asked what had come to mind to cause this reaction. She said that what she had seen made her think of how her sister had tried to hang herself. Her words came in seemingly unrelated fragments; she described how her mother used to beat her and how mean people could be towards children. When asked what she had meant about two children hanging, she denied saying that, and insisted that for her the card represented two people dancing.

The next day, she reported a dream of the old man saying angrily, "Let me take care of her." This time, however, there was a new element in her dream. A little boy crawled on the floor in the background. She identified him as her son. This was a startling bit of information because she had previously given a history of having two daughters without mention of a son. She reported a second dream of fighting with her sister. When asked what she thought these dreams might mean, she replied in an evasive manner:

> She (sister) hits when she gets mad. My sister was like that. I don't hit people when I get angry. No, oh, I guess I did throw a hanger at my husband. He slapped me because it nearly got into his eye, and I told him that I hated him. I cried for five hours. Then the old man said, "Who's that baby? He should have hit you more." The old man was real mean after that.

During subsequent psychotherapy sessions she described memories of various traumas at the hands of her sister, her mother, and her stepfather. Perhaps these were partly fantasy, partly real. She was regarded as the black sheep of the family and was accused of having an evil eye or being like a witch. She had rheumatic fever as a child and spent long periods alone in bed. As she recalls, she spent most of this time daydreaming in visual images. Being weaker than her sister when she emerged from bed, she was often beaten up. She sometimes hated all members of her family and attempted to suppress her rage.

During the research interviews in this phase, the interviewer asked her to draw pictures of the old man image. This she began with reluctance, but then continued with intensity. She said that drawing the images helped her to work through some of her feelings, and she hoped that she was now shielded from the images.

THIRD PHASE. Isabel continued to improve, her thinking seemed to be less confused, and she comported herself reasonably well on the ward. She was sent home for a trial period but returned after only a few hours, weeping and frightened. She spoke brokenly and would not report what had happened at home. The next day she remained unwilling to say what had happened or how she was feeling but did agree to repeat again the visual evocation task. Once again, the evocation task resulted in information. It was clear by this time that her thought was predominantly in visual images with poor capacity for abstract thought in lexical concepts. After repeating the stimulus phrase, "I feel lonely," she reported this image:

> My little boy, he's crawling. He fell off the bed, the crib. I didn't know what to do. He's crying, I'm trying to catch him, I wasn't there in time.

She indicated by her manner that this image represented something of considerable importance to her but refused to elaborate. The next day she reported a dream of the old man, lying in his bed saying that she had tried to kill him. As in the previous dream, she saw a little boy in the background and began to explain who he was. Her drawing of this dream is shown in Figure 2. Note the similar lines on the head of the old man and the boy; similar lines occur in the old man drawing of Figure 1.

The little boy was her son. Because of mental retardation and uncontrollable behavior, she and her husband had sent him to a State Hospital. She recalled the scene at a commitment hearing. The judge said that the boy looked too normal to be hospitalized. She replied that she was going to leave the boy there and let the judge see for himself. Her husband was surprised that she would just leave the boy, but she simply walked out. The boy, held for observation, was committed because he was violent.

She cried and said that she had to commit him because he was so violent, he would have killed someone; but she felt very badly. Then she blurted out, "Instead of hitting him or doing something drastic, I had to put him away." She then refused to talk further.

That night she dreamed of both her little boy and herself feeling anxious and crying. She said that now she thought of him whenever she saw children on the street. Also, instead of seeing the old man, she now had ugly images of her son eating disgustingly and sloppily as he used to.

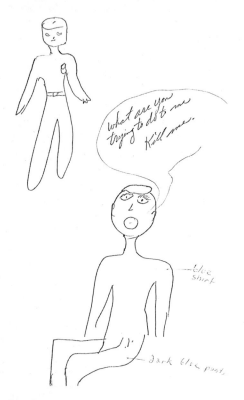

Fig. 2. The old man with a boy in the background.

She began to cry again and, in a fragmented manner, continued her story. When her son was only a few months old, she had left him in his crib with the railing down. While she sat across the room sewing, he squirmed to the edge of the crib and, as she watched horrified, fell to the floor hitting his head. After that he began to show signs of mental retardation.

Quite likely, the etiology of the mental retardation occurred at birth or before and the fall was incidental. Naturally, however, she experienced considerable remorse and sadness and felt at fault. She now told of a daydream she had had intermittently since the accident, in which she goes crazy, is sent to the same state hospital, is reunited with her son, and nurses him back to health.

During this phase, as she talked about her past history and her symptoms, there were juxtapositions of association and slips of the tongue suggesting the symbolic similarity of the old man and her son. It was shortly after the boy was committed that she asked the old man to move in, and the old man was given the boy's room. Both the boy and the old man had periodic rages and threatened violence. Both were sometimes incontinent of feces or urine, and she hated them both when she cleaned up their messes.

Next, in psychotherapy, she began to admit her fears that she might fall into a rage and hurt her two daughters. She had previously kept these ideas hidden, but her husband confirmed that she had spoken to him about them prior to that hospitalization, and that she did have periodic rages. She was afraid that she would become so intensely angry that she might assault her daughters and inflict upon them some injury equivalent to the ones she felt she had inflicted upon the old man and her son.

Isabel continued to improve, but, whenever the threat of discharge became too intense, her condition tended to deteriorate. She would become fearful and pleading, would sometimes say that she was now having the old man images again, and would act helpless and demanding. With each regression the fear she experienced about her aggressive impulses toward her two daughters was reinterpreted. Arrangements were made for a housekeeper and babysitter to be added to the household. With this buffer she was able to maintain her improvement and accept discharge from the hospital. During the ensuing period she continued psychotherapy, did well, and it was eventually possible to give up the housekeeper and babysitter.

DISCUSSION

In this section the clinical material is related to the explanatory points of view suggested in the previous chapter.

1. UNBIDDEN IMAGES AS SEQUELS TO TRAUMATIC PERCEPTIONS. The content of Isabel's unbidden images derived from the traumatic perception of the old man dead or screaming. But the images were not simply repetitions of trauma. The images returned a year after the old man's death when current strong hostile impulses towards her daughters had achieved dangerous proportions and she had a realistic need to avoid emergence of these impulses into behavior. The images of the old man served as a screen that partially expressed and partially prevented awareness of her dangerous impulses. The unconscious role structure or "latent thoughts" included an injuring party, herself, and an injured party, her children (earlier her son, now her daughters). In the images of the old man as dead, the injured party became the old man instead of her children. In the images of the old man screaming angrily at her, the roles were reversed: she became the injured party, he the one who would injure. By forming the image of his anger she frightened herself and scared away her own anger. This reversal of rules also correlated with childhood memories in which she identified herself as the injured party.

From this material, we can see that because of their special propensity for vivid revisualization, images of traumatic experiences may come to serve as symbols or screens for other concepts. The process may be retrospective or prospective: previous traumatic images may be revived to serve contemporary purposes (as in this case) or new traumas may tend to remain unmastered because they have become associated with previous memories and conflicts.

2. Expression of Repressed Ideas and Feelings. The image of the old man is at once a disguise and a breakthrough of repressed ideas and feelings. If, for conceptual clarity, we artificially label the repressed idea-feeling as "I'd like to hurt those girls (like my mother hurt me)," then in awareness the old man images express part of the repressed idea, "Somebody is angry, somebody is hurt." In an analogous compromise, the patient projects the impulsive feeling—anger—onto the old man. The defensive feelings—dread and guilt—she experiences as her own. In spite of partially successful defensive operations, the breakthrough of some of the repressed contents leads to her subjective sense of loss of control. Her dangerous ideas, denied expression in words, gain partial expression in images. Additional defensive efforts inhibited translation of the images into words.

The other repressed thoughts may be partially expressed in the image. She feels inadequate to the demands of taking care of small children and would like to be taken care of. If she were to scream crazily, like the old man, perhaps she would have her burdens lifted and be taken care of (e.g., by hospitalization). The recurrence of the images may be reinforced by this secondary gain.

3. Transformation and Disguise. The above case illustrates the disguise of roles and the transformation of hate to fear. Persons do sometimes reduce anger by making themselves afraid or, in other situations, may reduce fear by making themselves angry. Fear, guilt, and hate stand in a particular relationship to each other: any of these affects may be generated to avoid experience of the other two (Jones, 1929). A person may generate fear to reduce his own guilt or hate. He may make himself hate to reduce his guilt or fear or both.

Isabel projected her own rage onto the old man and formed images of him to produce a feeling of danger. Danger led to fright which, together with the resultant altered state of consciousness, reduced her feelings of hatred.

So far I have used traditional psychodynamic language to interpret or infer the latent meanings of the manifest images and the motives for the image formation. We have some idea why the images occurred and why they were subjectively experienced as unbidden. But we are not yet clear about the cognitive operations and sequences required in the image formation process. For example, some aspects of the repetition remain unexplained. The old man image expressed, yet disguised, dangerous ideas and feelings. It condensed past and impending traumas. But why was this one image so easily triggered?

This image recurs possibly because it is "tried and true." Put less colloquially, connecting links between elements in an ideational cycle that reduces displeasure or increases pleasure tend to remain in a state of latent facilitation. A predisposition to follow the same pathway in subsequent trains of thought remains. This predisposition can be considered to be a schema and will tend to structure subsequent ideational responses to similar stimuli. Thus, activation of the beginning of a train of thought may lead to the same end result, such as the same unbidden image. With repetition, the end result (the unbidden image) may come to stand as a symbol for the entire train of thought.

As described in Chapter 7, Klein (1967) suggests an ideational cycle model of peremptory ideation. He suggests a "primary region of imbalance" that leads to a series of ideas aimed at reducing the imbalance by producing some kind of switch-off thought, action, or perception. Following Klein, a provisional outline of an ideational cycle can be constructed. The region of imbalance consists of feelings of hatred which might lead to a certain expectable course of thought. The first element in this conjectured train of thought might be the idea of hurting her child. Next in this sequence might be a plan of how to hurt the child. These fantasies might lead to certain perceptual expectancies. For example, there might be the idea, "The next time I catch her doing something bad, I'll beat her." The need for the excuse, "when she does something bad," is the result of a compromise between raw aggression and mitigating forces such as conscience. When actual perceptions match expectancy, the plan of hurting the child may be released and the assault carried out. As a consequence of aggressive actions, hatred is reduced, and the cycle of ideas is temporarily deactivated because of the reduction in the pressure of the emotional motive.

The cycle of ideas that would diminish hatred by hurting a child is not carried out in awareness. The concept of hurting her child is too dangerous to contemplate, especially since Isabel realizes that her control is insufficient to contain her rage and since she still feels very guilty over the idea of damaging her son. To avoid completion of this ideational route, she transforms some of the ideas pressing for expression. The idea of hurting her daughter is transformed into the idea that she herself has been hurt, e.g., by the images of the old man. This is reinforced by her childhood memories of being hurt when she was a daughter.

In an alternate ideational cycle, the dangerous assaultive ideas are transformed into the concept of her being assaulted by using the vivid traumatic memories of the old man raging at her. The guilt feelings are expressed in the image of finding the old man dead. Both images lead to fright at an intense level. The fear, the warning pangs of guilt, and the secondary gain of being cared for herself diminish rage feelings. This secondary cycle can be activated to avoid the primary ideas of child assault. Repeating the thought cycle leads to condensation of the elements into a single symbol, the old man image. In a sense, she forms the image instead of the whole train of thought. Thus the images serve as a defensive mechanism against, as well as an expression of, primitive impulses.

CASE 2
Ned: A Beating Fantasy

The following case illustrates how unbidden images occur as a symptom in a schizophrenic patient. In contrast to Isabel, who was not schizophrenic, the communication is less clear, and the thought processes are less cohesive and organized. In spite of the basic difference in psychopathology, however, some of the same explanatory principles remain relevant to the symptom of unbidden images.

Ned, a 17-year-old, entered the psychiatric ward because his behavior had become progressively more withdrawn, aggressive, and strange. He was considered to have a schizophrenic reaction.

During his hospitalization, Ned revealed recurrent unbidden images in which he depicted his father beating his mother. The contents consisted of his mother bleeding from the nose, his father with an outstretched hand; and sometimes he depicted himself, as a small helpless bystander. These images sometimes lasted for the unusually long period of half an hour.

The presence of these images was not known to the staff during the first weeks of hospitalization. He entered the clinical research study because of his many bizarre statements about his body, which suggested a disturbed body image. Later, we found that these remarks also referred to the images. For example, he frequently repeated his initial complaints: his nose or his rectum was bleeding on the inside, someone had beaten him up, his nose was connected to his penis, his stomach and his bladder and his penis were connected.

Ned's bodily concern was not surprising, for he was abnormally short in height. For many years this impairment was thought to be due to impaired formative processes secondary to hormone imbalance. To correct the defect, he received weekly injections of hormones in the buttocks. After several years, his growth pattern and his X rays revealed that hormones were not to blame. He was told that the suspected disorder was not present and so he did not have to return for further treatment.

Ned had grown to like and depended upon his physician and the nurses of the clinic. He missed them when the regular visits stopped. After a few weeks he returned, complaining of a pain in his ear. Examination showed an infection and an antibiotic was prescribed. As a side-effect, Ned developed buzzing in his ear. This progressed to painful hearing and finally to auditory hallucinations. He would hear his uncle's voice saying, "You've got to be patient, Ned, you've got to be patient."

About this time he had outbursts of destructive behavior towards objects in the home. He stared into space, stayed in his room, and then stayed in bed. His speech was bizarre, and these symptoms led to the hospitalization.

THE BEATING IMAGES

Ned was seen in interviews that sometimes incorporated drawings, interaction drawings, or visual evocation procedures. The first indication of the images occurred during an interview on the 32nd day of hospitalization. He started to talk about having "crooked thoughts" which consisted of "pictures coming into his head by surprise." When asked what the pictures were about, he changed the topic abruptly. Later in the interview he was asked to do the visual evocation task and agreed. When asked to visualize a familiar person he said he could see (i.e., image) his father and his mother, and that both were red. His facial expression became distracted and he said, "No, maybe they were bright green."

When asked for a pleasant memory, he said he saw his mother kissing him a lot. For an unpleasant memory he reported, "Blood, just blood, it's red." In the second part of the visual evocation task, he was given various emotional words and asked to say whatever image came to mind about each. In response to the word "angry" he said only, "beat, pulling and kicking, she gets upset." At the end of the session he said plaintively, "My nose is bleeding from the inside, my bowels don't work. I'm bleeding on the inside. Can you help me with my crooked thoughts?"

There was little additional information about the images until the 53rd day of hospitalization. He saw two patients scuffling and became anxious. A nurse comforted him, and he told her it was like seeing his father beat his mother when he was a young boy. He added that he had continued to see his mother bleed ever since. In interaction drawings he drew a more striking picture than usual: a frog being cut open as in a dissection. On completing the drawing he looked up and said, very sincerely, that he realized his parents had a hard time so he wasn't going to let their arguments bother him anymore.

About a week later, I said that I noticed him lying in bed a lot and was interested in what went on in his mind. (His posture was unusual; he lay on his back but in a tense manner, with knees bent and hands very tightly clasped over his abdomen.) He said he stayed there to keep from thinking about his father hitting his mother. With encouragement, he then described how he once came home and found his mother covered with blood. It probably was because it came from her nose, he continued, because she didn't hold it up and because his father "did not keep patience."

He said he saw this again in his mind often, usually in color—the blood was very red. He also saw himself standing off to one side with a "question mark expression on my head." Talking of these images made him sad and anxious; those were his usual feelings while having them. He thought it might have happened when he was four or five. He then started talking about his hormone shots.

After talking of the injections he said that he had no thoughts while he was in bed, but sometimes he would just have the image for half an hour or so. I asked him to draw it sometime. He said he would if he could use stick figures; the image was not in stick figures but that was all he could draw. He drew the picture shown in Figure 3: his father with an arm into the face of his mother, the spiral of blood, himself off to one side. He said the drawing of the picture made him nervous, he had hit his father once, he had wanted to hit his father, but he was afraid his father would beat him into a nothing.

The next day he said he wished to stop drawing with me and just talk. He said the images troubled him whenever he was not doing much, like when he brushed his teeth. He knew he should just forget it, but when the images came his stomach hurt. He then drew pictures of how

Fig. 3. First drawing of the beating.

his internal organs were connected to his penis and to his nose. Then he reassured me: the images meant nothing; his father had told him his mother was having a bloody nose. Then he added wistfully, "But why was she crying?"

In later sessions he talked more of the images for a few days, then devoted his comments to other topics. A little over a month after telling me of the images he went on an extended home visit. He seemed relatively rational before leaving, but he returned in a regressive state before his pass was over. He reported having intrusive images of the blood and the beating.

The next day I found him in bed. He smiled, sat up, and said, "I was freezing out my thoughts." He was troubled by the image, so I said we could try and see if drawing it helped him control it. He seemed hesitant but agreed. He selected a yellow felt tip pen from several I carried with me. This gave the dimmest possible line. He drew his mother as a small figure (Figure 4). When asked to repeat the image, he took a purple pen and drew it twice the size (Figure 5). He was then asked to write words that described each person. The words for his father were "mean, ugly, filthy, dead, misunderstood and dishonest." The words for his mother were "helpless, innocent, helpful, means well, bad temper, and kind." He liked to describe himself with these same words.

I asked him to draw the image again. He did so showing only the head of his mother. He said that really she was kneeling down, but he didn't know how to draw it. Would I help? He gave me his pen saying

Fig. 4 (left). Second drawing of the beating. Fig. 5 (right). Third drawing of the beating.

Fig. 6 (left). Interaction drawing of the beating. Fig. 7 (right). His father beating his mother.

that "she faces towards him on her knees." I drew in a simple kneeling body (Figure 6) and asked him to draw it himself. He did and added blood pouring from his mother's head plus arms which he had previously omitted (Figure 7).

Ned went on to tell how the images sometimes came as the whole thing, sometimes only in pieces such as faces, or as just the red color. He drew some of the variations he experienced. In one there were two heads

Fig. 8 (left). A variation of the beating image. Fig. 9 (right). Only blood.

of different sizes and an elongated penis-like shape between them (Figure 8). He also drew the one as "only blood" (Figure 9).

In the days that followed our detailed redrawing of the images, Ned said they no longer bothered him. Perhaps he was able to suppress the image, perhaps this was a suggestion or positive transference, possibly he mastered the ideas and feelings, and possibly he simply wanted to avoid a repetition of our encounter together with the image. He improved gradually, as he had before the home visit, so there is no way to attribute this to the drawing intervention. He was discharged to out-patient treatment and, six months later, remained outside of the hospital and in school.

DISCUSSION OF NED

Ned's recurrent image of the beating can be considered under each of the points of view developed earlier.

THE IMAGE AS A REPETITION OF A TRAUMATIC PERCEPTION. As with Isabel, there was a possibility that Ned's images were memories of traumatic perceptions. We knew that violence in his family sometimes occurred, but there was no verification of the specific incident other than Ned's memory which could have confused fantasy with reality.

EXPRESSION OF REPRESSED MENTAL CONTENTS. The image returned again and again because it expressed strong urges that were never gratified. The emergence of the image was experienced as intrusive because Ned dreaded acknowledgement or experience of these urges; the idea and emotional content were too dangerous to think about. In a person with strong inhibitory capacity, such images might not emerge: the repression would be complete. In Ned, inhibition was attempted but was partially unsuccessful: part of the repressed ideas and emotions were expressed as the image. What were these repressed ideas and emotions?

The beating symbolized an aggressive assault, as is obvious, but also a sexual assault. This sexualization of aggression, or aggressivization of sexuality, is commonly called either sadism, if the urge is active; or masochism, if the urge is passive. In Ned the urge seemed to be both sadistic and masochistic. He wanted to be aggressive, and feared this urge because it could easily lead to uncontrolled rage. He wanted to receive pleasurable attention but feared the closeness threat (since there was an aggressive component) and the homosexual quality of his wishes. We can explore these themes more under transformation and disguise. As a breakthrough of repressive defenses per se, the image carried into awareness is a partial recognition of sexual and aggressive wishes as well as sexual and aggressive fears.

Transformation and Disguise. The recurrent image reflected the idea, "I am watching my mother being beaten by my father." Each person in the statement may stand for Ned himself, as pointed out by Freud (1919). Ned expresses and partially gratifies his sadistic impulses, in a disguised way, by identifying himself with his father as he holds the images in mind. His masochistic, passive, and homosexual impulses are similarly expressed and gratified by identifying with the role of his mother. This latter theme resonates with the situation that occurred before his hospitalization. He felt rejected by the doctor who prescribed injections. He wished to return to the state of being injected by the doctor. The image of "somebody" being beaten is a disguised version of his wish to submit, be injected (beaten), but attended to (nurtured, or loved) by the doctor. Deprived of the doctor, and withdrawn from father and mother, he must find a way to console himself. One way of self-consolation is fantasy and/or masturbation. Unfortunately, these processes were also dreaded as dangerous, and as symbols of guilty activity.

The timing of Ned's images provides a clue to their relevance to masturbatory wishes. The images came most often when he was alone in his room and unoccupied with a task. He usually would lie in bed, and at such times wanted to masturbate. As he described this in an interview, "I had to resist myself." He was afraid that he might have caused his deformity by excessive masturbation and was fearful of giving in to his urges. Another reason for his fear may have been guilt over the sado-masochistic fantasies that might have accompanied his masturbation. While he did not describe his masturbation fantasies in terms of content, he said that the excitement caused a turmoil of terrible thoughts. Note also, that the idea of a beating is a pun for masturbation: his age group uses such expressions as "to beat off" or "go beat your meat" to refer to this act. Paradoxically, while the beating images may signify masturbation, the anxiety they engender is used to nullify sexual arousal and to avoid masturbation.

To summarize, Ned's images expressed, in a disguised form, primitive sexual and aggressive themes. Ned could partially gratify his wishes by assuming various roles within the image drama. The images can also be considered as a thought process, apart from content. One aspect of Ned's thought disorder was a relative incapacity, at times, for thinking in orderly sequences of words. There were thoughts he wished to avoid, but he may also have had an incapacity to facilitate word organization. By facilitation of images he had a "fallback" position. He could think in images rather than face the danger of mental chaos: a turmoil of disorganized and dangerous lexical ideas and feelings. The images could be maintained with some clarity; they avoided verbal conceptualization of dreaded ideas but also avoided total disorganization.

CASE 3
Mary: The Earthquakes

The following case illustrates two interesting clinical phenomena: 1) how phases of repression may alternate with phases of recurrent intrusive images; and 2) how two sets of unbidden images, that superficially appear different, may have an underlying unity.

IDENTIFICATION OF THE PATIENT

Mary, a divorcee in her middle twenties, was admitted to the psychiatric ward shortly after childbirth. She had stayed at a home for unwed mothers until the child's birth. After delivery she was mute, apathetic, and remained in bed for days. She responded to encouragement by greater activity, but talked tangentially and bizarrely. When social workers asked her to decide the fate of her baby, she said she wanted to have the child adopted, but she refused to discuss necessary procedural details. Because of her recalcitrance, as an interim measure, the baby was sent to a foster home and Mary remained in the home for unwed mothers. Three weeks later, using an overdose of pills, she attempted suicide. After a day of intensive treatment on a medical ward, she was transferred to psychiatry.

THE SYNDROME OF UNBIDDEN IMAGES

One of Mary's chief complaints on entry to the psychiatric ward was that she was "having earthquakes" and wanted them to go away. These "earthquakes" were a synesthetic experience consisting of visual and kinesthetic images plus associated emotions. In the visual images of "the earthquake," she was injured or hollow in her abdomen and the victim of various crushing injuries (such as the ceiling falling in). Another version was that some bad organ or object was in her abdomen, such as "a yellow hair-ball." She also felt as if her abdomen were churning and as if she were shaking and the room were moving. The associated feelings were dread, fear of sudden death, depersonalization (a sensation of personal unreality), and feelings of hopelessness and emptiness. In addition, Mary reported distorted visual perception: when she looked at other people they appeared to twist at the stomach "as if they were being shifted or churned by an earthquake"; when she looked at the walls they seemed to buckle or move. Although these various experiences were frightening and seemed real, within moments she could check the sensations by carefully looking around, and would then decide that an earthquake was not really in process. Although her hospitalization occurred in San Francisco at the time of an earthquake scare, her symptom has other determinants.

In addition to her earthquakes, Mary later reported another set of unbidden images. In the second set she was not the injured victim, but the dangerous aggressor: she had repeated images of people, buildings, or cars exploding, or of herself shooting or stabbing people in their stomachs. She experienced these images as involuntary and intrusive but felt that she enjoyed them, "in a smirky evil way." The aggressive images seemed less peremptory than "the earthquakes" which frightened her the most.

Both sets of images recurred in spite of her efforts to suppress them. She was reluctant to say much about them other than giving brief descriptions of the content. She acted as if she did not acknowledge them as meaningful, purposive, or self-generated. Rather, they were alien, to be removed, mysterious, and not to be understood.

PAST HISTORY

Parental and environmental instability were important factors in Mary's early life according to the history given both by her parents and the patient herself. In her first year of life, several different persons cared for her. When she was a year old, she went to live with her grandparents. At age three she was returned to her parents for six months and then remitted back to the grandparents. Again at age five or six she returned to her parents' home. During this time a baby brother was born. Four additional younger siblings followed who occupied the center of attention. She was expected to care for all of them while she, herself, was very neglected.

Throughout childhood and adolescence she had a difficult time finding her own identity and role. She disliked her family and felt like Cinderella: always working on the chores and childcare, getting no love or attention. In adolescence she vacillated back and forth between "good" and "bad" identity sets. The "good" identity included religious activity, plans to become a missionary, and development of her musical and sewing talents to an above average degree. The "bad" identity included parental defiance and passive compliance with promiscuous and drug-taking friends. After two broken love affairs, several vacillations from positive to negative identity left her very depressed. She was married once, wanted children, but could not become pregnant. Her husband beat her, and she also was violent. After divorce she periodically felt very inadequate and, in dispair, attempted suicide at least twice.

She became pregnant in a passive happenstance manner, but decided to carry the baby to term. Shortly before delivery she said the baby was to be adopted, but refused to discuss matters beyond this point with a social worker. Following delivery, the topic of adoption of the baby was broached many times, but she would not discuss it beyond abrupt agreement. Instead she might withdraw, begin to talk in a bizarre manner, or have a temper tantrum. During this period her "earthquakes" became intense; she said she had had them on and off since adolescence.

THE MEANING OF THE IMAGES AND THE PSYCHODYNAMICS OF THE IMAGE FORMATION

Information obtained during her hospital stay, derived from both psychotherapeutic and cognitive research efforts, will be presented under the three main headings used for the previous case examples. Once again, I will regard unbidden images as the possible reexpression of traumatic perceptions, as breakthroughs in the face of repressive efforts, and as the result of various transformations and disguises of psychologic motives.

The way Mary labeled her unbidden images, "my earthquakes," suggests that she wished to communicate or (at least to herself) regard the experience as a disaster. The reasons for selecting the label "earthquakes" were revealed in the course of her hospitalization; the label reflects a traumatic experience which predates the symptom. The images, in turn, became "used" for screen purposes.

When Mary was 15 years old, a strong earthquake occurred. She was in a third-story school classroom at the time. For several seconds the blackboards moved on the walls, and the windows buckled, opened, and closed. The experience triggered a dangerous internal image. She realized it was an earthquake and had the sudden intensive thought, "I hope the house falls on them (her family) and crushes them all to death"; the thought was accompanied by a vivid visual image of such an event. She was very frightened, vowed to forget her thoughts, and made penances. One penance was to imagine herself as the victim in her earthquakes; she has the inner churning, she is crushed, she has the hole in her body.

Thus, as with Ned and Isabel, content derived from a "traumatic" perception is depicted in the intrusive images. The images are not, however, simply repetitions of the trauma. They are revived again and again as a vehicle and screen for the expression and concealment of other ideas and feelings. Her rage towards her parents, her repeatedly frustrated wish to have them take care of her, and her wish for revenge (at being neglected) were present at various times throughout her childhood, adolescence, and adult history. During the earthquake she experienced these ideas intensely, and the traumatic moment, with its associated fright, was recapitulated whenever some aspect of this set of ideas or whenever similar feeling states were triggered by current situations. The concept of the earthquake also serves as a useful symbol for other important ideas and feelings to be described below.

EXPRESSION OF REPRESSED IDEAS AND FEELINGS. In the previous cases, the sudden expression of images that partially expressed previously inhibited ideas or feelings led to the subjective feeling of unbiddenness or loss of control over thought. Mary is of special interest because during her hospitalization she had relatively clear phases in which unbidden images alternated with complete repression. These phases show the double-sided coin of loss of control: at times she could not think about certain concepts; at other times she could not prevent herself from thinking of them.

As indicated earlier, Mary had two sets of unbidden images. In one set her role was passive: she depicted herself as injured. These images expressed the latent idea that something inside her abdomen was missing or damaged. The latent emotions included anxious dread and depression related to feelings of being hopelessly deprived of nurturance or affection, and fear of losing herself and her baby. The image of her damaged belly symbolizes several themes: her overwhelming destructive hunger, her fear that she is beyond rescue, her wretchedness at having lost her baby, and possibly also her sensation of the baby kicking before she was "emptied" by childbirth.

Mary's second set of images makes her role active and destructive. She machine-guns people and blows the middle out of buildings and cars. These images express the latent idea of retaliation and the latent emotion of rage and blame towards others for not gratifying her needs.

Expression of such ideas and feelings had been a problem for Mary since childhood since her fear, helplessness, and rage were intense, persistent, and morally taboo. She was shuffled back and forth from parents to grandparents, feeling angry and depressed at each "rejection" and loss. When she returned to her parents, a new baby occupied their attention. She imagined she had been sent away because of the coming of this baby. For years after her return home, her mother continued to produce babies which, from Mary's point of view as a child, deprived her of love. In order to remove these rivals she developed fantasies of ripping the insides out of her mother. These thoughts were repressed since, as part of the talon principle (an eye for an eye), she feared that she would be destroyed in the same way because of her evil urges.

The above constellation of repressed ideas and feelings were, by and large, dormant until triggered by her pregnancy, isolation, and childbirth. These experiences excited implicit thoughts or questions such as: Who will feed the baby? Who will feed me? As she identified herself as both mother and baby, these questions generated dread, expressed in the passive set of images, and rage (no one will) expressed in the active images. These images partially express the dangerous ideas and emotions and hence are experienced as alien, intrusive, and menacing. She must disown the images to disown her impulses and her pain.

The phases noted in the course of Mary's hospitalization will be described next to illustrate successful and unsuccessful inhibition of the images. Such phases of symptom, symptom remission, and symptom recurrence are not uncommon in psychiatric hospitalizations. Acute symptoms subside in the safety of the ward leaving a plateau that includes denial of illness. This avoidance of thoughts or discussions relevant to illness distinguishes the plateau phase from stable reintegration of psychologic controls. Movement within psychotherapy or around discharge planning reactivates conflict and may lead to symptom flare-up. After such turbulance, patients commonly achieve a more stable integration.

PHASE 1: INTRUSIVE IMAGES, PASSIVE INJURED TYPE. On entry to the ward she complained of unbidden images and feelings that she labeled "earthquakes." She was cooperative, but passive, and periodically seemed to have a clouded state of consciousness during which she was withdrawn, inattentive, and unwilling or unable to concentrate. Her emotional expressions in her face, posture, and tone of voice indicated mild depression, but she would not speak about how she felt. This phase lasted three days.

With one of the nurses, she started interaction drawing to further communication of her current thoughts through pictures. Figure 10 is the first drawing produced. Mary drew a cracked head; the nurse drew a similar head with a similar line or crack. Mary added an icebag to her head and a flower to the head drawn by the nurse. Mary's later comments indicated that the cracked head was an earthquake reference.

PHASE 2: NO UNBIDDEN IMAGES. From the fourth through the eleventh days of hospitalization Mary seemed rational and cooperative. She recalled having the earthquakes but said the symptom was gone. She talked a little of her past history but specifically avoided mention of her pregnancy, the baby, her previous marriage, or plans for leaving the hospital or adopting the baby. She did report feeling sad and empty. When the psychotherapist referred to "forbidden" topics, e.g., the preg-

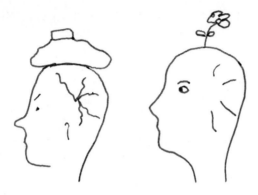

Fig. 10. The cracked head.

nancy, she cried and became silent. She remained rational, however, in all her communication and, on a questionnaire to assess confusion in thinking and intrusiveness of thought in general, she scored in a normal

Fig. 11. A drawing from a period without intrusive images.

range. Tasks that measured perceptual attention, memory, and perceptual matching were also performed with high levels of concentration, attention, and exclusion of intrusive thoughts.

Figure 11 is one of the interaction drawings from this plateau period. Mary drew mountains and a rising sun, the nurse a road. Mary drew pine trees and a walking figure. The nurse added another figure; Mary drew a detour sign. The nurse added a side road. Mary added a "Dairy Queen." Such food references were common; many of her drawings showed themes like a child who had dropped his ice cream cone. The nurse, as with the road after the detour sign, would add a helpful path. Mary would block this "help" in a passive-aggressive manner during this phase.

PHASE 3: ERUPTION OF HOSTILE IMAGES. During her psychotherapy hour, Mary was asked how she felt about her baby, and what was going to become of him. She wept, became angry, then confused, and stayed in a clouded state of consciousness for some hours. Thereafter, she reported intrusive, angry thoughts in the form of images. She saw herself machine-gunning people and blowing up buildings and cars. She visualized herself as having a hairy yellow mass in her abdomen; she saw others as plastic manikins without middle sections. She felt depersonalized, and others also seemed unreal. She threw a temper tantrum, threw her treasured musical instrument out the window, and messed up her room. During this period she did cooperate with cognitive testing: she reported herself confused and with intrusive thoughts on the questionnaire, made perceptual errors, and had intrusive thoughts while attempting to attend to the perceptual stimuli of the task.

Figures 12, 13, and 14 are the second, fifth, and sixth drawings from an interaction drawing session conducted immediately after the psychiatric interview in which the baby topic was brought up. The patient depicted an exploding building and car. She dropped a boulder on the ambulance "dispatched" by the nurse and depicted a fire behind a wall drawn by the nurse. In Figure 13 the nurse drew two figures fencing, referring to another drawing by the patient. The patient drew two "Camelot" figures walking away because "swordplay reminds me of that movie." The nurse added a child figure pointing at the fight; the patient dropped a bomb at it. In Figure 14 the nurse repeated the bomb theme. The patient drew a baby carriage where the bomb would drop into it. The nurse added a nurse and a warning figure which the patient labeled "deaf mute." She added a firecracker for good measure.

About two weeks after these drawings of "baby bombing," the patient asked to see her drawings. Her comments while looking them over were recorded. Here are her comments about this part of the series:

> Yeah. So I decided that they were fighting over a woman. And this was the knights of old. And it's sort of one of those ladies with pointed hats,

Fig. 12 (top). Explosion. Figs. 13 (middle) and 14 (bottom). Bombing the baby.

walking off with the man with the feather in his hat. And she drew this distressed little person trying to point out that they were fighting to the death. So I bombed him. I dropped a bomb on him. (Shown next picture.) Yeah. She decided to keep on with the bomb. So I decided to bomb the baby carriage. And she drew a man trying to warn the nurse about the bomb that was falling. Only he was a deaf-mute and couldn't say anything. And I threw a firecracker for him and then she drew glasses on the nurse. So I colored them in and said she was blind. It's going to get bombed anyway, I don't care.

The angry impulses are clearly depicted in these drawings. There is also a despairing quality of hopelessly intense, insatiable need. The "bombing" pictures were made on the first day of a three-day period of intrusive thoughts revolving predominantly around destructive visions. The airplane theme emerged again toward the end of this period in an image that expresses poignantly the feeling of hopeless dependency. During the visual evocation procedure she was asked to report whatever visual images might form in response to the stimulus concept, "I am afraid":

I am an airplane. Looking for a place to land, but no place to land. I do see two places, one bigger than the other, but can't land on either, running out of fuel. I am the plane, silver, the air is transparent black.

PHASE 4: REINHIBITION OF THE IMAGES ASSOCIATED WITH CONFUSION. The angry images subsided in three days. She reported no images and said she was hardly thinking at all. She sat staring at the floor and the wall and said there was a lid on her mind. During conversations and psychotherapy interviews she was dull, preoccupied, and confused. Apparently she inhibited the images but at the expense of a kind of confused "nonthinking." While she reported no intrusive images during this period, one of several interaction drawings made did show destructive themes. This is shown in Figure 15.* The nurse drew the figure outline. Mary drew in the face with crossed eyes, lines on the forehead, and the speech balloon, "my girdle is killing me." This remark was a joke about the slenderness of the figure but also a reference to her own abdomen (still distended from the postpartum period). The nurse drew a girdle, Mary added arms with knives that dripped blood.

This period lasted about a week, while the psychotherapist was supportive and deliberately avoided distressing themes. Then he again broached the "toxic" topics.

PHASE 5: REACTIVATION OF UNBIDDEN IMAGES. When the baby issue was brought up by the psychotherapist, Mary avoided talking. Afterwards she was angry and reported many intrusions of her "earth-

---

* The numbers in the illustration are annotations to indicate serial order. Circled numerals indicate Mary's drawing; uncircled numerals are the nurse's drawing.

Fig. 15 (above). A girdle that cuts. Fig. 16 (below). Man with a knife.

156

quakes." These were probably not only recurrent unbidden images; they were also used by Mary to punish the therapist and to look as if she were made ill by his intervention. The unbidden images were now, to an extent, "bidden unbidden images." Her drawings revolved largely around destructive and injured themes. While she would not discuss these ideas or feelings in words, she drew expressions of ideas of desertion, hunger and yearning, hopelessness and despair, and destruction involving the abdomen. Figure 16 provides one example. Mary drew a man holding a knife, and in his mouth is an uptilted cigarette. This upturned cigarette is a repetitive theme: note for comparison Figure 17. One head seems to be a rejecting male, the other the injured female.

PHASE 6: INHIBITION OF IMAGES AGAIN. Mary once again reported that the images were gone. She was confused, abstracted, and forgetful. At times she was overheard by staff groaning aloud or saying "no" to herself. This was now the sixth week of hospitalization. She flirted, at other times she had temper tantrums. She still refused to discuss her baby, so the adoption procedures could not proceed.

PHASE 7: HOSTILE IMAGES AGAIN. Then she began to report the hostile images again. They still came of their own accord, but she said she kind of enjoyed them "in a smirky evil way." She began to speak of the images as her own ideas and thought of producing the fearsome hole of the "earthquakes" in other persons (see Figures 18 and 19). In Figure 18 Mary drew a gun, and the nurse responded with a target. Mary made the target into a belt of a person and added a bleeding hole. The nurse added the head behind the gun. Then Mary changed to a new sheet of paper.

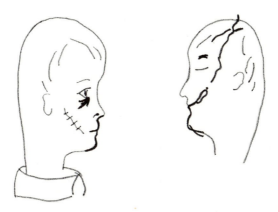

Fig. 17. The rejecting male and the injured female.

Fig. 18. Put the hole in others.

The nurse drew a circle (Figure 19). Mary scribbled inside it and drew worm-like forms (worms in holes was another repeated theme). The next day, Mary and the nurse drew Figure 20. It indicates Mary's passive-aggressive behavior and the hostile and orally deprived themes. Mary drew the artist, the nurse a picnic basket. Mary drew the bear, the nurse a box. Mary added honey in the bear's paws. The nurse added another "friendly" figure. Mary provided an alligator to threaten him, labeled the box "biskits," and staked down the figure so it could not escape. Finally, Mary drew a bird, the nurse added legs, and Mary drew a hunter with an arrow piercing the bird's belly.

PHASE 8: EMERGENCE OF THE UNDERLYING IDEAS, TURBULENCE, AND RESOLUTION. The above period lasted five days. Then an anniversary: two months after the birth of her baby. Mary berated her therapist for not curing her faster, had a temper tantrum, entered a state of clouded consciousness, and behaved in an infantile manner. She dreamt of floating away with her baby to another planet because she could not keep it on earth: this was her first deliberate mention of the baby. She said, "Now the stopper is out, and the poison gas is loose." She

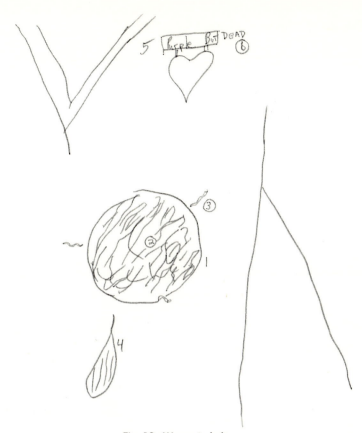

Fig. 19. Worms in holes.

Fig. 20. Food versus injury.

1 TON

Fig. 21 (above). Elephant stomping a man. Fig. 22 (left). Crushed head. Fig. 23 (below). Help.

HELP

felt very depressed and began talking of the baby. She also talked more of the earthquakes. In the drawings she showed an elephant stomping a man (Figure 21), a crushed head (Figure 22), and scenes of oral poignancy (Figure 23).

At times, while she was thinking of her troubles, she also avoided them by entering an altered state of consciousness. She did this by staring at some visual form such as a door jamb or a patch of sunlit floor. She said she felt "less awful while afloat" and that "when awake she feels disintegrated." She felt "phony" and "in parts," illustrating this with Figure 24 in the drawing sessions. The nurse added a feminine figure which Mary made toothless and breastless.

Mary began to talk things over in psychotherapy. She expressed the feelings previously depicted only in the images and her communication of their contents. She decided that her baby should have the permanent home that she herself had never had. She signed papers so that he could leave a temporary foster parent home and be adopted. In interaction drawings she deliberately depicted her earthquake-fear images (Figure 25), the hostile wish to do the same to others (Figure 26), and her split halves

*erased bust, made
bust flat, made
mouth toothless

Fig. 24. Herself in parts.

Fig. 25. Earthquake.

Fig. 26. Hurting others.

Fig. 27. Her split personality.

in the same picture (Figure 27). Mary began to experience and work with her feelings of yearning for the baby, her grief at giving it up, and her guilt for not keeping it. Some of these feelings were reflected in the interaction drawings of this period (Figures 28, 29, and 30).

After these therapeutic gains, Mary accepted encouragement to manage her own affairs. She sought work while still in the hospital. For a time she entered a kind of halfway house. Then she "graduated" to outpatient psychotherapy which will probably continue for some time.

TRANSFORMATION AND DISGUISE. In the set of images she found most distressing, Mary felt herself empty, damaged, and in danger

Fig. 28. The baby theme.

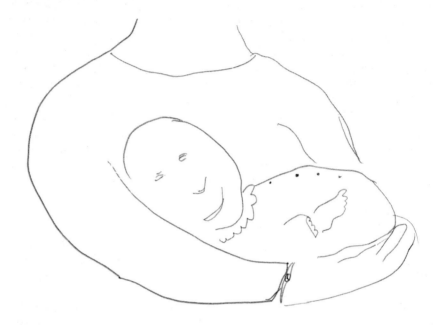

Fig. 29. The baby theme.

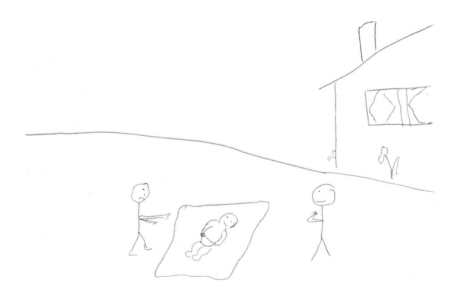

Fig. 30. The baby theme.

of disintegration. At an unconscious level she "preferred" to facilitate a cluster of emotions and self-concepts in which she imaged herself as a bad, dangerous, and angry person. Generation of anger and sadistic, revengeful satisfaction through the destructive images seemed semipurposive; she felt at least alive and personally intact when angry. Thus, one set of "unbidden images" seemed to be generated to suppress feelings expressed and aroused by a still more "unbidden" and intolerable set.

The bad identity, while in a sense a defense against the disintegrative despair, was also defended against; hence the dissociation of the images from her sense of self, from her thought, and from verbal communication. The bad identity was too close to painful feelings of being a bad mother, wishing to hurt her baby, deserting her baby, and being deserted by men and her parents.

Both sets of Mary's unbidden images had the same bipolar schema: an injured person and an injuring person. She could align her sense of self with either pole: she could be the injured person, as in the "earthquakes," or the injuring person, as in the hostile images. The two sets of images represent layers of the same formulation, which is why one set was labeled passive, and the other, active.

In the phase in which she aligns herself with the injuring pole, she forms active images in which she is a kind of phallic-destructive aggressor. In terms of unconscious metaphors, she may feel that she has inside herself, in place of emptiness, a powerful and destruction-wielding penis. In a sense she is strong because she is full of rage; others are weak victims. In the passive images she aligns herself with the injured pole. She is in danger of imminent harm or, more deeply, has been damaged beyond repair.

The dual roles leading to two sets of images demonstrate an important feature of image formation: image expression allows easy alternation between active and passive self-representations. Usually, in situations of fear of external persons, the preferred fantasy transformation is from passive victim to active persecutor (identification with the aggressor, A. Freud, 1946; see also Perry, 1970). For example, a child who has been afraid of his dentist may, in fantasy, image himself as the man who fixes the teeth of others (even if it hurts a little). The feared situation is depicted, but the role is changed from one of helplessness to mastery. This helps in adaptation; in the new fantasy role, the motives of the feared person may be understood as benign rather than malignant. Also, the rehearsal in an objective, external way of how another "victim" behaves and survives may lead to reduction of fear. On the other hand, when the active role is dreaded—as when anger, if expressed, would activate guilt—then the passive role may be fantasized. Recall how Isabel visualized the old man "haunting her" to disguise and avoid, and also to expiate in advance, her own assaultive impulses.

Mary's two sets of images, while "uncontrolled," were used by her to regulate feeling. When dangerously enraged, she could "punish" herself or warn herself with the passive images of being injured. When she felt injured, she was able to gratify herself in fantasy retaliation using the active images. When she felt guilty about rejecting or wanting to reject or harm her baby (or her own mother), she was able to inflict the same injury on herself with the passive images. A sample of transformation between active and passive role-structuring of the underlying injured-injuror schema is found in one of her dreams:

> I had a gun and was going to shoot a man. I pulled the trigger, but a hole in my own head occurred. Then I shot a woman in the belly. And there I was, holes in my own head, in my own belly, and no holes in them.

In this dream her rage is turned upon herself by role reversal. Also, this reversal of roles is important to the stress that preceded her symptoms: she has a baby she will not care for, thus reversing the situation from her own feelings of infantile neglect.

Why did Mary fall ill? She was, of course, engulfed in a life crisis, childbirth after an unwanted pregnancy. But why did she decompensate rather than experience emotional distress and adapt to her situation? Any woman might feel remorse, guilt, depression, and anger. A hypothetical normal woman might undergo a period of psychologic work, consisting of working through a grief reaction with, perhaps, periods of angry, anxious, or depressive moods. Mary required psychiatric hospitalization to work through her emotions. Why? Working through her problem requires thought and emotion. Mary may have a particularly low tolerance for unpleasant emotions and, rather than working through her experience, she avoids memory and feeling by withdrawal, mutism, altered states of consciousness, and suicide attempts. Partly this could be because her childbirth experience gave rise to unusually intense emotions. These would be hard to bear because they activate residues of her childhood deprivations. Rage, depression, and frustration are, by adulthood, "built in" to her character and any situation of rebuff, loss, or need will trigger these responses.

A second explanation of her symptom formation concerns her capacity for regulation. She attempts to use repression, but she seems to have a poor inhibitory capacity. It is hard for her to prevent images from entering awareness in the first place: instead, she has to avoid recognition or reaction to images that become conscious. This relatively low inhibitory capacity reduces her ability to "dose" the phases of any psychologic working-through process.

Consider again our hypothetic "normal" woman. In Mary's situation, she might have a grief reaction: she would think over her experience and try different means in thought of appraising it or reacting to it. When emotional responses such as shame or depression reached the level of tolerance, this "normal" woman might be able to inhibit further memories, thus, giving herself only tolerable doses of thinking-through. By repeated doses, within thresholds of tolerance, the working-through is gradually accomplished. If Mary cannot control the entry of memories or thoughts into awareness, she cannot so dose herself: to her, opening up to the experiences means overwhelming floods of painful feelings.

Mary must totally avoid reconsideration of her experience. Total avoidance means that the need to reconsider the experience is not reduced and the predispositions to develop the painful feelings remain at full strength. Mary falls ill, in a sense, because she has poor capacity for inhibition: this means she must totally inhibit rather than periodically "dose herself" with those painful experiences in need of mastery. The poor capacity for inhibition means this total avoidance is doomed to failure: aspects of the experience and her emotions do gain expression, albeit in the disguised form of the unbidden images.

The press towards expression is in conflict with motives of avoidance. This impulse-defense configuration undergoes various transformations as she uses different means of regulating what is represented in conscious thought. The first level of inhibition is repressive: no contents are allowed to "leak out." Her repressive inhibitory capacity is relatively inadequate, and she resorts to another level of inhibition, a form of denial. She describes her unbidden images as alien symptoms and denies to herself their implications. She does not translate their full meaning into words. Thus, she encapsulates the dreaded ideas and feelings as "foreign" images.

There is one additional historical contributant to Mary's tendency to deny, split, and dissociate mental concepts. When she returned home from her grandparents and felt parental neglect, there was a redeeming person, a bachelor friend of the family. He took her to work with him when she was six years old. She worked with him holding tools and was taken by him to enjoyable activities, such as the circus and the ice cream store (the source of the ice cream cones frequently shown in her drawings to depict both longing and gratification). While not directly molesting her sexually, as far as is known, this man used to fondle her, look at her body, and kiss her in a "sloppy, slobbery way." She was frightened and excited by these advances. To maintain the relationship, which she desperately needed, she encapsulated in one mental set the warm parental qualities of the man and held separately his sexual and exploitative qualities.

Like Isabel and Ned, Mary sometimes entered altered states of consciousness in which rational thought in words was diminished, fantasy amplified. Usually, in such states, images increase in vividness. But even if they do not, the loss of the sense of self-willed control over the course of thought lends the images a quality of quasi-reality: the images are not clearly demarcated from perceptions. This blurring of the boundaries between fantasy and reality may make internal images during altered states of consciousness both more gratifying and more terrifying, depending on their contents and on responses to the contents. Mary sometimes entered an altered state on purpose; she accomplished this by staring and repeating patterns of stimulation until they became meaningless. In clouded consciousness she could avoid thinking about unpleasant reality and dwell instead in fantasy. But once in the altered state, she could not necessarily rouse herself to full alertness when the images turned sour or activated too much responsive feeling.

DISCUSSION

The unbidden image is experienced subjectively as a surprise. The thought processes involved in image formation are not available to conscious appraisal, and the more unpleasant forms of unbidden images seem to occur in spite of conscious and deliberate efforts to avoid or dispel them. Nonetheless, clinical investigation of the underlying cognitive dynamics reveals that subjectively "unbidden" images are thought products which result from interactions between impulsive and defensive motives. In the case histories, impulsive motives and the transformations of these motives were described. Now I abstract from such clinical investigations how various defense mechanisms relate to image thinking.

Unbidden images are, first and foremost, a failure in *repression*. Usually dominant inhibitory influences over image formation give way to suddenly stronger facilitory influences. The sudden reversal of regulatory dynamics may be caused by intensification of impulsive motives, or waning of inhibitory capacity. In either event, the sudden entry into awareness lends the experience one aspect of its peremptory quality. When facilitation is relatively strong, the images are likely to be unusually vivid, hence more like perceptions and, therefore, easily regarded as some unpleasant aspect of the outer world rather than a dangerous part of the inner world. (This extrusion of the image contents from the concept of self is a *projective* operation). Once repression has failed, as a total inhibitory defense, then *denial* may be used as a supplement or substitute. In terms of image formation, denial works because of inhibitions that keep the conscious self-observing ego selectively unaware of a) the image formation process (and hence, the internal origin of the images), b) the motives for the expression, and c) the associations that might arise in response to the current image experience (denial of the meaning of the images). Denial of the internal source of images is analogous to the more familiar form of denial in which external perceptions, or their implications, are purposively ignored.

While inhibitory influences may fail to prevent image formation, such influences may still prevent lexical representation. The emerging contents may gain expression as images and yet be blocked from translation into word meanings. This form of *suppression* may contribute to the subjective regard of the images as mysterious and uncanny. In the presence of conflicted motives, the defensive maneuvers of *isolation* or *splitting* might result in one set of contents being expressed in the image system, another set in the lexical system, with avoidance of active conflict by inhibition of translation between the complexes. This would further contribute to the isolation of the images from a sense of meaning.

The revisualization of traumatic perceptions is explained as a particular example of repressive failure. The image records are incompletely mastered and press towards revisualization. This impulsive motive, described in detail in the next chapter, is countered by a motive for repression: the images, like the perceptions, are potentially overwhelming and certainly unpleasant. As with other failures in repression, the emergence of the traumatic images contributes to the sensation of loss of thought control. This adds to whatever emotions are already expressed (or evoked) by the images (usually fear).

Impulsive motives are repressed only when they cause some potential danger: they may seem too strong and, hence, potentially uncontrollable; they may conflict with other motives such as self-preservation, preservation of love by others, or moral standards. If the image contents partially express the impulsive motives, they are appraised as dangerous because the motives are dangerous. Further expression of the impulsive motives is prevented, insofar as possible, by disguise of the ideas and feelings through mechanisms such as *displacement* and *symbolization*. Because of differential abilities to disguise image contents and feeling states, some images may appear incongruent to the emotions that accompany them. When present, this incongruity contributes to the subjective strangeness of the unbidden image experience. Bland images may emerge with unpleasant feeling tones; horrible or lurid images may emerge without any accompanying emotion. This latter is a specific form of the defense of *intellectualization*.

If unbidden images were simply repressive breakthroughs they would be easy to explain. But the mind is very complex, even in psychosis, and there is often order in apparent chaos. Defensive motives may take an image, that in terms of content looks like the result of impulsive motives, and use it for defensive purposes. The basic versions of this defensive amplification are as follows:

1. The formation of a particular image may be facilitated to arouse a feeling of danger that in turn is used to motivate further defensive, controlling, or coping efforts. This is a specific form of *signal anxiety*.
2. The formation of a particular image may be facilitated to arouse feelings other than danger for the purpose of transforming more dreaded emotions and urges. This is a form of *reversal*. Fear may be generated to avoid anger as in (1), but anger may also be generated to avoid fear, guilt to avoid anger, and so forth. An important maneuver in this is the use of images to reverse roles from passive to active, or vice versa, so that passive fears become active urges, or active urges become passive fears. Sometimes this is a form of *displacement*, and sometimes it is a form of *undoing*.

Traumatic memories, with their propensity for formation of vivid images, are especially useful to the above defensive motives because they evoke intense fear and a sense of danger. Dormant traumas may be revived for this purpose, or contemporary traumas may remain unresolved, because they both trigger and screen internal conflict. Images that generate feelings such as fear, guilt, and hate, albeit for defensive purposes, will be regarded by the reflective self as unbidden and unwelcome.

Defensive motives tend to repeat trains of thought that end in images that successfully terminate tension states. Repetition results in condensation of the train of thought into the end symbol, the image. When similar tensions arise, the symbol may be activated without the original train of thought and the sudden, seemingly irrelevant, entry will lend the image-symbol a mysterious quality.

In the *defensive use of regression*, a person may deliberately let go of the sense of reflective self-awareness by blurring the boundary between percept and image (Schaffer, 1968). Thus, fantasies can be made to seem more real, and perception less real. Fantasy images can, through this defense, seem more gratifying, but they may also become more terrifying. Repressed images may emerge that "traumatize" the person from within. Images in regressive states seem to be unbidden because of the loss of reflective self-awareness and the reduced inhibition of contents and vividness.

The entry into regressive mental states is not always deliberate. A person may enter such a state because he lacks the capacity to organize thought into complex sequences. Even when this is due to an organic incapacity, seemingly unbidden images may be used for defensive purposes: to create emotion or to hold on to content that serves to stabilize cognitive organization and prevent further disintegration into chaos.

REFERENCES

Freud, S. (1919) A child is being beaten: A contribution to the study of the origin of sexual perversions. *Stand. Ed.*, 17, 1955.

Freud, A. 1946. *The Ego and the Mechanisms of Defense*. New York, International Universities Press.

Greenacre, P. 1949. A contribution to the study of screen memories. *Psychoanal. Stud. Child*, 3–4:78–84.

Horowitz, M. J. 1966. Visual imagery: an experimental study of pictorial cognition using the dot-image sequence. *J. Nerv. Ment. Dis.*, 141:615–622.

——— 1963. Graphic communication: A study of interaction painting with schizophrenics. *Amer. J. Psychother.*, 17:230–239.

Jacobson, E. 1957. Denial and repression. *J. Amer. Psychoanal. Ass.*, 5:61–92.

Jones, E. 1929. Fear, guilt and hate. *Int. J. Psychoanal.*, 10:383–397.

Klein, G. S. 1967. Peremptory ideation: Structure and force in motivated ideas. In Holt, R., ed. Motives and Thought: Psychoanalytic Essays in Honor of David Rapaport. *Psychol. Issues*, 5:80–128.

Perry, J. W. 1970. Emotions and object relations. *J. Anal. Psychol.*, 15:1–12.

Schafer, R. 1968. *Aspects of Internalization*. New York: International University Press, Inc.

CHAPTER

9

Experimental Research on the Revisualization of Traumatic Perceptions*

In the previous two chapters the observation was made that traumatic perceptions often return to mind as intrusive images. In this chapter, I present two experiments, designed to validate and expand clinical observations about unbidden images after psychic trauma. First I present some clinical material; then a discussion of theoretic issues followed by the experimental methodology and results.

FURTHER CLINICAL OBSERVATIONS

Psychoanalytic studies demonstrate the very long-lasting effects of some traumatic experiences. Niederland (1968) uses the term "survivor syndrome" to designate the group of symptoms formed in concentration camp victims. While various other symptoms are involved in this syndrome, relevant experiences include intrusive visual imagery of scenes seen decades before in the concentration camps, such as piles of corpses in Auschwitz, floggings and hangings of fellow prisoners, and other

* Portions of the research described in this chapter were supported by grants from Mount Zion Medical Center and the U.S. Public Health Service (NIMH 17373).

cruelties. Niederland's patients also report intensely vivid auditory and even olfactory experiences, such as hearing the crying and whimpering of the doomed women and children, the smell of burning flesh coming from the crematoriums and gas ovens, and so forth. Niederland has noted that these intrusive images may occur after a short or long, relatively free period, which he calls the "symptom free interval." Such patients commonly have sleep disorders and early morning awakenings because they fear the tormenting nightmares and the hallucinatory or semihallucinatory reliving of the past through imagery.

Murphy (1958) noted the central relationship of sensory perception to trauma and the compulsion to repeat or reenact traumatic events. He notes that a trauma in the present frequently acts as a screen for one in the past, as mentioned by Glover (1929), and that a trauma in the distant past can serve as a screen for one in the recent past. In several case illustrations, he notes how the persistence of traumatic effect may distort visual perceptions, such as heightening color perception in one eye as opposed to the other eye.

DEFINITION OF TRAUMA

Psychic trauma refers to an event or series of events that in some way causes subsequent psychic impairment. A frightening event is not necessarily traumatic. For example, if a child pets a dog and is bitten by it, the child's subsequent avoidance of the dog is not necessarily pathologic but adaptational. In order to label the inciting event a psychic trauma, there must be a later evidence of some response that is overreactive or underreactive. In the boy bitten by a dog, an overreactive response might be excessive fear upon seeing any animal, recurrent involuntary images of the dog's snarling face, or compulsive acting out of the event (or a symbolic substitute). Underreactivity might consist of excessive inhibition of a cognitive function, such as an amnesia for the event. Both types of psychic response may occur, either simultaneously or separately, after an overwhelming experience. For example, a person may repress the memory and be unable to revisualize the scene of the trauma; yet, at another time, the same person may have involuntary intrusions of traumatic images. Such impairments of cognition may be experienced subjectively as a loss of volitional control.

The above definition of trauma in terms of relatively enduring effects follows Freud and Breuer's (1895) clinical description. Freud (1920) also suggested a theoretic definition: traumatic impressions are those that breach "the stimulus barrier." * This second definition—of trauma as excessive stimulation—points the way to a theoretic schema to explain the tendency to repeat traumatic perceptions as unbidden images.

HYPOTHESIS

Chapter 7 provided a model of an image system that was partially differentiated in favor of perceptual input, partially in favor of internal memory input, and partially subservient to both inputs. One adaptational purpose for such a system would be the preservation of perceptual images until they were translated into word representation † and processed for memory storage by multiple coding systems (Tomkins, 1962; Underwood, 1969). A traumatic perception might overwhelm 1) perceptual processes, 2) the translation processes, and 3) coding processes. I hypothesize that overwhelming traumatic images enter into an active memory storage as visual images. Images held in this active storage system would be out of awareness but would press toward revisualization as mental images. This pressure would continue until translation and codification processes were completed.

The reentry of traumatic images into the image system and the translation into words meet with several kinds of resistance that provide motives for inhibition. One reason for resistance is that the reentry revives the unpleasant and potentially excessive emotions of the original experience. A person may still appraise these emotions as overpowering and as feelings to be avoided. A second reason for resisting revisualization is to prevent conceptualization of dangerous, associated ideas that might lead to other painful feelings. For example, if one witnesses a severe injury, he feels terror at the thought of suffering a similar injury. Mental images of the scene may cause not only terror but guilt as well, for being glad the injury happened to someone else.

This conceptual model suggests two opposing processes: one favors completion of unfinished business, i.e., translation, codification, and permanent storage, while the second favors continued inhibition to avoid emotional pain. If inhibition takes precedence, then the traumatic perceptions remain repressed, but active and unmastered—one has not learned to cope with them. If repression fails in spite of strong inhibition, one experiences intrusive images.

---

* The stimulus barrier is a kind of variable threshold that prevents excessive entry of perceptions and is analogous to inhibition of perception in the model of Chapter 7.
† As described in Chapter 5.

Predictions based upon this hypothesis should be testable in an experimental setting. As it happens, Lazarus and Opton (1968) and others (Folkins et al., 1968; Goldstein et al., 1965) have shown that witnessing unpleasant films can produce pronounced emotional and physiologic stress in the laboratory setting. Witkin and Lewis (1965) have demonstrated the impact of such films on subsequent images in hypnagogic reverie and dreams, and Cartwright et al. (1969) have shown a similar effect of arousing, erotic films. Thus, the stress film method may provide a useful means for experimental study of the clinical theory that trauma tends to return.

If a group of persons receives a traumatic perception and a nontraumatic perception, we would expect more reports of intrusive imagery and defensive activity in the posttraumatic period. Persons within the group, of course, would differ in outcome in terms of their subjective awareness, depending on the relative strengths of the impulsive, controlling, and defensive processes within the individual. Some persons might experience involuntary intrusions of imagery; other persons might repress the traumatic experience. Still other persons might have controlled returns of imagery which would not be experienced subjectively as a loss of control over the contents of awareness. Looking at the entire group, however, we would expect that after a traumatic film, significantly more involuntary intrusions of visual images would occur than after a neutral film.

EXPERIMENT 1: RETURN OF SCENES FROM A STRESS FILM*

Subjects, overall design, stimuli, and procedures will be discussed separately.

SUBJECTS

Eighteen male and four female college students volunteered to participate as a group in the experiment which involved the use of stressful and nonstressful films. One subject left during the experiment, and his incomplete data was not included in the data analysis.

---

* Originally published as "Psychic Trauma" in the *Arch. Gen. Psychiat.*, 20:552–559, May 1969. Judith Klein assisted with the data collection and analysis.

DESIGN

Research on thought experiences requires the use of introspective reports which are easily biased. For example, subjects may report more visual images when they believe this will please the investigator or when they share his predictions. On the other hand, if specific instructions are not given, introspective reports tend to be vague—to focus on content rather than the form or quality. In the present experiment, the tactic of increasing the specificity of instructions at certain key points was used in an attempt to maneuver between these two hazards in the use of introspective reports.

Mental contents reported after viewing a trauma film were compared with mental contents after a nontrauma film. Each subject was his own control and saw both films. To control for the effects of order of presentation of the films, half of the subjects viewed the neutral film first, half viewed the traumatic film first.

Before either film and after each film, subjects engaged in an auditory signal detection task which required them to pay close attention to stimuli from the external environment yet gave them a relatively meager supply of diverse information. The task required subjects to tune attention outwards rather than inwards, and led subjects to assume that, in part, the experimental goal was study of disruption in task performance secondary to stress. The task was interrupted at intervals, and subjects were asked to report all contents of their awareness during the preceding period.

During the tasks and report periods, no special emphasis was placed in the instructions on reporting visual imagery experience. Only after they had completed all the tasks of tone matching following the second film were the subjects informed that visual imagery was a focal interest. They were then asked to reconsider their subjective experiences and to write down on a separate paper all clear instances of visual imagery, amplifying their previous reports when necessary. This permitted analysis of the data as it stood prior to the introduction of the possible bias.

After obtaining the above data, still more instructions and questionnaires were given to subjects. The following additional data were obtained.

a. Rating of visual thought images for volitional control. The subjects compiled all of the visual images that they had recorded from their introspective reports after each task period and from their additional notes after having been informed that visual imagery was a focus of the study. Each image was rated on a 7-point scale, ranging from extreme control over imagery formation ("The image was deliberate.") to loss of control over imagery formation ("The image forced its way into my awareness," or "The image was insistent and hard to get rid of.")

b. Rating of intensity of scenes from the traumatic film. Subjects were given a form that listed 12 significant scenes in the traumatic film in the order of presentation. They rated each scene according to three somewhat overlapping qualities: the intensity of their emotional reactions while viewing the film, the intensity of their emotional reactions on recalling the scene now, and the vividness of their visual imagery on this recall.

c. Subjects completed a general questionnaire 24 hours after the experiment.

STIMULI

Subincision was used as the traumatic film because its wide use in film research attests to its traumatic impact—at least as measured by psychophysiologic indicators of stress. The film setting is the Australian bush, and it depicts naked natives engaged in a harsh puberty rite. Scenes of extensive penile surgery, bleeding wounds, and adolescents writhing and wincing with pain are repeated several times. The boys appear to volunteer for this painful procedure, which is conducted by older men.

The Runner was used as the non-traumatic film. The content is interesting, poignant and mildly humorous. A long distance race is depicted with repeated scenes of the runners jogging through a small town. Young and old men and women are the characters involved.

The films are of equal length, silent, and in black and white. Each repeats certain scenes and engages the viewer's interest. Also, both films involve groups of people and a feeling of suspense about what would happen next.

PROCEDURES

Before the films were shown, subjects were instructed in the auditory matching task and given two practice runs with repetition of instructions. The task before the first film, after the first film, and again after the second involved listening to tape-recorded musical tones. Then, without knowing which film they would see first or what the films would be about, half of the subject group faced a motion picture screen at the front of the room while half faced a similar screen at the rear of the room, and the films were shown using two projectors. Monitors watched to assure that the subjects did not turn their heads to see the second film prematurely. Later, the films were changed so that each group viewed the other film.

TASK

The tone task used is like that developed by Antrobus et al. (1966). In each of the three periods of tones, there were four two-minute segments, each composed of 23 tones. Five tones produced by an electric organ were used, each 1½ formal tonal intervals apart. Each tone sounded for approximately 2/10 second. While a set of five tones was used, the steps between successive stimuli were never more than 1½ intervals; that is, there was either no change or a change of one "step" higher or lower, at random. The intervals between successive tones were 3, 5 or 7 seconds (at random) and averaged 5 seconds per interval in each segment of 23 tones. Subjects were instructed to record whether the immediate tone was higher, lower, or the same as the preceding tone.

After each tone segment was completed, subjects were requested to recall and record in writing all their mental contents during the preceding tone-matching segment. They were told at this phase of the experiment that "mental contents" included awareness of thought in words, thought in images of various types, bodily sensations, feelings, and even fleeting or peripheral thoughts. They were asked not to make particular efforts to remember their thoughts during the task periods, but to rely on recall when the request was made to report mental contents. They were urged to listen diligently to the tones and perform the task as correctly as possible.

RESULTS

Sex Differences. Seventeen male and four female subjects comprised the final sample. Since the traumatic film depicted incision of the penis, males and females might be expected to have different reactions. Study of 26 male and female pilot subjects, however, indicated that intrusive returns of visual imagery from the film and defensive reactions such as mind wandering were distributed equally between the sexes, and that both found viewing the film to be stressful. The four female subjects, when compared to the 17 male subjects, had similar distributions of results on content analysis when comparing the post-traumatic and postneutral periods. In the discussion which follows, therefore, the sample group includes both the male and female subjects.

ERRORS IN TONE-MATCHING TASK. The matching of successive tones was scored in terms of the number of errors (see Table 1). The errors of all subjects in the four segments before the first film totaled 230. The group scored a composite of 234 errors after the neutral film and 258 errors after the stress film. This slight increase in errors after the stress film was not statistically significant.

CONTENT ANALYSIS OF INTROSPECTIVE REPORTS. The written reports that followed each tone-matching segment and were made by subjects prior to the announcement of the special interest in visual imagery were analyzed for content. The content analysts tallied separately: a) any reference to the film; b) any indicator of an intrusive or involuntary thought; c) any statement of thoughts irrelevant to the matching tone task; d) any type of visual image; and e) forgetting of thoughts. (The manual of the content analysis is presented at the end of this chapter.) The following brief operational definitions will indicate the basis for categorization.

1. Film reference: Any reference to either film, including references made before seeing either test film; for example, "Why don't they hurry up and show the film?" was scored as a film reference.

Table 1   Errors on Tone Matching by Performance Segment*

Group by Film Order†	Mean Errors (by Tone-Matching Segments)				
Before Films	1	2	3	4	Mean
Traumatic then neutral	2.6	2.4	3.0	1.6	2.4
Neutral then traumatic	3.1	2.4	3.8	3.0	3.1
After neutral film Traumatic then neutral	2.8	2.2	4.2	2.7	3.0
Neutral then traumatic	2.2	2.6	3.9	2.5	2.8
After traumatic film Traumatic then neutral	2.8	2.5	3.3	2.8	2.9
Neutral then traumatic	3.0	3.7	3.9	2.6	3.3
Mean	2.8	2.6	3.7	2.5	

*From Horowitz, 1969. Arch. Gen. Psychiat., 20:552-559.
†No. traumatic then neutral film = 11; No. neutral then traumatic film = 10.

2. Intrusive thought: Defined as any thought of a film during the tone task which was described by the subject as intrusive, as hard to push out of mind, or as distinctly unpleasant.

3. Task irrelevant thought: Any comment not related to task performance.

4. Visual image: A description implying a visual imagery experience such as "I saw," or "In my mind's eye," but not including "seeing-type" words used in a nonvisual sense such as "Now I see what you mean."

5. Forgetting: Any statement such as "My mind is blank," or "I forget what I was thinking."

Table 2 reports the total number of items tallied for each type of content in the three periods before and after films. These sums are based on division by two of a composite score obtained from two judges who independently rated all of the material. The period after the traumatic film led to more reports of film references, more intrusive thoughts, more visual images, and more instances of forgetting. In spite of the increases in these four categories, there was no significant difference in periods after stress and neutral films in terms of task irrelevant thoughts.

The significance of these findings is indicated in Table 3, which shows which condition led to the greatest frequency of reports using each subject as his own control. Ten subjects reported more visual imagery after the traumatic film than after the neutral film; one subject reported more visual imagery after the neutral film than after the traumatic film. Visual imagery, film references, and intrusive thoughts were reported with significantly greater frequency (p < 0.05) during post-traumatic periods than during postneutral periods. The post-traumatic period was also associated with more reports of forgetting in seven subjects, the postneutral period with more reports of forgetting in three

Table 2 Content Analysis of Introspective Reports*

Content Items	No. Items in Group by Period		
	Before	After Neutral Film	After Traumatic Film
Task irrelevant thoughts	78	67	75
Film references	12	48	64
Intrusive thoughts	0	4	30
Visual images	13	6	15
Visual images of film	0	1	13
Forgetting	2	3	9

*From Horowitz. 1969. Arch. Gen. Psychiat., 20:552-559.

Table 3   Content Analysis of Introspective Reports: Comparison of Periods Using Each Subject as His Own Control*

After Traumatic vs After Neutral Film

No. Subjects Reporting More of Item

Item Reported	After Traumatic Film	After Neutral Film	Significance†
Task irrelevant thoughts	10	6	NS
Film references	14	3	<0.006
Intrusive thoughts	16	0	0.002
Visual images	10	1	0.006
Forgetting	7	3	NS

After Traumatic Film vs Before Films

	After Traumatic Film	Prefilm	Significance†
Task irrelevant thoughts	12	7	NS
Film references	18	0	<0.002
Intrusive thoughts	16	0	0.002
Visual images	6	8	NS
Forgetting	7	1	0.04

After Neutral Film vs Before Films

	After Neutral Film	Prefilm	Significance†
Task irrelevant thoughts	13	5	NS
Film references	16	1	<0.002
Intrusive thoughts	2	0	NS
Visual images	2	9	0.03
Forgetting	2	3	NS

*From Horowitz. 1969. Arch. Gen. Psychiat., 20:552-559.
†By sign test.

subjects. The number of such reports of forgetting is small, and the probability by sign test that this difference is a chance occurrence is 17 percent (N.S.).

A comparison of the posttraumatic period with the prefilm period shows that significantly more subjects had more intrusive thoughts and more reports of forgetting after the traumatic period. Visual images were not significantly different in these two periods.

The postneutral film period was associated with significantly fewer visual images than the prefilm period; otherwise, there was no significant difference between the postneutral film period and the prefilm period.

RELIABILITY OF ANALYSTS. As a partial check on the capacity of analysts to agree on content analysis, two new analysts were given all items marked as visual images and all items marked as intrusive thoughts. The items were fragments of the introspective reports. Random ordering of items prevented bias, i.e., analysts did not know which items came from which subjects under which type of condition, or how they had been scored previously. On 64 items, the two analysts agreed 82 percent of the time as to whether or not it was a visual image and 96 percent of the time as to whether or not it was an intrusive thought.

ORDER EFFECTS. A few instances of imagery of the traumatic film were reported during the period after the neutral film. No imagery from the neutral film was reported after the traumatic film. Content analysis by order of film presentation, disregarding film type, showed no difference in the frequency of visual imagery but did show a difference in the frequency of intrusive thoughts. This difference is confined to the posttraumatic period, because intrusive thoughts after the neutral film were too sparse to consider. The subjects who viewed the stress film first were less likely to report intrusive thoughts than those who saw the traumatic film second. This suggests that fatigue may have increased the tendency to experience or report intrusive thoughts.

FURTHER DATA ON IMAGERY. The results so far concern subject responses during the perceptual tasks and the introspective report periods. After this data was recorded, subjects were given more specific instructions. A brief discussion of the subjective differences between thought in lexical and nonlexical form was a part of these instructions. Subjects were asked to record separately all mental contents that were clearly in the form of visual images. They could refer to their additional protocol if necessary, but not revise it. Hence, they might increase the detail of previous reports to indicate whether a given experience was a visual image or not; they might also add visual imagery experiences that they had not previously mentioned.

As expected, subjects reported more visual images after these instructions than content analysts tallied for their reports during general instructions. As shown in Table 4, this increase in visual images had a similar distribution to the data derived from reports from the period of general instructions. Under both conditions, more visual imagery was reported after the traumatic film.

Subjects were then asked to rate their list of visual images by a 7-point continuum from volitional to nonvolitional control over imagery formation. This involved a further specification of instructions through discussion of this dimension and the rating scale. (The reader should note that at this point in the experiment subjects could guess the purpose of the investigator, and the probability of bias increases accordingly.) Subjects rated images after the stress film as significantly more intrusive and involuntary than images after the neutral film (Table 5). While some bias effects are likely, this finding is entirely consistent with the results based on content analysis of reports during the phase of general instructions. Also, in postexperiment discussion many subjects stated that even at

Table 4   Comparison of Visual Images*

	No. Visual Images†		
	After Trauma Film	After Neutral Film	Frequency Ratio
Content analysts (general instructions)	15	6	0.40
Subjects report (specific instructions)	31	12	0.39
Frequency ratio	0.48	0.50	

*From Horowitz. 1969. Arch. Gen. Psychiat., 20:552-559.
†Tallied by content analysts for the period of general instructions with images as reported by subjects after increased specificity of instructions.

this point they had not reached any conclusions about the "purpose" or "right outcome" of the experiment.

SUBJECTIVE RATING OF EMOTIONAL AND VISUAL INTENSITY OF SCENES IN THE TRAUMATIC FILM

Subjects were given a form that listed each of the scenes and assigned an arbitrary intensity of "500" to the first rather neutral scene, in which men sit and beat sticks rhythmically on the ground. Subjects assigned a greater or lesser value as to whether each successive scene was relatively more or less intense than this standard. The "value" or number was used as a device to rank order scenes. Table 6 indicates the intensity of each scene of the traumatic film. The most "traumatic" scenes, selected by this method, were: the penis-bleeding scene (ranked highest by most subjects in all three categories), two separate scenes of boys writhing and wincing with pain, and three separate penis-cutting scenes. These were the scenes that had been reported previously to come back as unbidden visual images on the introspective reports.

EXTENDED EFFECTS OF THE EXPERIENCE. Subjects completed a questionnaire 24 hours after the experiment. The 22 questions were based on statements made by pilot subjects during an earlier pretest and concern recall of the film as well as emotional response to it.

All subjects reported that as time passed they had less and less thoughts about the film. About two-thirds of the subjects indicated that when they did recall the film the scenes returned to mind as vivid visual images. One quarter of the subjects reported that visual images of the

Table 5   Voluntary-Involuntary Ratings of
Control Over Imagery Formation*

| | No. of Times Cited | | |
Item on Scale	After Neutral Film	After Traumatic Film†	Total
1. The image was deliberate.	2	6	8
2. The image was related to the stream of thought at the moment.	2	1	3
3. The image happened to occur.	5	4	9
4. The image popped into mind.	2	4	6
5. The image intruded into mind.	1	6	7
6. The image forced its way into awareness.	0	5	5
7. The image was insistent and hard to get rid of (dispel).	0	5	5
Total	12	31	43

*From Horowitz. 1969. Arch. Gen. Psychiat., 20:552-559.
†Significance that images rated as more involuntary after traumatic film: $p < 0.05$ by point biserial coefficient of correlation.

film intruded into awareness in an involuntary or peremptory manner during this one-day period. Some subjects recorded their experiences in additional detail, and the following anecdotes convey the type of data.

Table 6   Intensity of Traumatic Film Scenes*

| | Mean Rank Order† | | |
Scene	Visual Vividness Now	Emotional Intensity While Viewing Film	Emotional Intensity Now
1. Standard scene—ground beating	12.5	12.0	10
2. Platform	10.0	11.0	11
3. Cutting‡	5.5	5.0	6
4. By fire	7.5	7.0	7
5. Platform	12.5	10.0	12
6. Cutting‡	5.5	4.0	4
7. In pain‡	1.0	2.0	3
8. By fire	9.0	8.5	9
9. Cutting‡	4.0	6.0	2
10. In pain‡	3.0	3.0	5
11. By fire	7.5	8.5	8
12. Bleeding‡	2.0	1.0	1
13. Hairbinding	11.0	13.0	13

*From Horowitz. 1969. Arch. Gen. Psychiat., 20:552-559.
†1 = most intense; 13 = least intense.
‡Most intense scenes.

A. A male subject related scenes from the traumatic film to a friend and tried to emphasize the pleasant, friendly quality of the old men in relation to the adolescents. Whenever he would call to mind such a positively charged scene, an unpleasant image (such as an image of the penis-bleeding scene) would interfere by intruding vividly into his awareness.

B. A male subject at a party was watching a pretty girl and having an erotic fantasy of caressing her leg when an unbidden image of a penis-cutting scene came to him, destroying the feeling of erotic arousal and evoking anxious feelings.

C. A male subject was taking a bath and had a similar intrusive image of a penis-cutting scene.

D. A female subject wrote: "Immediately following the film I experienced a trance-like situation in which I found myself staring into space visualizing quite vividly the actual act of subincision, the writhing agony of the victim afterward, and the ghastly bleeding, oozing wounds, over and over again. I had no control over this situation, and it was broken by others' attempts to engage me in conversation. Since then the same scenes have returned to my consciousness three or four times but I was in control of them. They are even recalled by my explaining my experiences to a friend."

DISCUSSION

These results support the hypothesis that a traumatic film is more likely to be followed by intrusive or unbidden visual images than a neutral film. Perceptual performance, however, was not impaired. Some individual subjects did make more errors after the traumatic film, but they were cancelled out by subjects who "tightened up" their performance and made fewer errors. The increase in errors during the third unit of each four-segment period of signal detection seems incidental. Possibly, this is a relaxation (or fatigue) effect: subjects knew there would be four segments, and they might have relaxed progressively only to alert themselves during the fourth segment to anticipate novel situations that might follow.

Could the data result from a nonspecific effect of trauma, such as a nonspecific increase in subsequent mental activity? If subjects increased their general response output and the experimenter only did a content analysis for specific contents, then a false impression of a specific increase in such responses might result. To partially control for such a source of error, the variation in reports of visual images was compared with the variation in reports of task irrelevant thoughts (as shown in Table 2). No significant variation in the number of task irrelevant thoughts between the post-traumatic and postneutral film periods was found, but a significant variation in the number of visual images was reported. This supports the thesis that the increase in reports of images and intrusive thoughts after the traumatic film was not due merely to a nonspecific increase in output after stress.

Another source of concern in interpretation of results is the possibility of a bias toward compliance in the subjects. Rosenthal (1966) has demonstrated how subjects and assistants may consciously or unconsciously comply with the wishes of the investigator. This experiment only partially controlled for such bias by gradually increasing the explicitness of instructions and comparing data from each phase of the experiment. The data on visual imagery from the period of general instructions did show a similar distribution to that of the later period of specific instructions. Subjects could, however, intuit expectations during the period of general instructions. Only replication with alteration of demand characteristics and personnel can fully control for this hazard of compliance.*

RECAPITULATION

Clinical studies suggest that traumatic visual perceptions have a tendency to return to awareness as unbidden visual images and that various defensive or controlling measures may be activated in response to this tendency. In this experimental study, it was predicted that subjects would report more unbidden images after seeing a stress film than after a neutral film. Twenty-one college students saw both a trauma film and a neutral film in a counterbalanced design. They reported more visual images and more intrusive thoughts after the trauma film but did not make more errors on a perceptual matching task or increase the number of task irrelevant thoughts during the post-trauma period. Subjects rated more of their visual images as having a peremptory quality after the trauma film than after the neutral film, and many subjects reported periodic returns of visual imagery from the trauma film during the ensuing 24 hours. These findings strengthen the theory that traumatic perceptions have a tendency to return to awareness as vivid and potentially intrusive images and, more generally, that psychic trauma tends to be reenacted.

---

* We have done such a replication. The results support the conclusions about return of intrusive images after a stress film.

EXPERIMENT 2: IMAGE FORMATION
AFTER STRESS FILMS*

Experiment 1 indicated that unbidden images tend to follow a traumatic film. These images penetrated into awareness while the subjects were engaged in a tone-matching task requiring direction of attention outward toward a series of external stimuli. The next study was undertaken to see if the unbidden image effect occurs when attention is not directed outward but rather inward during the postfilm period. The method involves a situation in which the experimenter structures the format of image formation but not the contents of images. My purpose was to see if an unbidden image effect would occur when subjects were instructed to engage in free image formation. A secondary purpose was to see if intrusive images (if observed) would be less prevalent after watching a stress film in a response-suppression condition.

SUBJECTS

Ten student nurses were asked to volunteer for an experiment on trauma. We selected this group because student nurses are especially trusting, frank, and open in their introspective reports. Other student nurses were paired with the subjects as observers; they looked at the experimental subjects, but not at the films.

STIMULI

Three films were used. Each was in black and white, cut to equal length, and shown without sound. The neutral film called *The Runner* was always shown on the first experimental day. On days two and three, one of two stress films were shown. One was *Subincision*, the film used in the previously described study. The other was *Accident*, which depicts a bloody series of three woodshop injuries.

---

* This study was undertaken in collaboration with Dr. Paul Ekman and Wallace Friesen, who wanted to study nonverbal behavior of subjects while watching stressful films. Sandra Newman and Judith Klein assisted throughout.

CONDITIONS

While seeing the film, the experimental subjects were watched by an observer who sat out of sight of the screen. On day one, while seeing the neutral film, and on day two, while seeing the first stress film—either *Subincision* or *Accident*—the experimental subjects were instructed to be naturally responsive to the experience and to be open to the observer in terms of their facial expression, muscular tension or movement, and verbal communication. On day three, on seeing the other stress film, they were instructed to suppress any stress responses and to appear to the observer as if they were viewing a neutral film.

PROCEDURES

Immediately after the films, the subjects had a brief interview to assess the degree of their immediate response to the films. Then they were instructed in the image formation task and, in every condition, were asked to be open and complete in their introspective reports.

The image formation task consisted of six segments. Each segment contained a 30-second period of silent imagery formation. The instructions were, "Don't try and form any particular image, let an image come spontaneously to your mind. Once an image comes to mind, let it become as vivid as possible." After 30 seconds the subject was asked to describe the image in detail, verbally. This was written down verbatim. The subject was asked to rest for 15 seconds, then asked to report what came to mind during the rest period. Before beginning, the subject was shown rating scales that she would use later to rate images for unbiddenness, vividness, duration, pleasantness, and unpleasantness. These ratings were retroactively applied after completion of the series of six images.

RESULTS

Table 7 condenses the outline of the experiment and the relevant data. Images formed after the stress film condition were rated by subjects as more "unbidden," on a 7-point scale, than images after the neutral film condition or the suppression condition. Vividness and duration ratings did not differ significantly. There were an increased number of images rated as unpleasant after the stress and suppression conditions, but, as

Table 7   Self Rating and Content Analysis of Images After the Films

		Self Rating	Content Analysis	
Day	Film Condition	Mean Rating of Unbiddenness	Mean, Film References	Mean, Intrusive Thoughts
1	Neutral (Runner)	3.3	1.7	0.6
		$-$p $<$ .01*	$-$p $<$ .01‡	$-$p $<$ .05
2	Stress (Accident or Subincision)	3.8	5.3	2.1
		$-$p $<$ .01	$-$NS	$-$NS
3	Stress-suppress (Subincision or Accident)	3.2	4.3	1.3

Each subject used as his own control, n = 10.
*Paired t tests.
‡Sign tests.

some images were also rated as more pleasant, the group means did not differ significantly. This is an interesting observation to be clarified by description of clinical data.

The content analysis manual was used to score images and "rest" reports for film references and intrusive thoughts. Because film references is a straightforward content item, only one judge, who was uninvolved in the experiment, counted these items. Intrusive thoughts require more refinement of judgment, so two content analysts independently tallied for this item. They had similar distributions, and the scores presented in Table 7 contain the mean of both judges.

In the period after seeing the stressful film, subjects had significantly more film references. As with self-reports, the effect is greater following the non-suppression stress condition than after the suppression condition.

More intrusive thoughts were tallied in the stress condition, a mean of 2.1 per subject. This was significantly greater than the mean of 0.6 for the neutral film condition and did not differ significantly from the mean of 1.3 for the stress-suppression condition. As an additional measure, subjects were rank-ordered according to their total scores for "unbiddenness" of images after stress, and this ranking was compared to their rank order by the number of intrusions tallied after stress conditions by the content analysts. These ranks correlated significantly: subjects who rated themselves higher on unbiddenness of images were tallied as having more intrusive reports by content analysts (Spearman rank correlation coefficient, $r = .647$, $p < .05$). Also, as would be expected, rank order determined by the number of intrusions after stress films correlated with that determined by the number of film references during imagery formation ($r = .782$, $p < .01$).

DISCUSSION

Two experiments support the hypothesis that traumatic films tend to be followed by intrusive revisualizations of unpleasant scenes. Experiment 1 obtained image reports from periods in which subjects were instructed to focus attention outward, while experiment 2 involved attention inward and specific instructions to form images.*

One subject's data are summarized here to provide illustrations of how images from the film return during the image formation period. The subject is a 24-year-old, married student nurse. She had just seen the nonstressful film before reporting these images during the six image-describe-rest-report-rate segments.

> Image 1: "I see something that related to the movie. A lady who was pushing a baby carriage.† See a child's birthday party, about 10 little girls, middle class, one girl opening gifts, in a living room." Rest period report: "I was recalling some of the pleasureful moments of the movie, country scenes, camera zeroed in on trees, pictured this in color." (Movie was in black and white.) She rated this first image on the un-biddenness scale as "6." A relatively intrusive rating: "The image forced its way into awareness." She added as a descriptive adjective the word "sad."

The remaining images after the neutral film are summarized:

> 2. A group of nursing students eating, in color. Rest—standing with her husband in a cave.
> 3. A nursery school with little kids. Rest—thinking of a coat.
> 4. Walking through a blizzard. Rest—the emergency room comes to mind.
> 5. A park with kids in funny clothes, a memory of a fight. Rest—wonders what's going on in the experiment.
> 6. A ski house in the mountains, herself singing. Rest—thought of her husband chasing a cat.

These five images were all rated "2" which signifies "related to the stream of thought." The next day this subject saw the subincision film. Here is her first image thereafter.

> 1. "I'm obviously thinking of that godawful gory movie. The boy's face screwed up in pain, from the waist up, everything the way it was on the screen."
> Rest: "I'm thinking I can't stand to see things like that. It ruins my day,

---

* Replication of both experiments using different subjects (30 in experiment 1, 20 in experiment 2) has yielded similarly significant results.
† A wistful scene in the nonstressful movie.

supposed to meet my husband. Don't feel so hot, I'm mad. The first movie wasn't unpleasant."
She rated this image as intrusive, "6, the image forced its way into awareness." The descriptive adjective was "helpless."

The succeeding images are summarized:

2. Sitting at dinner with husband; rated this as "1, the image was deliberate."
3. Little boy in pain, trying to forget it.* She rated this image as maximally intrusive "7, the image was insistent and hard to get rid of (dispel)."
4. A party, and a man playing guitar. Rated as "1, deliberate."
5. Husband lying in hospital bed, he's moaning. This image is rated as maximally intrusive "7."
6. Drawers, closets, and desks in her apartment. Things are broken. She rated this image as "2, related to stream of thought," on the unbiddenness scale, and reported her resting thoughts as: "I'm grasping at straws now. Glad I can think about (something) instead of about movie."

Even in this brief vignette, a common series of cognitive processes is illustrated. At first she has an intrusive image derived from one of the more shocking film scenes. She defends herself, perhaps, by seeing the scene only from the waist up. She then deliberately forms a pleasant image that is distant from the recent perceptions: dinner with her husband. The next image, however, is again a peremptory intrusion from the film. Following this, there is again an image more pleasant and distant. The fifth and sixth images apparently relate the concept of traumatization to herself and her husband.

This process is repeated after the third movie, *Accident,* seen in the stress-suppression condition. The first two images are rated as intrusive ("6" and "7") and are of the accidents depicted in the film. The third image was of herself being looked at by the observer and was rated as deliberate. The fourth image is again an intrusion: "Still seeing those men pushing boards, can't get rid of them, not really the bloody scene. Just the same as it was on the screen." This was rated "5, the image intruded into mind." The last two images, in which she visualizes herself as a patient in the hospital, and visualizes herself looking at her observer during the suppression period, are rated as deliberate.

This subject returned a questionnaire filled out by subjects 24 hours after seeing the last stress film. She reported that vivid remembrance of the film occurred and was hard to dispel, that she had flickering or very brief, hard-to-hold-onto images of the film, and that she was reluctant to let her thoughts just wander for a period of time after the film.

The counterbalancing, after the stress film, of intrusive, unpleasant images with deliberate, pleasant images is a very interesting feature seen

---

* Scene from stress film.

also in other subjects. The semistructured image formation task permits this type of observation. Perhaps it is merely an avoidance maneuver. Perhaps it is an adaptational technique that: a) permits dosing of re-visualizations within tolerable limits, and/or b) reduces anxiety by temporal association of unpleasant images with pleasant ones.*

APPENDIX TO CHAPTER 9
Manual for Content Analysis

You will be reading reports of thoughts by subjects in an experiment in which they see several films. You are asked to tally the number of times they have a task irrelevant thought, an intrusive thought, a visual image, a film reference, or forgetting. The order of the material as given to you is random and not that of production. Successive comments do not necessarily come from the same subjects. Please follow the enclosed guidelines for making judgments, whether or not you happen to agree with the theory behind the statement or the way in which the words are used.

In all that follows, you will be given a unit of thought that may be a phrase, a sentence, or a short paragraph. Score each unit separately in terms of each of the five categories, without regard to previous scorings. One unit of thought may be scored in more than one category. For example, a unit may be scored as a visual image, an intrusive thought, and a task irrelevant thought. Thus one unit may not be scored in any category, or it may be scored in one, two, three, four, or five categories.

Some judgments will be obvious; others will require more inferential decisions. Score each unit as accurately and fully as possible, being careful not to skip over any units. (Often reading the protocols out loud prevents skipping. This may seem tedious, but it prevents costly errors.) If you are in doubt, don't hesitate to refer back to this manual, and in general, refer back to the manual periodically. Above all, *please don't rush.*

HOW TO SCORE FOR FILM REFERENCES

Tally any unit that refers to the immediate films or the immediate film experience.

---

* This topic of dosing visualization of unpleasant scenes and of juxtaposing pleasant with unpleasant ones will be considered in terms of therapeutic techniques in Chapter 14 on guided image formation.

Score *anticipatory remarks* such as, "So, you're going to show us movies."

Score references to *film content*. (You will be given a description of the films used.)

Score references to *film setting*.

Do *not* score references to other film experiences such as, "I saw 'The Graduate' last night."

HOW TO SCORE FOR FORGETTING OR WANDERING ITEMS

Score as forgetting or wandering any evidence that the subject experienced forgetting of mental contents or loss of his train of thought. For example, *score* the following in this category:

"I forgot."

"I forgot something I was thinking of."

"My mind wandered."

"I went blank."

"I'm blank now."

"I don't remember."

"Something else, but can't get back to it."

"It's become too vague to recall now."

HOW TO SCORE FOR TASK IRRELEVANT THOUGHTS

The reports you are given may refer to a task in which subjects listen to auditory tones, match one tone with another, and record the symbols for "same," "higher," or "lower" on a form. A thought is task *relevant* if any element of it refers to any aspects of the tone matching task. A thought is *irrelevant* if there is no such reference. For example, *score* as *task irrelevant*:

"Wonder why we are shown these films"

"I thought of a jelly sandwich."

Do *not* score items which contain task referents even if the thought seems to wander off. For example, do *not* score:

"Matching the tones was boring."

"We did such matching in Psych. 1-A"

"I wish the tones came in waltz rhythm"

These statements do refer to the tone matching task and are therefore not task irrelevant.

HOW TO SCORE FOR INTRUSIVE THOUGHTS

This category is based less on content and more on inference about how the thought was experienced by the subject. We will consider a thought as "intrusive" if it has one or more of the following characteristics:

a. Non-volitional entry into awareness
b. Requires suppressive effort
c. The mental event of having the thought is experienced as something to be avoided (in the future)
d. The thought recurs

a. Categorize a thought report as intrusive if there is any evidence or inference of surprise or nonvolitional quality. Do so whether the thought content is pleasant or unpleasant. You may categorize a report as intrusive if it had any of these qualities: sudden entry into awareness, haunting, surprising, disclaimer of responsibility, not self-generated.

The following examples would be scored as intrusive:

"I was startled to find myself thinking of my childhood."
"The memory of her beautiful face haunted me."
"The answer came to me in a flash."
"I couldn't help seeing the scene again."
"Something made me think of spaceships."
"Wow! Why'd I think of Martians just then?"
"The radio-waves entered my head and made me think of . . ."

b. Call a report intrusive if there is any evidence that a thought was hard to dispel. Include suppressive efforts whether or not they are fully successful. For example, you would rate as intrusive:

"I can't get her out of my mind"
"I forced the thought from me."

Do *not* rate as intrusive remarks that only reflect *long-term character attitudes*. "I never think of sex" would not be categorized as an intrusive report. *However*, you would rate "I wouldn't think of sex at a time like this" if you think this statement indicates a current effort at suppression of ideas about sex. Mere illusions to propriety are not intrusive unless these are experienced by the subject as his own current attitude. For example, "One really shouldn't think of sex, heh! heh!" would not be rated.

c. Score as intrusive if in your judgment the subject experienced the thought as *something to be avoided* (in the future). Distinguish between the content of his thought and his reaction to the thought. Do not necessarily categorize thoughts with unpleasant content as intrusive. For example, *score* as intrusive: "I can't bear to think about the war," but do not necessarily so rate, "I thought of how terrible war is."

Other examples of intrusive thoughts are:

"I don't want to have to think about that thought again"

Extremely grisly and bizarre thoughts may be by definition categorized as intrusive unless they are reported in a bland manner. For example, *score:*

"My poor dog, squashed to death"

d. Score as intrusive a thought that recurs. Do not score the first thought, but *score* its *repetition.* For example,

"Thought of a baby carriage. Wonder why the tones are spaced so strangely apart. Thought of the baby carriage again."

The second reference to the baby carriage would be scored as an intrusive thought.

HOW TO SCORE FOR VISUAL IMAGES

The purpose of this item analysis is to assess the frequency of visual imagery reports in reports of introspective mental contents. Subjects differ in the style in which they report their mental contents and also in their style of linguistic usage. Two major problems arise in deciding to score a given report as a visual image:

a. Some visual images may be reported vaguely without definition of the sensory quality of the mental representation.

b. Some thoughts, those not experienced with visual sensory quality, may be described in the communicative process with words suggestive of the visual sphere such as "I see."

It is necessary to make a clinical "best guess" as to whether or not the subject has a visual thought image. The following offers some guidelines.

a. Remember in deciding to score a given fragment of report as visual imagery or not that subjects have not been given detailed instructions on how to describe their own reports. You may have to infer that they probably had a visual image and never can be sure if you are right or not.

b. Do not score an item as a visual image just because it has words in it such as "see," "saw" or similar visual words. For example: "Now I see why men from Mars landed on Earth." This should NOT be scored as a visual image. "I saw men from Mars" *should* be scored as a visual image.

c. If a subject describes a mental content with reference to its form, shape, color, or concrete quality, then this may be scored as a visual image even if its visual quality is not explicitly stated. For example: "Thought of men from Mars, dressed in blue," or ". . . a round spaceship moving slowly."

d. If a subject indicates a series of two or more associations that sound as though the thought process was visual, then score as a visual image. For example: "A doorway—then a man entering."

e. If a subject indicates that he tried to form a visual image or indicates efforts at visualization, then score this as a visual image. For example: "Tried to visualize the fourth dimension."

f. But, if a subject states he is avoiding a visualization (without indicating that he is having one), then do not categorize this as a visual image. For example, if he says, "I'm trying not to let myself see the spaceship again," don't call this a visual image. In contrast, a remark such as, "It's hard for me to dispel the spaceship image," should be called a visual image.

REFERENCES

Antrobus, J. S., Singer, J. L., and Greenberg, S. 1966. Studies in the stream of consciousness; experimental enhancement and suppression of spontaneous cognitive processes. *Percept. Motor Skills*, 23:399–417.

Cartwright, R. D., Bernick, N., Bokowitz, G., and Kling, A. 1969. Effect of an erotic movie on the sleep and dreams of young men. *Arch. Gen. Psychiat.*, 20:262–271.

Folkins, C. H. et al. 1968. Desensitization and the experimental reduction of threat. *J. Abnorm. Psychol.*, 73:100–113.

Freud, S. (1920) Beyond the pleasure principle. *Stand. Ed.*, 18, 1962.

—— and Breuer, J. (1895) Studies in hysteria. *Stand. Ed.*, 2, 1964.

Glover, E. 1929. The screening function of traumatic memories. *Int. J. Psychoanal.*, 10:90–93.

Goldstein, M. J., et al. 1965. Coping style as a factor in psychophysiological response to a tension-arousing film. *J. Pers. Soc. Psychol.*, 1:290–302.

Lazarus, R. S., and Opton, E. M. 1968. The use of motion picture films in the study of psychological stress: A summary of experimental studies and theoretical formulations. In Spielberger, C., ed. *Anxiety and Behavior*. New York, Academic Press.

Murphy, W. F. 1958. Character, trauma, and sensory perception. *Int. J. Psychoanal.*, 39:555–568.

Niederland, W. G. 1968. Clinical observations on the "survivor syndrome." *Int. J. Psychoanal.*, 49:313–315.

Rosenthal, R. 1966. *Experimenter Effects in Behavioral Research*. New York, Appleton-Century-Crofts.
Tomkins, S. S. 1962. *Affect, Imagery, Consciousness*. New York, Springer Publishing Co.
Underwood, B. 1969. Attributes of memory. *Psychol. Rev.*, 76:559–573.
Witkin, H. A., and Lewis, H. B. 1965. The relation of experimentally induced presleep experiences to dreams. *J. Amer. Psychoanal. Assoc.*, 13:819–849.

PART
III
Neurobiologic
Influences on
Image Formation

10

The Contribution of the Eye

In the previous chapter I described how intense perceptions emerged later as internal images. This chapter describes how perceptions can be made into internal images at once. These two processes, perception and image formation, occupy to some extent the same channels of consciousness and the same routes of information processing. Of course, some kinds of perceptual input reduce internal image formation by occupying channel capacity and attention. But other kinds of perceptual input augment internal image formation either by triggering motives or by providing a kind of sensory raw material for fantasy. The less definitive, in terms of configuration, the external input, the more likely that something of motivational relevance can be made out of it. The usual form of internal completion of an external stimulus is called an illusion and I shall begin with a general consideration of this phenomenon. Next I will consider in detail a special form of illusion in which the "external" source of perceptual raw material is inside the body, in the optic apparatus itself.

PERCEPTION AND ILLUSION

After considerable psychologic and neurobiologic research, it is now clear that perception is not a passive but an active process. An external signal undergoes many transformations, transportations, interpretations, and recombinations before a person experiences seeing, and any reader interested in image formation will eventually wish to consult texts on perception.*

We will begin our considerations at a point after perceptual processes have gathered a tremendous array of particulate information, some accurate and some inaccurate in terms of correspondence to external objects, and when cognitive processes strive to reduce and organize this information for meaningful labeling and conscious sampling. One means of organizing bits of perceptual stimuli is to assemble the stimuli according to patterns and forms. These forms may be inherent, part of the visual processing system built in by heredity, or they may be acquired through experience and perceptual learning (Koffka, 1935; Kohler, 1969).

The familiar patterns and forms serve as schemata or templates and those signals that fit the schemata may be facilitated while those that fall outside of its boundaries may be inhibited, a series of trials may establish the best fit of schemata to signal. The signals falling outside the schemata are regarded as "noise" and omissions from the usual pattern or form may be added to the perceptual image from internal rather than external sources. Without such schemata, perception might be, in the words of William James, "a blooming, buzzing confusion."

An example of the need for perceptual schemata is provided by Von Senden (Hebb, 1959) who removed the congenital cataracts that had blinded certain patients from birth. After surgical restoration of sight, these patients could not, at first, interpret with their eyes what they could interpret by touch. To label a block as "a square," a patient might not only have to look at it but count the corners and reason that four corners make a square, not a triangle.

Another example of the need for schemata of interpretation occurs in research on normally sighted persons. Kohler (1964) fitted his subjects with mirrors that altered their vision dramatically—the mirrors turned everything upside down. For several days his subjects were perceptually confused, but when their interpretive systems compensated for the altered format of stimuli, they once again used their eyes automatically to label visual stimuli. When the glasses were removed and the world resumed its "normal" tilt, the interpretation and labeling systems required a new period of adjustment.

Symmetry is important to schemata, as demonstrated by the completion effect. If a person cannot see part of his visual field, as in partial blindness, a form in the area of intact vision tends to be "seen" in the blind area, completed in a regular way (Williams and Gassel, 1962; Warrington, 1962).

---

* Excellent resources include texts by Neisser (1967), Haber (1968), Vernon (1962), Gregory (1966), Heaton (1968), and Granit (1955).

When a person misapplies old schemata to a new set of stimuli, we call the resulting image an illusion. In consensually valid illusions, certain configurations, such as unusual shifts in perspective, "play tricks" on the visual processes. Such illusions are usually geometric and are of interest because they indicate properties of the optical pathways. Like the examples so far, they are, in essence, errors of perception not necessarily bound into a person's feeling state or ideational state. The Müller-Lyer and Herring illusions are classic examples. Lines of equal length appear different because of differences in surrounding forms. These illusions are "consensually valid" because everyone can "see" the illusion (Luckiesh, 1922).

Idiosyncratic illusions commonly take place within an individual. One example is interpreting a shadow from a tree as a threatening human figure, another, identifying a stranger's face as that of a friend. These illusions are of interest to clinicians because they frequently reflect current motivations and concerns. The schemata for organization of signals into perceptual images are influenced by expectancy. Sometimes an illusion occurs because of wishful expectancy: a person tends to see what he desires. At other times expectancy is influenced more by fear than by wish, and a person may have an illusion of what he dreads. Logical reasoning, conditioning, and incipient conceptualizations also influence expectancy. I use this term, incipient conceptualizations, to indicate the press of certain ideas or feelings towards representation. In Chapter 5 I described how concepts may gain representation in thought through images, words, or anticipatory behaviors. Concepts may also gain representation through perception.

Suppose there is an incipient conceptualization—an idea or feeling not yet clearly represented in thought by words or images—that influences perceptual expectancy. A person may tend to focus selectively on some particular aspect of the environment that expresses the incipient idea. In a sense, the concept is projected onto the environment and "found" rather than "formed" as a thought. The woman who saw the sign "Evangelist's Services," in Chapter 6, is one example. Thus, a pre-representational thought can be represented through selective perception, and, in the case of defensive avoidance, the opposite process of selective nonperception may take place.

Ordinarily, selective perception does not grossly change the quality of external objects. In some states, however, perception is distorted by the incipient conceptualization, and an illusion occurs. Here is an everyday example:

> A young man had broken up with his girlfriend after a fierce fight. He dreaded the thought of running into her on the street because she might

continue to recriminate him. He also missed her and wanted to see her again. He was not thinking consciously of such matters, however, as he walked along a main boulevard. He thought he saw her half a block away walking towards him. His heart began to pound as he saw on her face a look of recognition and anger. Then he realized that he was staring at a stranger who was not looking at him and did not even resemble his girlfriend.

In the above illusion, the incipient conceptualization could continue to dominate the conscious perceptual image as long as the signal was relatively indistinct: as long as the real woman was so far away that he could not distinctly see her features. As the distance narrowed, the signals presenting her features became so clear that his conscious image shifted towards presentation of reality, and the girlfriend image was dispelled. This example illustrates the effects of both wishful and fearful expectancy and how they tend to increase the formation of illusions (Allport, 1955).

Illusions also tend to occur in states where signals are unclear because of dimness, brevity, or a low signal to noise ratio. Segal (1968a, 1968b, 1969) replicated and extended Perky's (1910) demonstration that normal subjects may confuse internal and external images when external signals are dim. In her experiment, a normal subject inserts his face into a partially translucent hood on which the experimenter can project various stimuli. The illumination of projections can be slowly increased until the stimuli are barely visible. Subjects can be told to imagine objects, to report any projections, and asked to differentiate the two sources. In this condition, subjects produce a variety of interesting illusionary effects. Sometimes a subject reports as an internal thought image what is actually being projected onto the hood. At other times, subjects report as stimuli projected on the hood, images that are in reality internally, and not externally, stimulated. A subject may combine the external and internal stimuli to form an illusion. For example, he might be trying to form an image of a red tomato when the experimenter projects, very dimly, an outline of the city skyline. The subject might then report that he sees the skyline of New York with a red sun setting.

Segal (1969) also found that when subjects form visual images, they score less correct reports on dim external visual perceptions; when they form internal auditory images, correct visual perception is not as impaired. These data show how image formation influences perception and how perception influences image formation.

Segal's experiments relate, in part, to subliminal perceptions, those registrations not recognized in conscious awareness which, nonetheless, influence subsequent image formation. Pötzl et al. (1960), working early in this century, found that subjects might not recognize certain visual stimuli, and yet evidence for these stimuli might be found in their subsequent internal images. Fisher and Paul (1959) replicated and extended this work. They found that very brief perceptions, that could not be consciously deciphered, emerged later in images and dreams and often were elaborated and transformed towards the subject's current motivational needs. Subjects tended to treat supraliminal or conscious perceptions logically, but they tended to absorb subliminal perceptions into fantasy thinking (Fisher and Paul, 1959; Paul and Fisher, 1959). Even when supraliminal stimuli are projected at the same time as subliminal stimuli, the impression of the subliminal stimuli is still incorporated into subsequent image formation and fantasy. Eagle (1962) found that simple, striking, emotionally-charged subliminal stimuli seemed to have greater subsequent effects on image formation and fantasy than well-defined and supraliminal stimuli. When supraliminal stimuli were vague, however, they too seemed to invite fantasy.

To summarize, perceptual events may influence image formation, and internal images may influence the interpretation of perceptual stimuli. People may get the two processes mixed up, and may interpret or appraise internal images as real perceptions, or real perceptions as internal images.

So far we have only considered stimuli from sources outside of a person's body. Perceptual stimuli may also arise from within the person's body and be formed into an illusion.

THE POSSIBLE INFLUENCE OF EYE MOVEMENTS ON IMAGE FORMATION

The reader may wish to recall, at this point, the possible relationship between eye movements and the formation of dream images described in Chapter 3. What is relevant to the topic of this chapter is that it has been occasionally possible to relate the direction of the eye movement to depictions of movement in the concurrent dream experience (Roffwarg et al., 1962). Are the eyes following the motions of hallucinatory dream objects? Or is it possible that the eye movements contribute stimuli that influence the selection of dream contents? Electroencephalographic data from electrodes placed in various brain locations of animals suggest that the subcortical events may arise first with cortical excitation appearing soon afterwards. It does seem possible, then, that the eye movements are not in pursuit of the already formed dream images but instead may influence or even evoke certain images.*

---

* The coincidence of visual hallucinatory dreaming with rapid eye movement sleep led to several speculations and studies concerning the possible coincidence of schizophrenic hallucinations with eye movements. For example, Wallach et al. (1960) report that there are involuntary eye movements similar to REMs in certain schizophrenics during periods of disturbed behavior. This study has not been replicated in the work of others, however, and correlations between eye movements and periods of wakeful visual thought images are inconclusive. Antrobus and Singer (1964) for example, find that eye movements are more likely to accompany efforts to suppress internal images than efforts to evoke them.

Whatever the role of eye movements, we know that the retina (or optical system) itself provides elementary sensations. The entoptic images are sometimes among the first subjective experiences during an altered state of consciousness that leads to hallucinatory images. For example, after taking LSD a person may have altered perception and entoptic images prior to experiencing hallucinations. A similar series of events occasionally occurs in hypnagogic states. Under certain circumstances, the raw sensory material supplied by entoptic phenomenon might be elaborated into a hallucinatory experience. As stated earlier, by very technical definition the elaboration of an entoptic image into an object-depicting image would be called an illusion. I use the word hallucination, however, because I will be discussing subjective experiences that are usually described by clinicians as hallucinations. Also the "external sensation" component is not external to the body, although it is peripheral to the psyche or mind. The remainder of this chapter considers this possibility.

ENTOPTIC PHENOMENA AS PERCEPTUAL CONTRIBUTANTS TO IMAGE FORMATION*

As early as 1887, Hoope suggested that the physical eye might furnish the material on which hallucinations are based (Klüver, 1942) and Hughlings Jackson (1932) described how floaters (muscae volitantes) in the eye might develop into visions of rats. My own clinical experiences suggest the same hypothesis: that some complex image experiences contain a nidus or matrix of simple sensations.

When first questioning patients about their visual experiences, I found it helpful to persist beyond initial verbal descriptions of hallucinations, and to insist that the patient draw exactly what he imaged. For example, verbal description of "vicious snakes" might be drawn as wavy lines; the visual images of moving sets of dots might translate verbally to "two armies struggling over my soul"; "spiders" might reduce to a few radiating lines. Patients could sometimes distinguish a form that they "saw with their eyes" from the more elaborate images described as their hallucinations. If the same hallucination recurred, it might become simpler as their clinical state improved. Below are some case examples.

* Portions of the following material were reported in a paper published and copyrighted by the Williams and Wilkins Co. in the *J. Nerv. Ment. Dis.*, 138:513–520, 1964. The research was supported by a grant from the Office of Naval Research (NR 105 156).

CASE 1

A young man was diagnosed as having a borderline and schizoid personality underlying an acute psychotic episode. The first symptom occurred when he had been brooding over the traumatic death of his older brother and staring at the fire in a fireplace. He saw the jagged peaks of the flames as the shape of a menacing dragon and, in spite of his efforts to blink it way, the dragon spontaneously reappeared before his eyes several times during the next few days. During the acute state of his illness, he again felt threatened by "heads" which were prominent afterimages or double visions of real objects. Figure 1A represents the patient's drawing of the dragon event and Figure 1B, the transition of a faucet into a head.

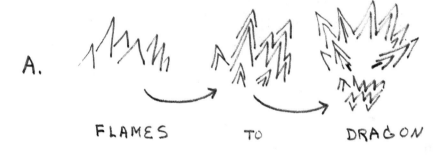

A.

FLAMES   TO   DRAGON

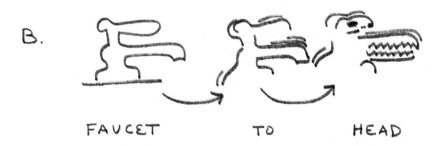

B.

FAUCET   TO   HEAD

Fig. 1. From the patient's drawings of his development of hallucinations (Case 1).

Fig. 2. From drawings of hallucinations of "Bugs" and of "The Holy Trinity" (Case 2).

(DRIFT)

EYEBALL
BURNING

FLAMES

WAVY
LINES

Fig. 3. Excerpts from the patient's drawings showing the transition from the image of "an eyeball burning" to "just wavy lines" (Case 3).

CASE 2

A patient having a schizophrenic episode jerked his gaze to one side periodically during an office interview. When asked why, he replied, "You've got bugs over there!" On another occasion he stated that he saw the faces of the Holy Trinity. The drawings from both occasions of what he saw are identical (Figure 2). Ophthalmologic examination recreated "the bugs," and the same floater configuration seemed to provide the signal basis or matrix for the "bugs" and the "Holy Trinity" images.

CASE 3

A chronic schizophrenic patient told people that he could see his "eyeball burning." Figure 3 represents his drawing; the heavy lines are what he "really saw." As his clinical state improved, he reported that he no longer thought of his eyeball burning and that he saw "just flames" or "just wavy lines."

CASE 4

An 18-year-old enlisted man in the Armed Forces was hospitalized when discovered roaming the streets in a confused and disoriented state. He had "hallucinations" of dots in the corner of his visual field (Figure 4A) which occurred almost constantly during certain hours of the day, especially if he were not occupied in some distracting activity. During an interview he pointed to them with his finger but, when he attempted to focus them, they drifted to the periphery of his visual fields. At times he was convinced they were "cosmic balls of fire sent to punish me." Treatment was started with chlordiazepoxide (Librium), 20 mg four times daily. He reported a marked worsening of the visual disturbances and made drawings of what he saw (Figure 4B). Examination of his visual fields showed a left central scotoma which was confirmed by campimetry (a special study of visual fields) during an ophthalmologic consultation. With the opposite eye closed he could see different figures in each eye (Figure 4C). With an exclamation of surprise, he identified the figure in his right eye as "the snakes" he had been "hallucinating." He then reported a psychotic episode, one and a half years previously, which he had kept secret hoping to remain in the service. He stated he had not had visual hallucinations then until he received medication which, by his description of the capsule colors and recognition of the current medication, had been chlordiazepoxide. After chlordiazepoxide was discontinued, the visual phenomena diminished markedly although the dots persisted; the scotoma disappeared subjec-

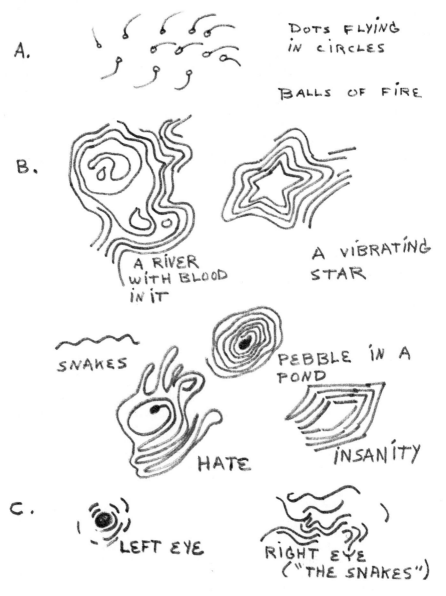

Fig. 4. From the drawings of hallucinations A, B, & C (Case 4).

tively and by campimetry. Later, another dose of chlordiazepoxide caused these particular symptoms to recur, and this medication was permanently discontinued. When the patient was treated with thioridazine, there were no similar effects.

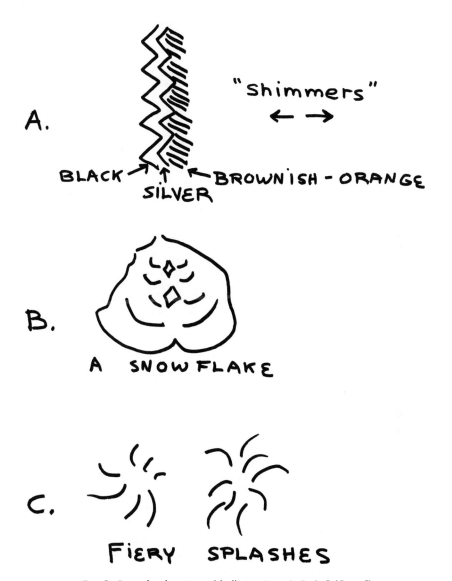

Fig. 5. From the drawings of hallucinations A, B, & C (Case 5).

CASE 5

The patient is a 69-year-old woman with a 20-year documented history of Meniere's disease (a disease of the middle ear that includes dizziness as a major symptom). Her first symptom occurred at the age of 40.

While she was outside gardening, a shrub seemed to move; then, falling black spots appeared from above; then her vision became obscured by what appeared to be smoke and fog. She experienced a tremendous spinning sensation, characterized by the world moving clockwise. As the "fog" cleared, she saw brilliant herringbone scintillations in the periphery of the right eye's visual field and a bright halo around objects (Figure 5A). The attack lasted 20 minutes and recurred two to five times a year thereafter, with some variations. She was intensely frightened, mostly by the herringbone scintillations which she originally interpreted as fire and icicles of metaphysic origin. Occasionally, instead of snow flakes, she would see fiery splashes (Figures 5B and 5C).

CASE 6

A 37-year-old man had a syndrome of severe migraine headaches for 15 years. He knew the onset of the headaches because of a visual aura: whatever he was looking at seemed to become pockmarked or rippled. It was as if drops of rain had fallen onto his perceptual image and caused tiny concentric circles of perceptual distortion in many areas. Then, he often noted bright, fluorescent, starlike flashes. On occasion he had, with his auras, the visual sensation of looking at six-sided honeycomb figures that could create "an endless wallpaper effect."

REDUNDANT ELEMENTS OF FORM

Clinical descriptions such as those illustrated above suggest that some entoptic event, usually ignored, might provide a nidus around which hallucinations, pseudohallucinations, or (technically) illusions develop. Since people commonly experience entoptic phenomena, such as "floaters" or after-images, the following questionnaire was distributed to 80 psychiatric staff members in order to obtain drawings of these experiences in normal subjects.

QUESTIONNAIRE—VISUAL IMPRESSIONS

Name: _____ Age: ____ Sex: ____ Date: _____
1. Draw and describe the visual impressions you sometimes have while falling asleep or waking up.
2. Draw and describe the visual impressions you have had while looking at bright spaces such as the sky, clouds, walls, etc.
3. Draw and describe the visual impressions you have had on being struck on the eyes or head, or on seeing a very bright light.
4. Close your eyes and press on your eyeballs with your thumbs. Draw and describe the visual impressions you get.

5. Have you ever had unusual visual experiences when:
    a. Delirious or confused   d. Alone for a long time
    b. Intoxicated   e. Unrested for a long time
    c. Very ill or feverish   f. Isolated
    Draw and describe your impressions.

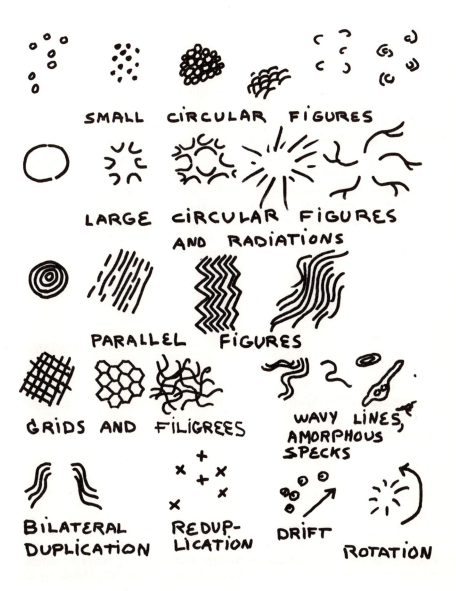

Fig. 6. Redundant elements in hallucinations and visual imagery.

The completed forms and drawings resembled the verbal and graphic descriptions of patients who reported visual hallucinations. The staff tended to interpret visual forms, e.g., calling flashes "stars," wavy lines "snakes," or circular figures "marbles," but this was less pronounced than in the descriptions elicited from patients.

Certain words and graphic forms appeared regularly in the data from normals and in interviews with schizophrenics and other patients. Some redundant words and forms were stars, pinwheels, wheels, marbles, dots, specks, circles, snakes, spiders, worms, bugs, spots, swirls, wavy lines, and filigrees. Many of the descriptions could be categorized as one of Klüver's hallucinatory form constants: spirals, funnels, cobwebs, or lattices. In Figure 6, I show the redundant figural elements in their simplest and most common forms; at times they appear as overlapping, combined, or multiplied. These forms also appear frequently in physiologic or biochemical disturbances as in chemogenic hallucinations (Maclay and Guttman, 1941; Malitz, Wilkens & Esecover, 1962), lesions or stimulation of the brain (Horowitz et al., 1968), retinal stimulation (Horowitz, 1967), toxic or starvation deliria (Miller, 1962; West et al., 1961), and sleep deprivation (Luby et al., 1962). Similar figural elements also occur in eidetic imagery (Nickols, 1962), blank screen effects, hypnogogic hallucinations (Isakower, 1938), the visions in sensory deprivation (Miller, 1962; Solomon et al., 1961), schizophrenic hallucinations (Arieti, 1962; Bleuler, 1950), artistic imagery (Arnheim, 1954; Holstijn, 1951; Langui, 1959); psychotic art (G. Adler, 1948; Anastasi and Foley, 1944; Stern, 1952), and even mystical or "visionary experiences" (Stace, 1960).

DISCUSSION

Clinical material suggests that visual hallucinations and other image experiences may be elaborated from elementary sensations. These elementary sensations might arise either 1) in the retinal ganglionic and post-retinal neural network and/or 2) from anatomic bodies within the eyeball.

RETINAL AND POSTRETINAL GANGLIONIC NETWORK

This is the complicated circuitry of interlacing neurons which is fed by stimuli from the rods and cones and, in turn, connects with the optic nerves. Knoll (1962) and his coworkers (Knoll et al., 1963) continued the nineteenth century work of Volta, Purkinji, and von Helmholz by studying the subjective visual images which arise on mild electric or mechanical stimulation of the optic system. The drawings and descriptions of their subjects are very similar to the descriptions reported earlier and are composed largely of the figures abstracted in Figure 6. Knoll suggested that such experiences arise from the effect of the electrical stimulus on the retinal ganglionic network. Similar effects were achieved with flickering light (Horowitz, 1967) produced by a photostimulater, covered with a sheet of paper. The frequency dial was manipulated slowly back and forth (in a random manner) between 10 and 100 flashes per second. The light appeared steady (flicker fusion) between 75 and 90 flashes per second. Below 15 flashes per second most subjects merely saw the lamp going on and off.

In the intervening ranges all subjects (n = 20) reported visual sensations of various types and to a varying degree. These sensations were probably caused by rapid on and off stimuli affecting the more distal circuitry of the retino-cortical pathways and consisted of fluorescent colors, myriad parallel lines (both straight and curvilinear), mosaics, reticulated designs, and the other multiplied geometric figures illustrated earlier. Colors were seen as expanding and contracting, and the formed elements were seen as swirling, vibrating, counterrotating, and scintillating. At frequencies of 20 to 40 flashes per second, 8 of 20 subjects experienced a feeling of arousal described as anxiety, fearful expectancy, increased excitement, or joyfulness. In this range, subjects sometimes exclaimed with surprise, they often spoke with a more aroused vocal tone and inflection in reporting, and they occasionally reported visual images of objects rather than patterns, for example, "Oh, a hand is coming out at me," "I see faces disappearing," "there is a kitten with a hernia," "a horrible face," and so forth. These idiosyncratic visual images seemed to originate from forms supplied by elementary sensations.

The early view of the optic pathway, as being a kind of telegraphic system with point-to-point retinal-cortical representations, has been discarded. The retina appears to do more work in terms of codifying information through special receptivity to patterns in the complex tangle of retinal neurons, feedback circuits, and ganglia (Granit, 1955; Letvin et al., 1959). It is postulated that the basic coding forms include: 1) straightness of line, regularity of arc; 2) circularity; 3) parallelisms of straight lines, arcs, and circles; and 4) congruence of figures, equidistance, and equiangularity (Figure 7) (Pitts and McCulloch, 1947; Platt, 1960). These forms resemble, in part, the images abstracted earlier from clinical material, and they also fulfill the Gestalt criterion of pregnanz and figural goodness—the qualities found in figures most readily perceived (Attneave, 1955; Hochberg and McAlister, 1953; Woodworth, 1958). It is conceiv-

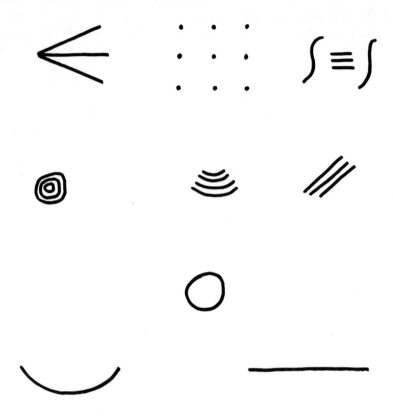

Fig. 7. Hypothesized patterns of special retinal receptivity.

able, then, that the images so repetitive in the clinical material may relate to the nature and function of retinal circuitry and to pattern receptivity.

ANATOMIC STRUCTURE OF THE EYE

The eye usually does not see its own contents, yet most people have visualized one or another of their entoptic elements. These are usually called floaters and are commonly seen while staring at a blank source of illumination such as an overcast sky or a sunlit wall. It seems likely that the figures abstracted earlier (Figure 6) could arise, in part, from anatomic forms. The patterns of the retinal blood vessels affect the light-sensitive rods and cones peripheral to the *macula lutea*, the area of precise vision. The shadows of such vessels could give rise to the wavy, radiating, filigreed elements; the blood cells within them might produce dot-like apparitions. The optic disc, that is the central scotoma, could give rise to the large circular figures and the layers of rods, cones, and neural bundles to the parallel figures. The fibers of the lens are arranged around six diverging axes, and they cause the rays seen around distant lights (giving them a star-like luster) and can also produce a sense of parallel fibers, swirls, or spots when such defective structures are present in the lens (von Helmholtz, 1962). The *muscae volitantes*, or floaters in the vitreous humor, like the artifacts in the lens, are produced by the invagination of integument during embryonal development of the eye and can give rise to oval or irregular shapes in entoptic visions. The movement of dots could be the flow of formed blood elements. The constant variations in optic movement caused by tremor, flicker, and drift would also impart a sense of movement to the elements. Optic rotation could cause circling effects, and bilateral orbital stimuli could result in the reciprocal duplications. Other features of imagery might be related to such optical phenomena as the production of figural aftereffects (Hanawalt, 1954; MacKay, 1961).

To restate the hypothesis, redundant clinical material of visual images can be abstracted into simple forms, and the origin of such forms may be entoptic—either from the anatomic characteristics of the eye or arising in the bioelectrical circuits for pattern receptivity in the retinal ganglionic network.

Why are entoptic images not usually consciously perceived? Images that are stationary on the retina fade out in six seconds. The natural involuntary movements of the eye, especially flicker and tremor, regenerate the image and compensate for drift (Ditchburn et al., 1959; Pritchard, 1961). Certain entoptic elements, especially the optic disc and the retinal blood vessels, would not generate many impulses because of their relatively stable retinal position. Their shadows, however, would shift under certain circumstances of moving illumination. In addition to fadeout, then, there must be other ways of limiting the penetration of such stimuli.

There is continuous retinal activity, even with the eye at rest, and there are continuous forces of inhibition and facilitation which alter receptivity to various stimuli and patterns (Bartley, 1959; Granit, 1955). It is known that the visual field varies with the deployment of attention and that receptivity to visual messages depends on the state of visual pathway excitability (Callaway, 1962; Lindsley, 1956; Oswald, 1963; Williams and Gassel, 1962). With the evidence for centrifugal control, that is, for optic nerve impulses moving toward the retina, comes the realization that inhibition and facilitation may operate at a peripheral locus as well as in the brain (Granit, 1955; Pitts and Mc-Culloch, 1947). Cortical responses to stimulation of the retina show: 1) a topographic, organized process and 2) a slower, more diffuse process, partially intraretinal, which activates major portions of the visual cortex (Doty, 1960). Vision is a complex transactional process with the eye telling the brain what it sees and the brain telling the eye what it should look for, and what it should not look for. Stimuli originating within the eyeball would register at the retinal level but could be kept from being perceived, under normal circumstances, by active inhibition or lack of facilitation. Such inhibition and facilitation probably take place at both the retinal and higher levels of the nervous system and represent the somatic equivalents of the deployment of attention. Under conditions of increased need to see, as in sensory deprivations, entoptic imagery would be facilitated or "tuned up." The somatic purpose would be to prevent optically dependent areas of the brain from being lulled by insufficient afferent stimulation.

What might happen when entoptic images or vague "noisy" perceptions are disinhibited or especially facilitated? This raw material would then impinge on higher centers for image representation and undergo a variety of secondary elaborations leading to the final conscious image. The nature of the secondary elaborations would depend on current motivational states and also on current regulatory capacity. In persons with a relatively well functioning ego, simple and momentary illusions or hypnagogic images of pleasing lights and patterns might result. With further regression of regulatory function (or intensification of motives) the images might become illusions or pseudohallucinations of current wishes, needs, or fears. In states of impaired control (as described in Chapter 7) hallucinations might be elaborated out of the entoptic raw material. I tentatively suggest, also, the possibility that entoptic sensations contribute sensory quality to dream images. Some subjects, awakened from dreaming sleep, have reported to me an increase in entoptic sensations as they look with open eyes into the darkness of their room.

Entoptic phenomenon may, as illustrated in several of the case vignettes, contribute a vivid raw material that is elaborated into a hallucination while awake in certain schizophrenic patients. This phenomenon could be explained in two ways: one way suggests impairment of control capacity, the second suggests a purposive regression to primitive levels of regulation of perception and image formation.

Perhaps some schizophrenic syndromes contain an impairment of inhibitory capacity. Many patients do describe being swamped by an incoming tide of sensations, especially during the early phases of decompensation (Goldstein, 1944; McGhie and Chapman, 1961). In this state they seem either unable or unwilling to screen out meaningless stimuli to focus their visual attention on meaningful stimuli. Also, their labeling, interpretation, and elaboration of incoming signals follows regressive lines, approximating the rules of the "primary process" (as described in Chapter 6).

The second possibility, in addition to that of ego-impairment, is that there is a regression of regulatory capacity for defensive purposes. Thus, to avoid an environment perceived as hostile or empty, to avoid an environment that triggers dangerous motives within, the schizophrenic person may regress to a style of diffuse perception and image-formation with blurring of the distinction between what is within and what is without. Entoptic images, for example, might be used as a focus of interest to defensively withdraw from external perceptions (Arlow and Brenner, 1964). Once facilitated or disinhibited, these images might undergo the archaic elaborations just mentioned. These two possibilities are not contradictory and follow the outlines of schizophrenic thought postulated by Von Domarus (1946) and Arieti (1961). They also correspond with ideas concerning other, nonvisual, modalities of representation. Luby (1962) suggested that disrupted body input mechanisms, such as in audition, are responsible for some of the disturbances of schizophrenia. Hoffer and Osmond (1962) accounted for olfactory hallucinations by a hypothesis of lowered olfactory threshold.

Sullivan postulated a loss of inhibitory ability as the cause of schizophrenic language. When inhibition is lowered, language regresses to its primal purpose—the establishment of a sense of security with others rather than the transmission of information. Such a process, he continued, goes on at all times but is screened out as unreasonable as long as one is alert. Should a person fall asleep while talking, however, he may awaken to find himself talking schizophrenic language (Sullivan, 1946). Shakow summarized the disorganization in schizophrenia as the inability to maintain a major or generalized set in conjunction with a trend to establish minor sets—to segmentalize both the external and internal environments. Thus, "there is an increased awareness of, and preoccupation with, the ordinarily disregarded details of existence—the details which normal people spontaneously forget, train themselves, or get trained rigorously to disregard" (Shakow, 1962). To summarize, schizophrenic persons may selectively "adapt-in" entoptic visions as an environmental avoidance defense (i.e., perceptual withdrawal) or they may be physiologically unable to "adapt-out" entoptic visions as can normal persons.

None of the above comments are, of course, specific to schizophrenic syndromes. Any type of regression or impairment of regulatory capacity might lead to both increased visual "noise" and a greater propensity to elaborate the sensory material into vivid images. Normal persons may experience identical phenomena in altered states of consciousness. Of interest, a very similar line of reasoning has been advanced for auditory hallucinations. Gross et al. (1963) and Saravay and Pardes

(1967) postulate that elementary auditory sensations such as buzzing or popping noises may contribute to the auditory hallucinations seen in alcohol withdrawal psychoses.

It is wise for clinicians to be alert for the redundant visual forms described in this chapter. Sometimes these pinwheels, hexagons, or wavy lines in the description of an animated hallucination indicate a physical basis for the hallucinatory syndrome. Also, some patients are reassured and relieved of disorganizing degrees of anxiety when the "spots in front of their eyes" are explained as actual physical bodies within the eyes. The following vignette is illustrative:

> A middle aged woman rushed to see her minister whom she consulted intermittently for recurrent anxiety and depression. When she told him she was "seeing the blood of Christ" and seemed very distraught, he sent her for a psychiatric consultation, for he feared this was the onset of a hallucinatory psychosis. The psychiatric resident recognized her distress but wondered about possible organic contributions to the reddish color she described as "the blood of Christ," which began with a shower of sparks and a sensation of darkness. Her eyes were examined, and she was found to have a retinal hemorrhage and a partial retinal detachment which needed immediate treatment. When this was explained to her she was, of course, realistically apprehensive, but she was also very relieved that she was not losing her mind.

REFERENCES

Adler, G. 1948. *Studies in analytical psychology*. London, Routledge & Kegan Paul.

Allers, R., and Teller, J. (1924) On the utilization of unnoticed impressions in associations. *Psychol. Issues, Monogr.* 7, 2:121–155, 1960.

Allport, F. H. 1955. *Theories of Perception and the Concept of Structure*. New York, John Wiley & Sons.

Antrobus, J. S., and Singer, J. L. 1964. Eye movements accompanying day-dreaming, visual imagery & thought suppression. *J. Abnorm. Soc. Psychol.*, 69:244–252.

Anastasi, A., and Foley, J. P. 1944. An experimental study of the drawing behavior of adult psychotics in comparison with that of a normal control group. *J. Exp. Psychol.*, 34:169–194.

Arieti, S. 1962. The microgeny of thought & perception. *Arch. Gen. Psychiat.*, 6:454–468.

———1961. The loss of reality. *Psychoanalysis*, 48:3–25.

Arlow, J. A., and Brenner, C. 1964. *Psychoanalytic Concepts and the Structural Theory*. New York, International Universities Press.

Arnheim, R. 1954. *Art and Visual Perception: A Psychology of the Creative Eye*. Berkeley, University of California Press.

Asher, H. 1963. Experiment with LSD: They split my personality. *Saturday Review*, 39–43, June 1, 1963.

Attneave, F. 1955. Symmetry, information & memory for patterns. *Amer. J. Psychol.*, 68:209–222.

Bartley, S. H. 1959. Some facts and concepts regarding the neurophysiology of the optic pathway. *A.M.A. Arch. Ophth.*, 60:775–791.

Bleuler, E. 1950. *Dementia Praecox*. Translated by J. Zinkin. New York, International Universities Press.

Callaway, E. 1962. Factors influencing the relationship between alpha activity and visual reaction time. *Electroenceph. Clin. Neurophysiol.*, 14:674–782.

Ditchburn, R. W., Fender, D. H., and Mayne, S. 1959. Vision with controlled movements of the retinal image. *J. Physiol.* 145:98–107.

Von Domarus, E. 1944. The specific laws of logic in schizophrenia. In Kasanin, J. S., ed. *Language and Thought in Schizophrenia*. Berkeley, University of California Press.

Doty, R. W. 1960. Functional significance of the topographic aspects of the retino-cortical projection. In Report of Symposium: *The Vision System: Neurophysiology and Psychophysics*, pp. 228–245. Freiburg, Germany.

Eagle, M. 1962. Personality correlates of sensitivity to subliminal stimulation. *J. Nerv. Ment. Dis.*, 134:1–17.

Fisher, C. and Paul, I. H. 1959. The effect of subliminal visual stimulation on images and dreams: A validation study. *J. Amer. Psychoanal. Ass.*, 7:35–83.

Granit, R. 1955. *Receptors and Sensory Perception*. New Haven, Yale University Press.

Gregory, R. L. 1966. *Eye and Brain: The Psychology of Seeing*. New York, McGraw-Hill.

Gross, M. M., et al. 1963. Hearing disturbances and auditory hallucinations in the acute alcoholic psychoses: I. Tinnitus: incidence and significance. *J. Nerv. Ment. Dis.*, 137:455–465.

Goldstein, K. 1944. A methodological approach to the study of schizophrenic thought disorder. In Kasanin, J. W., ed. *Language and Thought in Schizophrenia*, pp. 17–40. Berkeley, University of California Press.

Haber, R. N. 1968. *Contemporary Theory and Research in Visual Perception*. New York, Holt, Rinehart, and Winston.

Hanawalt, N. G. 1954. Recurrent images: New instances and a summary of older ones. *Amer. J. Psychol.*, 67:170–174.

Heaton, J. M. 1968. *The Eye: Phenomenology & Psychology of Function & Disorder*. Philadephia, J. P. Lippincott Co.

Hebb, D. O. 1959. A neuropsychological theory. In Koch, S., ed. *Psychology: A Study of a Science*, Vol. I, pp. 622–643. New York, McGraw-Hill.

Helmholtz, H. von. 1962. *Popular Scientific Lectures*. New York, Dover Publications.

Hochberg, J., and McAlister, E. A. 1953. A quantitative approach to figural "goodness." *J. Exp. Psychol.*, 46:361–364.

222/Neurobiologic Influences on Image Formation

Hoffer, A., and Osmond, H. 1962. Olfactory changes in schizophrenia. *Amer. J. Psychiat.*, 119:72–75.

Holstijn, A. J. 1951. The psychological development of Vincent van Gogh. Translated by H. P. Winzen. *Amer. Imago.*, 8:239–273.

Horowitz, M. J. 1967. Visual imagery and cognitive organization. *Amer. J. Psychiat.*, 123:938–946.

———— Adams, J. E., and Rutkin, B. B. 1968. Visual imagery on brain stimulation. *Arch. Gen. Psychiat.*, 19:469–486.

———— Adams, J. E., and Rutkin, B. B. 1967. Dream scintillations. *Psychosom. Med.*, 29:284–292.

Isakower, O. A. 1938. A contribution to the patho-psychology of phenomena associated with falling asleep. *Internat. J. Psychoanal.*, 19:331–345.

Jackson, J. H. (1932) *Selected Writings of John Hughlings Jackson*, Taylor, J., ed., Vol. II. New York, Basic Books, 1958.

Klüver, H. 1942. Mechanisms of hallucinations. In McNemar, Q., and Merrill, M. A., eds. *Studies in Personality*, pp. 175–207. New York, McGraw-Hill Book Co.

Knoll, M., et al. 1963. Effects of chemical stimulation of electrically induced phosphenes on their bandwidth, shape, number, and intensity. Confinia. Neurol., 23:201–226.

———— et al. 1962. Note on the spectroscopy of subjective light patterns. *J. Anal. Psychol.*, 7:55–70.

Koffka, K. 1935. Principles of Gestalt Psychology. London, Routledge and Kegan Paul.

Kohler, W. 1969. *The Task of Gestalt Psychology*. Princeton, Princeton University Press.

———— 1964. The formation and transformation of the perceptual world. *Psychol. Issues.*, 3:1–164, Monograph 12, No. 4.

Langui, E. 1959. *Fifty Years of Modern art*. New York, Praeger.

Letvin, J. Y., et al. 1959. What the frog's eye tells the frog's brain. *Proc. Inst. Radio Engs.*, 47:1940–1945.

Lindsley, D. B. 1956. Basic perceptual processes and the electroencephalogram. *Psychol. Res. Rep.*, 6:161–170. Washington, D.C.

Luby, E. D., et al. 1962. Model psychoses and schizophrenia. *Amer. J. Psychiat.*, 119:61–67.

Luckiesh, M. (1922) *Visual Illusions*. New York, Dover, 1965.

Maclay, W. S., and Guttmann, E. 1941. Mescaline hallucinations in artists. *A.M.A. Arch. Neurol. Psychiat.*, 45:130–137.

MacKay, D. M. 1961. Interactive processes in visual perception. In Rosenblith, N., ed. *Sensory Communication*. Cambridge, Mass., MIT Press.

Malitz, S., Wilkins, B., and Escover, H. 1962. A comparison of drug induced hallucinations with those seen in spontaneously occurring psychoses. In West, L. J., ed. *Hallucinations*. New York, Grune & Stratton.

Miller, S. C. 1962. Ego autonomy in sensory deprivation, isolation and stress. *Int. J. Psychoanal.*, 43:1–20.

McGhie, A., and Chapman, J. 1961. Disorders of attention and perception in early schizophrenia. *Brit. J. Med. Psychol.*, 34:103–116.

Neisser, U. 1967. *Cognitive Psychology*. New York, Appleton-Century-Crofts.

Nickols, J. 1962. Eidetic imagery synthesis. *Amer. J. Psychother.*, 16:76–82.

Oswald, I. 1963. *Sleeping and Waking: Physiology and Psychology*. New York, Elsevier.

Paul, I. H., and Fisher, C. 1959. Subliminal visual stimulation; a study of its influence on subsequent images and dreams. *J. Nerv. Ment. Dis.*, 129:315–340.

Perky, C. W. 1910. An experimental study of imagination. *Amer. J. Psychol.*, 21:422–452.

Pitts, W., and McCulloch, W. S. 1947. How we know universals: The perception of auditory and visual forms. *Bull. Math. Biophysics.*, 9:127–147.

Platt, J. F. 1960. How we see straight lines. *Sci. Amer.*, 202:121–129.

Pritchard, R. M. 1961. Stabilized images on the retina. *Sci. Amer.*, 204:72–78.

Pötzl, O. (1917) The relationship between experimentally induced dream images and indirect vision. *Psychol. Issues*, Monograph 7, 2:41–120, 1960.

Rapaport, D. 1942. *Emotions and Memory*. Baltimore, Williams & Wilkins.

Roffwarg, H. P., et al. 1962. Dream imagery: Relationship to rapid eye movement of sleep. *Arch. Gen. Psychiat.*, 7:235–258.

Saravay, S. M., and Pardes, H. 1967. Auditory elementary hallucinations in alcohol withdrawal psychosis. *Arch. Gen. Psychiat.*, 16:652–658.

Segal, S. J. 1969. Imagery & reality: Can they be distinguished. Presented at conference of the Eastern Psychiatric Research Association. New York, Nov. 1969.

—————— 1968a. Patterns of response to thirst in an imaging task (Perky technique) as a function of cognitive style. *J. Personality*, 36:574–588.

—————— 1968b. The Perky effect: Changes in reality judgments with changing methods of inquiry. *Psychon. Sci.*, 12:393–394.

Shakow, D. 1962. Segmental set. *Arch. Gen. Psychiat.*, 6:1–18.

Silberer, H. 1951. Report on a method of eliciting and observing certain symbolic hallucination-phenomena. In Rapaport, D., ed. *Organization and Pathology of Thought*, pp. 195–207. New York, Columbia University Press.

Solomon, P., et al. 1961. *Sensory Deprivation*. Cambridge, Harvard University Press.

Stace, W. T. 1960. *The Teachings of the Mystics*. New York, New American Library.

Stern, M. 1952. Free painting as an auxiliary technique in psychoanalysis. In Bychowski, G., and Despert, J. L., eds. *Specialized Techniques in Psychotherapy*, pp. 68–85. New York, Basic Books.

Sullivan, H. S. 1946. The language of schizophrenia. In Kasanin, J. S., ed. *Language and Thought in Schizophrenia*, pp. 8–13. Berkeley, University of California Press.

Vernon, M. 1962. *The Psychology of Perception*. Boston, Penguin.

Wallach, S., Wallach, M., and Yessin, G. 1960. Observations of involuntary eye movements in certain schizophrenics: A preliminary report. *J. Hillside Hosp.*, 9:224–227.

Warrington, E. K. 1962. The completion of visual forms across hemianopic field defects. *J. Neurol. Neurosurg. Psychiat.*, 25:208–217.

West, L. J. et al. 1961. The psychosis of sleep deprivation. *Ann. N.Y. Acad. Sci.*, 96:66–71.

Williams, D., and Gassel, M. 1962. Visual function in patients with homonymous hemianopia. Part I: the visual fields. *Brain*, 185:175–251.

Woodworth, P. S. 1958. *Dynamics of Behavior*. New York, Henry Holt & Co.

CHAPTER

11

Influence of the Brain
on Image Formation*

We know that the neurobiology of the brain influences image formation, but the precise nature of these influences is yet unknown. Regulation of image formation is a complex process that probably requires mass
action of nets of nerve tissue in many parts of the brain. When some aspect of the brain's structure or function is abnormal, then a person may
experience a large range of visual images and perceptual distortions, or he
may experience a loss of certain image-forming capacities.

We can use two approaches to study the relationship between brain
function and structure, and image formation. One approach would be to
alter image formation and observe what happens to brain functions. The
second approach would be to alter brain functions and then to observe
image formation.

RELATIONSHIP BETWEEN CHANGES IN IMAGE
FORMATION AND THE ELECTROENCEPHALAGRAM

While at rest, with their eyes closed, many persons have an electroencephalographic pattern known as the alpha rhythm, a brain wave with

* Portions of this chapter were published in the paper "Visual Imagery on Brain
Stimulation," coauthored with John E. Adams, M.D., and Burton Rutkin, that
appeared in the *Arch. Gen. Psychiat.*, 19:469–486, 1968. The research work was supported by research grants from the U.S. Public Health Service (V.R.A.: RD-2211-P
and RD-1225-M).

eight to twelve peaks per second. Investigators have noted a relationship between the alpha rhythm and image formation. Lehmann et al. (1965) find that as images disappear alpha rhythm appears and vice versa. Costello and MacGregor (1957) report that the alpha rhythm is suppressed as image experiences increase in vividness. Kamiya and Zeitlan (1963) found that subjects could increase alpha by avoiding images and decrease alpha by forming images and focusing attention on them.

Some researchers have tried to typologize people as verbalizers or visualizers on the basis of the relative frequency of alpha waves on their resting EEG and on the degree to which this alpha wave is blocked when subjects follow instructions to form mental images (Golla et al., 1943; Short, 1953). Slatter (1960) finds that his visualizer subjects are likely to block alpha on image formation, while verbalizer subjects do not show this effect as readily.*

Most researchers agree that as awareness of images increases, the alpha rhythm of the EEG tends to decrease. But not all persons have a resting alpha rhythm; those persons who show alpha may not show a block of alpha on image formation; and those who do block alpha with image formation may on occasion have alpha and report conscious images. Thus, there is no decisive correlation between these variables and, quite possibly, the alpha rhythm does not correlate directly with image formation, but with some relevant variable such as perceptual alertness or mental effort (Oswald, 1957). For example, the alpha rhythm might be produced by synchronous activity of large masses of resting cells. An effort of perception, of forming images, or of thinking may disrupt the synchronous activity that produces the alpha rhythm. However, until we have more data, we can make no firm conclusions about a one-to-one relationship between image formation and any electrophysiologic measures.

CLINICAL OBSERVATIONS OF ALTERED STRUCTURE AND FUNCTION: ORGANIC BRAIN DISEASE

Organic brain disease includes either permanent or transient changes in structure or function. These changes may arise from many causes including physical trauma, atrophy, infection, inflammation, intoxication, vascular disturbances, tumors, degenerations, or metabolic shifts such as vitamin, oxygen, or blood sugar deficiencies. In general, pathology in the nondominant hemisphere impairs the visual and spatial tasks that require

---

* Categorization of persons as visualizers and verbalizers presents phenomenologic problems, as cited in Chapter 4.

image formation.* Although a disturbance that alters or destroys nerve tissue in any anatomic site may influence control of image formation, the *site* and *nature* of the pathology determine (with wide variations and exceptions) the changes that take place.

For example, the geniculocalcarine pathway goes from the input of the optic tracts into the midbrain to the cortical receptive areas in the occipital lobe. Pathology anywhere along this pathway, or in the calcarine cortex, results in blindness or visual symptoms that correlate highly with the size and exact location of the lesion. Irritative lesions usually give rise to elementary sensations, similar to the entoptic type experience reported in the previous chapter. About one-quarter of patients with tumors along the geniculocalcarine pathway report such elementary sensations (Bailey, 1948; Williams and Gassel, 1962). Such patients usually report the sensations as occurring on the side of their vision opposite to the site of pathology, although sometimes the sensations are straight ahead or even on the same side as the pathology. At one time it was believed that this pathway supplied all of the visual information available to the brain and was wired like a telegraph system, one point on the retina corresponded with one point in the calcarine cortex. Recent work suggests, instead, that there are multiple areas for registering information from the retina. For example, Sprague (1966) reported that removal of one side of the occipito-temporal neocortex results, as is well known, in total blindness in the opposite visual field (a contralateral hemianopia). Sprague demonstrated this effect in cats but then, in a second operation, he removed the opposite sided superior colliculus, a structure in the midbrain involved in visual perception. Remarkably, there appeared to be a return of vision in the blind field. Apparently, the initial blindness is due to inhibition of function rather than total loss of function.

From the calcarine cortex there extend nerve bundles to various cortical areas considered to be visual association areas. These extend into the temporal lobe of the brain. Pathology centered in or near the temporal lobe commonly gives rise to complex hallucinations of persons, places, or things. A temporal lobe epileptic seizure, for example, may consist of a hallucinatory experience.

Epileptic or migraine seizures may be preceded by an aura that can include perceptual distortions, intrusive images, elementary sensations, or hallucinations. The cause may be transient impairment of brain function, or the resultant altered state of consciousness (Whitten, 1969). Like the images in a recurrent dream, the images of the aura in successive seizures may always be similar. Sometimes the images are simple and discrete;

---

* The dominant hemisphere is more likely to have pathology when there is impairment of lexical thinking, as outlined for aphasia in Chapter 5. For a review of the literature on psychologic impairment with lesions in either hemisphere see Horowitz et al., 1970.

sometimes they are miniature fantasies or "micro-dreams"; or sometimes they take the form of "dream scintillations," in which images seem to pass through consciousness in rapid succession but escape recollection.

Frequently noted varieties of perceptual auras include illusions, micropsia, macropsia, change in brightness of color, movement, shimmering, distortion, and alterations in body image. Jackson (1932) described these phenomena in the nineteenth century and noted the occasional occurrence of a sequential elaboration progressing from crude sensations, such as sensations of color, to formed images, such as fearsome faces.

Hallucinatory states can also be caused by shifts in metabolism, such as low blood sugar, low blood oxygen, excessive hormone levels, vitamin deficiencies, fevers, poisonings, or withdrawal from habitually used sedatives or narcotics. Delirium tremens and acute alcoholic hallucinosis are prime examples: the pink elephants and the numerous small carnivorous animals of the DT's are part of our cultural lore. Visual hallucinations are more common than auditory hallucinations in delirium tremens, and include themes of dismemberment, being devoured, small animals, and castration. More common in acute alcoholic psychosis are auditory hallucinations (Bromberg and Schilder, 1933).

The above examples demonstrate general tendencies for what frequently happens with specific brain pathology. But there are many exceptions, and each case should be carefully reviewed for its individual idiosyncrasies. For example, transient impairment of brain function leading to hallucinations may require both neurobiologic and psychologic levels of explanation. Hallucinations of sparks and flashes to the right of the person's visual field may suggest pathology somewhere in the left optical-cortical pathway. But such hallucinations could also arise without brain pathology. A hallucination of a pink elephant might arise because of a particular set of psychologic motives, but it also might indicate the presence of acutely impaired neurophysiologic functions in centers that regulate and control image formation.

Usually, with organic brain disease, impaired image formation is associated with other symptoms, such as loss of memory; orientation for time, place, and person; intellectual deficiencies; and emotional lability. Sometimes, however, there may be a discrete loss of image formation (Brain, 1954). Such syndromes, though rare, support the notion that image formation can be regarded as a separable system from lexical representation (as suggested in the model presented in Chapter 5). The following clinical example shows a case that began with the loss of the ability to form visual images:

A 42-year-old man had a brain tumor (an angioblastoma) that destroyed cortical tissues in the ventral-parietal and dorsal-temporal regions of his right cerebral hemisphere. His earliest symptom was loss of ability to visualize memories or to form visual thought images. He also reported a reduction in visual dreaming. As the disease advanced, he developed a spatial disorientation, later followed by loss of memory, speech impairment, partial deafness, and progressive dementia. In the early stages, the patient could not recognize his own children, but relied on hearing them speak to identify them by their tone and inflection of voice. Later he required a guide whenever he left his home, as he could not retain spatial relationships and would get lost immediately.

While clinically we observe natural changes in the brain's structure and function, experimentally we can initiate functional alterations in order to study further how the brain influences image formation. The clearest and most discrete change in terms of image formation is localized electrical brain stimulation.

IMAGES ON BRAIN STIMULATION

Penfield and his associates (Penfield, 1966; Penfield and Jasper, 1954; Penfield and Rasmussen, 1950) found that stimulations of the calcarine cortex produced simple visual sensations in the contralateral visual field. One type of report included simple visual sensations: stars, balls, disks, wheels, wavy lines, honeycombs, outlines, black forms, flashes, and colors which were either stationary, moving, or rotating. These forms are common in various hallucinations and deliria and have been discussed in Chapter 10. Stimulation of the extracalcarine cortex of the occipital lobe produced similar sensory experiences, ipsilateral or bilateral as well as contralateral to the side stimulated. Stimulation of the superior and lateral cortical surfaces of either the right or left temporal lobe produced more complex visual hallucinations of objects, faces, persons, or scenes.

Penfield was impressed by what he labeled "experiential hallucinations," which sometimes combined vivid sensations of several modalities simultaneously. Of 453 patients who had electrical exploration of the temporal lobe cortex, 38 (8.4 percent) reported very vivid and lifelike flashbacks of their past lives. When the same point was restimulated after a few seconds, the same experience was usually repeated. After more time had elapsed, another experience appeared on restimulation. Other electrical stimulations at times produced distortions of actual perception. An object viewed might appear to have unusual alterations in distance, size, shape, movement, or clarity, or change in its reality-sense. It might appear either uncannily familiar, or very strange, even unreal.

Although Penfield speculated that these perceptual-cognitive experiences might be due to the hallucinatory evocation of memories by stimulus activation of their neurophysiologic substrate, he did not presume that

the electrode was necessarily placed on the specific site of memory storage: "The psychical or interpretive areas of the temporal cortex produced
recall of past experiences, or illusions of interpretation by conduction to
some distant zone, such as the hippocampus" (Penfield, 1958). He believed that some memory storage site was activated and that an actual
perceptual memory was then rerun.

In addition, he postulated a "scanning mechanism," at least partially
resident in the temporal lobes, that compared present experiences with
past similar experiences (Perot and Penfield, 1960). This scanning of past
experiences would usually be at a level subliminal to subjective consciousness. However, during the alteration in function provoked by the electrical stimulations, the past experiences might reach hallucinatory vividness.
Penfield and his associates carefully emphasized that hallucinations
of prior experience were evoked from persons with temporal lobe epilepsy who had long histories of brain malfunction.

The postulate that these experiences were reruns of memory engrams
is attractive, but it does not explain all of the phenomena. For example,
some of Penfield's subjects saw themselves in the visual images they reported. Other than memories of self-perceptions in a mirror or photo-
graph, this could not be derived from an actual perception that was laid
down directly as an engram. Rather, it was derived from a reconstruction
of various actual perceptions into imaginative images. The imagination
can use such bits and pieces of prior perceptions (Rapaport, 1959).

The occasional progression from simple sensations to complex hallucinations reported by Penfield, and noted by Hughlings Jackson for
auras, suggests that, as described in Chapter 10, some of the animated
imagery is elaborated out of a matrix provided by the elemental sensations of colors and of geometric forms.

Jasper and Rasmussen (1958) inserted electrodes in structures deep
within the temporal lobes in persons with temporal lobe epilepsy. They
reported that stimulations of the amygdaloid regions sometimes produced
confusion, diminished awareness, amnesia, and/or automatic behavior.
Some hallucinations or illusions were produced from stimulations deep
in the Sylvian area and, the peri-insular regions, as well as from surface
stimulations. Amygdala stimulations of 46 patients rarely produced visual
events. One patient reported a visual distortion: one patient seemed to
have a visual hallucination, but his report was vague and uncertain. No
visual effects were reported for hippocampal stimulation.

Mahl and his co-workers (1964) reported the results in a single patient who underwent psychologic interviews during stimulation sessions.
This patient reported auditory hallucinatory experiences when deep
structures of the temporal lobe were stimulated using a needle electrode.
While no visual experiences were reported, we are interested in Mahl's

data because he was led to modify Penfield's hypothesis that stimulations activated memory traces in the neural record. The hallucinatory experiences could be shown often to relate to the patient's mental content before the stimulation. Repeated stimulation at short time intervals tended to elicit responses with related content. If the time intervals were long, then thematic content was unrelated. Also, the relationship between the prestimulation mental content and the sensory experience resembled the processes of dream construction: displacement, distortion, and condensation were prominent, and ideas were translated into sensory images. Mahl concluded from these observations that

> electrical stimulation of the temporal lobe does not directly activate memory traces in the ganglionic record. Instead it induces a state of consciousness which makes it more probable that primary-process modes of functioning will prevail. If there is a background of subliminally excited memory traces in the ganglionic record at the time of stimulation, then all the conditions exist for the occurrence of hallucinatory experiences, and the content of these experiences would necessarily be related to the prestimulation mental events, for it would be determined partly by them. (p. 361)

All of the studies cited so far have concerned patients with temporal lobe epilepsy, since the hazards of stereotactic surgery forbid its use with normal human subjects. Each group of investigators carefully pointed out the danger of considering their results from stimulation of an abnormally functioning brain to be equivalent to the results of stimulating a nonepileptic brain. However, a group in Japan has reported the results of stimulation of both the temporal cortex and deep structures of the nondominant temporal lobe in persons with chronic schizophrenia and hallucinatory symptoms, in order "to treat the auditory hallucinations" (Ishibashi et al., 1964). Visual hallucinations were reported in 5 of 17 cases (29 percent). Elementary visual hallucinations—those of color or simple geometric forms—did not result from surface stimulation but did arise from stimulation of the depth structures. Only one of their cases showed clearly clouded consciousness.

To summarize, electrical stimulation to the temporal lobe cortex may give rise to formed and meaningful visual hallucinations. The temporal lobe is apparently the only portion of the cortex where stimulation may evoke such phenomena. Stimulation of the deep structures of the temporal lobe gives rise to conflicting findings: some investigators report evoked hallucinations; others do not.

Two major theoretic explanations of the phenomena have been offered. One theory suggests that a memory "engram" from an actual past experience is activated by the stimulations and is rerun with perceptual vividness. The second theory suggests that stimulation produces an altered state of consciousness with a concomitant shift toward primary-process thinking. In work previously reported in association with Dr. John Adams * and Mr. Burton Rutkin (Horowitz et al., 1968) we hoped to see which theoretic explanation seemed most correct.

RESEARCH PLAN

Depth electrodes were implanted in patients with long-term intractable temporal lobe epilepsy for diagnostic and therapeutic reasons. This afforded the invaluable opportunity for research into the behavioral and experiential effects of stimulations. We hoped particularly to derive answers to the following questions.

1. Would the stimulation of the deeper limbic system structures such as the hippocampus, hippocampal gyrus, and amygdala of persons with temporal lobe epilepsy: (a) produce visual events similar to those elicited by Penfield on his stimulation of the surface of the temporal lobes; (b) resemble the results of Jasper and Rasmussen whose stimulations of depth structures were fairly negative for visual events; or (c) follow the results of those groups who reported both simple and complex visual hallucinations on depth stimulation?

2. If fully formed hallucinatory events were reported by the patient subjects, would the contents and the dynamics of the formation of the hallucination support the memory trace hypothesis of Penfield or the motivational construction and altered state of consciousness hypotheses of Mahl?

METHOD

The 16 subjects were patients with intractable temporal lobe epilepsy who (after appropriate clinical study) underwent implantation of depth electrodes in order to obtain data about possible focal sites of epileptogenesis. The methods involved in stereotactic electrode placement are detailed elsewhere (Adams, 1966).

Bipolar electrode pairs were used to pick up electrographic data and to deliver electrical stimuli.† Figure 1 illustrates several electrodes stabilized within the temporal lobes.

---

* Guggenhime Professor of Surgery, University of California Medical School, San Francisco.
† The bipolar spacing was 2 mm, and the pairs were from 4 to 10 mm apart. Each electrode consisted of a strand of stainless steel wire, 0.0032 inches in diameter, wrapped several times around a tiny cylinder which supported seven electrodes.

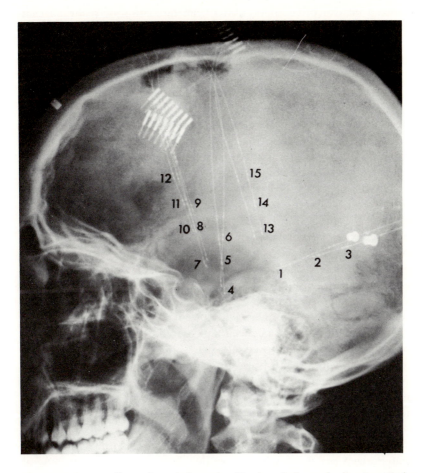

Fig. 1. Stereotactically implanted electrodes. Numbers indicate the location of electrode pairs. Final anatomical locations are established by comparison of pneumoencephalograms with a brain atlas. The usual locations are: (1) posterior hippocampus; (2) posterior hippocampus; (3) optic radiation; (4) hippocampal gyrus; (5) hippocampus; (6) globus pallidus; (7) amygdala; (8) putamen; (9) corona radiata; (10) anterior commissure; (11) ventricle; (12) corpus callosum; (13) basal medial nucleus; and (15) cingulum bundle. (From Horowitz, Adams, and Rutkin. 1968. *Arch. Gen. Psychiat.*, 19:469–486.)

The subjects' responses to stimulation were recorded on magnetic tape, and in some patients, synchronized video tape. Thus it was possible to record simultaneously electrocardiogram (EKG), electroencephalogram (EEG), vocal, and behavioral responses. These taped records were reviewed subsequently. Each sensory event was recorded and categorized on edge-punched cards with appropriate notation of the stimulation in terms of duration, voltage, and amperage; the observed behavioral effect; the reported introspective effect; and a brief indication of recorded electroencephalographic effect.

The patients were fully conscious and seated semiupright in hospital beds during recording and stimulation sessions. A microphone was positioned about 10 inches in front of the patient, and a video camera was about 9 feet away. The stimulation switches and an oscilloscope for electrographic monitoring of the EEG were positioned behind the patient. The investigator sat beside the bed observing the face and body of the patient and the monitor oscilloscope. The location, order, and parameters of stimulations were predetermined; the timing of stimulus delivery was up to the interviewer.

A stimulation was delivered at a moment when the interviewer had an idea of what to expect from the patient in terms of continuous behavior. Thus the effect of a stimulation could be judged from changes in behavior as well as from introspective reports. Most of the performance tasks were verbal, ranging from nondirective psychiatric interviews to counting and remembering situations. Occasionally, perceptual-motor tasks were used. (Because of our focus on visualization processes, we will report only the introspective reports of visual events.)

Most stimulations were given without specific warning. The patient knew that stimulations might occur at any time during a 1½- to 2½-hour session, but he did not know precisely when they would occur. At times after a given site had already been stimulated without the patient's foreknowledge, the patient would be told exactly when stimulation was on and off. This was done: (1) to increase the patient's awareness of his experiences and (2) to see if the patient would report differently when he knew he was receiving a stimulation.

Visual sensations that subjects reported during or after stimulations were categorized as "A," "B," "C," or "D." We classified events "A" if visual hallucinations were described by the patient as externally placed with contents related to formed objects. We classified events as "B" if visual imagery experiences were reported with formed, object-related content in which the images were not clearly projected onto the external environment. The differentiation of "A" and "B" events depended on the quality of description given by subjects. If a sensation was not described as having apparent reality or external spatial location, it was classified as a "B" event. We classified events as "C" if they consisted of elementary sensations such as colored lights, geometric forms, and amorphous shapes —that is, visual sensations that did not represent objects or scenes. The fourth classification, "D," was used for visual distortions of actual perceptions.

RESULTS

Patients described many varieties of sensory, motor, and emotional experiences as a consequence of electrical stimulations. Here, only the visual events are reported.

Table 1 shows the total number of stimulations for all anatomic sites in each of 16 patients, the total number of visual events, and a breakdown of visual events into types "A" through "D."

Ten percent of 1,509 stimulations in all subjects resulted in some type of visual event. Most of the events were elementary sensations ("C" events). Less than 1 percent of the stimulations resulted in events that could be categorized as formed hallucinations of an object or scene ("A"). Less than 1 percent of the stimulations led to reports of vivid visual thought images ("B"). While we attempted an impartial survey of all electrode points, we did tend to repeat stimulations of sites where

Table 1   Visual Events*

Patient	Total Stim all Sites	Number of Visual Events Reported					
		Type A (Halluc)	Type B (Images)	Type C (Colors & Geom)	Total A+B+C (% of Stim)	Type D (Percept Distort)	Total A+B+C+D (% of Stim)
1	88	2	0	3	5 (6)	1	6 (7)
2	137	0	1	7	8 (6)	0	8 (6)
3	78	0	0	12	12 (15)	0	12 (15)
4	84	0	0	14	14 (2)	0	14 (2)
5	90	2	0	1	3 (3)	1	4 (4)
6	104	0	0	1	1 (1)	1	2 (2)
7	89	1	3	6	10 (11)	1	11 (12)
8	109	0	0	13	13 (11)	6	19 (17)
9	57	0	0	1	1 (2)	1	2 (3)
10	176	2	4	9	15 (9)	4	19 (11)
11	55	2	0	13	15 (27)	0	15 (27)
12	65	0	0	1	1 (2)	0	1 (2)
13	176	2	0	19	21 (12)	1	22 (13)
14	101	1	1	0	2 (2)	0	2 (2)
15	52	0	4	1	5 (10)	0	5 (10)
16	48	1	0	1	2 (4)	1	3 (6)
Totals (% of stim)	1,509 (100)	13 (1)	13 (1)	102 (7)	128 (8)	17 (1)	145 (10)
Median	88-89	0-1	0	3-6	5-8 (6-10)	1	5-8 (6)
Mean	94	1	1	6	8 (9)	1	9 (10)
Range	48-176	0-2	0-4	0-19	1-21 (1-27)	0-6	1-22 (2-27)

*From Horowitz, Adams, and Rutkin. 1968. <u>Arch. Gen. Psychiat.</u>, 19:469-486.

previous stimulations resulted in reports of a visual sensation. This increased the percentages of reports of visual events beyond the percentages likely to occur from random and equal frequent stimulations of each anatomic site. This should be kept in mind when evaluating percentage data in the following sections.

Anatomic Correlates of Events. The anatomic sites that were thought to have received stimulations were the anterior (pes) hippocampus, the posterior hippocampus, the hippocampal gyrus, the amygdala, the globus pallidus, the anterior commissure, the optic radiation, the corpus collusum, the caudate nucleus, the putamen, the cingulum bundle, and occasionally the anterior thalamus and the temporal lobe cortex. The number of visual events in each category and the number of patients reporting such events are shown as related to the presumed site of stimulation in Figure 2. The optic radiation stimulations produced many "C" events but did not produce any "A" (hallucinatory) or "B" (image) events in any subject. The posterior hippocampus was the site of

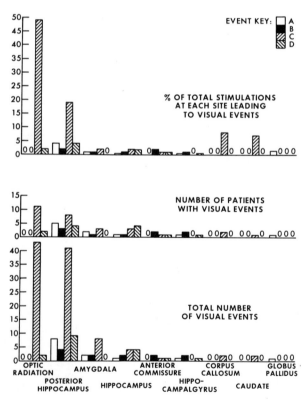

Fig. 2. Anatomic correlates of visual events. (From Horowitz, Adams, and Rutkin. 1968. Arch. Gen. Psychiat., 19:469–486.)

greatest interest in terms of visual events. Stimulations of the posterior hippocampus led to 8 of the 13 "A" events in addition to many "C" events. Five of the 13 "B" events were from stimulation of the posterior hippocampal site. Thus, 13 of 26 (50 percent) of the fully formed imagery events ("A" and "B") occurred from stimulations of the posterior hippocampus while only 4 (15 percent) occurred from stimulation of the amygdala, the second most productive site.

In scattered instances the visual imagery occurred in conjunction with an electrically evoked aura or seizure, but usually the visual events had no observable relationship to suspected areas of focal epileptogeneses. Nor did the frequency of visual events have any consistent relationship to the side of the brain stimulated or to the presence or absence of visual events in the aura (Table 2).

ELECTROGRAPHIC CORRELATES OF SUBJECTIVE VISUAL SENSATIONS. Recordings from the site of a stimulation frequently showed a high voltage, rapid, "spiking" after-discharge which lasted from several seconds to a minute or more after the end of the stimulus train. Such after-discharges were frequent, but they did not always occur after a stimulation had evoked a visual event. (Because of stimulus artifacts it was not possible, usually, to record electrographic data until the stimulus was over.) After-discharges accompanied subjective visual phenomena 33 to 100 percent of the time in the 16 patients, and the median patient had a 75 percent likelihood of an after-discharge.

Table 2 Relationship of Aura to Visual Events on Stimulation*

Patient	Aura†	No. Stim	No. Vis Events	Object-bound A + B
1	Fear, tingling head, epigastric	88	6	2
2	Funny throat, shoulder feeling, woozy	137	8	1
3	Tingling of leg	78	12	0
4	Feels angry	84	14	0
5	**Distorted vision, micropsia**	90	4	2
6	None	104	2	0
7	Fear	89	11	4
8	**Flashing light, distorted vision**, goofy	109	19	0
9	Epigastric	57	2	0
10	Epigastric, **recurrent visual image**	176	19	6
11	Shrinking, fear, lightheaded	55	15	2
12	Fear	65	1	0
13	Woozy, left-sided sensations	176	22	2
14	Epigastric, dreamy state	101	2	2
15	Fear, **distorted vision, hallucinations, illusions**	52	5	4
16	Epigastric	48	3	1

*From Horowitz, Adams, and Rutkin. 1968. Arch. Gen. Psychiat., 19:469-486.
†Visual auras are indicated in boldface type.

After-discharges were not restricted to the site of stimulation but spread at times to other areas of the same hemisphere or crossed over to the limbic system of the opposite hemisphere. Since many of the visual events arose from stimulation of the posterior hippocampus, we assessed stimulation of other sites for spread of after-discharge to the posterior hippocampus. Of 81 visual events produced by stimulations in sites other than the posterior hippocampus, 18 (22 percent) were accompanied by an after-discharge recorded from posterior hippocampus electrodes.

Certain visual events were very brief and occurred only during the period of stimulation. Others persisted during the period of the after-discharge. Several patients reported subjective visual experience ceased at a time coincident with the observed cessation of the after-discharge (Table 3).

SUBJECTIVE EXPERIENCES. We anticipated that some brain stimulations would lead to hallucinatory experiences. We hoped to relate the hallucinatory content to the patient's prestimulation stream of thought. Constant verbalization in a nondirective interview was our goal. Organic brain damage, psychopathology, and situational stress interfered, and directive questioning was frequently necessary.

In spite of many communication difficulties, we felt that reports were reasonably reliable and that errors, when present, were on the side of omission (false negatives). False positives, that is, reports of imagery in the absence of brain stimulation, occurred twice to our knowledge and may have been due to a hypnagogic or regressive mental state.

Table 3 Correlation of Visual Events With After-Discharge*

	Category of Visual Event			
	A (Halluc)	B (Image)	C (Elem Sens)	D (Distort)
	No. of Events (No. of Patients)			
Event during period of stimulation only (no recorded EEG change)	0 (0)	3 (3)	46 (11)	4 (1)
Event endured after stimulation, no AD present	1 (1)	0 (0)	10 (5)	0 (0)
Event reported to cease before AD ends	3 (2)	1 (1)	3 (3)	2 (2)
Event reported to cease coincident with end AD	4 (4)	1 (1)	10 (7)	4 (4)
Event continued after end of AD	3 (3)	1 (1)	9 (5)	2 (2)
Unable to determine relationship of cessation event to AD	2 (2)	6 (3)	24 (9)	5 (4)

*From Horowitz, Adams, and Rutkin. 1968. Arch. Gen. Psychiat., 19:469-486.

Not all stimulations led to some sort of subjective or behavioral effect. Some stimulations led to subjective experiences that patients did not report immediately: instead, the patient might finish a sentence he had started before telling his experience. We instructed patients to report always and immediately any sensation, but "rules" of courtesy and grammar sometimes prevailed. Frequently, stimulations that resulted in some subjective experience also led to speech interruption. If the patient became unresponsive, he was asked firmly what he was experiencing, and if he was still unresponsive, he was asked to give some body movement signal—for example, raising a hand to show that he could hear us. As soon as possible we obtained the patient's introspective report. In spite of persistent questioning, one out of four instances of visual experience was impossible to locate in time (see also Table 3). Additional communication difficulties were created by the psychomotor retardation, increased speech pathology, perseveration, and loosened associations that followed some stimulations, especially those stimulations followed by an after-discharge. This suggests that the after-discharge may be a sign of cognitive disorganization.

A striking finding concerned memory for the hallucinatory experience. Several of the "A" (hallucination) events were forgotten by patients from 10 to 15 minutes after occurrence. When questioned the next day, patients still could not recall the experience. If, however, they were given partial contents as clues and if they were encouraged repeatedly to remember, then they sometimes reconstructed other portions of the experience.

The same object-related visual event ("A" or "B") was never repeated in our sample by subsequent stimulation of the same site with the same parameters of stimulation. As mentioned above, we tried to reproduce events by repeated stimulation of the same site later the same day or during subsequent sessions. Sometimes nothing was reported, while at other times another type of visual event was reported. Sometimes the same category of event was repeated but with a shift in content.

The following sections review perceptual distortions and elementary sensations briefly and then describe the formed imagery.

"D" EVENTS—PERCEPTUAL DISTORTIONS. The perceptual distortions reported during brain stimulation resemble certain apparently psychogenic visual disturbances and perceptual distortions occurring during auras and regressive experiences. Stationary objects appeared to move or to bend, reduplicate (e.g., double vision), or to develop a halo. Occasionally micropsia or tunnel vision was reported. (Macropsia was not reported.) Sometimes a portion of the visual field was lost: one patient reported a spotty, "here and there" loss of his visual field during a stimulation. Such perceptual distortions arose most frequently on stimulation of the optic radiation, the hippocampus, or the posterior hippocampus.

"C" EVENTS—ELEMENTARY SENSATIONS. As indicated earlier, most "C" events were elicited from the optic radiation and appeared usually in the contralateral visual field. Flashes of blue or white light, described as splashes or starbursts, were common. Colors of gold, red, green, and orange were reported less often. At times, the lights, "splashes," or "balls" were reduplicated so that two, three, or even a dozen lights were seen. Klüver has noted that reduplication is one of the "constancies" of hallucinatory experiences of any origin (Klüver, 1942). Flickering and moving lights were common. One subject reported a "rolling X," another, "vibrating, wavy lines." Several subjects saw "lines" or "circles." An example of a "C" event as described by a patient is presented below.

REPORT OF "C" EVENT. Note the directive style of "question and answer" interview structure necessary with this patient and the apparent repetition of a similar elementary sensation on repeated stimulation of the same site.

Prior to stimulation, the patient had been talking sporadically about other people in her hospital room. Many questions were needed to encourage her to speak. She then received a stimulation of the right optic radiation at 3 volts, 0.5 milliamps, 100 cps for 5 seconds and fell silent, staring fixedly ahead.

> What's happening now?
> "I have a—some kind of light—"
> You had a light?
> "Yeah, over here." (Points to left field.)
> What was it like?
> "Sort of blue—"
> What was its shape?
> "Round."
> Round?
> "Yeah."
> Did it move?
> "No."
> Stayed perfectly still?
> "Yeah."
> Tell me if you see it again. (Pause) Do you see it now?
> "No." (Stimulation is repeated.) "Yeah, it's right over there." (Points toward left visual field.)
> Tell me when it's gone.
> "It's gone."
> Is it different from the one you saw before?
> "No, the same."
> Did it stay perfectly still?
> "Yeah. It kind of went like this, though." (Indicates by opening and closing fingers that it was changing size, probably flashing or twinkling.)

"B" EVENTS—PSEUDOHALLUCINATIONS. A gross idea of the types of images reported can be obtained from a brief list of the "B" events. For brevity and clarity, the patients' words are condensed.

1. An elephant, something on its back, associated with the world of crime.
2. A doctor, name forgotten, but you find him over there (Dr. H.). I recognized him as a radio signal.
3. An animal, maybe a monkey; it has something to do with my spells. (The patient stated that he saw this regularly as part of his aura although previously he had never mentioned it.)
4. A series of numbers—"30," "40"—moving and changing size. (Previously the patient had performed a counting task.)
5. My sons.
6. Walking in the park. I see a park.
7. I see myself having a spell in the hospital corridor and hitting my head.
8. Flashes—mother talking on phone with doctor; next, people from school—waxes and wanes; now it flashes.
9. My sons flying.
10. A symptom, a base plate, mountains like triangles.
11. An upright pig, talking. (This was reported also as an aura. See an elaboration below.)
12. A closet, familiar, not empty.
13. A room, familiar.

Whether or not a person reported a visual event did not have any observable relationship to his prestimulation reports of the phenomena of his auras and seizures (described in Table 2). On the other hand, precipitation of an aura-like sensation by electrical stimulation led some patients to say, "This is what I have all the time." They then proceeded to tell us of phenomena that they had not described previously in spite of repeated, careful questioning during the preimplantation work-ups. This may be attributed to the poor memory for events occurring during auras and seizures.

EXAMPLE OF A "B" EVENT. On stimulation of the right occipital optic radiation, a young female patient reported that she saw pulsating circles that were composed of fluctuating, unusually fluorescent colors. This type "C" report occurred on repeated stimulation of the same electrode at 5 and 8 volts, 3 and 5 milliamps. However, on stimulation of the right portion of the anterior commissure at 8 volts, 5 milliamps for 15 seconds (an unusually long stimulation), the patient seemed startled and said that she felt as she did just before a seizure. As shown in Figure 3, there were some "spikes" following the stimulation but no after-discharge. (The heavy band to the left of the figure is stimulus artifact. It obscures the patient's EEG during the period of stimulation.)

While the patient was responsive to instructions during this period (opening and closing her eyes, moving her hands correctly according to

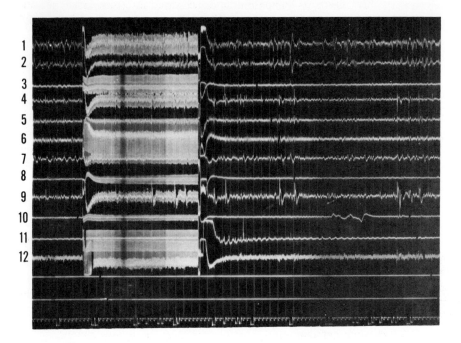

Fig. 3. Vivid thought image. Electrographic record showing effects of stimulation of right anterior commissure at 8 v, 5 ma, 100 cps for 15 seconds. Sensitivities of channels 1-12 are 500μv, full scale. Vertical lines are 1 second apart. Key: (1) right posterior hippocampus; (2) probable right posterior hippocampus; (3) probable right optic radiation; (4) left posterior hippocampus; (5) probable left posterior hippocampus; (6) probable left optic radiation; (7) probable right hippocampal gyrus; (8) probable right hippocampus; (9) left hippocampal gyrus; (10) left anterior hippocampus; (11) right anterior commissure; and (12) probable right cingulum. (From Horowitz, Adams, and Rutkin. 1968. *Arch. Gen. Psychiat.,* 19:469–486.)

instructions), she appeared unable to deliver an introspective report in words. A few seconds later, she said she had seen "pigs walking upright like people" and that she saw such images frequently during her auras. Further questioning clearly revealed that the pigs were not hallucinations, since she did not project them into external reality or think that they were real perceptions. Yet, the pigs were very vivid visually, more so than her usual pictorial ideation. Her association to the pigs was:

> They called me a pig a lot; it got me upset. I'd seen the image of a pig
> —standing on two legs—dressed in clothes—staring at me—as if it were
> saying to me, "You're not a pig. You don't belong with us even if they
> call you a pig."—Like myself talking to myself. The pig was me, but
> telling me I wasn't a pig—but I see it all the time before spells.

The content of the vivid thought image, apparently initiated by the electrical stimulation, is not derived directly from a perceptual experience.

Even if she had seen pigs in storybook illustrations, any perceptual source was reworked in the construction of the imagery that the patient reported. This alone does not indicate that the experience could not be a rerun of a memory. The patient might have been reexperiencing a memory of an imaginary experience. She might have developed a specific fantasy image that compounded various ideas and affects, and this fantasy image might have become a symbolic substitute for a more extended train of thought—a condensation of various ideas, affects, defensive attitudes, and so forth. The symbol might then have been rerun into visual imagery when the systems of visualization were activated, when the underlying affects or ideas were activated, or when the substrates of that particular symbol were activated.

This incident of the pigs was reported only once during the stimulations and recording sessions, although the same site was stimulated twice more with similar stimulus parameters.

"A" EVENTS—HALLUCINATION. A condensed list of the visual hallucinations reported will give an overview. The last four events will be described in greater detail.

1. Round room off to the side, remembered from when a little girl.
2. A dog and a man.
3. Self sitting, giving sister a "sickle cell" treatment (injection).
4. A man wearing a brown sports outfit, sitting in a chair. Seemed to be Dr. A.
5. A cherry grove, familiar—near home, changing into a single tree, then into a wire (attached to the TV camera at which the patient had been staring).
6. Three boys playing on a swing in the yard. One was the patient's youngest son. (Patient did not recall ever seeing this.)
7. A white number moving. (Patient had performed a counting task previously.)
8. Flashes of light becoming a doorway, then becoming flashing light again.
9. A "No Smoking" sign. (There was such a sign on the surgery room door.)
10. Gold color becoming an invitation—then a boy and girl—then Dr. H. and someone else getting papers.
11. Orange color—becoming people.
12. A spinning phantom, assuming the shape of the overhead light fixture.
13. Lady with a pink dummy.

EXAMPLE OF AN "A" EVENT—TWO HALLUCINATIONS EVOKED BY REPEATED STIMULATION OF THE SAME SITE. The patient was an 18-year-old boy who received a stimulation of the left posterior hippocampus at 17 volts, 11 milliamps, 100 cps for 2.5 seconds. At the onset of stimulation, the patient's facial expression changed, and he began to look and turn his head to the right. He said that he saw the investigator's

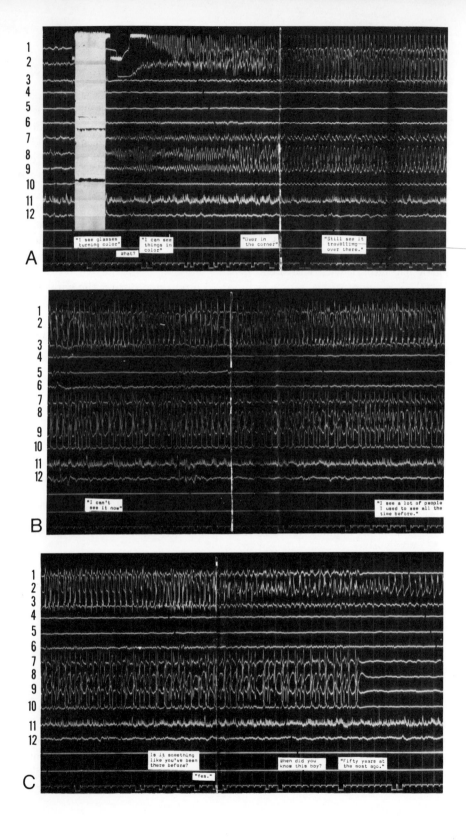

glasses turning an orange color that changed shape "every split second" and continued to "travel" to the right. Approximately a minute later he reported seeing people he knew "50 years ago," one of them a boy standing on a street. This was associated with unusually prolonged left limbic after-discharge that lasted 4 minutes and 30 seconds while the patient responded to questions in a more obtunded manner than prior to the stimulation. He seemed to comprehend some of the meaning of the questions, but his verbal contents and tonal inflections resembled those found in aphasia, sleep-talking, or hypnagogic speech. (The electrical concomitants are represented in Figure 4A–C.)

During the following day, the same electrode within the left posterior hippocampus was stimulated at 11 volts, 10 milliamps for 12 seconds.

The following notes are taken from the transcript.

(Stimulus on. Patient looks and turns his head gradually to the right, gazing intently at blank spaces on the wall. He stopped talking with the onset of stimulation.)

Do you see anything now?
"I see, uh, up against that canvas there, there's, uh—" (points toward the wall)
What do you see?
"What's that?"
What do you see?
"A gold drovoil (sic)—you see, it's moving."
What's moving?
"The sign—it's—"
It's moving?
"Yeah."
It's a gold sign?
"Yeach, goldvoy (sic). It's still moving."
And what does the sign say?
"Uh, it's, uh—seems like—uh—(unclear word) invit—invitation for, uh—for, uh—"
What?
"I can't even describe it right now—a thing—invi—initation."
The sign (or invitation) then became "some guy" and the images apparently persisted when he shut his eyes:

Fig. 4. Hallucinatory event. Electrographic record showing effects of stimulation of left posterior hippocampus at 17 v, 11 ma, 100 cps for 2.5 seconds. Sensitivities of channels 1-10 are 500μv, full scale, channels 11 and 12 are 200μv, full scale. Heavy vertical line indicates omission of 30 seconds of record. Light vertical line indcates 1 second of time. Key: (1) left inferior hippocampus; (2) probable left posterior hippocampus; (3) probable left posterior hippocampus; (4) right anterior commissure; (5) probable right lateral ventricle; (6) right junction of corpus callosum and cingulum bundle; (7) left hippocampal gyrus; (8) probable left hippocampus; (9) left hippocampal gyrus; (10) probable left globus pallidus; (11) right amygdala; and (12) right globus pallidus. The record continues sequentially in 4A-C. Some of the patient's remarks are inserted at the appropriate times. (From Horowitz, Adams, and Rutkin. 1968. *Arch. Gen. Psychiat.*, 19:469–486.)

Is it anybody you know?
"Yeah, but I can't recall the name. That's just the funny thing about
it."
It's a boy?
"Yeah."
Where is he?
"He's going, uh, I—"
Shut your eyes. Do you still see him?
(eyes shut) "Uh—yeah, I can still see it."
The boy?
"Uh, yeah—"

The patient was then asked to open his eyes. He reported a boy and
girl "traveling a lot together."

They're traveling a lot together?
"Yeah."
And?
"This is all it." (sic)
You see two of them?
"Yeah. . . . Kind wonder if, uh—the dear, the idea about them, ya'-
know. . . ."
Well, was it a boy and another boy, or a boy and a girl?
"It was a boy and a girl."
How old were they?
"Uh—really couldn't say."
Were they wearing clothes?
"Yeah—"
Can you describe them?
"Uh, no, not really. I can't describe it, I don't—really pay much attention
to what they're wearing. I do know they didn't come here naked or
nothing."

The patient drifted off into a semistuporous but wakeful state in
which he continued to respond to questions with replies such as "I'm
completely lost. I don't know how many, nary a thing. I feel real weird
right now. I can't stray" (he meant 'say') and "feel like I'm—feel all like
I'm ready to go to sleep." He apparently continued to form visual
images for, after a pause, he continued:

"I mean this picture—uh, you and somebody else—picking up papers (an
unclear, mumbled phrase)"
Me and someone else getting papers?
"Yeah—I don't even know if I'm—uh saying anything that makes sense
or not—"
It seems funny to you, your thinking?
"Yeah."

(The initial visual events seemed to be of hallucinatory intensity and
projected into the external environment; the latter event of picturing
"you and somebody else" is more likely a visual thought image than a
hallucination.)

The depth EEG showed high-voltage, rapid spiking activity in both the left inferior and posterior hippocampus and the left hippocampal gyrus. Fifteen minutes after this visual event, the subject was asked if he remembered seeing anything. He replied, "I did remember seeing it, but I can't remember what it was." The early electrical events are indicated in Figure 5.

The two preceding episodes are illustrative of a frequent occurrence: an initially unformed, geometric, or colored visual sensation occurred, probably because of excitation in some section of the visual pathways, then was elaborated into "what it looks like." The elaboration followed the form of the initial elementary impression but was also guided by other psychologic processes. The after-discharge continued throughout the period of elaboration of the images. Both visual hallucinations were forgotten about 15 minutes after occurrence.

As mentioned, the hallucinatory quality of thought seems to have, at times, a crude coincidence with the intense after-discharge that often follows stimulation. This after-discharge may be followed in turn by a period of low-voltage, irregular EEG activity. The patient mentioned above continued to be responsive during this period of relatively quies-

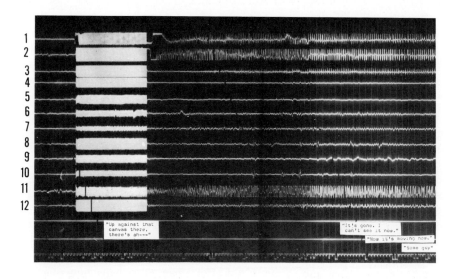

Fig. 5. Hallucinatory event. Electrographic record showing effects of stimulation of left posterior hippocampus at 11 v, 10 ma, 100 cps for 12 seconds. Sensitivities of channels 1, 2, and 3 are 500μv, full scale; channels 4–12 are 200μv, full scale. Vertical lines are 1 second apart. Key: (1) left inferior hippocampus; (2) probable left posterior hippocampus; (3) probable left posterior hippocampus; (4) right anterior commissure; (5) probable right lateral ventricle; (6) right junction of corpus callosum and cingulum bundle; (7) right hippocampal gyrus; (8) right lateral amygdala; (9) right amygdala; (10) right globus pallidus; (11) left hippocampal gyrus; and (12) probable left globus pallidus. (From Horowitz, Adams, and Rutkin. 1968. *Arch. Gen. Psychiat.*, 19:469–486.)

cent EEG activity. He answered questions in a rational manner, but the quantity of mental contents seemed to be reduced. Some patients reported the experience of a haunting sensation—"trying to grab hold of my memory but can't"—or the flickering of images through consciousness that has been labeled "dream scintillations." (Forbes, 1949; Saul, 1965; Horowitz et al., 1968) In short, there is at times a quality suggestive of a regressive state of consciousness following electrical stimulation of structures deep within the temporal lobe.

EXAMPLE OF AN "A" EVENT WITH PSYCHOMOTOR SEIZURE. The patient was a 40-year-old man who received an electrical stimulation of the left posterior hippocampal gyrus of 10 volts, 100 cps for 1 second. As an immediate consequence, both a generalized electrical spiking discharge and a psychomotor seizure developed for a period of 1 minute, in which the patient looked about with a startled expression, saying, "who, who, who," and fumbled with his clothes. Following this he returned to the coherent, alert, and communicative mental state that preceded the stimulation. He reported having seen an attractive woman, whom he identified as a hospital worker, enter the room carrying a pink, plaster dummy in the form of a woman. She appeared to be smoothing over the plaster just as the doctor had done when applying his cast "to mend his arm." While telling this, the patient patted the plaster cast of his broken arm, saying, "like this." He stated that the woman was going to "fix things up." The dummy he associated with the manikins he worked with in a department store. He lost his job because of a psychomotor seizure in the company cafeteria, but it was the best job he had ever had and he wished he had one like it now.

Just prior to the stimulation, the patient had been looking carefully at his broken arm and talking of his inability to work because of it. Just after the seizure, he asked if he was going to be cured of his spells. He also reached absently for the arm of a nurse with whom he had been indulging in a mild flirtation during intervals before the stimulation. He seemed to provide a cover for this gesture by looking at her watch. The content of the hallucination seemed to be a highly condensed pictorialization of his motivational state at the time of the stimulation.

Another "A" event was produced upon repeated stimulation of the right posterior hippocampus on another day. The patient reported a visual phantom that spun around and then assumed a shape like that of the overhead fixture. There was an after-discharge at the site of stimulation but no general discharge and no psychomotor activity.

COMMENT

In our study, stimulation of deep structures of the limbic system produced a variety of visual events that resembled in phenomenology the events reported as a consequence of surface stimulations. Psychologically, we were most interested in those visual events that depicted formed objects. Penfield had found that stimulation of the temporal cortex of epileptics occasionally evoked hallucinations (Penfield, 1958). He suggested that experiential hallucinations might be activations of the engrams of perceptual memories. He was careful to point out that such activation of mnemic engrams might be true only of epileptics since normative data was not available. In the foregoing description of our clinical results, I made several comments on the relationship of the events to current percepts and motives. In this discussion, I would like to speculate further into the processes involved in the formation of images and hallucinations and into the ingredients that supply the content.

THE PROCESSES OF IMAGE FORMATION. According to the memory-"engram" model, perceived events are stored as memories in some sort of neuronal or molecular site. Activation of the storage site evokes the memories and may lead to hallucinatory reenactments of the perceptions. The subject reports these perceptual reruns as reliving a past experience.

Several of our observations have led us to believe that this model is too simple.

1. No two stimulations at the same anatomic point produced the same images or hallucinations. This in itself, however, does not necessarily contradict the memory-"engram" model since the same site is never in the same state of excitation and since, as Penfield (1966) pointed out, it is doubtful that stimulations are of the memory sites directly.

2. Images and hallucinations were reported that probably were never actually seen in prior experience. Sometimes the self was seen in a way which would not be possible by self-perception: sometimes imaginary scenes were depicted. Again, this in itself does not necessarily refute the memory-"engram" model, for to retain a memory of a previous fantasy or dream is possible. Such a memory of an imaginary product could conceivably be aroused by stimulations.

3. Many of the images were related to recent perceptions, active ideas, or current motives. Of course, perceptions, ideas, emotions, and motives may all "prime" certain memories subliminally, in this way rendering such engrams more likely to be selected for further activation into psychic representation. Many of the visual events were also produced in association with an altered state of awareness. In such states, image formation is enhanced and increased influence of primary-process prevails.

4. At times the image or hallucination seemed to be elaborated out of a matrix provided by elementary sensations such as light, color, or amorphous shape. Such progressive elaborations (and simplifications in some instances) are very similar to the descriptions in the previous chapter.

To summarize, the relatively few hallucinations and pseudohallucinations found in our study could be due simply to a loss of inhibition over image formation and to, in some instances, the elaboration of elementary sensations evoked by irritation of the optic radiations. Our results thus support the hypothesis of Mahl et al. (1964) that brain stimulations may lead to regressive alteration of the state of consciousness and regressive alteration of the organization of thought. Since we tentatively use loss of inhibition as an explanatory principle, let us permit some further speculation as to the possible role of hippocampal structures in the regulation of image formation. Because, however, our findings are based on the introspective reports of persons prone to episodes of clouded consciousness and primary process thinking, and because our patients probably all have some degree of diffuse organic brain damage, any remarks based on the evidence reported above must be regarded with caution.

THE HIPPOCAMPUS.   We found that a relative preponderance of reports of formal visual sensations occurred after stimulation of the posterior hippocampal gyrus in comparison with other limbic sites of stimulation. MacLean and his coworkers, using microelectrodes in waking animals, found that the cortex above and below the calcarine fissure was found to "fire" into the posterior hippocampal gyrus and this gyrus in turn was found to "fire" into the hippocampus (Pribram and MacLean, 1953). In squirrel monkeys, photostimulation evoked discharge in the posterior hippocampal gyrus and the adjoining lingual cortex (Cuenod et al., 1965). A class of cells in the posterior hippocampal gyrus that responded to slowly adapting "on" cells of the retinae was also identified (MacLean, 1966). The findings of our empiric study and the neurophysiologic work of MacLean et al. suggest that there are visual pathways to the posterior hippocampal gyrus or that this area is, in some way, involved in the regulation of image formation.

What possible role does the posterior hippocampus structure play in image formation processes? Douglas (1967) reviewed the literature on hippocampus function in man. Four theories survive his analysis.

1. The hippocampus appears to be involved in working memory in relating present situations to previous ones. In terms of the model of image formation advanced in Chapter 7, the process would involve holding an image of a perception, forming images based on similar schemata, and comparing and modifying the external and internal images until a match occurs, and the current situation is deciphered according to relevance and similarity to past memories and perceptual schemata.

2. The hippocampus appears essential to internal and external inhibitory processes. In terms of image formation this process would involve preserving the autonomy of images of internal and external origin. That is, when the image formation apparatus was in perceptual use, in-

ternal images would be inhibited. When daydream images were the content of attention, then perceptual images might be inhibited.

3. The hippocampus is believed to be involved with suppression of conditioned responses. Suppression of conditioned responses in image formation would involve the capacity to preserve the independence of images of perception from schemata of prior sensory memory. This suppression capacity makes it possible to recognize a *novel* perceptual image and avoids an imperative or erroneous transformation of a novel image into a false correspondent to a memory image or traditional schemata.

4. The hippocampus may exert inhibitory control over attention, possibly by means of inhibitory control over incoming sensations (Douglas and Pribram, 1966; Gerbrandt, 1964).

In image formation, this inhibitory control would allow a flexible shift between fantasy and assessment of external reality without confusion between the two or excessive centering on one activity.

In summary, the hippocampus apparently serves a regulatory role. Possibly the posterior areas of the hippocampal formation are relatively devoted to the regulation of image formation. Disrupting the function of this area, as by electrical stimulation, might alter controls. Images of perceptions might be confused with images of memory resulting in poorly differentiated composites or illusions (failure of Function 1 above). In a sequence of thought in images there might be a failure to connect together and keep separate those images derived from sequential perception from those in a fantasy (failure of Function 2). Similarly, the person would be unable to suppress the peremptory interpretation of external signals according to currently active internal schemata (Function 3) and would lose the power to shift at will from perception to fantasy and back (Function 4). The results could be the perceptual distortions, elementary sensations, illusions, pseudohallucinations, and hallucinations reported by our patients.

CONCLUSION

Electrical stimulation of structures deep within the temporal lobes of persons with long-term temporal lobe epilepsy resulted in visual events. Ten percent of 1,509 stimulations in 16 patients produced some type of visual event. When these events were divided into categories of hallucinations, vivid thought images, elemental sensations, and visual distortions, about 1 percent of stimulations produced hallucinations and 1 percent produced vivid thought images. Such object-related images were most likely to be reported following stimulation of the posterior hippocampus. Many of the visual events were associated with an after-discharge at the site stimulated. Visual events had no clear relationship to the side stimulated or to areas of epileptogenic pathology.

Examination of the content of the imagery and hallucinatory-type events indicates that object-related contents are sometimes evolved from a matrix or gestalt provided by elemental sensations. These images and hallucinations may also relate to current motivational dynamics. They cannot be explained entirely by the theory that stimulation activates memory "engrams" that are then rerun. The stimulations, at least at times, produced an altered state of consciousness in which lexical cognition was reduced and image formation was enhanced or disinhibited.

The contents of the last two chapters illustrate the usefulness and necessity of the concept of regulatory controls. The inhibition and facilitation of image formation can be influenced by psychologic motives, and these motives involve change in neurophysiologic variables. The inhibition and facilitation of image formation is influenced by neurophysiologic factors, and these factors change the current state of psychologic motives. In sum, then, whether we can figure it out or not, any given image experience is a result of both psychologic and neurobiologic influences and their interrelationship.

REFERENCES

Adams, J. E. 1966. Future of stereotaxic surgery. *J.A.M.A.*, 198:648–652.

Bailey, P. 1948. *Intracranial Tumors.* Springfield, Ill., Charles C Thomas Co.

Bender, M. B. 1965. Neuroophthalmology. In Baker, A. B., ed. *Clinical Neurology*, 3rd ed. New York, Hoeber Medical Division, Harper & Row Publishers.

Brain, R. 1955. *Diseases of the Nervous System.* London, Oxford University Press.

———— 1954. Loss of visualization. *Proc. Roy. Soc. Med.*, 47:288–290.

Bromberg, W., and Schilder, P. 1933. Psychologic considerations in alcoholic hallucinosis—castration and dismembering motives. *Int. J. Psychoanal.*, 14:206–224.

Costello, C. G., and MacGregor, P. 1957. The relationships between some aspects of visual imagery and the alpha rhythm. *J. Ment. Sci.*, 103:786–795.

Cuenod, M., Casey, K. L., and MacLean, P. D. 1965. Unit analysis of visual input to posterior limbic cortex: I. photic stimulation. *J. Neurophysiol.*, 28:1101–1117.

Douglas, R. J. 1967. The hippocampus and behavior. *Psychol. Bull.*, 67:416–442.

———— and Pribram, K. H. 1966. Learning and limbic lesions. *Neuropsychol.*, 4:197–220.

Feldman, M., and Bender, M. 1969. Hallucinations and illusions of parieto-occipital lobe origin. Paper presented to the Eastern Psychiatric Research Association Meeting on Origin and Mechanisms of Hallucinations. New York, Nov. 1969.

Fisher, C., and Paul, I. H. 1959. The effect of subliminal visual stimulation on images and dreams: A validation study. *J. Amer. Psychoanal. Assoc.*, 7:35–83.

Forbes, A. 1949. Dream scintillations. *Psychosom. Med.*, 11:160–162.

Golla, F. L., Hutton, E. L., and Walter, W. G. 1943. The objective study of mental imagery. I. physiological concomitants. *J. Ment. Sci.*, 89:216–223.

Gerbrandt, L. K. 1964. Generalizations from the distinction of passive and active avoidance. *Psychol. Rep.*, 15:11–22.

Horowitz, M. J. 1964. The imagery of visual hallucinations. *J. Nerv. Ment. Dis.*, 138:513–523.

———— Adams, J. E., and Rutkin, B. B. 1968. Visual imagery on brain stimulation. *Arch. Gen. Psychiat.*, 19:469–486.

———— Adams, J. E., and Rutkin, B. B. 1967. Dream scintillations. *Psychosom. Med.*, 29:284–292.

———— Cohen, F. M., Skolnikoff, A., and Saunders, F. A. 1970. *Psychosocial function in epilepsy.* Springfield, Ill., Charles C Thomas Co.

Ishibashi, T., et al. 1964. Hallucinations produced by electrical stimulation of the temporal lobes in schizophrenic patients. *Tohoku. J. Exp. Med.*, 82:124–239.

Jackson, J. H. (1932) *Selected writings of John Hughlings Jackson.* Taylor, J., ed., Vol. 1. New York, Basic Books Inc., 1958.

Jasper, H. H., and Rasmussen, T. 1958. Studies of clinical and electrical responses to deep temporal stimulation in men with some considerations of functional anatomy: The brain and behavior. *Res. Publ. Ass. Res. Nerv. Ment. Dis.* 35:316–334.

Kamiya, J., and Zeitlin, D. 1963. Learned EEG alpha wave control by humans. Report #182, Dept. of Mental Hygiene, Research Div., State of California.

Klüver, H. 1942. Mechanisms of hallucinations. In *Studies in Personality.* New York, McGraw-Hill.

Lehmann, D., et al. 1965. Changes in patterns of the human electroencephalogram during fluctuations of perception of stabilized retinal images. *Electroenceph. Clin. Neurophysiol.*, 19:336–343.

MacLean, P. D. 1966. The limbic and visual cortex in phylogeny: Further insights from anatomic and microelectrode studies. In Hassler, R., and Stephan, H., eds. *Evolution of the Forebrain.* Stuttgart, Georg Thieme Verlag.

Mahl, G. F., et al. 1964. Psychologic responses in the human to intracerebral electrical stimulation. *Psychosom. Med.*, 26:337–368.

Oswald, I. 1957. The EEG: Visual imagery and attention. *Quart. J. Exp. Psychol.*, 9:113–118.

Penfield, W. 1966. Speech, perception and the cortex. In Eccles, J. C., ed. *Brain and Conscious Experience*, pp. 217–237. New York, Springer-Verlag.

——— 1958. *Temporal Lobe Epilepsy*. Baldwin, M., and Bailey, P., eds. Springfield, Ill., Charles C Thomas, Publisher.

——— and Jasper, H. 1954. *Epilepsy and the Functional Anatomy of the Human Brain*. Boston, Little, Brown & Co.

——— and Rasmussen, T. 1950. *The Cerebral Cortex of Man*. New York, MacMillan Co.

Perot, P., and Penfield, W. 1960. Hallucinations of past experience and experimental responses to stimulation of temporal cortex. *Trans. Amer. Neurol. Ass.*, 85:80–84.

Pribram, K. H., and MacLean, P. D. 1953. Neuronographic analysis of medial and basal cerebral cortex: Monkey. *J. Neurophysiol.*, 16:324–340.

Rapaport, D. (1959) The theory of attention cathexis: An economic and structural attempt at the explanation of cognitive processes. In Gill, M., ed. *The Collected Papers of David Rapaport*, pp. 778–794. New York, Basic Books, 1967.

——— 1942. *Emotions and Memory*. Baltimore, Williams & Wilkins.

Saul, L. J. 1965. Dream scintillations. *Psychosom. Med.* 27:286–289.

Sedman, G. 1966. Being an epileptic. *Psychiat. Neurol.*, 152:1–16.

Short, O. 1953. The objective study of mental imagery. *Brit. J. Psychol.*, 44:38–51.

Slatter, K. H. 1960. Alpha rhythms & mental imagery. *Electroenceph. Clin. Neurophysiol.* 12:851–859, 1961–62.

Sprague, J. M. 1966. Interaction of cortex and superior colliculus in mediation of visually guided behavior in the cat. *Science*, 153:1544–1547.

Stepien, L., and Sierpinski, S. 1964. Impairment of recent memory after temporal lesions in man. *Neuropsychologia*, 2:291–303.

Whitten, J. R. 1969. Psychical seizures. *Amer. J. Psychiat.*, 126:560–564.

Williams, D., and Gassel, M. 1962. Visual function in patients with homonymous hemianopia. Part I: The visual fields. *Brain*, 185:175–250.

CHAPTER

12

Psychedelic Images
and Flashbacks*

Psychedelic agents evoke many unusual experiences, but none as dazzling as the visual images which sometimes reach hallucinatory proportions. Even before any increase in images, the psychedelic experience alters perception. Colors may take on a new vividness or meaning; illusions are common, so that the outline of objects may appear haloed, or telephone wires may look like snakes. Images often contain reduplication of figural elements as illustrated in Figures 1 and 2. At the height of the experience, images flow effortlessly, often into complicated and bizarre stories, and seemingly without voluntary control. Reality testing is often lost so that it becomes difficult to distinguish internal or fictive images from external perceptions. Factors such as mood, current motivational states, expectancy, and environment largely determine image contents. Indeed, environment may be crucial, for example, persons taking LSD in laboratory experiments report much different imagery than those in a candle-lit room with friends, music, and incense. Because a person loses his sense of volitional direction of thought, he may be amazed at the content of his images, but in spite of this nonvolitional sensation, images can be altered to some degree by voluntary effort. This "march of experience" from perceptual distortion, through perception and image

* Portions of this chapter were published in the *Amer. J. Psychiat.*, 126:565–569, 1969. Copyright 1969 by the American Psychiatric Association, and are reproduced by permission.

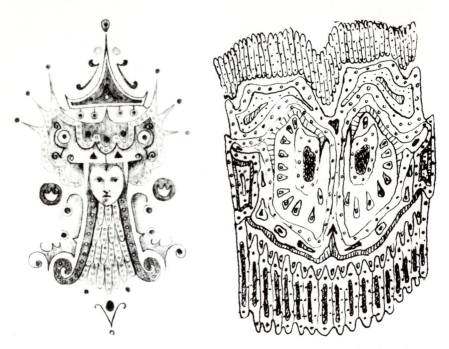

Fig. 1 (left) and 2 (right). An artist's drawing of two of his images under the influence of LSD.

fusion, to hallucination occurs in many organic conditions, intoxications, and in certain brain stimulation experiences. The resemblance of the phenomena in these conditions suggests that drug action effects the organic substrates of control image formation and perception.

Frequently, as volition decreases, people report ideas and feelings that are usually repressed. Under benign conditions, a person may "trip" on pleasantly gratifying wish fulfillments (as in a dream), accompanied by associated bliss and distortions of memory and time. Afterwards, a person may remember that he had unusual visions of great personal wonder and relevance, but he often will forget the details. Sometimes the release of normally inhibited ideas leads to new symbol formations which work to resolve defensive and impulsive conflicts (again, as with a good dream). On the other side of the coin, the release of what has been dormant or buried can result in a "bad trip," and, instead of a successful compromise among previously irreconcilable motives, there may be an excessive eruption of fear, hatred, or guilt.

After a trip, some persons increase their sensitivity to internal and external sensations. They may become more observant of their mental life (particularly images) or notice new sounds in music or new forms or colors in nature. Usually most of the contents from a trip are forgotten except for fragmentary memories. But sometimes people have intrusive returns of sensations which they first experienced during the drug state. "Flashbacks" can be extremely unpleasant, and are often symbolic of current psychologic problems. The remainder of this chapter will focus on that topic.

DESCRIPTION

Flashbacks (flashes, flashing) may persist for weeks or months after the last drug experience. The most common and clearest content of the flashbacks seems to involve the visual sensory system, but flashbacks have been reported in every sensory modality: taste, smell, touch, kinesthetics, vestibular changes, auditory images. In addition, distortions of time sense, self-image, or reality sense may occur. The most important variety of visual flashbacks consists of repeated intrusions of frightening images in spite of volitional efforts to avoid them. First, however, I describe two lesser variants.

1. SPONTANEOUS RETURN OF PERCEPTUAL DISTORTIONS

Distortions of perception experienced during the drug experience may recur long afterward, as previously reported (Horowitz, 1964). Subjective experiences include halo effects, blurred vision, shimmering, reduplications of percepts, distortion of spatial planes, and changes in normal coloration. Micropsia, macropsia, and tunnel vision may also appear during the period "off" drugs. Examples of such perceptual distortions and elementary sensations are:

EXAMPLE A

"Now I often see a bright shiny halo around people, especially at the dark edges—sometimes it's rainbow colors—like during the trip."

EXAMPLE B

"Sometimes the sidewalk seems to bend as if it's going downwards—even when I'm not on anything—or it just kinda vibrates back and forth."

2. INCREASED SUSCEPTIBILITY TO SPONTANEOUS IMAGERY

Some persons report that after repeated use of hallucinogens they find visual imagery occupies a greater proportion of their thinking than formerly. They also state that their imagery now has a different quality: it is more vivid, seems to spring from some nonvolitional source, and is less readily suppressed than formerly. The incidence of this type of flashback appears related to total dose over time.

Example C

"I see this giant iguana, all the time, man. Green. In corners. Like under your chair.
(Are you putting me on about that?)
No—you mean about under your chair like? No. I see it all right—sometimes even when I want to. It used to be fierce; now it's friendly.
(Used to be fierce?)
Well, like when I first had it—it was a monster from the dark lagoon (laugh) and then it came at me sometimes.
But now it's okay.
(Well, didn't you see stuff like that in your mind's eye all the time before any trips?)
Not like this, man. Not like this—it's real green.
(You mean, it's different?)
Oh, I see other things—this one's different—more so, I guess, more often, and clearer."

Example D

"Now I see things—walls, and faces, and caves—probably imprinted on my thalamus from the prehistoric past. Sometimes as clear as on a trip, but mostly not. My dreams sometimes are really spectacular now."

3. RECURRENT UNBIDDEN IMAGES

As described in Chapters 7 and 8, unbidden images are those that repeatedly coerce their way into awareness, demanding attention and resisting efforts to dispel them. They have been described by those who experience them as having "a will of their own." Some persons are frightened by their incapacity to dispel the images. Anxiety reactions, even psychotic reactions, may result.

Three examples clarify the recurrent and unbidden imagery of the flashbacks:

Example E

A 17-year-old boy who had taken marihuana, DMT, methedrine, LSD, and LSD with arsenic ("for that special kick").
Although his behavior was noted by his friends to be "freaky when he was flashing," he was able to deliver his thoughts in a rational manner.

He described his theme song as "LSD and speed are all that there is for me" and spent most of his time drawing morbid and bizarre references to death. His costume was black with steel link chains. During a recent "trip" he hallucinated a dark scorpion on the back of his hand and experienced terror: "It had many legs, and I was worried it might sting me." In the five weeks after the "trip" he claimed to have ingested no drugs, but the scorpion continued as "flashings," sometimes in a changed position, but always brown or black in color.

Example F

A 21-year-old man had numerous trips on LSD and marihuana. He described himself as preoccupied with life and death. After taking STP for the first time he had repeated visual and kinesthetic images of himself crashing through the window of his car. He had never had such an accident in reality, yet during the flashbacks he felt fear at the vividness of the experience. He was sensitive about his flashback and said it was *not* a symptom but a "release of the within" from the drug. The image appeared symbolic of repressed fears of losing control and of self-destructiveness.

Example G

A 16-year-old male high school drop out living in the Haight-Ashbury community reported an estimated 10 LSD trips and 100 marihuana smokings. He denied use of other drugs. Generally, during LSD trips he experienced interesting, wild, intense, and usually pleasant visual imagery. Recently, however, he had a "bad trip" with images of a human figure being sucked into the vortex of a whirlpool. Returns of this image began three weeks after the LSD trip and persisted for about three additional weeks. Five to ten times a day the vivid, black and white images interrupted whatever he was thinking. These images were more pressing when he was "high" on marihuana. Whenever he had the flashback he felt frightened and unsuccessfully tried to get rid of it. Although the time seemed very long, he knew that after approximately 15 to 20 seconds the image would leave of its own accord.

Since leaving home a year previously, he had stayed in various places, having incidental sexual and drug experiences without forming any intimate emotional attachments to anyone. However, in the "pad" (living place) where he had been staying most recently he had formed a close relationship with a particular boy and girl. Further discussion revealed that he had recently been asked to leave this pad. While denying that this had had any emotional impact on him, his tone of voice and facial expression indicated his sadness.

Later he began to talk of his loneliness and feelings of rejection with considerable feeling. Thereafter, he reported no more flashbacks. Possibly this symptom relief was due to working through his feelings and having a positive (substitute) relationship with the psychotherapist. The flashback seemed to symbolize three trends of his feelings: 1) loneliness, despair, and helplessness on being removed from a situation that had been homelike for him; 2) his feelings of being sucked down by drugs and lack of plans or structure in life; and 3) his dread of being overwhelmingly incorporated by getting too close to others.

INCIDENCE OF FLASHBACKS

The frequency of flashbacks is hard to assess because the phenomenon is subjective, difficult to describe, and not always inquired about by professional interviewers. In their 1967 review of the literature, Smart and Bateman (1967) reported only 11 cases of spontaneous recurrence of LSD effects. In contrast, a recent questionnaire survey of professionals revealed a very high rate of reports of "flashbacks" in patients who had used LSD (Ungerlider et al., 1968). Robbins et al. (1967) and his associates found that 11 of 34 patients admitted to a psychiatric ward because of LSD had some kind of reappearance of LSD effects after the drug had worn off. Keeler et al. (1968) state that spontaneous recurrence of marihuana effects are relatively common and, when associated with severe anxiety, constitute a psychiatric emergency.

My best source of information on the general incidence of flashbacks has been older hippies who function as fantasy guides during trips and as wisemen to the community at large. They estimate conservatively that flashbacks occur in about 1 out of 20 users, at least in the milder form of recurrence of perceptual distortions. The more severe forms appear to be more common with repeated use of hallucinogens, although each kind of flashback has been reported to occur after a single drug experience.

Recently, in cooperation with the Haight Ashbury Research Project,* a detailed study of flashback phenomena has begun. While only preliminary data are now available, they are consistent with the above remarks. Thirty-one persons, not contributors to the clinical data reported above, were interviewed as representative members of the drug-using community. As it happened, these persons split into three rather discrete groups with reference to use of hallucinogens. Twenty-two had massive drug use defined as a history of more than 15 LSD "trips" and considerable use of other agents, three had between 3 and 8 LSD "trips," and six had used various drugs such as marihuana and amphetamines but not LSD, DMT, or other hallucinogens. Of these 31 persons, eight reported one or more of the three types of flashbacks described in this chapter. Seven of these eight persons had massive drug intake; the remaining per-

* Supported by an NIMH grant (MH 15737-01A1) through Mount Zion Medical Center. R. Wallerstein, M.D. and S. Pittel, Ph.D., principal investigators.

Table 1 **Incidence of Visual Flashbacks in a Sample of 31 Persons with Chronic Drug Use***

Type of Flashback	More than 15 Hallucinatory Trips (M = 22)	Less than 8 Hallucinatory Trips (n = 9)	Total
Perceptual Distortion	3	0	3
Heightened Imagery Formation	4	1	5
Recurrent Unbidden Images	1	1	2
Totals	8 (in 7 persons)†	2 (in 1 person)	10 (in 8 persons)

*From Horowitz. 1969. Amer. J. Psychiat., 126:565-569. Copyright 1969, the American Psychiatric Association.
†The preponderance of flashbacks in the massive drug use group was not statistically significant (chi square).

son was from the group who had not used hallucinogens. Diagnostically, of the eight persons with flashbacks, two received diagnoses of ambulatory schizophreniform psychosis, four received personality pattern or neurotic diagnoses, and two were felt to have no evidence of psychiatric pathology sufficient to merit diagnosis. These data are summarized in Table 1.

Any of the major hallucinogens may be followed by flashbacks. The phenomenon was not reported after repeated marihuana use earlier in my subject sample, but now, with more potent forms of marihuana, cases are emerging. Keeler et al. (1968) also have reported similar events in four users of marihuana. Marihuana, seconal, physical fatigue, or stress may produce a state in which flashbacks from previous LSD "trips" are more likely to recur. I have only two reports of such recurrence with alcohol intoxication.

Persons with flashbacks insist that the imagery of the flashback has a different quality from thought images experienced prior to drug use. Usually the content of the flashbacks is derived from frightening imagery experiences during drug intoxication; less commonly, new images may be produced.

EXPLANATORY THEORIES

Several theories can be put forward to explain why recurrent unbidden images, often of identical context, may intrude into awareness for an extended period after the immediate effects of drugs have worn off.

1. THE RELEASE THEORY

The release theory is similar to that described in Chapters 7 and 11, and suggests that psychedelic agents may produce changes at the neurophysiologic level in the processes that regulate image formation (Freedman, 1968). Repeated toxic effects may lead to enduring changes in such processes although blood levels of LSD rapidly diminish (Aghajanian and Bing, 1964). The neurophysiologic changes, just as in brain stimulations, may create a situation in which image formation is disinhibited. Of interest, it has recently been suggested that a therapeutic agent in psychiatry, chlordiazepoxide, might result in release of image formation processes leading to hallucinations (see Case 4, Chapter 10; also Viscott, 1968).

The content of the flashbacks lends some support to the release theory. Hallucinatory constants (see Chapter 10; also Klüver, 1966) are common (the spiral shapes of the whirlpool, the radiating lines of the scorpion, and the broken windshield). Elementary sensations, such as these forms, and perceptual distortions, such as those of the first examples, are also reported during the auras of epilepsy or migraine and on electrical stimulation of the eye or brain, as described in the previous chapters. When the same object-depicting image occurs repeatedly, however, this suggests the presence of a meaningful set of psychologic motives in addition to whatever neurophysiologic "release" may be in operation.

2. DECONDITIONING THEORY

During the drug experience the person becomes aware of certain subjective sensations such as visual images to a heightened degree. Once such sensations have been noted, it is not quite so easy to ignore lesser degrees of the same event (Keeler et al. 1968). As in the release theory, the substrates of attention may be altered leading also to lessened capacity to ignore image formation. In addition, the repetition of frightening images could be an automatic effort at desensitization.*

3. PSYCHODYNAMIC THEORY

Even if the release and the deconditioning theories are correct, it would be necessary to describe a psychologic theory that considers

---

* Desensitization, a method used by behavior therapists, will be described in Chapter 14.

control in terms of cultural, and personal factors (such as those described in Chapters 7 and 8).

Interest in imagery is great in the drug community. Various means of promoting imagery experiences are experimented with. The richness of imagery experience, induced by hallucinogens and reinforced by the values of the subculture, probably enhances both the capacity to form images (through training) and the attention given to such forms of psychic representation. Also, some persons turn away from the external world and relationships with persons and preoccupy themselves with their own inner world.

Psychotherapeutic study of persons with recurrent unpleasant images suggests that cultural style, however influential, is not the only determinant. In some flashbacks, the image content seems to be a symbolic depiction of an affect state or situational crisis (e.g., despair and hopelessness). In some flashbacks, the recurrent images seem to be a return of traumatic perceptions—images of the drug experience that were overwhelmingly frightening at the time they were hallucinated. When the trauma is worked through by repeated discussion of the affects involved or when the repressed ideas were worked through, the flashbacks ceased. It is quite possible, however, that elimination of the symptom is accomplished through establishing a positive relationship rather than through resolution of trauma or lifting of repression per se.

Recurrent flashbacks bear some resemblance to other clinical phenomena such as peremptory ideation, obsessive rumination, and repetitive visual pseudohallucinations (as in hysterical psychosis). The experience is felt as a loss of volitional control over the contents of awareness, and this sensation of loss of control contributes to the attendant anxiety or loss of reality sense. As with unbidden images, the contents seem to be returns of traumatic perceptions, breakthroughs of repressed ideas or affects, or screen images to symbolize but conceal emotional conflicts. In particular, many of the images reported symbolized feelings of disintegration or impending doom, fears characteristic of persons undergoing an identity diffusion.

4. THE MYSTIC THEORY

The hippies believe that the mind has imprinted upon it memories of all ages past and possibly projections of the future as well. These prehistoric and archetypic perceptions are released, it is thought, by psychedelic experience. Once the images have learned the route to awareness, they press for remembrance. Perhaps, if we substitute "childhood" or "unconscious fantasy" for "prehistoric," "archetypic," and "ages past," this mystic theory is not as incompatible with psychologic theories as it might seem.

SUMMARY

Flashbacks are returns of images for extended periods *after* hallucinogens have worn off. The most symptomatic form consists of recurrent intrusions of the same frightening image into awareness without volitional control of this event. Like the imagery of the "trip," and the imagery on brain stimulation described in Chapter 11, the image experience may arise because of alteration of the neurobiologic capacity to use various regulatory controls over image formation. The image contents, however, and the secondary usage of the experience relate to psychodynamic motives for expression and control of expression. While chemotherapy, as with phenothiazine medication, may terminate the immediate experience of peremptory images, psychotherapy seems helpful for flashbacks, especially if there is a focus on traumatic and screening aspects of the imagery.

REFERENCES

Aghajanian, G. K., and Bing, O. H. 1964. Persistence of lysergic acid diethylamide in the plasma of human subjects. *Clin. Pharmacol. Ther.*, 5:611–614.

Freedman, D. X. 1968. On the use and abuse of LSD. *Arch. Gen. Psychiat.*, 18:330–347.

Heaton, J. M. 1968. *The Eye: Phenomenology & Psychology of Function & Disorder*. Philadelphia, J. B. Lippincott Co.

Horowitz, M. J. 1964. The imagery of visual hallucination. *J. Nerv. Ment. Dis.*, 138:513–523.

Keeler, M. H., Reifler, C. B., and Liptzin, M. B. 1968. Spontaneous recurrence of marihuana effect. *Amer. J. Psychiat.*, 125:384–385.

Klüver, H. 1966. *Mescal and Mechanisms of Hallucination*. Chicago, University of Chicago Press.

Robbins, E., Frosch, W. A., and Stern, M. 1967. Further observations on untoward reactions to LSD. *Amer. J. Psychiat.*, 124:149–151.

Schilder, P. 1942. *Mind: Perception & Thought in Their Constructive Aspects*. New York, Columbia University Press.

Smart, R. G., and Bateman, K. 1967. Unfavorable reactions to LSD. *Canad. Med. Ass. J.*, 97:1214–1221.

Ungerlider, J. T., Fisher, D. D., et al. 1968. A statistical survey of adverse reactions to LSD in Los Angeles county. *Amer. J. Psychiat.*, 125:352–356.

Viscott, D. S. 1968. Chlordiazepoxide and hallucinations. *Arch. Gen. Psychiat.*, 19:370–376.

13

Graphic Products

Painting or drawing furthers expression and evaluation of emotional ideas by allowing participation of the motor and perceptual systems. The construction of an external picture modifies the internal image; the external picture may stimulate further image formation which is then used to elaborate the external picture. The process is thus one of ever-expanded and more concrete expression and representation. Unlike internal images, external pictures can be viewed directly by other persons. Indeed, the person who produces the pictures communicates with himself by regarding the picture as an external object. Also, others may react to pictures, thus further influencing the image formation of the picture maker.

Some patients communicate graphically better than verbally. A mute person may draw or paint, incoherent patients may make understandable pictures. A patient who does not respond to words may acknowledge a picture drawn by a therapist. Thus, graphic products may offer a communicative medium that is a shift from a distrusted verbal medium.

Some concepts are poorly labeled with words and yet may be well depicted graphically. Take for example the body image. Sometimes a drawing of a person's body may convey to the observer an impression that is hard to describe in words, either by the patient or the observer—note the eerie effect of Figure 1. The same patient on the same day also made the drawing in Figure 2. While the style is different, both figures have a floating and unstable quality characterizing this patient's bizarre and unstable self-representation.

Fig. 1. A person drawn by a schizophrenic man.

Fig. 2. Another person drawing by the same patient that drew Figure 1.

DISADVANTAGES OF GRAPHIC PRODUCTS

While pictures can be useful tools for the communication of internal images, they do not necessarily depict such images accurately. Several filtering processes distort or elaborate the experience between image formation and graphic production. As Gombrich (1969) notes, drawing skills require not only accurate perception but also the acquisition of conventional graphic schemata. Thus, many persons draw not the flower they see but the one they were taught to draw by their kindergarten teacher: a stalk, a blob, two leaves.

In addition to the requirement of graphic schemata, a person must be able to use his hand and eye to make the representation. An alcoholic

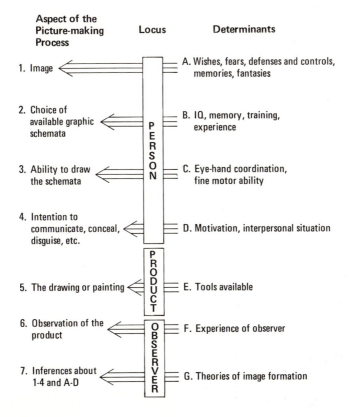

Fig. 3. Minimal complexity of process required to form, communicate, and interpret a graphic product.

trying to draw his hallucinatory experience may have learned enough drawing schemata to produce his image yet make a drawing far from his intention because of his trembling hands.

Figure 3 shows the minimal complexity of processes required to produce a drawing of an image. Motivation is included as an important factor. Many persons are reluctant to draw because they anticipate ridicule. They defend themselves by resorting to stereotypes as shown in Figure 4. Because of wide variation in filter processes, graphic products are useful in the hands of experienced clinicians who interpret them in

Fig. 4. Stereotypes used defensively in compliance with request to draw.

the light of other information about the patient. On the other hand, in research studies where only judgments of the graphic products are made, the results are often unreliable. A prime example is the figure-drawing or draw-a-person test which has generated a large literature of advocates and critics (Swenson, 1965; Witkin, 1962).

PSYCHOTIC ART *

Before modern psychiatric hospitals were available, some patients made pictures on their walls with food, blood, or feces. More advanced institutions supplied patients with proper materials in response to this apparent pressure towards graphic expression. The superintendents of these early asylums collected the resultant art works as curios and sometimes studied them in search of clues to the nature of insanity. More recently, efforts have been made to see if psychotic persons produce consistently different forms or contents than do normal persons. In terms of diagnostic use, other than deepened understanding of a single individual or separation of large groups, the results are disappointing.†

Expert judges can sometimes reliably separate drawings by schizophrenic persons from drawings or paintings by normal persons (Anastasi and Foley, 1940, 1941a and b, 1944; Anastasi, 1943; Levy and Ulman, 1967; Burton and Sjöberg, 1964). But there are too many false positives and negatives: some schizophrenic drawings appear normal, some normal drawings contain elements common in schizophrenic drawings.

In one study, I attempted to increase the information available from graphic products by increasing the number of drawings and by asking that drawings be produced in a reverie-like state (Horowitz, 1966). I based my task, the "dot-image sequence," on results of Corman et al. (1964) and Caligor (1957) which suggested that sequential drawings gave more information about preconscious mental processes.

The methods are described in detail elsewhere (Horowitz, 1965) and resulted in a series of six free drawings. Sixteen schizophrenic patients and 16 nonpatient subjects of equivalent age, sex, education, and social class were asked to put their minds at rest, stare fixedly at a central dot, and draw whatever came to mind or suggested itself upon a page of white paper. When each page felt finished they were to go on to the next. Six drawings were completed, taped together in order, and examined by

---

* The reader interested in the psychology of creative art is advised to consult Kris (1965), Arnheim (1966), Gombrich (1969), or Freud (1962).
† Kiell (1965) provides a bibliography of over 7,000 citations on the psychology of art, esthetics, and psychopathology and art.

Table 1   Rank Data from the Judging of Sets

Judges	Rank Average*		Rank Significance†
	Nonschiz.	Schiz.	
	n = 16	n = 16	
Expert			
A. Psychiatrist	11	22	p <.01
B. Psychiatrist	10	24	.01
C. Psychiatrist	11	22	.01
D. Psychiatrist	10	23	.01
Average	10	23	
Experienced			
E. Psychiatric technician	10	23	.01
F. Psychiatric nurse	12	21	.01
G. Chaplain	11	22	.01
H. Psychiatric nurse	12	21	.05
I. Psychiatric administrator	14	19	NS
J. Student technician	14	19	NS
K. Resident psychiatrist	15	18	NS
L. Psychiatric social worker	16	17	NS
Average	13	20	
Inexperienced			
M. Internist M.D.	11	22	.01
N. Internist M.D.	20	13	NS
O. Internist M.D.	22	11	.01 (significantly wrong)
Average	18	15	
Overall average	13	20	

*Sum of ranks divided by n.
†Rank-sum test.

judges at various levels of clinical sophistication. Each judge worked separately to rank order the 32 sets of six drawings so that the "most schizophrenic" set was number 1, the "most normal" number 32. The results appear in Table 1; more experienced judges could separate the dot-image sets beyond chance expectations, but some false categorizations were made.

How did the experienced clinicians separate the sets of drawings? They used various clues found in the contents of pictures, the form or style of drawing, and the nature of the sequential organization (the type and degree of change from one picture to the next). These clues are general tendencies in psychotic drawings and paintings. In what follows, I summarize such clues as found in this study, in my ongoing examination of graphic products, and in the reports by many others who have studied patient productions. The statements are generalizations; they reflect the tendency of groups of schizophrenic persons rather than individuals. No feature is diagnostic; the elements of style and content to be described can also be found in the art work of nonschizophrenic persons.

rig. 5. This drawing preceded a violent episode by two days. Note the overdrawing of the M in harm.

FORM

Persons in a schizophrenic episode usually behave with greater variation than normal persons. While they are more impulsive, they are also more inhibited. This general tendency is reflected in their graphic products.

Impulsive modes of production are revealed in harsh angular lines, scribbling, marking over, abrupt erasures, violent color combinations, and disregard for the conventional use of materials. Usually, impulsiveness in drawing or painting correlates with impulsiveness in general behavior or speech. Sometimes, however, a patient may be subdued in all other respects and only permit discharge of impulses in painting or drawing. Occasionally, pictures may be a useful barometer. For example, Figure 5 was done by a patient during a period in which he was overtly quiet on a psychiatric ward. Internally, there was a build up of paranoid rage, and an episode of violent behavior occurred the next day.

At the other end of the spectrum, overorganization and elaboration are also frequent in the graphic products of schizophrenics. Sometimes,

Fig. 6 (left). First painting during a psychotic episode. The patient depicted her initials clearly. Fig. 7 (right). Second painting during a psychotic episode. The patient has disguised and elaborated her initials. They are at once collapsed and ornamentalized.

intricate filigrees are produced as shown in Figures 6 and 7. A psychotic woman painted her initials very carefully with many tiny lines in Figure 6. On the same day, she did the figure shown in Figure 7, which also is based on her initials. The elaboration is so great that they would be unrecognizable without the previous graphic product. The "E" has collapsed and, as if in restitution, it is ornamentalized endlessly. The reader is reminded again of the nonspecific quality of such overelaboration: many a doodler fills telephone pads with similar drawings.

CONTENT

Bizarre contents characterize many drawings by schizophrenics. In schizophrenic episodes there seems to be a special tendency to decompose or distort the body. Drawings may contain anatomic deformities, transparencies, impossible positions, fragmentations, and depictions of sexual or aggressive assault to humans, animals, or things. Scenes of desolation and loneliness also appear (as they do commonly in depressive illnesses). Figures 8–13 show the dot image sequence from a young schizophrenic man. The series depicts story-like content. Relationship with a girl is threatening, the male face changes from happy to unhappy in Figure 8. The mouth has both expressions in Figure 9—the girl, although she looks coquettish in the drawing, is turned away from his sexual arousal. The next four drawings show permutations of the idea of harsh or dangerous women. Figure 10 is an evil-looking woman drawn with very hard and angular lines. Figures 11 and 12, his fourth and fifth drawings of the series, are less evil looking, but there are still aggressive aspects in the harshness of the hair lines and possibly the mouth of Figure 13. In Figure 13 the face is drawn violently with scribbling and hard lines.

The dot image sequence from another schizophrenic patient, again an extreme instance, is shown in Figures 14 through 19. Note the elaboration of the flame-like forms of the first drawing. In the second drawing there is a form that looks like a mouth with sharp teeth. (In psychoanalytic symbolism this frequently appearing form may either be a devouring mouth, or a devouring vagina: the *vagina dentata*). This dangerous form is softened, perhaps, into a rabbit-like figure. But the ears of the rabbit (if this interpretation is correct) develop evil-appearing eyes, and the forms undergo an elaboration that conveys to the viewer a weird impression. This series of drawings resembles the kind of hallucinatory elaboration described in chapter 10.

Themes of disintegration are common in schizophrenic graphic products, but it is important to note the frequency of an opposing con-

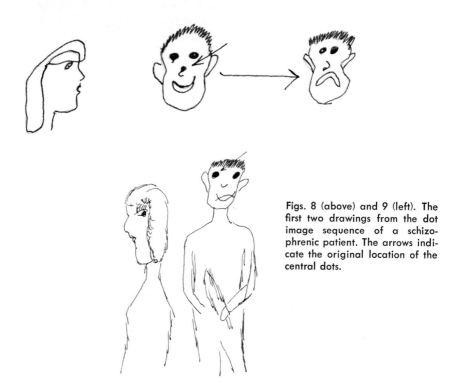

Figs. 8 (above) and 9 (left). The first two drawings from the dot image sequence of a schizophrenic patient. The arrows indicate the original location of the central dots.

tent: themes of reconstruction and integration: They may consist of inscription of the alphabet, the series of numerals, all the states of the union, addresses, names, or mathematical figures. Of larger proportion, entire cosmologies may be drawn, or systems involving religious figures, metaphysical symbols, or fantastic machines. I believe these all may be grouped as symbolic efforts at integration, control, organization, and reconstitution of the self. Figure 20 may combine both disintegrative and reconstructive aspects in simple form: the human figure has a detached and bizarrely constructed penis and testis. Note also the asymmetry between right and left limbs. Various abstract symbols are added: a cylinder, a square, a plus, and the sign for infinity. It seems likely these symbols are added to give a feeling of definitiveness and labeling, a sense of mastery as when one first learned the multiplication table or how to draw a square in school.

The extreme variation in form and content from impulsivity and disaster to control and reconstruction may reflect the psychologic struggle of a person in the midst of a schizophrenic psychosis. At the onset of the break with reality, the person is dimly aware of, and alarmed about, the

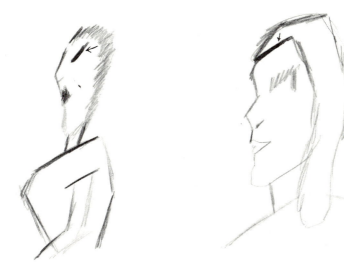

Figs. 10 (upper left), 11 (upper right), 12 (lower left), and 13 (lower right). The third to the sixth picture of the series begun in Figure 8. The arrows indicate the original location of the central dot.

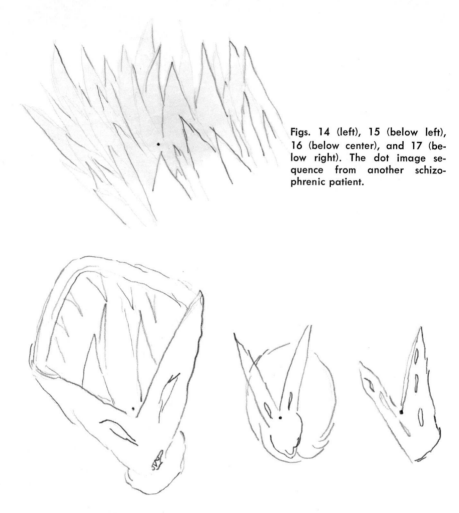

Figs. 14 (left), 15 (below left), 16 (below center), and 17 (below right). The dot image sequence from another schizophrenic patient.

dissolution of his mental capacities. To express this sense of psychologic disintegration he may use concrete symbols such as the body. Instead of thinking "my mind is coming apart," the person may draw his body, or the world, coming apart. Such drawings may represent subjective feelings, hypochondriacal delusions, or bodily hallucinations. The danger may be projected outwards, onto other persons or things which are shown in states of destruction. These destructive themes may also be motivated by intense and primitive hostile impulses that are poorly controlled.

In a similar manner, the feeling of despair and isolation leads to pictures such as lonely broken trees in desolated landscapes or figures lost

Figs. 18 (right), and 19 (below).
Continuation of the dot image
sequence begun in Figure 14.

in space. Again, such themes occur at some time in the life of all persons. Every amateur picture gallery will show paintings of the lonely tree (perhaps at sunset on a lonely mountain) and the sad clown who makes everyone else laugh while his heart is breaking.

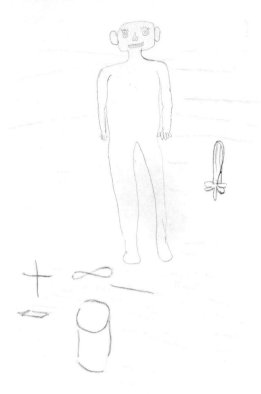

Fig. 20. A picture combining bodily fragmentation—separation of the penis—with abstract symbols. The symbols may serve as a pseudoexplanation for the loss.

The response to feelings of coming apart, to fears of destroying the world because of primitive inner rage, and to despair is to attempt reparation or restitution (Arlow and Brenner, 1964). This restitutional desire leads to the creative strivings in psychosis and couples with efforts to control impulses. The result is the spiritual, metaphysical, idealized contents and the careful, overdrawn, and excessively ornamental forms. In the process of drawing curlicues everywhere in a drawing, a person may gain feelings of organization and productivity that counteract his dread of chaos. The metaphysical symbols serve to heal the world a patient feels he menaces with his destructive impulses. Symbolically, the careful construction makes his own body and ideational structure intact and secure.

ART THERAPY

Early in dynamic psychiatry, reliving of experiences and ventilation of feelings (abreaction and catharsis) were regarded as powerful therapeutic tools. Art therapy began as an effort to provide an avenue for such discharge and expression.

The use of art therapy in the United States was pioneered by Margaret Naumberg (1950, 1953, 1966). She encouraged the patient to paint at home and in her office and regarded the pictorial products as equivalent to the free associative method of psychoanalytic treatment. The trusting relationship with the therapist, the development of expressive clarity, the interpretation of the meaning of symbols, and the working through of troubled emotions and painful memories were regarded as the therapeutic agents. (See also Stern, 1952 and Pickford, 1967.)

Other art therapists, such as Elinor Ulman (1953), focus on art therapy as a means of fostering growth and maturation. The effort to produce clear pictorial symbols is believed to help the patient gain a sense of identity, self-esteem, esthetic pleasure, and creativity.

In adults, as in children (Kramer, 1965; Kellog, 1967), art therapy may also foster a sense of mastery and control. To some extent, impulses, unclear but dreaded urges, and disquieting fears can be tamed by actively drawing or painting them.

Most art therapists encourage patients to use various modes of graphic depiction. They may suggest what medium to use, what subject matter to attempt, or give advice on technique. Art therapists more experienced in psychodynamics and trained in psychotherapy may encourage associations and offer interpretative remarks that seek to clarify further the meaning of the patient's expressions. The conventional art therapy situation, in which the patient draws or paints and the therapist observes or talks, has always seemed limited to me, especially in the treatment of severely disturbed individuals. I therefore tried a technique of interaction painting or drawing in which the therapist uses the same media of communication as the patient.

INTERACTION PAINTING AND DRAWING

The patient and I usually sit side by side and use the same media, either paints or felt tipped pens or pencils. I encourage the patient to begin, then try to respond. Most of the time we take turns; sometimes we both work at once. When we finish the activity, we discuss the product or separate until the next session. These sessions last 15 to 30 minutes and are generally repeated three to five times each week.

Many schizophrenic patients resist this procedure at first, and the following principles make its establishment easier. After the patient knows what to expect, I approach him with a positive and simple statement: "Let's go to my office now." On the rare occasion that a patient refuses, I ask him several times the same day or let him watch me paint for a while. I touch very withdrawn patients to establish contact in a friendly way and direct them to the painting table. Clean and bright materials in a simple arrangement and with only a few colors stimulate interest and reduce confusion. If the patient is reluctant to begin, I suggest: "Just blob on some paint," or I begin myself. My conversation is kept to a minimum. Praise, criticism, or posting of the results is avoided because the products are not intended to be "art" works but only a record of our communication. Immediately after each picture, after separation from the patient, I record the sequence of events. I note any pertinent happenings before or after the picture, my clinical observations of the patient's affective states, and my memories of my reactions during the picture production. Frequent review of the entire series clarifies what is happening and reveals overall patterns. One example of this technique was included in Chapter 8 (Mary). Here is another.

> The patient, a late adolescent male, was placed in a psychiatric inpatient treatment unit became of bizarre behavior, seeming disintegration of thought processes, preoccupation with his body, and withdrawal from his usual activities and interpersonal relations. Once on the ward he was unable to speak coherently, avoided the gaze of other persons, and turned his body away from them when approached. Periodically he stared at the ceiling or wall and moved his lips wordlessly—we wondered if he was hallucinating, but he was so verbally unresponsive that we could not tell. Interviews with his family indicated that periodically he had been verbally abusive and had kicked furniture; what he said at such times is unclear as his speech was incoherent or severely fragmented into unrelated phrases. It is clear that he had always been withdrawn, had never formed close friendships, and lived in a disturbed family. After an initial turbulent period in which he stubbornly resisted the hospital program (for example, by sitting up in a chair all night or not coming for meals), he settled down and went about with the other patients. He did not speak in group meetings or in individual interviews. When spoken to he sometimes looked up and stared for a long time at the other person with a suspicious and sour expression. On occasion he would say yes or no or make a tangential statement, usually with reference to the diseased state of his body.
>
> At this point verbal communication was a one way channel, and we were uncertain even as to the clarity of his reception of what was said to him. He did not reply. Even his nonverbal communications were reduced; he maintained a wooden face and a rigid, protective, and withdrawn type of posture. He made few gestures. Staff received the message that he wished to keep his distance from us and, if we were to get close, that he wished to repel us. We knew little else about what went on in his mind and, since this was not a satisfactory situation for therapeutic interventions, since neither milieu or drugs seemed to be altering the picture, another form of communication was attempted. Instead of words, visual symbols, colors, and lines were used. The patient was asked to sit down and paint with me.

At first it seemed that this, too, would fail to establish a network of give and take communications. With a certain forcefulness of approach, on my part, he was willing to enter the office, but sitting side by side was apparently too threatening for him. He sat at another table and watched me paint. I made a few abstract dabbings of colors. He watched with apparent interest when my gaze was on what I was doing, and looked away when I glanced at him.

We did this for two sessions. On the third he was willing to paint too—although separately from me. He used only a corner of the painting paper, at times ignoring the boundary and extending a line onto the desk top. After some time at this level of activity he let me approach closer to him, and we began to paint on the same panel. He painted on his side of the paper, and I got the message that I was to paint on my side. Generally, he copied what I did, but whenever he added something different I copied that. This developed into a kind of game. The feeling of cooperation was my main indicator; I tried anything that maintained contact between us and avoided things that increased his apparent tension or withdrawal. From an esthetic point of view our paintings were nothing to look at—just lines and dots of color at two sides of the paper.

After this had gone on for awhile and I thought I had his confidence—at least a little bit of trust—I allowed one of my lines to advance into what had become his territory. He withdrew his hand from that area. By now we were painting in sequence one after the other. At this point he stopped. But the next day his first stroke was a heavy black line down the middle of the paper. For a few sessions I resumed painting on "my" side, but as soon as it seemed permissible I painted something adjacent to his last effort. He added a series of dashes surrounding it as if it were a foreign body, and this began a new kind of game. He painted in my half of the paper, I approached it, then he jumped back to his side. If I followed, he circled my line. At times he got so involved that he grunted or laughed. Occasionally I tried verbal communication: "That was interesting," and at times he answered, "Yes."

In the next phase we were building up complex abstract structures of shape and color. We worked together and even talked a little bit before and after. When he seemed comfortable with this activity, I took an opportunity to paint over an area that he had done. He was shocked and stopped, peering at me suspiciously. I smiled a little and nodded. I hoped this communicated that he was to go on. He did and painted over something I had done. He looked at me intently. I went on painting. Then he demolished parts of the construction with great gusto. I made no verbal interpretations.

In subsequent phases we made stick figures. I started this and he copied. In time we began talking more, and eventually he was able to tell me some of his feelings.

I have presented this illustration because the communicative process clearly proceeds in graphic form with minimal content. The paintings were composed of areas of color with various shapes, primarily just dots and lines. They became more complex and appeared to be more integrated when the patient and I began working together. Florid content and bizarre symbols were not present. What was recorded in the series of pictures was the working through of an early phase in a therapeutic relationship. What was communicated was interpersonal intentions: I intended to work with him, to avoid threat situations, but to push against his withdrawal. I tried to indicate I was trustworthy. He tested me and then gradually expressed some of the feelings he had so tightly inhibited.

Of course, in many other patients this kind of work takes place using recognizable graphic forms, especially depictions of human figures in various types of relationships. In such instances the therapist and the patient gradually progress through phases. The first phase almost invariably seems to be a testing phase.

TESTING PHASE

During this phase the communication networks of territory, time, symbols, and modes are used guardedly until they are anxiety free and successful in transmitting messages. My efforts center around demonstrating the possibilities, encouraging the patient to be free in his expression, and establishing interaction. During initial encounters many patients resist interaction. At first they prefer to paint independently; then they may copy or tolerate being copied. Later, play and cooperative interactions emerge.

The testing phase lasts from five to ten sessions and then merges into the expressive phase. Usually by that time there is a feeling of rapport and collaboration, and direct expressions gradually emerge.

During the testing phase, spatial considerations are also important as indicated in the foregoing example by the patient's reluctance to sit together at the same table and also his concern for territories during the joint efforts. Interpersonal distances that seem natural and comfortable for the therapist may seem threateningly close to some schizophrenic patients: this spatial sensitivity applies both to interpersonal distance and to the use of space on the drawing or painting. Therapists should be alert to this spatial aspect of nonverbal behavior, and avoid infringing prematurely on the patient's "body-buffer zone" (Horowitz, 1964 and 1968).

EXPRESSIVE PHASE

Establishing a safe relationship with another human being protects patients from their conflicts and troubled feelings to the extent that they allow themselves a greater range of expression. The expressive phase varies from patient to patient. The patterns that emerge in a series of paintings with any one patient are naturally related to my reactions and interventions as well as to the patient's psychologic and psychopathologic characteristics. Nevertheless, each patient often develops a characteristic theme that emerges in a series of pictures related to his life style, conflicts, or clinical state. Some patients paint symbolic reparations of lost objects. Some draw their fears or traumas. Others concentrate more on the relationship with the therapist.

PHASE OF THERAPEUTIC INTERVENTIONS

When the therapist has sufficient insight into the problems of the patient, he may attempt to help the patient clarify his expression. This may involve confrontation with the patient's defensive operations. For example, if a patient blocks his own expression by repetition of just a few symbols. The therapist may attempt to develop the range of available symbols by drawing different elements. Here is one illustration:

> In a series of interaction paintings, a young adolescent patient had gradually increased his openness so that he and the therapist now mutually executed pictures. Landscapes were the repetitive theme. These landscapes consisted of green meadows, trees, blue skies, the sun, and mountains. The patient showed no indication to express anything further. The therapist began to introduce animals into the pictures. At first the patient merely watched the therapist's activities. After a while he also drew animals. When the patient was comfortable with this, the therapist began to add human figures. The patient seemed uneasy. Then he drew in not a single figure but an army complete with spears, bows and arrows, and machine guns. A series of "fighting" pictures developed: airplanes were shot down in flames, tanks and ships were blown up, people were killed. The patient seemed alternately uneasy and excited about these pictures, but gradually seemed to experience a sense of control over his hostile impulses. Only then did he begin to discuss his intense rage towards his parents.

Therapeutic interventions in art therapy are not very different from those in conventional verbal psychotherapy. The therapist tries to understand the current situation. In general he tries to work on the surface first and to avoid excessively "deep" interpretive thrusts. He seeks to effect a more effective and adaptive use of the patient's control and defensive capacity. When he thinks the patient can tolerate it, he may encourage him to consider troublesome topics. In art therapy he can introduce these topics gradually through pictorial symbols. Some of the methods for guiding image formation, to be discussed in the next chapter, will clarify the other options of the art therapist.

CONCLUSION

At the present time, no reliable and objective diagnostic use for graphic products has been found. On the other hand, such products, either drawings or paintings, offer to the therapist a wide range of useful information for clinical interpretation. The information contained in graphic products has a different mode of communication and representation than the face-to-face verbal interview. Contents may be expressed in pictures that go unmentioned verbally.

The patient may record his ideas and feelings while alone or in a group with other patients. He does not have to be there when the communication is "received." This indirectness of communication may allow increased message sending in patients who are regressed, withdrawn, frightened, or overly aroused during contact. It is possible to use art therapy in a wide range of interpersonal settings ranging from a kind of meditative self-communicative process, while alone, to the interaction drawing or painting described in the latter half of the chapter. The method seems especially useful in mute, withdrawn, or very blocked patients.

REFERENCES

Anastasi, A., and Foley, J. 1943. An analysis of spontaneous artistic productions by the abnormal. *J. Gen. Psychol.*, 28:297–313.

———— and Foley, J. P. 1944. An experimental study of the drawing behavior of adult psychotics in comparison with that of a normal control group. *J. Exp. Psychol.*, 34:169–194.

———— and Foley, J. 1941a. A survey of literature on artistic behavior in the abnormal. I. Historical and theoretical background. *J. Gen. Psychol.*, 25:111–142; II. Approaches and interrelationships. *Ann. N.Y. Acad. Sci.*, 42:1–112.

———— and Foley, J. 1941b. A survey of literature on artistic behavior in the abnormal. IV Experimental investigations. *J. Gen. Psychol.*, 25:187–237.

———— and Foley, J. 1940. A survey of literature on artistic behavior in the abnormal. II. Spontaneous productions. *Psychol. Monogr.*, 52(6).

Arieti, S. 1955. *Interpretation of Schizophrenia*. New York, Brunner.

Arlow, J., and Brenner, C. 1964. *Psychoanalytic Concepts and the Structural Theory*. New York, International Universities Press.

Arnheim, R. 1966. *Toward a Psychology of Art*. Los Angeles, University of California Press.

Burton, A., and Sjöberg, B. 1964. The diagnostic validity of human figure drawings in schizophrenia. *J. Psychol.*, 57:3–18.

Caligor, L. 1957. *A New Approach to Figure Drawing*. Springfield, Ill., Charles C Thomas, Publisher.

Corman, H. H., et al. 1964. Visual imagery and preconscious thought processes. *Arch. Gen. Psychiat.*, 10:160–172.

Freud, S. (1910) Leonardo Da Vinci and a memory of his childhood. *Stand. Ed.*, 11, 1962.

Gombrich, E. H. 1969. *Art and Illusion: A Study in the Psychology of Pictorial Representation*. New York, Pantheon.

Horowitz, M. J. 1968. Spatial behavior and psychopathology, *J. Nerv. Ment. Dis.*, 164:24–35.

———— 1966. Visual imagery: an experimental study of pictorial cognition using the dot image sequence. *J. Nerv. Ment. Dis.*, 141:615–622.

———— 1965. Notes on art therapy media and techniques. *Bull. Art Therapy*, 4:70–73.

———— 1964a. Body-buffer zone. *Arch. Gen. Psychiat.*, 11:651–656.

———— 1964b. The imagery of visual hallucinations. *J. Nerv. Ment. Dis.*, 138:513–523.

———— 1963. Graphic communication: A study of interaction painting with schizophrenics. *Amer. J. Psychother.*, 17:230–239.

Kellog, R. 1967. Understanding children's art. *Psychol. Today*, May, 1967, 16–25.

Kiell, N. 1965. *Psychiatry and Psychology in the Visual Arts and Aesthetics*. Madison, University of Wisconsin Press.

Kramer, E. 1965. Art therapy and the severely disturbed gifted child. *Bull. Art Therapy*, October, pp. 3–20.

Kris, E. 1965. *Psychoanalytic Explorations in Art*. New York, International Universities Press.

Levy, B., and Ulman, E. 1967. Judging psychopathology from paintings. *J. Abnorm. Psychol.*, 72:182–187.

Naumberg, M. 1966. *Dynamically Oriented Art Therapy: Its Principle and Practice*. New York, Grune and Stratton.

———— 1953. *Psychoneurotic Art: Its Function in Psychotherapy*. New York, Grune and Stratton.

———— 1950. *Schizophrenic Art: Its Meaning in Psychotherapy*. New York, Grune & Stratton.

———— 1947. Studies of the "free" art expression of behavior problem children and adolescents as a means of diagnosis and therapy. *J. Nerv. Ment. Dis.*, Monogr. 71.

Pickford, R. W. 1967. *Studies in Psychiatric Art*. Springfield, Ill., Charles C Thomas, Publisher.

Stern, M. 1952. Free painting as an auxiliary technique in psychoanalysis. In Bychowski, G., ed. *Specialized Techniques in Psychotherapy*. New York, Basic Books.

Swenson, C. H. Jr. (1957) Empirical evaluations of human figure drawings. In Murstein, B. I., ed. *Handbook of Projective Techniques.* New York, Basic Books, 1965.

Ulman, E. 1953. Art therapy at an outpatient clinic. *Psychiatry,* 16:55–64.

Witkin, H. A., et al., eds. 1962. *Psychological Differentiation: Studies of Development.* New York, John Wiley and Sons.

CHAPTER
14
The Use of Image Formation in Psychotherapy

Psychotherapists of different persuasions use image formation for various purposes. Some use images to explore dimly recognized or repressed ideas, feelings, memories, and fantasies. Others attempt to transform current attitudes, emotions, and behavioral patterns by the use of image formation. In what follows, I first discuss general reasons for the employment of images in psychotherapy; then I describe some of the technical variations used.

PURPOSES

The formation and communication of images can 1) yield information, 2) establish empathic understanding, 3) release and work through emotions, and 4) transform mood or attitude. Any therapeutic effort may use each of these effects to a greater or lesser degree.

1. INFORMATION

The therapist constructs within his own mind a model of the patient's world. The model ideally includes the nature of the patient's self-images,

289

the residues of previous relationships, the expectancies toward future relationships with others, the standards of proper conduct, the typical needs and fears, the quality and intensity of urges and feelings, the habitual style of coping and defense during conflict situations, and important fantasies and memories.

Ordinary social communication usually avoids these topics but, with time and help, verbal communication in therapy can convey this information. Sometimes, however, images are especially useful message units. In diagnostic sessions, especially, certain information is hard to translate in words, and the therapist may seek additional data by asking about dreams, fantasies, or earliest childhood memories. Such memories are usually recalled in visual images (Lewin, 1968). Sometimes, in addition to recollection, image formation during the interview may yield useful impressions as in the following example:

> A teenage girl with vague medical complaints was referred for psychiatric consultation. Her response to a nondirective psychiatric interview technique was desultory. When specific questions were asked, she seemed cooperative and not overtly evasive but gave meager information. For example, when asked about her mother she said, "She's OK." When asked about their relationship, she said, "Pretty good." She was asked to form an image of herself together with her mother. She reported a detailed image of her mother and herself in the kitchen, her mother's face angry and yelling something at her, her own face cast down and sullen.

> Similarly, when asked about her father, she gave nonspecific information of a general, socially expectable, socially acceptable type: "He's OK, we get along so-so, et cetera." When asked for an image of herself with her father, she described herself walking down a stairway, blushing; her father is making a dirty comment about her tight sweater.

> Later, when asked to form an image of her school friends, whom she had described verbally as "just a bunch of the girls," she cried and said she was always left out of the group at lunch time and stood apart, watching the laughter of a group of girls.

In the above example, the request for image formation released information. The effect, of course, was not due merely to the emotion-evocation power of images. As it happened, the patient habitually thought in images. Discourse in words was, for her, a distant and relatively nonmeaningful social activity. Images, on the other hand, contained her rich inner fantasy life: the interviewer's request for images meant to her that he was interested in her inner life. Thus, the release of information was due not only to the transition to image formation from word formation, but also to an expression of meaningful interest on the part of the interviewer. The interviewer's request meant "O.K., now let's really talk about what's on your mind."

In diagnostic or early sessions, while the therapist may wish to gather maximal information, the patient may not have developed a trusting relationship and may wish, consciously or unconsciously, to withhold some information. Censorship over verbal communication is keen. Censorship over images is often less meticulous, and the patient may convey information without acknowledgment or without having to recognize officially the implications of the images. In the above example of the patient describing the scene with her father and her tight sweater, the patient did not have to recognize her feelings of sexual excitation, prohibition, shame, and anger. (These feelings are not clearly expressed in the single image but were inferred from other patterns within the interview.)

Because of the relatively lower threshold of censorship, the therapist may use images to learn about the deeper levels of a patient's mental life. In the topographic model of psychoanalytic theory, three levels of thought processes are considered: conscious, preconscious, and unconscious. Knapp (1969) distinguishes sets of mental images or predispositions to certain image contents at each of these levels. The easiest to distinguish is the conscious or fully emergent layer which consists of the person's overt images of himself and others. Behind this is a preconscious layer that is partially emergent and partially hidden. In this fringe, or background layer, daydreams of being a super-spy or a cowboy hero may lurk and enter consciousness periodically. In this preconscious layer of images, the boundaries between the self and others may be unclear, as described in the example of the patient with "earthquakes" (in Chapter 9). Knapp describes a third layer of unconscious, hidden images. These express primitive urges and fears, and must be inferred by unraveling the disguises of reported images. Fully conscious images usually can be readily translated into verbal metaphors. The preconscious and unconscious levels may be approachable by direct description of the image contents, and the patient may remain unaware of the verbal meanings or implications of these images.

2. EMPATHY

A therapist listens to his patient. As the patient describes the images of a dream or fantasy, the therapist may passively allow himself to form an image like the one described. These images within the therapist may serve to generate empathic understanding. Also, these images provide the therapist with a set of memories that he can review later and repeatedly for additional understanding. When a therapist is accustomed to using such images in his work, and encounters a situation in which he feels blocked in responsive imaging or finds his images are not congruent with a patient's descriptions, he may suspect that empathic understanding is not present (Greenson, 1960). When incongruence if images appears, the therapist may ask himself whether the patient is being clear, whether there is some resistance within the patient or some difficulty in the relationship, or whether the therapist is having some countertransference reaction (Ross and Knapp, 1962).

The therapist will generally scan his own images but seldom report them to the patient directly. At times, however, the therapist's internal image response may contain the kernel of an interpretation that is not only correct but phrased with a useful degree of simple, concrete clarity. Sometimes this concrete casting of information is more convincing to patients than an abstract interpretive remark.

3. EXPRESSION AND WORKING-THROUGH

Image formation is closely linked with emotion. In some persons this linkage has been split-off so that images are produced without associated feeling. Generally, however, image formation may propel a patient towards expression of previously restrained emotions.

Once conflicted feelings are clearly labeled and expressed, the useful tool of rational thought is available for resolving as much of the conflict as possible, and for accepting realistic limitations. Unfortunately, we do not yet have a clear route-map of the optimum ways for a given personality to work through conflicts, traumas, and losses. But we do clinically recognize the importance of many-faceted expression. By many-faceted expression I mean that the previously uncognized, or not fully cognized, ideas and feelings should be labeled in many flexible ways: in words as well as images, in images as well as words. When the patient has the cognitive security of clear labels, a powerful constellation of feelings and ideas can be "tamed," as Freud (1895) put it, by being broken down into acceptable doses. Once there is a breakdown into tolerable components he can achieve new plans for action, new routes of expression, or new tolerances for frustration.

Isolation, intellectualization, splitting, and denial are defense mechanisms that interfere with many-faceted expression. In intellectualization, for example, ideas emerge but there is continued repression of feelings. Using this unconscious defensive maneuver, some persons can conceptually review a recent loss or a traumatic experience without emotion. Their blandness or numbness is not the consequence of completely worked-through feelings but rather a defense against potentially powerful and painful emotions. Because of the defense against expression of their grief or fear in therapy, they may repeatedly describe important past experiences, but always with numbness of feeling. Sometimes a visualization of the experience, when the patient is ready to tolerate the unpleasant feelings because of his good relationship with the therapist, may release emotions and permit grieving or trauma-mastery to task place.

Sometimes image formation will circumvent a defense such as denial, isolation, or repression. Here is an example in which the defense of denial was extreme and prevented the working-through of grief:

> A young woman had an argument with her husband as to whether or not he should go out late in the evening to obtain medicine recently prescribed for their sick daughter. He left angrily to do her bidding but was killed in his car in a head-on collision. She refused to believe he was dead when she was informed. She even denied his death during his funeral. She claimed the body was not his because it did not look like him: his face had been badly shattered by the accident and was poorly reconstructed by a mortician.

> She developed a delusion that she was pregnant following the accident and was afraid people would accuse her of being a whore because she had no husband. This delusion was partly restitutional: her husband lived on inside of her. She had no menstrual periods although she had negative pregnancy tests on several occasions. A gynecologist recommended a dilatation and curettage which showed only normal, non-pregnant uterine tissue. She reported suicidal thoughts and was seen by a resident psychiatrist in consultation. She seemed bland and to be flagrantly denying any depressive feelings, although she described her suicidal impulses. He prescribed outpatient psychotherapy and gave her tranquilizers. She took all of the tranquilizers at once in a suicidal effort and was admitted to the hospital. During the drug-induced deliria, she had visual hallucinations of her husband's face talking to her, telling her to come with him to the land of the dead. These apparitions persisted after the drug effects had worn off.

> She denied her husband's death and asked the psychiatric staff not to mention such unpleasant topics, because her husband would only visit her when she was not feeling depressed or planning suicide. After several days she was told firmly that her husband had died, that this was so painful to her that she was trying to ignore it, but that she would have to accept it and begin to talk about her emotional reactions. She did not acknowledge this intervention directly. Yet the next time she experienced the visual hallucination of her husband's face, according to her description, she screamed "go away! I'm not going with you!" Thereafter she reported no further hallucinations but continued to deny that he was dead. She was then asked to visualize him as she had last seen him. She burst into tears and could not describe her image. Later she drew it (Figure 1), a picture of him in his coffin. (A flag is present because he had a military funeral.) She then described the argument before the crash and her feelings that if she had not been so vehement he would have stayed home and remained alive. Her guilt, her sadness, and a delayed grief response to her tragic loss could then begin to be worked through in psychotherapy.

Fig. 1. The acknowledgment and acceptance of loss in a patient with a delayed grief reaction.

4. TRANSFORMATION OF FEELINGS OR ATTITUDES

The power of images to evoke emotion may be used to alter emotional states. Indeed, the counsel of friends, relatives, and bartenders often takes this form: a despondent person is told to "buck up" and to imagine some pleasant time in the past or future to change his mood. The bigot, in order to diminish his biases, is told, "imagine yourself in their shoes." This trial in imagination is a kind of internal psychodrama that lets him experience the difficulties of others and, therefore, feel greater understanding and tolerance for their responsive behavior. In a similar manner, patients may be encouraged to try out possible future courses of action. When they imagine "the worst possible" outcome of a dilemma, they may find that it is improbable or, if probable, that they will be better able to cope than they had previously thought. Also, they may find that they can envision plausible behavior that will solve current dilemmas. Rehearsal of such behavior, in the imagination, may provide encouragement for later implementation as real behavior.

TECHNIQUES

Many of the techniques that I will describe are quite new. Some are faddish; others may prove useful. While I shall make some comments, I cannot give all the pros or cons, or even a very detailed description of each technique. I caution the reader against any ready acceptance or premature trial of the more radical techniques. Image formation can be a powerful tool, and one that may go out of control. Telling a patient what to image, for example, exerts many complex effects on the patient-therapist relationship that extend beyond the obvious. Deep exploration, emotional discharge, altered states of consciousness, and regression should be postponed until the patient has established a secure and confident relationship with the therapist and until there is the assurance of adequate time for follow-up and integration of the released emotions and ideas. With these cautionary words, I will first describe the least directive techniques—those which ask the patient to image, but do not effect much guidance of the image contents by the therapist. Then I discuss more manipulative techniques in which the therapist suggests specific contents.

THE SHIFT TO IMAGE FORMATION

A. INQUIRY

Inquiry has few dangers. As part of a clinical interview, one merely inquires about descriptions of dreams, daydreams, and other varieties of image experiences. Some patients do not include such experiences in their ordinary communications and will not tell of such events unless asked. Sometimes an inquiry about images is necessary, even in the psychoanalytic situation in which the patient has already been told that free association is the major means for production of material. Some patients assume that reporting what comes to mind applies only to words, and not to images which they regard as peripheral and irrelevant. This assumption would allow some ideas and feelings to be isolated from the realm of communication and to "hide" in images. The interpretation and working through of the images communicated, upon inquiry, is described adequately in earlier chapters and I will not repeat it here.

B. SUGGESTION OF SHIFT IN MODE OF REPRESENTATION FROM WORDS TO IMAGES

In a technique more directive than inquiry, the therapist may suggest that the patient allow himself to form images and to describe them. Freud (Freud and Breuer, 1895) used this technique to explore repressed memories during a period of transition, in his technique, from hypnosis to free association. He found that some patients were difficult to hypnotize, and, to unravel the meaning of a hysterical symptom, he asked the patient to form an image relevant to the time when the symptom first began. He enforced his request with the power of suggestion. The patient reclined on a couch, and Freud placed his hand on her forehead and pressed firmly. He then commanded the patient that when he lifted his hand a memory would form as a visual image. The patient was further instructed to report all the details of the image and the associated emotions. When associational connections were made, the symptom, hopefully, was relieved after a period of abreaction, catharsis, and interpretation. We now know that the addition of suggestion is not usually necessary; the therapist may merely ask that the patient allow images to spring spontaneously to mind and to report them without discrimination.

Freud later rejected this technique because, while initially expedient, it led to increased resistance and difficult transference effects later in treatment. While contemporary psychoanalysts seldom suggest a deliberate shift from words to image formation, they do pay attention to when such shifts spontaneously occur and try to understand what motivates this shift and the latent meanings of the images. Image contents tend to be analyzed in terms of underlying defensive motives as well as (often disguised) sexual and aggressive impulses or derivative childhood memories. Thus the analyst may be interested in 1) the reasons for use of an image at that point in treatment; 2) the sources of content in terms of perceptual memories and previous fantasies; 3) the emotional, impulsive, and defensive meanings represented in the images; 4) the defensive or cognitive style manifested in the (inferred) process of image formation, and; 5) the organizational structure or pattern of the image in terms of object relations (how primitive versus how differentiated, how human versus inanimate, how close versus distant, and the characteristic role structure, such as who does what kinds of things to whom, what is wished, what is feared, and so on).

Jung, in 1916 (Jung, 1959; Adler, 1967), developed a means of focusing on image formation that he called *active imagination*. The purpose of Jung's active imagination was to encourage a patient to get in touch with his "unconscious" and to narrow the gap between conscious and unconscious mental contents. The therapist instructs the patient to allow a deliberate dimming down of conscious mental activity and to concentrate passively on the "unconscious background to mental life." The technique involves a kind of active passivity, a setting aside of planful or organized thought. In this state, previously hidden contents emerge, often with intense emotion, and often in the form of visual images. Then the conscious mind takes over again and cooperates in the analysis of the images.

G. Adler (1967) states that the products of images produced by this Jungian technique carry a quality of inner conviction that differs subjectively from reactions to ordinary daydreams. In such Jungian therapy, *archetypal images* tend to emerge as a consequence of active imagination: witches, devils, tempters, sorcerers, magicians, princes, heroes, wisemen. Archetypal images refer to universal themes that emerge in similar form in many patients because persons share a racial unconscious memory. Non-Jungians agree with the prevalence of archetypes in fantasy images, but trace this symbolic similarity to the basic patterns of the human life situation rather than to a collective unconscious. For example, almost all children are raised in a family where there are dominant figures who are good or bad, and often both. The child may permit himself to think dangerous thoughts about such persons by using the guise of displacements to imaginary figures, either his own or those supplied by myths and fairy tales. Thus, a bad parent may become a witch in fantasy, a powerful parent a magician, and a good parent a fairy godmother. When childhood fantasy continues to direct behavior patterns in adults, the emergence of the fantasy may again take "archetypal" form. The active imagination technique, coupled with a style of interpretation that labels archetypes, has a propulsive quality: the patient is encouraged to develop the images further and, in essence, to "lure out" all the characters of the drama.

Kubie (1943), a Freudian analyst, suggested that inducted *hypnagogic reverie* might enhance image formation. He found his technique invaluable with patients who had not revealed the roots of their neurosis in an analysis that seemed too prolonged. Kubie used suggestion and the Jacobson (1942) method of progressive muscular relaxation * to induce the reverie state and asked the patient to allow and report a free and spontaneous flow of images. Kubie found that the fantasies that emerged were often clearer, in terms of apparent meaning of the latent contents, than the dreams reported by patients.

Other therapists such as Reyher (1963) report the usefulness of asking for image formation within the first few interviews to find out hidden motives and memories. Reyher asks his client to close his eyes and report free images, the same as Jung and Kubie. He finds that one of three outcomes usually occurs: the patient resists, he has an acute abreaction of pent-up emotions, or he undergoes some form of regression. The abreaction and the regression are productive of therapeutic movement, however, only if the patients have good ego strength, good motivation for therapy, and a high tolerance for anxiety. When the opposites pertain, treatment failures can occur.

Sacerdote (1967, 1968) reports a technique that he calls *induced dreams*. The patients are induced into a hypnotic trance and asked to dream. Sacerdote then uses free associative methods to unravel the mean-

---

* Progressive muscle relaxation produces a sense of serenity and calm in most persons, and a deeply altered state of consciousness in a few. The method consists of focusing attention on various muscle groups and trying to "let go" of those that are tense. In one technique, the specific muscle group under attention is lightly tensed during the inspiratory phase of respiration, which involves muscle action, and then released during expiration, which can take place passively due to the elastic contraction of the lungs.

ings of the dreams. In addition, he attempts to interconnect a series of dreams so that each successive dream completes the understanding of a previous induced or spontaneous dream. Also, he may instruct a patient in a general way to dream about a current conflict or problem area. Sacerdote points out that this active technique is used only in persons who are poor candidates for more orthodox, less directive forms of therapy or analysis. One problem with hypnosis is that the patient surrenders ownership of the mind to the therapist. Sacerdote compromises with this hazard by telling them to form images, but leaving the contents largely to the patient.

C. DRUGS

Sodium amytal has been used intravenously to reduce defensive aspects of cognition and evoke the abreactive memory of previous traumatic experiences. These memories often emerge as visual images. Amytal was used widely in World War II to treat combat neurosis but has since been largely abandoned. It is still occasionally used in civilian practice although it is only infrequently mentioned in the professional literature. Instead, attention was focused on hallucinogenic drugs such as LSD until their use was declared illegal except for limited research purposes.

Mescaline, peyote, and other hallucinogens have been around for centuries and used for various ritualistic and mystic purposes. The emergence of vivid images, subjectively experienced as nonvolitional, naturally predisposed persons to consider the possibility of spiritual or transcendental causation to the images. Discovery of LSD rocketed the use of hallucinogens. While these drugs have many effects, one is some kind of change in image formation. Many persons take such drugs in the hope of increasing image experiences and, from the image contents, gaining insights that have been hidden from them.

In view of the profound symbolic and transcendental quality of images and experiences while on hallucinogens, it is not surprising that these agents would be experimentally used for psychotherapeutic purposes. The use of hallucinogens to produce images and feelings follows two main techniques: the *psychedelic* and the *psycholytic* (Leuner, 1967).

In the *psychedelic technique*, a fairly high dose is given to produce, if possible, a "consciousness-expanding peak experience." The goal is self-understanding, rejuvenation, enhancement of self-esteem through a sense of spiritual relevance, decrease of despair through a sense of greater relatedness to persons or "the world-order," and hope because of feeling there is "a way." Some claim that after such an experience a person is more self-accepting, loving, less hostile, and less indifferent to others. The image formation is usually not directed in this technique; however, an effort is made to insure that the setting is warm, supportive, and non-hostile. This technique is sometimes used as a kind of experiential shock therapy in persons who are locked into a self-impairing behavior pattern and are near the end of the road. The hope is that the person will discover new meanings and a new way of self-acceptance and self-change.* The use of LSD in chronic severe alcoholism is one example (Hoffer and Osmond, 1967; Abramson, 1967). LSD has also been used in the psychotherapy of terminal cancer patients (Pahnke et al., 1969).

The *psycholytic technique* seeks not so much to "expand consciousness" as to break into repressed and compartmentalized memories and fantasies. (Crocket et al., 1963). The dosage level of the hallucinogen is usually less, a therapist is usually present, and several sessions with or without the drugs are generally used. The emergence of repressed material is often in symbols that depict both the defensive and impulsive arms of a conflict. These symbols are often carried into both cosmic and primal form: e.g., supernatural powers may provide guidance, and birth and death may be enacted. Emergence of previously hidden or dormant images can be frightening; in a later section of this chapter, techniques in use for guiding images will be discussed. These are sometimes necessary because the patient is in a regressive state and has a low capacity to control either the vividness or the contents of his experiences.

The general criticism of psychedelic and psycholytic therapy is that too much enters awareness too soon. The images often contain elements of repressed ideas, feelings, memories, and fantasies. For the procedure to be fully useful, the images should be translated into word meanings—this is often impossible while on the drug. Also, the emotions cannot be worked through, since this usually means gradual and repetitive assimilation. I believe that, in general, the result of the average treatment with these agents is not durable emotional insight, although intellectual knowledge of conflicts may be produced. The impulse-defense configurations cannot be worked through, new coping styles cannot develop in the regressive state, and the "new material" may be rigidly compartmentalized or else largely forgotten.

Even advocates such as Buckman (1967) caution that the low level of control by either patient or therapist indicates a need for careful selection of patients. Buckman states that important factors in successful psycholytic treatment are positive motivations to get better, a capacity to gain insight, and an ability to tolerate stress and depression. I believe he

---

* For a philosophic and psychoanalytic study of man's enduring wish to see his own thinking, his own meaning, and his own history in the form of mental images see Lewin (1968).

should add, as necessary safeguards, a capacity to master the experience and an enduring, protective relationship with an expert on psychodynamics.

DIRECTING THE CONTENTS OF IMAGES

A. IMAGE EVOCATION

In Chapter 8, I described an image evocation task that suggested certain categories of images. For example, the patient might be asked to form spontaneous images of all the important persons in her life, of earliest memories, or of images in response to certain emotions. In therapy, one need not follow a research-oriented structure, of course. If the patient is talking in a guarded way about a given topic, the therapist has the choice of interpreting the resistance or, in less analytically oriented therapies, he may wish to skirt the defensive maneuver by asking the patient to form an image. For example, suppose the patient has reported a dream and does not report many associations. The therapist may ask him to attempt to reexperience right now the images of the dream and to associate to this experience. Or, if the patient is talking abstractly of some dreaded situation, the therapist may ask him to visualize and describe some specific version of it. Even when the patient is talking of some abstract concept such as "venting aggression" or "being more self confident," the therapist may ask him to imagine what that might be like. The concreteness of visual images helps to define abstractions and also to propel the patient into some clear statement of his current concerns.

B. "FORCED FANTASIES"

Ferenczi (1950) wrote a paper in 1923 that he called "On Forced Fantasies." Patients who had poor fantasy production were "forced" to recover emotional reactions to previous situations by the analyst insisting that they visualize the situations during the analytic hour. At first he found his patients only rarely cooperative. In time, however, they became more courageous and fabricated experiences of almost hallucinatory distinctness. These were accompanied by unmistakable signs of anxiety, rage, or erotic excitement.

The reader should realize, however, that while a patient complies and produces a volley of emotions and images, there may be a certain "transference expense." That is, the patient is complying with an instruction and may expect a reward, may feel he is submitting to a sadistic attack, may feel humiliated, or may try a new defense: excessive material as avoidance, to achieve the same effect as too little material. The net effect may be to make some progress in therapy at first with limitation of what can be accomplished in the long run, because of transference complications.

C. IMAGE THERAPY

Biddle (1963) suggests a form of group therapy for psychotic persons in which instructions are issued to change the contents of dreams and hallucinations. He conducts his image therapy in groups of as many as 20 patients in a one-hour session. Discussion within the group is limited to dream material, and patients are instructed to carry out a series of events in their dreams or hallucinatory images. As the first step, they are encouraged to see and eat food; next they are urged to include money in the dream; and finally to include depictions of clothes. Biddle's rationale regards image formation as a means of conflict resolution, and, through food, money, and clothes, he hopes to take the patients through conflicts of the oral, anal, and genital stages of psychosexual development.

This approach seems naive: food, clothes, and money may appear as symbols in the context of oral, anal, or genital contexts, but certainly they do not invariably symbolize or activate such conflicts. Even if they did, taking patients "back" over presumed developmental sequences and "working forward" is not necessarily therapeutic in and of itself. The method seems unrealistically simple, but perhaps much is left out of Biddle's report.

Biddle apparently continued to work on his idea of image therapy because, in 1969, he proposed technical revisions: a new purpose is to help the mental images of patients conform more realistically to external persons. The therapist regards all external objects as either parental or self symbols. In the imagining of objects, the therapist encourages the patient to correct the bad internal parent and self-images so that interpersonal relationships will be regarded as safe. Nine basic characters are involved in this internal image cast: good, bad, and realistic representations of mother, father, and the self. When a patient dreamt that she saw a man throw a dead rat under a door, Biddle interpreted the dead rat as the bad self-image, the man as the bad father, and the room behind the door as the mother. He urged the patient to a more realistic appraisal of herself and her potential relationships with men.

The advantages of this type of technique are that interpretation is easy because it follows simple rules, the therapist sets clear goals, and the suggested image formation probably does improve the patients mood. Possibly, with careful work, this method may indeed help stabilize object and self representations and may help the patient differentiate reality from fantasy. Also, the supportive relationship may be quite helpful.

The principle disadvantages rest with an oversimplified, unsophisticated theory and a cavalier approach to interpretation of symbols that uses a set formula. Many patients, even psychotic patients, disguise the meaning of images by reversal: father figures may stand for mother and so forth. This type of intervention may gain some ground by allowing partial expression, yet continued partial disguise, of an impulse. The unexpressed portion of the impulse can then be more vigorously repressed. The result is a firming up of defensive avoidances. In conventional treatment of neurosis, we generally do not wish to foster increased avoidance. In treatment of psychotic patients, however, we do sometimes wish to shift impulse-defense configurations in the direction of greater defensive stability, and Biddle's suggestion may eventually prove useful there.

Image instruction techniques, like those to be described subsequently, may have the unspoken effect of encouraging the patient to gain control over image formation. They may motivate the patient to a maximum regulatory effort so that his thinking is less dominated by unbidden images and more occupied by the images suggested by the therapist. By telling the patient what to image, the therapist is also telling him that he, the patient, can come to be in control of his own image formation and could, thus, be in a position of freedom—either to image or not image certain contents.

Beck (1970) uses a variety of image formation tasks to gain information, pinpoint vagueness, release emotion, and to teach patients that they can control their thought processes. Some of his patients who complained of "free floating anxiety" were having uncontrolled visual images of imminent danger. He found that clapping his hands, for example, might dispel the image in the patient's mind. The patient could learn this technique and do it himself. Beck also encouraged patients to form their unpleasant and unwanted images over and over again, at will. They learned the image formation process was under their control and learned also to dispel unwanted images as soon as they formed. Furthermore, Beck found that repetition reduced the unpleasant emotions related to the images. While he noted the similarity of some of his techniques to systematic desensitization, a procedure to be described, he also clearly indicated that he used his techniques in a psychodynamic framework. Whatever emerged in the course of image formation, was worked on cognitively and verbally to establish its relationship to other behaviors, attitudes, feelings, and memories.

Gestalt therapists, as one of their techniques, direct a patient to report a dream fragment or a fantasy image. First, the patient is asked to report the image in exquisite detail: like free associations, this often adds revealing information. As part of this detailed report, the therapist asks the patient to re-experience the image or dream "here and now." Next the patient is asked to speak, or to act, as if he were each aspect of the image content, again in the immediate present (Perls, 1970). For example, if the dream fragment or fantasy contained the scene of a man shooting a horse, the patient would be instructed to speak as if he were the man: to say what he feels in that role as he experiences it now. Then he would be successively told to repeat the process while imagining himself to be the gun, the bullet, and the horse. For instance, while "being the bullet" he might speak of himself tearing into flesh. This directive technique forces the patient to speak ever more clearly of the ideas and feelings that are expressed unclearly in the manifest image. This type of image technique differs from the psychoanalytic *use* of free association. Gestalt therapists, such as Perls, do not interpret—instead they act in such a way as to propel the patient towards clear expression. When defensive maneuvers obstruct this goal, they push through them or go around them. In contrast, the major activity of a psychoanalyst is interpretation: the goal is to help the patient become aware of and modify defenses that have prevented clear expression of ideas and feelings. Then expression can occur spontaneously.

D. DIRECTED DAYDREAM AND GUIDED AFFECTIVE IMAGERY TECHNIQUES

In the directed daydream technique the therapist encourages a flow of images, as in the therapies suggested by Ferenczi, Jung, Sacerdote, Biddle, and others. In these techniques, the therapist provides even more content material than in those just described. Then, as the story line is reported by the patient, the therapist suggests various maneuvers that the patient may use, to change the image contents.

Hammer (1967) and Gerard (1963) attribute aspects of the guided daydream technique to Jung, Leuner, Desoille, and Assagioli. Leuner (1969) bases an entire system of psychotherapy on what he calls GAI, for guided affective imagery. The patient reclines or sits comfortably, and relaxes his body. Deep breathing is used to deepen the relaxation and may also achieve an altered state of consciousness that increases the vividness and reduces the control over image formation.

Once the patient is suitably relaxed, the therapist suggests rather open-ended imaginary situations or symbolic themes. The patient fills in the details, continues the daydream, and reports his images as he goes along. Thus, the therapist may begin by suggesting that the patient visualize a door and step through it, or imagine himself in some setting such as a meadow, mountains, cave, forest, or at the bottom of the sea. The patient then describes what he encounters in his fantasy.

Most patients are afraid of some inner image, frightening memory, or external possibility. The "bad" parts of the self and "bad" parent images are often externalized and disguised. Thus, it is not surprising that, in the daydream during therapy, the patient imagines himself encountering something frightening such as a monster. Hammer (1967) and Leuner (1969) suggest five or six "basic" ways of guiding and managing the course of the ongoing "symboldramatic" events. The therapist may guide the patient with instructions to confront the symbol, to feed the symbol, to reach reconciliation with the symbol, to use magical fluids, or to engage the symbol so that exhaustion and killing take place. For example, a person may imagine himself confronting a huge snake. The therapist may say, "Try offering him a piece of candy." The patient may comply and subdue the snake through friendship. Leuner couples this technique with psychoanalytic methods. He may ask patients to produce associations to the daydream images, or he may use GAI at moments of resistance in regular therapy.

Hammer notes the danger of these techniques in the hands of inexperienced but adventurous psychotherapists. He says that confrontation with monsters or symbols is an active and strong technique that may produce strong emotional outbursts, especially if death or violence occurs. Inexperienced therapists should, he suggests, try a milder procedure such as suggesting feeding the monster. Leuner suggests avoidance of this technique when treating psychotics or addicts.

This type of guidance of image formation is sometimes used by "trip guides" in counseling persons on a drug-induced hallucinatory trip. For example, a person on a "bad trip" may hallucinate that he is about to jump from a frightening height. In response to hearing a description of such image contents, the trip guide may suggest that the person can try flying safely. The feelings of intense fear may then change, with the permission and suggestion of the guide, to the ecstasy of flight.

Gerard (1963) gives an example of how directed daydreaming may transform emotional states. A married woman in his care was frustrated and angry because her husband did not express warm feelings towards her. While contemplating divorce, she had the image of a wooden heart. The therapist suggested that she imagine a door in the heart, that she open it, and report what she found on the other side. There she reported a wasteland of snow and ice; she saw a man bundled in a heavy overcoat which concealed his face. The therapist told her to dig into the ice and see what was underneath. She did so in her fantasy and reported that she found green grass underneath the ice. Then, to her amazement, the ice receded, and she found herself in a green meadow. To her surprise the man's face became that of her husband. Despite the warm sunshine, he seemed unable to remove his overcoat. The therapist encouraged the patient to help her husband. As she helped him take off the overcoat, he responded warmly. They embraced and decided to build a home on the spot. In the following session, the patient reported experiencing warm feelings towards her husband who was responding in kind.

While advocates of this technique may not agree, we should note that the therapist uses the directed daydream technique to deliver a trial suggestion: why not try harder? Try and get through to your cold husband in a warm, positive way. Perhaps the image formation allows this suggestion to be tentative and somewhat covert. This could allow the patient to rehearse the possibility of accepting the suggestion in fantasy before implementing it in actuality. I suspect that many forms of image therapy are veiled modes of offering suggestion and support to patients.

Lazarus (1968) a behavior therapist, reports a similar technique for transforming emotion in depressed patients. In one of his examples, a girl patient was acutely depressed after being rejected by her boyfriend. Lazarus hypnotized the patient and suggested that she image herself as he projected her forward into the future. He suggested what she might be doing days and weeks later. Finally he suggested images six months in the future. At that point, he asked her to reflect back on the "previous," actually the current, incident. After dehypnotizing, the patient reported that she realized that she was overreacting and that there were other things to do with herself. This treatment, according to Lazarus, completely overcame her depression. Lazarus concludes that "contemplation of future positive reinforcements may diminish depressive responses."

The reader should note, once again, the establishment of a warm, protective, giving, and suggestive relationship which may contribute to a "transference cure." This relationship could certainly be expected when a male therapist offers to take care of and hypnotize a female patient who has lost her boyfriend. Behavior therapists, however, usually do not report or acknowledge transference issues in their scientific publications.

E. BEHAVIOR THERAPY

Systematic desensitization is one of the major techniques used by behavior therapists. Joseph Wolpe (1958) developed it after experimentally inducing and treating "neurosis," in cats. According to Rachman (1967), who reviewed the literature on experimental tests of the efficacy of desensitization, Wolpe, following the techniques of Masserman, traumatized cats and then cured them. The cure was aimed at desensitizing the cat's "neurotic" fear when returned to the site of the painful stimulation used to traumatize the cats. This desensitization was first achieved through gentle feeding in a neutral situation but gradually, in stages, by feeding them in the traumatic situation. Feeding was pleasurable and secure, it opposed and inhibited the anxiety, and thus broke the conditioned association between anxiety and the traumatic environment.

In extending his work to humans, Wolpe, like Kubie, used Jacobson's (1942) method of progressive relaxation. He hoped, through relaxation, to produce calm and oppose anxiety. Persons, in the relaxed state, could then be reintroduced to objects that tended to provoke anxiety. The difficulty in really presenting people with traumatic or frightening objects led him to the use of imaginary objects, and he found this could be done by asking them to form visual images.

Thus, the method developed into its present form. The procedure begins with a discussion of the patient's problems. Then patients are instructed in how to achieve muscular relaxation, a procedure that is somewhat similar to the first stages of hypnotic induction, although the goal is not achievement of a trance. When fully and comfortably relaxed, patients are told to imagine items from a hierarchy ranging from very mild versions of their phobia (for example) to extreme versions. Gradual steps are used so that the patient learns to remain calm. Whenever anxiety is elicited, the therapist instructs the patient to stop the image formation and relax further. Relaxation is deepened, and the same image offered again. According to Wolpe's theory, the superimposition of relaxation on the conditioned anxious response dissipates the anxiety by reciprocal inhibition. As anxiety to the milder images on the hierarchy diminishes, more frightening images are suggested until the patient can tolerate, remaining relaxed, vivid visualization of what he has previously found anxiety provoking. Theoretically, and as some experiments demonstrate, there is a carry over from fearless image formation to reduction of anxiety on encountering the object in reality. Behavior therapists also claim that there is no substitution of other symptoms once relief is obtained (Rachman, 1967).

Take, for example, a patient with a phobia about cats. He might first be asked to visualize a cat several hundred yards away. After suggesting this image, the therapist might remain silent, observing meanwhile the patient's nonverbal responses. If the patient remains relaxed, the therapist might then suggest visualization of holding a stuffed cat. Eventually he would lead up to an image of holding or fondling a cat.

What happens during the period of suggested image formation? Weitzman (1967) has asked patients this question after sessions of systematic desensitization. He found that they were not restricted to the image given by the therapist. Instead, the patients reported that other images and associations occurred during the period of silence which moved rather far in content from the initial suggestion. Weitzman's findings suggest that the method of suggestion of anxious images in a relaxed state is not dependent for its effects on "reciprocal inhibition" but may also encourage the patient to review his problems conceptually. Brown (1969) has observed Wolpe conducting systematic desensitization therapy, and he also underscores the role of cognitive exploration as the patient describes and discusses his experiences with the therapist.

These observations suggest that desensitization procedures may involve a thinking-through of emotionally tense topics, a facet that many behavior therapists tend to minimize. The patient might have avoided this working-through on his own because thinking of his problems was too threatening or unpleasant. With instruction, encouragement, and support from the therapist, however, the patient can begin to experience avoided ideas and feelings. Note that this technique covertly teaches the patient that he can start or stop images that previously were experienced as a lapse of control. He has them when the therapist instructs him to, and presumably stops them when the therapist says to. The patient learns, first under the protective umbrella of the relationship with the therapist, that he can think of forbidden or unpleasant topics and indeed does so on specific instruction from an admired authority.

Images can generate emotions, and these emotions can change conditioned responsivity. Kolvin (1967) uses this principle in a form of *aversive training* in adolescent behavior disorders in which the patients are poorly communicative or intellectually dull. The therapist first finds out from the patient which images are most unpleasant to contemplate. Then the patient is instructed to conjure up such images in association with ideas the therapist wishes to render nonpleasurable. If the patient has a perversion, he is instructed to visualize images related to the perversion while lying in a relaxed state with his eyes closed. When it is noted that the patient is becoming erotically aroused by his perverse images, the aversive image is suddenly introduced in a vividly descriptive manner. For example, Kolvin reports a patient who assaulted women by suddenly slipping his hand up under their skirts. First the patient was told to image a woman in a skirt. Then, when the patient seemed to be aroused, he was suddenly told to visualize an unpleasant falling experience that he had previously revealed to be frightening. The juxtaposition of the unpleasant affect with the aroused affects was believed to account for the reduction in symptoms.

Marks and Gelder (1967) carry this aversive technique even further. Patients with transvestism or fetishism were given electrical shocks while carrying out their deviant behavior in images. The authors report that the deviant images became indistinct and transient, lost their pleasurable quality, and ceased to be accompanied by erections.

F. IMPLOSIVE THERAPY

Stampfl (Stampfl and Lewis, 1967) has advanced an "implosive" method of psychotherapy that is similar to behavior therapy in its reliance on learning theory yet uses a rather divergent technique of instructed image formation. Instead of the patient forming the suggested images in a state of calm relaxation, the therapist uses the images to create a situation of intense anxiety, hoping to "implode" away symptom formation.

Here is a résumé of Stampfl's theory. A painful experience has caused an association between certain ideas and feelings of anxiety. This conditioned association of anxiety in response to certain objects or situations does not undergo extinction because the person represses memory of the original painful experience. Unfortunately, the person has overgeneralized the painful experience, and current stimuli subliminally activate the anxiety without remembrance of the original events.

Stampfl reasons that bringing the traumatic events into consciousness may allow extinction of the conditioned anxiety when this anxiety is not reinforced by the contemporary experience. Thus, the goal of his therapy is reinstatement or symbolic reproduction of the cues to which the anxiety is conditioned. This reproduction is achieved by suggesting the anxiety-provoking images to the patient. As the patient experiences the images he becomes very anxious, but the situation is not "really" anxiety provoking (according to Stampfl) because no ill befalls the patient, the relationship is supportive, and the activity is fantasy rather than reality. Thus, Stampfl asserts, the anxious response gradually diminishes or implodes in on itself.

Stampfl begins implosive therapy with diagnostic interviews during which the therapist forms an idea of what cues are avoided or are anxiety provoking. In later sessions, the therapist tells the patient to image these cues as vividly as possible, giving his own version of lurid detail to maximize the patient's anxiety. The therapist tries throughout to guess what the patient is avoiding and then to make him image it. Thus, for example, the therapist may tell a person with rat phobia to image a rat touching them, running across their hand, biting them on the arm, piercing them viciously, devouring their eyes, and jumping down their mouths to destroy internal organs (Hogan and Kirchner, 1967). Stampfl relies heavily on his knowledge of general psychodynamics and states that, in general, he will touch upon most of the following categories of images: aggression, punishment, oral material (eating, biting, spitting, cannibalism, sucking), anal material, sexual material, rejection, bodily injury, loss of control, acceptance of conscience (scenes of confessing, being guilty, courtrooms, after death before God), and physical feelings.

Stampfl's implosive therapy rests, in part, on shock value. His technique forcibly undermines the patient's defenses of conceptual avoidance: the patient visualizes vividly all that he has wished to avoid thinking about. Perhaps the experience is less anxiety provoking than the patient has feared, and perhaps it is less anxiety provoking to think the unthinkable in the presence of an authority figure who orders you to do it. The patient not only gains official permission to think all sorts of thoughts; he may also learn that his fearsome thoughts can be controlled. He can form the images on instruction; perhaps he can also instruct himself when to form or not form the thoughts. Also, the images are fantasy, and the procedure may help the patient to distinguish between fantasy and reality.

CRITICISM OF IMPLOSIVE THERAPY AND BEHAVIOR THERAPY

The principle disadvantage of implosive therapy and behavior therapy is that they tend to regard a patient's symptoms as passive "happenings" rather than the creative, if pathologic, cognitive response to psychologic conflict. When psychodynamics are considered at all they are considered in a general, nonindividualized form. Also, the behavioral schools of therapy tend to minimize the viscissitudes of relationship between therapist and patient. Decades of experience in therapy suggest that this relationship is of great importance and that distortions of it are ignored by the therapist at the patient's expense.

Therapists committed to the use of systematic desensitization and to implosive therapy claim very good results with these methods. To some extent placebo effects, the positive expectations of patients, and the powers of persuasion, personality, and suggestion may contribute to the therapeutic change. Other factors, operating in addition to or separate from the theoretic deconditioning process, may include exploration of hidden feelings, ideas, fantasies, and memories.

In following the instructions of the respected healer or authority figure, the patient thinks of ideas and feelings, in the form of images, that he has been prohibiting himself from expressing. The prohibition may have arisen by internalization of real or imagined parental or social attitudes. Now a new powerful and superior figure is changing the censorship. Instead of being told not to think of sex or aggression, for example, the person is being told to think vividly of every aspect of sex and aggression. Instead of prohibited fantasy, the patient is told to fantasize. The therapist replaces the earlier introjects (internal "presences" of parents and important figures) and, thus, alters the internal psychodynamic configuration. His influence reduces inhibition and helps the patient recognize previously hidden wishes and fears.

In psychoanalytic therapies, the important role of the internalized image of the therapist is recognized, and part of the work may deal with seductive or resistant motives of the patient towards the imagined therapist. Behavior and implosive therapists, in their theoretic statements, do not explore this relationship, but in their activities they probably use it. The procedures not only "decondition," they also illustrate for the patient his current internal and external sources of stress. By learning to turn imagination on and off, the patient learns to clearly demarcate and separate reality and fantasy. The real relationship with the therapist bolsters his defenses and his self-esteem. Under this "protective umbrella," he is encouraged to work through his conflicts and anxieties, even if these trends are not overtly labeled in the therapeutic transactions or in theoretic writings. Finally, the power of suggestion is present: the patient and therapist believe that if they follow the procedures, fear will diminish and assertive responses will be enhanced.

DISCUSSION

Image formation is a form of thinking. When a therapist of any theoretic persuasion suggests, encourages, or inquires about an image he is, in effect, asking the patient to think. Furthermore, because patients seek help and therapists wish to help, the thinking usually focuses on problem areas: the facets of the patient's life and behavior pattern that he is presently having trouble thinking clearly about or wishes to avoid thinking about because of his associated feelings. Whatever other factors may be involved, this encouragement of thinking facilitates conceptual and emotional change. Image formation, as a particular form of thinking, may be a route to expression of emotional conflict and to expression of distortions or instability of self and object representations.

In summary then, the image formation maneuvers described in this chapter have certain similarities: they encourage the patient to express ideas and feelings that may have been avoided or distorted. Also, whether the therapist explicitly focuses on interpretive cognitive work or not, the average patient will, himself, review his images and work them over conceptually and emotionally. He will develop associational connections and, perhaps, think of alternative routes towards fulfillment or pain reduction. To some extent he may observe more clearly his own impulses, emotions, traits, motives, and behavior patterns. Unresolved but repressed issues, such as object loss or traumatization may be reexpressed and the cognitive-emotional resolution completed.

The patient will also be considering his image productions in a communicative network: he will have to ask himself what another person thinks about his images. He will wonder if the ideas expressed are realistic or fantastic sounding to the therapist; he will wonder if the therapist likes him better for having the images, or likes him less. Thus, the patient's internal image of the therapist begins to influence the cognitive working-through. The idealized image of the therapist, through identification contributes to the patient's own ideals. If a previous internalized parental figure (an introject) is one source of blocking a thought cycle, this effect may be attenuated by the current "power" of the introject of the therapist. That is, if mother said, "Don't even think dirty thoughts," and the therapist says, "Think anything and tell me everything you think," the growing influence of the therapist immediately changes the cognitive dynamics of the patient: to the extent that the patient identifies with or internalizes the therapist, he is permitted to think sexually or aggressively "dirty" thoughts.

Thus, through image formation, as through any form of thinking, the individual acquires the capacity to gain control over his internal motives and, by action, over external reality. When we add to the power of cognition the influence of magical expectation and the healing power of persuasion (Frank, 1961), when we mix in suggestion and charisma, when we add accurate empathy, nonpossessive warmth, and genuineness of relationship on the part of the therapist (Rogers, 1951; Truax and Wargo, 1966), we are prepared to believe that some of these therapeutic attempts are successful.

In my opinion, two factors are crucially important. One is the conceptual process of working-through. Working-through consists of repeatedly reviewing active ideas and feelings, translating expression of these contents into various modes of representation and meaning, and relating the contents to various memories, self-images, images of other persons, values, attitudes, and fantasy of the past, present and future. These various "cognitive structures" are then revised and aligned with the active ideas and feelings.

The second crucial factor is the relationship between the patient and the therapist. This relationship is based partially on current reality and partially on the transference of attitudes towards previously important figures. If the relationship with the therapist is good in the mind of the patient, then the patient will increase his tolerance for unpleasant or dangerous emotions because he is not alone and can, therefore, stand the pain previously avoided. Increased tolerance of emotions permits the conceptual work just mentioned.

Thus, use of a powerful procedure such as evocation of images, or uncovering of images can be therapeutically valuable in persons with sufficient cognitive capacity for the issues at hand. With sufficient trust in the therapist, these patients will take the cognitive risks of thinking clearly of their worst fears. If one of these crucial factors is relatively absent, however, the use of powerful uncovering or regressive procedures is unwise: true, some "unconscious" material will emerge, but it cannot be integrated into the overall cognitive structure, will have little if any therapeutic worth, and may be harmful.

I believe that therapeutic errors are made when the goal is to uncover inner images "at all costs." Hidden images are inhibited for some reason. They probably cannot be assimilated until the reasons for avoidance are attenuated. When these reasons for avoidance are reduced (as in change in defenses), images emerge more spontaneously. Once the person integrates his defenses so that they are conscious controls rather than unconscious avoidances, childhood memories, old traumas, and current wishful fantasies become far more accessible without any special "techniques" (Weiss, 1967).

The integration of defenses usually takes place in insight therapy. Many patients do not wish or cannot use or cannot obtain insight therapy. When the goal is not insight but change in behavior or emotion, there is still a need for the *therapist* to be insightful. He should realize that any efforts involving image formation may be evocative of concealed feelings, impulses, or ideas, and he should appraise the patient's capacity to cope with these emergent contents. For example, if the therapist is going to suggest angry or destructive images, he must assess the degree of guilt the person may feel in response to these images. My position, then, is that whether or not the patient is going to "know," the therapist should. Any therapy that avoids giving the therapist time to get to know his patient and yet uses uncovering techniques is liable, in my opinion, to be potentially harmful to some patients.

Image forming techniques may be contraindicated in some patients for reasons other than those indicated above. Some patients habitually use images as fantasy substitutes for life. They dull the edge of real effort by daydreaming, they use fantasy to withdraw from perception of hurtful reality. Encouraging such patients to use imagery may be nontherapeutic. Also, some patients readily blur the distinction between image and percept, and encouragement of image formation may lead to a loss of reality testing capacity.

CONCLUSION

Image formation samples the real and fantasy past, and pre-experiences the many possible futures. The closeness of images to sensory perception evokes emotional responses and cognitive processes associated with real experience. Thus, a patient can relive and complete events and fantasies that were too overwhelming for him in the past. As to the future, he can obtain courage, stamina, and discretion to try the possible, accept the inevitable, and avoid the hazardous. Because much remains to be learned about the indications and contraindications and the optimum techniques for individual cases, therapists should use *all* modes of representation to tailor the treatment to individual patients.

REFERENCES

Abramson, H. A., ed. 1967. *International Conference on the Use of LSD in Psychotherapy and Alcoholism.* Indianapolis, Bobbs-Merrill Co.

Adler, G. 1967. Methods of treatment in analytical psychology. In Wolman, B. B., ed. *Psychoanalytic Techniques.* New York, Basic Books.

Beck, A. T. 1970. Role of fantasies in psychotherapy and psychopathology. *J. Nerv. Ment. Dis.*, 150:3–17.

Biddle, W. E. 1969. Image therapy. *Amer. J. Psychiat.*, 126:408–411.

——— 1963. Images. *Arch. Gen. Psychiat.*, 9:464–470.

Brown, B. M. 1969. Cognitive aspects of Wolpe's behavior therapy. *Amer. J. Psychother.*, 124:854–859.

Buckman, J. 1967. Theoretical aspects of LSD therapy. In Abramson, H. A., ed. *International Conference on the use of LSD in psychotherapy & alcoholism.* Indianapolis, Bobbs-Merrill Co.

Crocket, R., Sandison, R. A., and Walk, A., eds. 1963. *Hallucinogenic drugs and their psychotherapeutic use.* In Proceedings of the Royal Medico-Psychological Association. London, H. K. Lewis & Co.

Ferenczi, S. 1950. *Further Contributions to the Theory and Technique of Psychoanalysis.* London, The Hogarth Press.

Frank, J. 1961. *Persuasion & Healing.* Baltimore, Johns Hopkins Press.

Freud, S. (1895) Project for a scientific psychology. In Bonaparte, M., Freud, A., and Kris, E., eds. *The Origins of Psychoanalysis.* New York, Basic Books, 1954.

——— and Breuer, J. (1895) Studies on hysteria. *Stand. Ed.*, 2, 1955.

Gerard, R. 1963. Symbolic visualization—A method of psychosynthesis. *Top. Probl. Psychother.*, 4:70–80.

Glover, E., ed. 1955. *The Technique of Psychoanalysis.* New York, International Universities Press.

Greenson, R. 1960. Empathy and its vicissitudes. *Int. J. Psychoanal.*, 41:418–424.

Hammer, M. 1967. The directed daydream technique. *Psychother: Theory, Res. & Prac.*, 4:173–181.

Hogan, R., and Kirchner, J. 1967. Preliminary report of the extinction of learned fears via short-term implosive therapy. *J. Abnorm. Psychol.*, 72:106–109.

Hoffer, A., and Osmond, H. 1967. *The Hallucinogens.* New York, Academic Press.

Jacobson, E. 1942. *Progressive Relaxation*. Chicago, University of Chicago Press.

Jung, C. G. 1959. *The Archetypes and the Collective Unconscious*. New York, Pantheon.

Knapp, P. H. 1969. Image, symbol and person. *Arch. Gen. Psychiat.*, 21:392–406.

Kubie, L. S. 1943. The use of induced hypnagogic reveries in the recovery of repressed amnesic data. *Bull. Menninger Clinic*, 7:172–182.

Kolvin, I. 1967. Aversive imagery treatment in adolescents. *Behav. Res. Ther.*, 5:245–248.

Lazarus, A. 1968. Learning theory & the treatment of depression. *Behav. Res. Ther.*, 6:83–89.

Leuner, H. 1967. The present state of psycholytic therapy & its possibilities. In Abramson, H. A., ed. *International Conference on the Use of LSD in Psychotherapy and Alcoholism*. Indianapolis, Bobbs-Merrill Co.

——— 1969. Guided affective imagery (GAI). A method of intensive psychotherapy. *Amer. J. Psychother.*, 23:4–22.

Lewin, B. D. 1968. *The Image and the Past*. New York, International Universities Press.

Marks, I., and Gelder, M. G. 1967. Transvestism & fetishism: Clinical & psychological changes during faradic aversion. *Brit. J. Psychiat.*, 113:711–729.

Pahnke, W. N., et al. 1969. LSD assisted psychotherapy with terminal cancer patients. In Masserman, J. H., ed. *Curr. Psychiat. Ther.*, 9:114–152.

Perls, F. S. 1970. Dream seminars. In Fagan, J., and Shepherd, I. L., eds. *Gestalt Therapy Now*. Palo Alto, Calif., Science & Behavior Books, Inc.

Rachman, S. 1967. Systematic desensitization. *Psychol. Bull.*, 67:93–103.

Reyher, J. 1963. Free imagery: An uncovering procedure. *J. Clin. Psychol.*, 19:454–459.

Rogers, C. R. 1951. *Client Centered Therapy*. Boston, Houghton-Mifflin.

Ross, W. D., and Knapp, F. T. 1962. A technique for self analysis of counter transference. *J. Amer. Psychoanal. Ass.*, 10:643–657.

Sacerdote, P. 1968. Induced Dreams. *Amer. J. Clin. Hypn.*, 10:167–173.

——— 1967. *Induced Dreams*. New York, Vantage Press.

Stampfl, T. G., and Lewis, D. J. 1967. Essentials of implosive therapy: A learning theory based on psychodynamic behavioral therapy. *J. Abnorm. Psychol.*, 72:496–503.

Truax, C. B., and Wargo, D. 1966. Psychotherapeutic encounters that change behavior: For better or worse. *Amer. J. Psychother.*, 20:499–520.

Weiss, J. 1967. The integration of defenses. *Int. J. Psychoanal.*, 48:520–524.

Weitzman, B. 1967. Behavior therapy & psychotherapy. *Psychol. Rev.*, 73:300–317.

Wolpe, J. 1958. *Psychotherapy by Reciprocal Inhibition*. Palo Alto, Stanford University Press.

Bibliography

Abramson, H. A., ed. 1967. *International Conference on the Use of LSD in Psychotherapy and Alcoholism.* Indianapolis, Bobbs-Merrill Co.

Ach, N. (1905) Awareness. In Mandler, J., and Mandler, G., eds. *Thinking: From Association to Gestalt.* New York, John Wiley & Sons, 1964.

Adams, J. E. 1966. Future of stereotaxic surgery. *J.A.M.A.*, 198:648–652.

Adler, G. 1967. Methods of treatment in analytical psychology. In Wolman, B. B., ed. *Psychoanalytic Techniques.* New York, Basic Books.

———— 1948. *Studies in analytical psychology.* London, Routledge & Kegan Paul.

Allers, R., and Teller, J. (1924). On the utilization of unnoticed impressions in associations. *Psychol. Issues,* Monogr. 7, 2:121–155, 1960.

Allport, F. H. 1955. *Theories of Perception and the Concept of Structure.* New York, John Wiley & Sons.

Amadeo, M., and Gomez, E. 1966. Eye movements, attention and dreaming in subjects with lifelong blindness. *Canad. Psychiat. Ass.* J., 11:500–507.

Anastasi, A., and Foley, J. P. 1944. An experimental study of the drawing behavior of adult psychotics in comparison with that of a normal control group. *J. Exp. Psychol.*, 34:169–194.

———— and Foley, J. 1943. An analysis of spontaneous artistic productions by the abnormal. *J. Gen. Psychol.*, 28:297–313.

———— and Foley, J. 1941a. A survey of literature on artistic behavior in the abnormal. I. Historical and theoretical background. *J. Gen. Psychol.*, 25:111–142; II. Approaches and interrelationships. *Ann. N.Y. Acad. Sci.*, 42:1–112.

———— and Foley, J. 1941b. A survey of literature on artistic behavior in the abnormal. IV Experimental investigations. *J. Gen. Psychol.*, 25:187–237.

315

———— and Foley, J. 1940. A survey of literature on artistic behavior in the abnormal. II. Spontaneous productions. *Psychol. Monogr.*, 52(6).

Angell, J. C. 1910. Methods for the determination of mental imagery. *Psychol. Monogr.*, 13:61–107.

Anthony, J. 1959. An experimental approach to the psychopathology of childhood: Sleep disturbances. *Brit. J. Med. Psychol.*, 32:19–36.

Antrobus, J. S., and Singer, J. L. 1969. Mind wandering & cognitive structure. Paper presented to N.Y. Acad. Sci., Oct. 20, 1969.

———— and Singer, J. L. 1964. Eye movements accompanying daydreaming, visual imagery & thought suppression. *J. Abnorm. Soc. Psychol.*, 69:244–252.

———— Singer, J. L., and Greenberg, S. 1966. Studies in the stream of consciousness; experimental enhancement and suppression of spontaneous cognitive processes. *Percept. Motor Skills*, 23:399–417.

Arieti, S. 1967. *The Intrapsychic Self.* New York, Basic Books.

———— 1962. The microgeny of thought and perception. *Arch. Gen. Psychiat.*, 6:454–468.

———— 1961. The loss of reality. *Psychoanalysis*, 48:3–25.

———— 1955. *Interpretation of Schizophrenia.* New York, Brunner.

Aristotle. Thinking; Recollection. In Mandler, J., and Mandler, G., eds. *Thinking: From Association to Gestalt.* New York, John Wiley & Sons, 1964.

Arlow, J. 1969. Unconscious fantasy & disturbances of conscious experience. *Psychoanal. Quart.*, 38:1–27.

———— and Brenner, C. 1964. *Psychoanalytic concepts and the structural theory.* New York, International Universities Press.

Arnheim, R. 1966. *Toward a Psychology of Art.* Los Angeles, University of California Press.

———— 1954. *Art and Visual Perception: A Psychology of the Creative Eye.* Berkeley, University of California Press.

Aserinski, E., and Kleitman, N. 1953. Regularly occurring periods of eye motility and concommitant phenomena during sleep. *Science*, 118:273–274.

Asher, H. 1963. Experiment with LSD: They split my personality. *Saturday Review*, 39–43, June 1, 1963.

Attneave, F. 1955. Symmetry, information & memory for patterns. *Amer. J. Psychol.*, 68:209–222.

Bailey, P. 1948. *Intracranial Tumors.* Springfield, Ill., Charles C Thomas Co.

Bakan, D. 1967. *On Method.* San Francisco, Jossey-Bass, Inc.

Barber, T. X. 1969. *A Scientific Approach to Hypnosis.* Princeton, Van Nostrand.

———— and Calberley, D. S. 1965. Hypnotizeability, suggestibility, and personality. II. An assessment of previous imaginative-fantasy experiences by the As, Barber-Glass, and Shor questionnaires. *J. Clin. Psych.*, 21:57–58.

Bartley, S. H. 1959. Some facts and concepts regarding the neurophysiology of the optic pathway. *A.M.A. Arch. Ophth.*, 60:775–791.

Beck, A. T. 1970. Role of fantasies in psychotherapy and psychopathology. *J. Nerv. Ment. Dis.*, 150:3–17.

Bender, M. B. 1965. Neuroophthalmology. In Baker, A. B., ed. *Clinical Neurology*, 3rd ed. New York, Hoeber Medical Division, Harper & Row Publishers.

Beres, D. 1965. Symbol and object. *Bull. Menninger Clin.*, 29:3–23.

———— 1960. Perception, imagination, and reality. *Int. J. Psychoanal.*, 41:327–334.

Berger, R. J., Olley, P., and Oswald, I. 1962. The EEG, eye-movements and dreams of the blind. *Quart. J. Exp. Psychol.*, 14:183–186.

Beritashvili, I. S. 1969. Concerning psychoneural activity of animals. In Cole, M., and Maltzman, I., eds. *A Handbook of Contemporary Soviet Psychology*. New York, Basic Books.

Betts, G. H. 1909. *The Distribution and Functions of Mental Imagery*. New York: Columbia University Teacher's College Press.

Bexton, W. H., Heron, W., and Scott, T. H. 1954. Effects of decreased variation in sensory environment. *Canad. J. Psychol.*, 8:70–76.

Bibring, E. 1943. The conception of the repetition compulsion. *Psychoanal. Quart.*, 12:486–519.

Biddle, W. E. 1969. Image therapy. *Amer. J. Psychiat.*, 126:408–411.

———— 1963. Images. *Arch. Gen. Psychiat.*, 9:464–470.

Bleuler, E. 1950. *Dementia Praecox or The Group of Schizophrenias*. New York: International Universities Press.

Brady, J. P., and Leavitt, E. E. 1966. Hypnotically induced visual hallucinations. *Psychosom. Med.*, 28:351–363.

Brain, R. 1955. *Diseases of the Nervous System*. London, Oxford University Press.

———— 1954. Loss of visualization. *Proc. Roy. Soc. Med.*, 47:228–290.

Brauchi, J. T., and West, L. J. 1959. Sleep deprivation. *J.A.M.A.*, 171:11–14.

Breger, L. 1967. Function of dreams. *J. Abnorm. Psychol., Monogr.*, 72 (5, Whole #641).

Breuer, J., and Freud, S. (1895) Studies on hysteria. *Stand. Ed.*, 2, 1954.

Bromberg, W., and Schilder, P. 1933. Psychologic considerations in alcoholic hallucinosis. *Int. J. Psychoanal.*, 14:206–224.

Brower, D. 1947. The relative predominance of various imagery modalities. *J. Gen. Psych.*, 37:199–200.

Brown, B. M. 1969. Cognitive aspects of Wolpe's behavior therapy. *Amer. J. Psychother.*, 124:854–859.

Bruner, J. S. 1964. The course of cognitive growth. *Am. Psychol.*, 19:1–15.

Buckman, J. 1967. Theoretical aspects of LSD therapy. In Abramson, H. A., ed. *International Conference on the use of LSD in psychotherapy & alcoholism*. Indianapolis, Bobbs-Merrill Co.

Bühler, K. (1907) Tatsachen und probleme zu einer psychologie der denkvorgänge. I. uber gedanken. In Mandler, J., and Mandler, G., eds. *Thinking: From Association to Gestalt*. New York, John Wiley & Sons. 1964.

Burton, A., and Sjöberg, B. 1964. The diagnostic validity of human figure drawings in schizophrenia. *J. Psychol.*, 57:3–18.

Caligor, L. 1957. *A New Approach to Figure Drawing*. Springfield, Ill., Charles C Thomas, Publisher.

Callaway, E. 1962. Factors influencing the relationship between alpha activity and visual reaction time. *Electroenceph. Clin. Neurophysiol.*, 14:674–782.

Cartwright, R. D., Bernick, N., Bokowitz, G., and Kling, A. 1969. Effect of an erotic movie on the sleep and dreams of young men. *Arch. Gen. Psychiat.*, 20:262–271.

Caston, J. 1969. Completion effects and attention in hallucinatory and non-hallucinatory patients and normal subjects. *J. Nerv. Ment. Dis.*, 148:147–157.

Chodoff, P. 1970. The German concentration camp as a psychological stress. *Arch. Gen. Psychiat.*, 22:78–87.

Clark, B., and Graybiel, A. 1957. The breakoff phenomenon. *J. Aviat. Med.*, 28:121–126.

Cobb, S., and Lindeman, E. 1943. Neuropsychiatric observation after the Coconut Grove fire. *Ann. Surg.*, 117:814–824.

Cohen, L. H. 1938. Imagery and its relations to schizophrenic symptoms. *J. Ment. Sci.*, 84:284–346.

Cordeau, J. P. 1964. Abstracted in *Electroenceph. Clin. Neurophysiol.*, 17:442–443.

Corman, H. H., et al. 1964. Visual imagery and preconscious thought processes. *Arch. Gen. Psychiat.*, 10:160–172.

Costello, C. G., and MacGregor, P. 1957. The relationships between some aspects of visual imagery and the alpha rhythm. *J. Ment. Sci.*, 103:786–795.

Crocket, R., Sandison, R. A., and Walk, A., eds. 1963. *Hallucinogenic drugs and their psychotherapeutic use*. In Proceedings of the Royal Medico-Psychological Association. London, H. K. Lewis & Co.

Cuenod, M., Casey, K. L., and MacLean, P. D. 1965. Unit analysis of visual input to posterior limbic cortex: I. photic stimulation. *J. Neurophysiol.*, 28:1101–1117.

Davis, D. R. 1966. *An Introduction to Psychopathology*, 2nd Ed. London, Oxford University Press.

Dement, W. 1955. Dream recall and eye movements during sleep in schizophrenic subjects and normals. *J. Nerv. Ment. Dis.*, 122:263–269.

––––––– and Wolpert, E. 1958. The relation of eye movements, body motility, and external stimuli to dream content. *J. Exp. Psychol.*, 55:543–553.

––––––– and Kleitman, N. 1957. The relation of eye movements during sleep to dream activity. *J. Exp. Psychol.*, 53:339–346.

Deno, S. L. 1968. Effects of words and pictures as stimuli in learning language equivalents. *J. Educ. Psychol.*, 59:202–206.

Deutsch, F. 1953. Instinctual drives and intersensory perceptions during the analytic procedure. In Lowenstein, R. M., ed. *Drives, Affects, Behavior*, Vol. 1. New York, International Universities Press.

Ditchburn, R. W., Fender, D. H., and Mayne, S. 1959. Vision with controlled movements of the retinal image. *J. Physiol.* 145:98–107.

Domarus, E. von. 1944. The specific laws of logic in schizophrenia. In Kasanin, J. S., ed. *Language and Thought in Schizophrenia*. Berkeley, University of California Press.

Domhoff, B., and Kamiya, J. 1964. Problems in dream content study with objective indicators. *Arch. Gen. Psychiat.*, 11:519–532.

Doty, R. W. 1960. Functional significance of the topographic aspects of the retino-cortical projection. In Report of Symposium: *The Vision System: Neurophysiology and Psychophysics*, pp. 228–245. Freiburg, Germany.

Douglas, R. J. 1967. The hippocampus and behavior. *Psychol. Bull.*, 67:416–442.

———— and Pribram, K. H. 1966. Learning and limbic lesions. *Neuropsychol.*, 4:197–220.

Eagle, M. 1962. Personality correlates of sensitivity to subliminal stimulation. *J. Nerv. Ment. Dis.*, 134:1–17.

———— Wolitsky, D. L., and Klein, G. S. 1966. Imagery: Effects of a concealed figure in a stimulus. *Science*, 151(2):837–839.

Eissler, K. R. 1966. A note on trauma, dream, anxiety, and schizophrenia. *Psychoanal. Stud. Child*, 21:17–50.

Ellinwood, E. H. 1967. Amphetamine psychosis: 1. Description of the individuals and process. *J. Nerv. Ment. Dis.*, 144:273–283.

Erikson, E. H. 1954. The dream specimen of psychoanalysis. In Knight, R. P., and Friedman, C. R., eds. *Psychoanalysis, Psychiatry, and Psychology*, Vol. 1. New York, International Universities Press. 1954.

Evarts, E. V. 1962. A neurophysiologic theory of hallucinations. In West, L. J., ed. *Hallucinations*, New York, Grune & Stratton.

Feldman, M., and Bender, M. 1969. Hallucinations and illusions of parieto-occipital lobe origin. Paper presented at Eastern Psychiatric Research Association meeting, New York, November, 1969.

Ferenczi, S. 1950. *Further Contributions to the Theory and Technique of Psychoanalysis*. London, The Hogarth Press.

Fisher, C. 1960. Subliminal and supra-liminal influences on dreams. *Amer. J. Psychiat.*, 116:1009–1017.

———— 1959. The effect of subliminal visual stimulation on images and dreams: A validation study. *J. Amer. Psychoanal. Assn.*, 7:35–83.

———— 1954. Dreams and perception: The role of preconscious and primary modes of perception in dream formation. *J. Amer. Psychoanal. Assoc.*, 2:389–445.

———— and Dement, W. 1963. Studies on the psychopathology of sleep and dreams. *Amer. J. Psychiat.*, 119:1160–1168.

———— and Paul, I. H. 1959. The effect of subliminal visual stimulation on images and dreams: A validation study. *J. Amer. Psychoanal. Ass.*, 7:35–83.

Fisher, S., and Cleveland, S. E. 1958. *Body Image and Personality*. Princeton, N.J., D. Van Nostrand Co.

———— Goldberg, F. H., and Klein, G. S. 1963. Effects of subliminal stimulation on imagery and discrimination. *Percept. Motor Skills*, 17:31–44.

Fiss, H., Ellman, S. J., and Klein, G. S. 1968. Effects of interruption of rapid eye movement sleep on fantasy in the waking state. *Psychophysiology*, 4:364 (Abstract).

Folkins, C. H. et al. 1968. Desensitization and the experimental reduction of threat. *J. Abnorm. Psychol.*, 73:100–113.

Forbes, A. 1949. Dream scintillations. *Psychosom. Med.*, 11:160–162.

Forgus, R. H., and Dewolfe, A. S. 1969. Perceptual selectivity in hallucinatory schizophrenics. *J. Abnorm. Psychol.*, 74:288–292.

Frandsen, A., and Holder, J. 1969. Spatial visualization in solving complex verbal problems. *J. Psychol.*, 73:229–233.

Frank, J. 1961. *Persuasion & Healing*. Baltimore, Johns Hopkins Press.

Freedman, D. X. 1968. On the use and abuse of LSD. *Arch. Gen. Psychiat.*, 18:330–347.

Freedman, S. J., and Greenblatt, M. 1960. Studies in human isolation, II. Hallucinations and other cognitive findings. *U.S. Armed Forces Med. J.*, 2:1479–1497.

Freeman, T., Cameron, J. L., and McGhie, A. 1966. *Studies on Psychosis*. New York, International Universities Press.

Freud, A. 1946. *The Ego and the Mechanisms of Defense*. New York, International Universities Press.

Freud, S. (1923) The ego and the id. *Stand. Ed.*, 19, 1961.

—————— (1922) Some neurotic mechanisms in jealousy, paranoia, and homosexuality. *Stand. Ed.*, 18, 1962.

—————— (1920) Beyond the pleasure principle. *Stand. Ed.*, 18, 1962.

—————— (1919) A child is being beaten: A contribution to the study of the origin of sexual perversions. *Stand. Ed.*, 17, 1955.

—————— (1916) A mythological parallel to a visual obsession. *Stand. Ed.*, 14, 1962.

—————— (1911) Formulations on the two principles of mental functioning. *Stand. Ed.*, 12, 1958.

—————— (1910) Leonardo Da Vinci and a memory of his childhood. *Stand. Ed.*, 11, 1962.

—————— 1908. Hysterical phantasies and their relation to bi-sexuality. *Stand. Ed.*, 9, 1959.

—————— (1901) The psychopathology of everyday life. *Stand. Ed.*, 6, 1960.

—————— (1900) The interpretation of dreams. *Stand. Ed.*, 5, 1953.

—————— (1899) Screen memories. *Stand. Ed.*, 3, 1962.

—————— (1898) The psychical mechanism of forgetfulness. *Stand. Ed.*, 3, 1962.

—————— (1895) Project for a scientific psychology. In Bonaparte, M., Freud, A., and Kris, E., eds. *The Origins of Psychoanalysis*. New York, Basic Books, 1954.

—————— and Breuer, J. (1893–1895) Studies on hysteria. *Stand. Ed.*, 2, 1955.

Friedman, P. and Linn, L. 1957. Some psychiatric notes on the Andrea Doria disaster. *Amer. J. Psychiat.*, 114:426–432.

Furst, S. S. 1967. *Psychic Trauma*. New York/London, Basic Books, Inc.

Galton, F. 1919. *Inquiries into Human Faculty*. New York, E. P. Dutton & Co. (Everyman).

Gardner, R. W. 1969. Organismic equilibration and the energy structure duality in psychoanalytic theory. *J. Amer. Psychoanal. Ass.*, 17:3–40.

Gerard, R. 1963. Symbolic visualization—A method of psychosynthesis. *Top. Probl. Psychother.*, 4:70–80.

Gerbrandt, L. K. 1964. Generalizations from the distinction of passive and active avoidance. *Psychol. Rep.*, 15:11–22.

Gill, M. M. 1967. The primary process. *Psychol. Issues*, Monogr. 18/19, 5:60–298.

———— 1963. Topography & systems in psychoanalytic theory. *Psychol. Issues*, 3(2): Monogr. 10.

Glover, E., ed. 1955. *The Technique of Psychoanalysis*. New York, International Universities Press.

———— 1929. The screening function of traumatic memories. *Int. J. Psychoanal.*, 10:90–93.

Goldberger, L. 1961. Homogeneous visual stimulation (Ganzfeld) and imagery. *Percept. Motor Skills*, 12:91–93.

———— and Holt, R. 1961. *A comparison of isolation effects and their personality correlates in two divergent samples*. New York: N.Y. Univ. ASD Technical Report, 61–417.

Goldstein, K. 1944. A methodological approach to the study of schizophrenic thought disorder. In Kasanin, J. W., ed. *Language and Thought in Schizophrenia*, pp. 17–40. Berkeley, University of California Press.

Goldstein, M. J., et al. 1965. Coping style as a factor in psychophysiological response to a tension-arousing film. *J. Pers. Soc. Psychol.*, 1:290–302.

Golla, F. L., Hutton, E. L., and Walter, W. G. 1943. The objective study of mental imagery. I. physiological concomitants. *J. Ment. Sci.*, 89:216–223.

Gombrich, E. H. 1969. *Art and Illusion: A Study in the Psychology of Pictorial Representation*. New York, Pantheon.

Gordon, R. A. 1950. An experiment correlating the nature of imagery with performance on a test of reversal perspective. *Brit. J. Psychol.*, 41:63–67.

———— 1949. An investigation into some of the factors that favor the formation of stereotyped images. *Brit. J. Psychol.*, 39:156–167.

Granit, R. 1955. *Receptors and Sensory Perception*. New Haven, Yale University Press.

Greenacre, P. 1949. A contribution to the study of screen memories. *Psychoanal. Stud. Child*, 3–4:73–84.

Greenberg, R. 1966. Cerebral cortex lesions: The dream process and sleep spindles. *Cortex*, 2:357–366.

———— et al. 1968. The effects of dream deprivation. Presented to American Psychoanalytic Association 1968 Annual Meeting, Boston, Mass.

Greenson, R. 1960. Empathy and its vicissitudes. *Int. J. Psychoanal.*, 41:418–424.

Gregory, R. L. 1966. *Eye and Brain: The Psychology of Seeing*. New York, McGraw-Hill.

Griffitts, C. H. 1924. *Fundamentals of Vocational Psychology*. New York, MacMillan.

Gross, J., et al. 1965. Eye movements during emergent stage I EEG in subjects with lifelong blindness. *J. Nerv. Ment. Dis.*, 141:365–370.

Gross, M. M., et al. 1963. Hearing disturbances and auditory hallucinations in the acute alcoholic psychoses: I. Tinnitus: incidence and significance. *J. Nerv. Ment. Dis.*, 137:455–465.

Guilford, J. P. 1959. Three faces of intellect. *Amer. Psychol.*, 14:469–479.

Haber, R. N. 1968. *Contemporary Theory and Research in Visual Perception*. New York, Holt, Rinehart, and Winston.

Hall, C. S., and Vander Castle, R. L. 1964. A comparison of home and monitored dreams. Paper presented at the Association for the Psychophysiological Study of Sleep, Palo Alto, Calif., March, 1964.

Hammer, M. 1967. The directed daydream technique. *Psychother: Theory, Res. & Prac.*, 4:173–181.

Hanawalt, N. G. 1954. Recurrent images: New instances and a summary of the older ones. *Amer. J. Psychol.*, 67:170–174.

Havens, L. L. 1962. Placement and movement of hallucinations in space: Phenomenology & theory. *Int. J. Psychiat.*, 43:426–435.

Hartley, D. (1834) Excerpts from "Observations on Man." In Mandler, J., and Mandler, G., eds. *Thinking: From Association to Gestalt*, pp. 72–92. New York, John Wiley & Sons, 1964.

Hartmann, H. 1964. Comments on the psychoanalytic theory of the ego. In *Essays on Ego Psychology; Selected Problems in Psychoanalytic Theory*. New York, International Universities Press.

———— 1958. *Ego Psychology & the Problem of Adaptation*. New York, International Universities Press.

Heaton, J. M. 1968. *The Eye: Phenomenology & Psychology of Function & Disorder*. Philadelphia, J. B. Lippincott Co.

Hebb, D. O. 1959. A neuropsychological theory. In Koch, S., ed. *Psychology: A Study of a Science*, Vol. I, pp. 622–643. New York, McGraw-Hill.

Helmholtz, H. von. 1962. *Popular Scientific Lectures*. New York, Dover Publications.

Hernandez-Peon, R. 1964. Psychiatric implications of neurophysiological research. *Bull. Menninger Clin.*, 28:165–185.

Hochberg, J., and McAlister, E. A. 1953. A quantitative approach to figural "goodness." *J. Exp. Psychol.*, 46:361–364.

Hoffer, A., and Osmond, H. 1967. *The Hallucinogens*. New York, Academic Press.

———— and Osmond, H. 1962. Olfactory changes in schizophrenia. *Amer. J. Psychiat.*, 119:72–75.

Hogan, R., and Kirchner, J. 1967. Preliminary report of the extinction of learned fears via short-term implosive therapy. *J. Abnorm. Psychol.*, 72:106–109.

Hollender, M. H., and Boszormenyi-Nagy, I. 1958. Hallucination as an ego experience. *Arch. Neurol. Psychiat.*, 80:93–97.

Holstijn, A. J. 1951. The psychological development of Vincent van Gogh. Translated by H. P. Winzen. *Amer. Imago.*, 8:239–273.

Holt, R. R. 1968. Comments made during the panel "Psychoanalytic Theory of the Instinctual Drives in Relation to Recent Developments." Reported by Dahl, H. *J. Amer. Psychoanal. Ass.*, 16:613–637.

—— 1967. The development of the primary process: A structural view. *Psychol. Issues*, Monogr. 18/19, 5 (2–3):344–383.

—— 1964a. Imagery: The return of the ostracized. *Amer. Psychologist*, 19(4):254–264.

—— 1964b. The emergence of cognitive psychology. *J. Amer. Psychoanal. Ass.*, 12:650–665.

—— 1962. A critical examination of Freud's concept of bound versus free cathexis. *J. Amer. Psychoanal. Ass.*, 10:475–525.

Horowitz, M. J. 1968. Visual thought images in psychotherapy. *Amer. J. Psychother.*, 22:55–59.

—— 1968. Spatial behavior and psychopathology. *J. Nerv. Ment. Dis.*, 164:24–35.

—— 1967. Visual imagery and cognitive organization. *Amer. J. Psychiat.*, 123:938–946.

—— 1966. Visual imagery: an experimental study of pictorial cognition using the dot-image sequence. *J. Nerv. Ment. Dis.*, 141:615–622.

—— 1966. Body image. *Arch Gen. Psychiat.*, 14:456–460.

—— 1965. Notes on art therapy media and techniques. *Bull. Art Therapy*, 4:70–73.

—— 1964a. Body-buffer zone. *Arch. Gen. Psychiat.*, 11:651–656.

—— 1964b. The imagery of visual hallucinations. *J. Nerv. Ment. Dis.*, 138:513–523.

—— 1963. Graphic communication: A study of interaction painting with schizophrenics. *Amer. J. Psychother.*, 17:230–239.

—— Adams, J. E., and Rutkin, B. B. 1968. Visual imagery on brain stimulation. *Arch. Gen. Psychiat.*, 19:469–486.

—— Adams, J., and Rutkin, B. 1967. Dream scintillations. *Psychosom. Med.*, 29:284–292.

—— Cohen, F. M., Skolnikoff, A., and Saunders, F. A. 1970. *Psychosocial function in epilepsy*. Springfield, Ill., Charles C Thomas Co.

Hume, D. (1739) Excerpt from "A treatise of human nature." In Mandler, J., and Mandler, G., eds. *Thinking: From Association to Gestalt*, pp. 51–69. New York, John Wiley & Sons, 1964.

Humphrey, G. 1951. *Thinking: An Introduction to Experimental Psychology*. New York, Wiley and Sons.

Humphrey, M. E., and Zangwill, O. L. 1951. Cessation of dreaming after brain injury. *J. Neurol. Neurosurg. Psychiat.*, 14:322–325.

Isakower, O. A. 1938. A contribution to the patho-psychology of phenomena associated with falling asleep. *Int. J. Psychoanal.*, 19:331–345.

Ishibashi, T., et al. 1964. Hallucinations produced by electrical stimulation of the temporal lobes in schizophrenic patients. *Tohoku. J. Exp. Med.*, 82:124–239.

Jackson, J. H. (1932) *Selected writings*, Taylor, J., ed., Vol. 2, New York, Basic Books, 1958.

Jacobson, E. 1957. Denial and repression. *J. Amer. Psychoanal. Ass.*, 5:61–92.

Jacobson, E. 1942. *Progressive Relaxation*. Chicago, University of Chicago Press.

Jaensch, E. R. 1930. *Eidetic Imagery & Typological Methods of Investigation.* London, Kegan, Paul, Trench and Truber & Co.

Janis, I. L. 1958. *Psychological Stress.* New York, John Wiley and Sons.

Jansson, B. 1968. The prognostic significance of various types of hallucinations in young people. *Acta. Psychiat. Scand.,* 44:401–409.

Jarvis, J. H. 1967. Post mastectomy breast phantoms. *J. Nerv. Ment. Dis.,* 144(4):266–272.

Jasper, H. H., and Rasmussen, T. 1958. Studies of clinical and electrical responses to deep temporal stimulation in men with some considerations of functional anatomy: The brain and behavior. *Res. Publ. Ass. Res. Nerv. Ment. Dis.* 35:316–334.

Jaspers, K. 1962. *General Psychopathology.* Manchester, England, Manchester University Press.

Jenkins, J. R., et al. 1967. Differential memory for picture and word stimuli. *J. Educ. Psychol.,* 58:303–307.

Jones, E. 1953. *The Life and Work of Sigmund Freud,* Vols. I, II, III. New York, Basic Books, Inc. 1953, 1955, 1957.

——— 1948. *Papers on Psychoanalysis,* 5th ed. Baltimore, Williams & Wilkins.

——— 1929. Fear, guilt, and hate. *Int. J. Psychoanal.,* 10:383–397.

Joseph, E. D. 1959. An unusual fantasy in a twin with an inquiry into the nature of fantasy. *Psychoanal. Quart.,* 28:189–206.

Jung, C. G. 1959. *The Archetypes and the Collective Unconscious.* New York, Pantheon.

Kafka, E., and Reiser, M. 1967. Defensive and adaptive ego processes: Their relationship to GSR activity in free imagery experiments. *Arch. Gen. Psychiat.,* 16:34–40.

Kamiya, J., and Zeitlin, D. 1963. Learned EEG alpha wave control by humans. Report #182, Dept. of Mental Hygiene, Research Div., State of California.

Kandinski, V. 1880. Zur lehre von jen halluzinationen. *Arch. Psychiat.,* 11:453.

Kanzer, M. 1958. Image formation during free association. *Psychoanal. Quart.,* 27:465–484.

Kellog, R. 1967. Understanding children's art. *Psychol. Today,* May, 1967, 16–25.

Kepecs, J. G. 1954. Observations on screens and barriers in the mind. *Psychoanal. Quart.,* 23:62–77.

Kiell, N. 1965. *Psychiatry and Psychology in the Visual Arts and Aesthetics.* Madison, University of Wisconsin Press.

Klein, G. S. 1967. Peremptory ideation: Structure & force in motivated ideas. *Psychol. Issues,* 5:80–128.

Klüver, H. 1942. Mechanisms of hallucinations. In McNemar, Q., and Merrill, M. A., eds. *Studies in Personality,* pp. 175–207. New York, McGraw-Hill Book Co.

Knapp, P. H. 1969. Image, symbol and person. *Arch. Gen. Psychiat.,* 21:392–406.

Knoll, M., et al. 1963. Effects of chemical stimulation of electrically induced phosphenes on their bandwidth, shape, number, and intensity. *Confinia. Neurol.*, 23:201–226.

————— et al. 1962. Note on the spectroscopy of subjective light patterns. *J. Anal. Psychol.*, 7:55–70.

Koffka, K. 1935. Principles of Gestalt Psychology. London, Routledge and Kegan Paul.

Köhler, W. 1969. *The Task of Gestalt Psychology*. Princeton, N.J., Princeton University Press.

————— 1964. The formation and transformation of the perceptual world. *Psychol. Issues.*, 3:1–164, Monograph 12, No. 4.

Kollar, E. J., et al. 1969. Psychosis in dream deprivation. "Psychological, psychophysiological, and biochemical correlates of prolonged sleep deprivation." *Amer. J. Psychiat.*, 126:488–497.

Kolvin, I. 1967. Aversive imagery treatment in adolescents. *Behav. Res. Ther.*, 5:245–248.

Kramer, E. 1965. Art therapy and the severely disturbed gifted child. *Bull. Art Therapy*, October, pp. 3–20.

Kramer, M. 1970. Manifest dream content in normal and psychopathologic states. *Arch. Gen. Psychiat.*, 22:149–159.

Kris, E. 1965. *Psychoanalytic Explorations in Art*. New York, International Universities Press.

————— 1950. On preconscious mental processes. In Rapaport, D., ed. *Organization and Pathology of Thought*, pp. 474–493. New York, Columbia University Press, 1951.

Krystal, H. K., ed. 1968. *Massive Psychic Trauma*. New York, International Universities Press.

Kubie, L. S. 1967. The relation of psychotic disorganization to the neurotic process. *J. Amer. Psychoanal. Ass.*, 15:626–640.

————— 1958. *Neurotic Distortion of the Creative Process*. Lawrence, University of Kansas Press.

————— 1943. The use of induced hypnagogic reveries in the recovery of repressed amnesic data. *Bull. Menninger Clinic*, 7:172–182.

Kubzansky, P. E. 1964. Discussion of papers presented at symposium, Sensory deprivation research: Where do we go from here? American Psychological Association Convention.

Külpe, O. (1922) The modern psychology of thinking. In Mandler, J., and Mandler, G., eds. *Thinking: From Association to Gestalt*. New York, John Wiley & Sons, 1964.

Lacan, J. 1966. The insistence of the letter in the unconscious. *Yale French Studies: Structuralism*, Issues 36 and 37, pp. 112–147.

Langui, E. 1959. *Fifty Years of Modern art*. New York, Praeger.

Lazarus, A. 1968. Learning theory & the treatment of depression. *Behav. Res. Ther.*, 6:83–89.

Lazarus, R. S., and Opton, E. M. 1968. The use of motion picture films in the study of psychological stress: A summary of experimental studies and theoretical formulations. In Spielberger, C., ed. *Anxiety and Behavior*. New York, Academic Press.

Lehmann, D., et al. 1965. Changes in patterns of the human electroencephalogram during fluctuations of perception of stabilized retinal images. *Electroenceph. Clin. Neurophysiol.*, 19:336–343.

Letvin, J. Y., et al. 1959. What the frog's eye tells the frog's brain. *Proc. Inst. Radio Engs.*, 47:1940–1945.

Leuner, H. 1969. Guided affective imagery (GAI). A method of intensive psychotherapy. *Amer. J. Psychother.*, 23:4–22.

———— 1967. The present state of psycholytic therapy & its possibilities. In Abramson, H. A., ed. *International Conference on the Use of LSD in Psychotherapy and Alcoholism*. Indianapolis, Bobbs-Merrill Co.

Levy, B., and Ulman, E. 1967. Judging psychopathology from paintings. *J. Abnorm. Psychol.*, 72:182–187.

Lewin, B. D. 1969. Remarks on creativity, imagery and the dream. *J. Nerv. Ment. Dis.*, 149:115–121.

———— 1968. *The Image and the Past*. New York, International Universities Press.

———— 1955. Dream psychology & the analytic situation. *Psychoanal. Quart.*, 24:169–199.

———— 1948a. Inferences from the dream screen. *Int. J. Psychoanal.* 29:224–231.

———— 1948b. Reconsideration of the dream screen. *Psychoanal. Quart.*, 22:174–199.

———— 1946. Sleep, the mouth and the dream screen. *Psychoanal. Quart.*, 15:419–434.

Lindauer, M. 1969. Imagery and sensory modality. *Percept. Motor Skills*, 29:203–215.

Lindsley, D. B. 1956. Basic perceptual processes and the electroencephalogram. *Psychol. Res. Rep.*, 6:161–170. Washington, D.C.

Linton, H., and Langs, R. 1962. Subjective reactions to lysergic acid diethylamide (LSD-25). *Arch. Gen. Psychiat.*, 6:352–368.

Locke, J. (1690) Excerpts from "An essay concerning human understanding." In Mandler, J., & Mandler, G., eds. *Thinking: From Association to Gestalt*. New York, John Wiley & Sons, 1964.

Luby, E. D., et al. 1962. Model psychoses and schizophrenia. *Amer. J. Psychiat.*, 119:61–67.

Luckiesh, M. (1922) *Visual Illusions*. New York, Dover, 1965.

Lukianowicz, N. 1960. Visual thinking and similar phenomena. *J. Ment. Sci.*, 106:979–1001.

Luria, A. R. 1968. *The Mind of a Mnemonist*. New York, Basic Books.

———— 1966. *Higher Cortical Functions in Man*. New York, Basic Books, Inc.

———— and Vinogradova, O. S. 1959. An objective investigation of the dynamics of semantic systems. *Brit. J. Psychol.*, 50:89–105.

Maclay, W. S., and Guttman, E. 1941. Mescaline hallucinations in artists. *Arch. Neurol. Psychiat.*, 45:130–137.

MacKay, D. M. 1961. Interactive processes in visual perception. In Rosenblith, N., ed. *Sensory Communication*. Cambridge, Mass., MIT Press.

MacLean, P. D. 1966. The limbic and visual cortex in phylogeny: Further insights from anatomic and microelectrode studies. In Hassler, R., and Stephan, H., eds. *Evolution of the Forebrain*. Stuttgart, Georg Thieme Verlag.

Maher, B. A. 1966. *Principles of Psychopathology*. New York, McGraw-Hill.

Mahl, G. F., et al. 1964. Psychologic responses in the human to intracerebral electrical stimulation. *Psychosom. Med.*, 26:337–368.

Mahler, M. S. 1960. Symposium on psychotic object relationships. III. Perceptual de-differentiation and psychotic "object relationships." *Int. J. Psychoanal.*, 41:548–553.

Malev, M. 1969. Use of the repetition compulsion by the ego. *Psychoanal. Quart.*, 38:52–71.

Malitz, S., Wilkens, B., and Esecover, H. 1962. A comparison of drug induced hallucinations with those seen in spontaneously occurring psychoses. In West, J., ed. *Hallucinations*. New York, Grune & Stratton.

Mandler, J. M., & Mandler, G., eds. 1964. *Thinking: From Association to Gestalt*. New York, John Wiley & Sons.

Marbe, K. (1901) The psychology of judgements. In Mandler, J., and Mandler, G., eds. *Thinking: From Association to Gestalt*. New York, John Wiley & Sons, 1964.

Marks, I., and Gelder, M. G. 1967. Transvestism & fetishism: Clinical & psychological changes during faradic aversion. *Brit. J. Psychiat.*, 113:711–729.

Marrazzi, A. S. 1962. Pharmacodynamics of hallucination. In West, L. J., ed. *Hallucinations*. New York, Grune and Stratton.

Martin, R. M. 1968. The stimulus barrier and the autonomy of the ego. *Psychol. Rev.*, 75:478–493.

McGhie, A., and Chapman, J. 1961. Disorders of attention and perception in early schizophrenia. *Brit. J. Med. Psychol.*, 34:103–116.

McKellar, P. 1957. *Imagination & Thinking*. New York, Basic Books.

Mendelson, J. H., et al. 1963. Effects of visual deprivation on imagery experienced by deaf subjects. In Wortis, J., ed. *Recent Advances in Biological Psychiatry*, Vol. 6. New York, Plenum Press, 1964.

Messer, A. (1906) Experimental psychological investigations on thinking. In Mandler, J., and Mandler, G., eds. *Thinking: From Association to Gestalt*. New York, John Wiley & Sons, 1964.

Mill, J. (1829) Excerpts from "Analysis of the phenomena of the human mind." In Mandler, J., and Mandler, G., eds. *Thinking: From Association to Gestalt*, pp. 94–124. New York, John Wiley & Sons, 1964.

Miller, S. C. 1962. Ego autonomy in sensory deprivation, isolation and stress. *Int. J. Psychoanal.*, 43:1–20.

Murphy, W. F. 1961. A note on trauma and loss. *J. Amer. Psychoanal. Ass.*, 9:519–532.

Murphy, W. F. 1958. Character, trauma, and sensory perception. *Int. J. Psychoanal.*, 39:555–568.

Naumberg, M. 1966. *Dynamically Oriented Art Therapy: Its Principle and Practice*. New York, Grune and Stratton.

——— 1953. *Psychoneurotic Art: Its Function in Psychotherapy*. New York, Grune & Stratton.

——— 1950. *Schizophrenic Art: Its Meaning in Psychotherapy*. New York, Grune & Stratton.

——— 1947. Studies of the "free" art expression of behavior problem children and adolescents as a means of diagnosis and therapy. *J. Nerv. Ment. Dis.*, Monogr. 71.

Neisser, U. 1967. *Cognitive Psychology*. New York. Appleton-Century-Crofts.

Niederland, W. G. 1968. Clinical observations on the "survivor syndrome." *Int. J. Psychoanal.*, 49:313–315.

Nickols, J. 1962. Eidetic imagery synthesis. *Amer. J. Psychother.*, 16:76–82.

Noy, P. 1969. A revision of the psychoanalytic theory of the primary process. *Int. J. Psychoanal.*, 50:155–178.

Offenkrantz, W., and Rechtschaffen, A. 1963. Clinical studies of sequential dreams. I: A patient in psychotherapy. *Arch. Gen. Psychiat.*, 8:497–508.

——— and Wolpert, E. 1963. The detection of dreaming in a congenitally blind subject. *J. Nerv. Ment. Dis.*, 136:88–90.

Orne, M. T. 1962. On the social psychology of the psychological experiment: with particular reference to demand characteristics and their implications. *Amer. Psychologist*, 17:776–783.

——— 1959. The nature of hypnosis: Artifact or essence? *J. Abnorm. Soc. Psychol.*, 58:277–299.

Oswald, I. 1963. *Sleeping and Waking: Physiology and Psychology*. New York, Elsevier.

——— 1957. The EEG: Visual imagery and attention. *Quart. J. Exp. Psychol.*, 9:113–118.

Pahnke, W. N., et al. 1969. LSD assisted psychotherapy with terminal cancer patients. In Masserman, J. H., ed. *Curr. Psychiat. Ther.*, 9:114–152.

Paivio, A. 1969. Mental imagery in associative learning and memory. *Psychol. Rev.*, 76:241–260.

Parkes, C. M. 1964. Effects of bereavement on physical and mental health: A study of the medical records of widows. *Brit. Med. J.*, 2:274–294.

Paul, I. H. 1964. The effects of a drug-induced alteration in state of consciousness on retention of drive-related verbal material. *J. Nerv. Ment. Dis.*, 138:367–374.

——— and Fisher, C. 1959. Subliminal visual stimulation: A study of its influence on subsequent images and dreams. *J. Nerv. Ment. Dis.*, 129:315–340.

Penfield, W. 1966. Speech, perception and the cortex. In Eccles, J. C., ed. *Brain and Conscious Experience*, pp. 217–237. New York, Springer-Verlag.

——— 1958. *Temporal Lobe Epilepsy*. Baldwin, M., and Bailey, P., eds. Springfield, Ill., Charles C Thomas, Publisher.

——— and Jasper, H. 1954. *Epilepsy and the Functional Anatomy of the Human Brain*. Boston, Little, Brown & Co.

——— and Rasmussen, T. 1950. *The Cerebral Cortex of Man*. New York, MacMillan Co.

Perky, C. W. 1910. An experimental study of imagination. *Amer. J. Psychol.*, 21:422–452.

Perls, F. S. 1970. Dream seminars. In Fagan, J., and Shepherd, I. L., eds. *Gestalt Therapy Now.* Palo Alto, Calif., Science & Behavior Books, Inc.

Perot, P., and Penfield, W. 1960. Hallucinations of past experience and experimental responses to stimulation of temporal cortex. *Trans. Amer. Neurol. Ass.*, 85:80–84.

Perry, J. W. 1970. Emotions and object relations. *J. Anal. Psychol.*, 15:1–12.

Piaget, J. 1930. *The Child's Conception of Physical Causality.* New York, Harcourt.

Pickford, R. W. 1967. *Studies in Psychiatric Art.* Springfield, Ill., Charles C Thomas, Publisher.

Pitts, W., and McCulloch, W. S. 1947. How we know universals: The perception of auditory and visual forms. *Bull. Math. Biophysics.*, 9:127–147.

Pivik, T., and Foulkes, D. 1966. "Dream deprivation": Effects on dream content. *Science*, 153:1282–1284.

Platt, J. F. 1960. How we see straight lines. *Sci. Amer.*, 202:121–129.

Popovic, M., and Petrovic, D. 1964. After the earthquake. *Lancet.*, 2:1169–71.

Pötzl, O. (1917) The relationship between experimentally induced dream images and indirect vision. *Psychol. Iss.* Monograph 7, 2:41–120, 1960.

Pribram, K. H., and MacLean, P. D. 1953. Neuronographic analysis of medial and basal cerebral cortex: Monkey. *J. Neurophysiol.*, 16:324–340.

Pritchard, R. M. 1961. Stabilized images on the retina. *Sci. Amer.*, 204:72–78.

Rachman, S. 1967. Systematic desensitization. *Psychol. Bull.*, 67:93–103.

Rapaport, D. 1967. *Emotions and Memory.* New York, International Universities Press.

——— (1960) On the psychoanalytic theory of motivation. In Gill, M., ed. *The Collected Papers of David Rapaport*, pp. 853–915. New York, Basic Books. 1967.

——— (1959) The theory of attention cathexis: An economic and structural attempt at the explanation of cognitive processes. In Gill, M., ed. *The Collected Papers of David Rapaport*, pp. 778–794. New York, Basic Books, 1967.

——— 1958. The theory of ego autonomy: A generalization. *Bull. Menninger Clin.*, 22:13–35.

——— (1957) Cognitive structures. In Gill, M., ed. *The Collected Papers of David Rapaport.* New York, Basic Books, 1967.

——— 1954. The conceptual model of psychoanalysis. In Knight, R. P., and Friedman, C. R., eds. *Psychoanalytic Psychiatry and Psychology.* New York, International Universities Press.

——— 1951. Consciousness: A psychopathological & psychodynamic view. In Abramson, H. A., ed. *Problems of Consciousness*, pp. 18–57. New York, Josiah Macy Jr. Foundation.

——— 1951. The autonomy of the ego. *Bull. Menninger Clin.*, 15:113–123.

——— 1951. *The Organization and Pathology of Thought.* New York, Columbia University Press.

Rapaport, D. 1942. *Emotions and Memory.* Baltimore, Williams & Wilkins.

Rechtschaffen, A., Vogel, G., and Shaikun, G. 1963. Interrelatedness of mental activity during sleep. *Arch. Gen. Psychiat.*, 9:536–547.

Reider, N. 1960. Percept as a screen; economic & structural aspects. *J. Amer. Psychoanal. Ass.*, 8:82–99.

Reyher, J. 1963. Free imagery: An uncovering procedure. *J. Clin. Psychol.*, 19:454–459.

Richardson, A. 1969. *Mental Imagery*. New York, Springer Publishing Co.

Roe, Anne. 1951. A study of imagery in research scientists. *J. Personality*, 19:459–470.

Roffwarg, H. P., et al. 1962. Dream imagery: Relationship to rapid eye movements of sleep. *Arch. Gen. Psychiat.*, 7:235–258.

Rogers, C. R. 1951. *Client Centered Therapy*. Boston, Houghton-Mifflin.

Roman, R., and Landis, C. 1945. Hallucinations and mental imagery. *J. Nerv. Ment. Dis.*, 102:327–331.

Rosenthal, R. 1966. *Experimenter Effects in Behavioral Research*. New York, Appleton-Century-Crofts.

Ross, W. D., and Knapp, F. T. 1962. A technique for self analysis of counter transference. *J. Amer. Psychoanal. Ass.*, 10:643–657.

Rossi, A. M., Sturrock, J. B., and Solomon, P. 1963. Suggestion effects on reported imagery in sensory deprivation. *Percep. Motor Skills*, 16:39–45.

Ruesch, J. 1957. *Disturbed Communication, the Clinical Assessment of Normal & Pathological Communicative Behavior*. New York, Norton.

Sacerdote, P. 1968. Induced Dreams. *Amer. J. Clin. Hypn.*, 10:167–173.

———— 1967. *Induced Dreams*. New York, Vantage Press.

Sachs, L. J. 1956. A case of obsessive-compulsive neurosis showing forced visual imagery. *J. Hillside Hosp.*, 5:384–391.

Sampson, H., 1966. Psychological effects of dreaming sleep. *J. Nerv. Ment. Dis.*, 143:305–317.

Saravay, S. M., and Pardes, H. 1967. Auditory elementary hallucinations in alcohol withdrawal psychosis. *Arch. Gen. Psychiat.*, 16:652–658.

Sarbin, T. R. 1967. The concept of hallucination. *J. Personality*, 35(3):359–380.

———— and Juhasz, J. B. 1970. Toward a theory of imagination. *J. Personality*, 38(1):52–76.

Saul, L. 1965. Dream scintillations. *Psychosom. Med.*, 27:286–289.

———— Snyder, T., and Shepard, E. 1956. On reading manifest dreams and other unconscious material. *J. Amer. Psychoanal. Ass.*, 4:122–137.

Schafer, R. 1968. *Aspects of Internalization*. New York, International Universities Press.

Scheibel, M., and Scheibel, A. 1962. Hallucinations and brain stem reticular core. In West, L., ed. *Hallucinations*, New York, Grune & Stratton.

Schilder, P. 1950. *The Image and Appearance of the Human Body: Studies in the Constructive Energies of the Psyche*. New York, International Universities Press.

———— 1942. *Mind: Perception and Thought in Their Constructive Aspects*. New York, Columbia University Press.

Schultes, R. E. 1969. Hallucinogens of plant origin. *Science*, 163:245–254.

Schur, M. 1966. *The Id and the Regulatory Principles of Mental Functioning*. New York, International Universities Press.

———— 1953. The ego in anxiety. In Lowenstein, R. M., ed. *Drives, Affects, Behavior*, Vol. 1, pp. 67–103. New York, International Universities Press.

Sears, R. R. 1936. Functional abnormalities of memory with special reference to amnesia. *Psychol. Bull.*, 33:229–274.

Sedman, G. 1966. A comparative study of pseudohallucinations, imagery and true hallucinations. *Brit. J. Psychiat.*, 112:9–17.

———— 1966. Being an epileptic. *Psychiat. Neurol.*, 152:1–16.

Segal, S. 1969. Imagery & reality: Can they be distinguished? Paper presented at conference of the Eastern Psychiatric Research Association on Origin and Mechanisms of Hallucinations, New York, 1969.

———— 1968a. Patterns of response to thirst in an imaging task (Perky technique) as a function of cognitive style. *J. Personality*, 36:574–588.

———— 1968b. The Perky effect: Changes in reality judgments with changing methods of inquiry. *Psychon. Sci.*, 12:393–394.

Seitz, P. F., and Molholm, H. B. 1947. Relation of mental imagery to hallucinations. *Arch. Neurol. Psychiat.*, 57:469–480.

Selz, O. (1927) The revision of the fundamental conceptions of intellectual processes. In Mandler, J., and Mandler, G., eds. *Thinking: From Association to Gestalt*. New York, John Wiley & Sons, 1964.

Shakow, D. 1962. Segmental set. *Arch. Gen. Psychiat.*, 6:1–18.

Shapiro, D. 1965. *Neurotic Styles*. New York, Basic Books.

Sharpe, E. F. (1937) *Dream Analysis*. London, The Hogarth Press, 1949.

Sheehan, P. 1967a. A shortened form of Betts' questionnaire upon mental imagery. *J. Clin. Psychol.*, 23:386–389.

———— 1967b. Reliability of a short test of imagery. *Percept. Motor Skills*, 25:744.

Shevrin, H., and Stross, L. 1964. The fate of fleeting impressions in dreams, waking images and hypnosis: A study of thought organization in different states of consciousness. Unpublished progress report.

———— and Luborsky, L. 1961. The rebus technique: A method for studying primary-process transformations of briefly exposed pictures. *J. Nerv. Ment. Dis.*, 133:479–488.

———— and Luborsky, L. 1958. The measurement of preconscious perception in dreams and images, and investigation of the Pötzl phenomenon. *J. Abnorm. Soc. Psych.*, 56:285–294.

Short, O. 1953. The objective study of mental imagery. *Brit. J. Psychol.*, 44:38–51.

Silberer, H. (1909) Report of a method of eliciting and observing certain symbolic hallucination phenomena. In Rapaport, D., ed. *The Organization and Pathology of Thought*. New York, Columbia University Press. 1951.

Singer, J. 1966. *Daydreaming*. New York, Random House.

Slater, P. E., Morimoto, K., and Hyde, R. W. 1957. The effect of group administration upon symptom formation under LSD. *J. Nerv. Ment. Dis.*, 125:312–315.

Slatter, K. H. 1960. Alpha rhythms & mental imagery. *Electroenceph. Clin. Neurophysiol.* 12:851–859, 1961–62.

Small, I. F., et al. 1966. Clinical characteristics of hallucinations of schizophrenia. *Dis. Nerv. Syst.*, 27:349–353.

Solomon, P., et al., eds. *Sensory Deprivation*. Cambridge, Mass., Harvard University Press, 1961.

Soltis, J. F. 1966. Seeing, Knowing & Believing: *A Study of the Language of Visual Perception*. Reading, Mass., Addison-Wesley.

Spanos, N., and Barber, T. 1968. Hypnotic experiences as inferred from subjective reports: Auditory and visual hallucinations. *J. Exp. Res. Personality*, 3:136–150.

Sperry, R. W. 1969. A modified concept of consciousness. *Psychol. Bull.*, 76:532–536.

———— (1964) Brain bisection and mechanisms of consciousness. In Eccles, J. C., ed. *Brain and Conscious Experience*. New York, Springer-Verlag, 1966.

Sprague, J. M. 1966. Interaction of cortex and superior colliculus in mediation of visually guided behavior in the cat. *Science*, 153:1544–1547.

Stace, W. T. 1960. *The Teachings of the Mystics*. New York, New American Library.

Stampfl, T. G., and Lewis, D. J. 1967. Essentials of implosive therapy: A learning theory based on psychodynamic behavioral therapy. *J. Abnorm. Psychol.*, 72:496–503.

Stekel, W. 1951. The polyphony of thought. In Rapaport, D., ed. *Organization and Pathology of Thought*. New York, Columbia University Press.

Stepien, L., and Sierpinski, S. 1964. Impairment of recent memory after temporal lesions in man. *Neuropsychologia*, 2:291–303.

Stern, M. 1952. Free painting as an auxiliary technique in psychoanalysis. In Bychowski, G., and Despert, J. L., eds. *Specialized Techniques in Psychotherapy*, pp. 68–85. New York, Basic Books.

Suedfield, P., and Vernon, J. 1964. Visual hallucinations during sensory deprivation: A problem of criteria. *Science.*, 145:112–113.

Sullivan, H. S. 1946. The language of schizophrenia. In Kasanin, J. S., ed. *Language and Thought in Schizophrenia*, pp. 8–13. Berkeley, University of California Press.

Swenson, C. H. Jr. (1957) Empirical evaluations of human figure drawings. In Murstein, B. I., ed. *Handbook of Projective Techniques*. New York, Basic Books, 1965.

Titchener, E. B. (1909) Imagery and sensationalism. In Mandler, J., and Mandler, G., eds. *Thinking: From Association to Gestalt*. New York, John Wiley & Sons, 1964.

Todd, J., and Denhurst, K. 1955. The double: its psychopathology and psychophysiology. *J. Nerv. Ment. Dis..* 122:47–55.

Tomkins, S. 1962. *Affect, Imagery, Consciousness*. New York, Springer Publishing Company.

Truax, C. B., and Wargo, D. 1966. Psychotherapeutic encounters that change behavior: For better or worse. *Amer. J. Psychother.*, 20:499–520.

Tversky, B. 1969. Pictorial and verbal encoding in a short term memory task. *Percept. Psychophysics*, 6:225–233.

Ulman, E. 1953. Art therapy at an outpatient clinic. *Psychiatry*, 16:55–64.

Underwood, B. 1969. Attributes of memory. *Psychol. Rev.*, 76:559–573.

Underwood, H. W. 1960. The validity of hypnotically induced visual hallucinations. *J. Abnorm. Soc. Psychol.*, 61:39–46.

Verdone, P. 1965. Temporal Reference of manifest dream content. *Percept. Motor Skills*, 20:1253–1268.

Varendonck, J. 1921. The psychology of daydreams. In Rapaport, D., ed. *Organization and Pathology of Thought*. New York: Columbia University Press, 1951.

Vernon, J. A., Hoffman, J., and Shiffman, H. 1958. Visual hallucinations during perceptual isolation. *Canad. J. Psychol.*, 12:31–34.

Vernon, M. 1967. Relationship of language to the thinking process. *Arch. Gen. Psychiat.*, 16:325–333.

———— 1962. *The Psychology of Perception*. Boston, Penguin.

Wallach, S., Wallach, M., and Yessin, G. 1960. Observations of involuntary eye movements in certain schizophrenics: A preliminary report. *J. Hillside Hosp.*, 9:224–227.

Warren, M. 1961. The significance of visual images during the analytic session. *J. Amer. Psychoanal. Ass.*, 9:504–518.

Warrington, E. K. 1962. The completion of visual forms across hemianopic field defects. *J. Neurol. Neurosurg. Psychiat.*, 25:208–217.

Watt, H. J. (1905) Experimental contribution to a theory of thinking. In Mandler, J., & Mandler, G., eds. *Thinking: From Association to Gestalt*. New York, John Wiley & Sons, 1964.

Weiss, J. 1967. The integration of defenses. *Int. J. Psychoanal.*, 48:520–524.

Weissman, P. 1969. Creative fantasies and beyond the reality principle. *Psychoanal. Quart.*, 38:110–123.

Weitzman, B. 1967. Behavior therapy & psychotherapy. *Psychol. Rev.*, 73:300–317.

Werner, H. 1957. *Comparative Psychology of Mental Development*. New York, International Universities Press.

West, L. J. 1962. A general theory of hallucinations and dreams. In West, L. J., ed. *Hallucinations*. New York, Grune & Stratton.

———— et al. 1961. The psychosis of sleep deprivation. *Ann. N.Y. Acad. Sci.*, 96:66–71.

Whitten, J. R. 1969. Psychical seizures. *Amer. J. Psychiat.*, 126:560–564.

Williams, D., and Gassel, M. 1962. Visual function in patients with homonymous hemianopia. Part I: the visual fields. *Brain*, 185:175–251.

Willinger, R., and Klee, A. 1966. Metamorphopsia and other visual disturbances with latency occurring in patients with diffuse cerebral lesions. *Acta. Neurol. Scand.*, 42:1–18.

Witkin, H. A., and Lewis, H. B. 1965. The relation of experimentally induced presleep experiences to dreams. *J. Amer. Psychoanal. Assoc.*, 13:819–849.

———— et al., eds. 1962. *Psychological Differentiation: Studies of Development*. New York, John Wiley and Sons.

Wolpe, J. 1958. *Psychotherapy by Reciprocal Inhibition*. Palo Alto, Stanford University Press.

Woodworth, P. S. 1958. *Dynamics of Behavior*. New York, Henry Holt & Co.

Zern, D. 1968. Freud's considerations of the mental process. *J. Amer. Psychoanal. Ass.*, 16:749–782.

Zilboorg, G. 1941. *A History of Medical Psychology*. New York, W. W. Norton & Co.

Ziskind, E. 1965. An explanation of mental symptoms found in acute sensory deprivation: Researches 1958–1963. *Amer. J. Psychiat.*, 121:939–947.

———— and Augsburg, T. 1962. Hallucinations in sensory deprivation—method or madness? *Science*, 137:992–993.

Zubek, J. P., ed. 1969. *Sensory Deprivation: Fifteen Years of Research*. New York, Appleton-Century-Crofts.

Zuckerman, M., and Cohen, N. 1964a. Is suggestion the source of reported visual sensations in perceptual isolation? *J. Abnorm. Soc. Psychol.*, 68:655–660.

———— and Cohen, N. 1964b. Sources of reports of visual and auditory sensations in perceptual-isolation experiments. *Psychol. Bull.*, 62:1–20.

———— et al. 1962. Stress and hallucinatory effects of perceptual isolation and confinement. *Psychol. Monogr.*, 76:30, 1–15.

Author Index

Todd, J., 25
Tomkins, S., 101, 174
Truax, C. B., 311
Tversky, B., 71

Ulman, E., 271, 281
Underwood, B., 174
Underwood, H. W., 46
Ungerlider, J. T., 260

Vander Castle, R. L., 33
Varendonck, J., 32
Verdone, P., 33
Vernon, J., 40–41
Vernon, M., 70, 202
Vinogradova, O. S., 76
Viscott, D. S., 262
Vogel, G., 33–34

Walk, A., 299
Wallach, M., 205
Wallach, S., 205
Walter, W. G., 226
Wargo, D., 311
Warren, M., 102
Warrington, E. K., 202

Watt, H. J., 58
Weiss, J., 312
Weissman, P., 119
Weitzmann, B., 306
Werner, H., 70
West, L. J., 36, 108, 116, 214
Whitten, J. R., 227
Wilkens, S. B., 37, 214
Williams, D., 202, 227
Willinger, R., 17
Witkin, H. A., 175, 271
Wolitsky, D. L., 48
Wolpe, J., 305
Wolpert, E., 33, 35
Woodworth, P. S., 215
Wundt, W., 57

Yessin, G., 205

Zangwill, O. L., 77
Zeitlin, D., 226
Zern, D., 85
Zilboorg, G., 8
Ziskind, E., 40, 41
Zubek, J. P., 51
Zuckerman, M., 40, 41

Subject Index

341